Tense Past

Tense Past

Cultural Essays in Trauma and Memory

EDITED BY
PAUL ANTZE & MICHAEL LAMBEK

ROUTLEDGE
New York • London

Published in 1996 by

Routledge
29 West 35th Street
New York, NY 10001

Published in Great Britain by

Routledge
11 New Fetter Lane
London EC4P 4EE

Copyright © 1996 by Routledge, Inc.

Printed in the United States of America on acid-free paper

Library of Congress Cataloging-in-Publication Data

Tense past : cultural essays in trauma and memory / edited by Paul
    Antze & Michael Lambek.
        p.   cm.
    Includes bibliographical references.
    ISBN 0–415–91562–7. — ISBN 0–415–91563–5 (pbk.)
    1. Memory—Social aspects. 2. Recovered memory. 3. Psychic
trauma. I. Antze, Paul, 1943–   . II. Lambek, Michael.
    BF378.S65T46   1996
    153.1´2—dc20
95–26249

Contents

Contents

Preface

We live in a time when memory has entered public discourse to an unprecedented degree. Memory is invoked to heal, to blame, to legitimate. It has become a major idiom in the construction of identity, both individual and collective, and a site of struggle as well as identification. Memory has found a prominent place in politics, both as a source of authority and as a means of attack; one need think only of recent controversies over museum exhibits commemorating the bombing of Hiroshima or the legacy of Freud. Indeed, we now have not only a politics but a forensics of memory, in which conflicts over memory become matters for litigation and in which talk about memory is increasingly driven by the jural obsession with matters of fact. These developments raise troubling questions. How is our experience of memory being altered by the new political burdens thrust upon it? And what are the moral implications?

This book is an attempt to understand the new importance that memory has assumed in contemporary culture. It attends especially to the central role that trauma and victimization have come to play within a politics of memory. Our basic premise is that memories are never simply records of the past, but are interpretive reconstructions that bear the imprint of local narrative conventions, cultural assumptions, discursive formations and practices, and social contexts of recall and commemoration. When memories recall acts of violence against individuals or entire groups, they carry additional burdens—as indictments or confessions, or as emblems of a victimized identity. Here, acts of remembering often take on performative meaning within a charged field of contested moral and political claims. They do so, moreover, in ways that reflect specific beliefs about the nature of memory itself and about its relationship to identity. Drawing on cases ranging from child abuse to the Holocaust, some of the chapters that follow attempt to illuminate the complex relationship between this performative aspect of memory and its capacity to recall the truth about literally "unspeakable" events. Others consider ways in which memories of violence and victimhood have been shaped by expert discourses or by local idioms of distress.

We approach our subject by triangulation, as a space defined by three converging perspectives. From one side, we examine memory as a signifying practice and an index of identity, as part of a moral discourse taken up by individuals and groups, often unself-consciously, as a means to articulate, legitimate, and even constitute their selfhood and relationships to others. From another, we examine the disciplines through which the very idea of memory has been constructed and through which the memories of individuals and collectivities are objectified and explored in scientific and clinical discourse. Thirdly, we consider some of the ways in which collective assumptions and concerns shape commemorative practices in different cultural contexts, both Western and non-Western.

A concern with the interplay between individual and collective memory in practice runs through the volume. We consider the mutual influence of these two kinds of memory in the constitution of theoretical discourses such as psychiatry and history. We examine the discursive and narrative practices that have a stake in particular constructs of memory. We also examine the part played by constructs of memory in moral practice and judgment, in spheres ranging from autobiography, embodied "symptoms," and psychotherapy to the more public realm of rituals and national memorials. The chapters explore how these various memory practices draw from and refer to one another in complex exchanges of metaphor, authority, and power.

Our purpose here is to develop an approach to memory which is anthropological in the broadest sense and hence transdisciplinary. We undertake a conversation among anthropologists and contributors from the fields of history of science, philosophy of science, and psychiatry. The individual contributions stand on their own but also speak to each other. Indeed, the contributors *have* been speaking to each other for some time. The places where our paths have crossed and our papers have been rehearsed include a symposium we organized on "Trauma, Narrative, and the Politics of Memory" at the joint annual meeting of the Canadian Anthropological Association (CASCA) and the Canadian Association of Medical Anthropology (CAMACAM) in May, 1993; a workshop on "The Texture of Time: Memory, Narrative, and Dissociation," organized by Laurence Kirmayer for the Society for Psychological Anthropology, September, 1993; Ian Hacking's seminar at the University of Toronto during the winter semester of 1993; Paul Antze's panel on "Life Stories: Trauma, Memory, and the Politics of Identity" at the CASCA/CAMACAM meeting of May, 1994; and our graduate seminar on "Culture, Memory, and the Politics of Identity" at the University of Toronto during fall semester of 1994.

We are indebted to all the participants at these events and especially to our contributors for their advice, enthusiasm, and faith in our enterprise. We would like to acknowledge Mikkel Borch-Jacobsen, whose work could not be included here for lack of space. We would also like to single out Ian Hacking for both the intellectual stimulation his work has provided and his personal support. Our thanks to the members of our graduate seminar for listening so carefully and debating with us so vigorously. Nancy Lewis and Glynis George offered extremely helpful responses to an earlier version of the introduction. Gillian Gillison graciously responded to the frequent disruption of her office space with lively discussion of the intellectual issues. Annette Chan has provided unfailing assistance with secretarial matters and Deidre Rose assisted ably with typing, indexing, and editing. We would also like to express our gratitude to the Social Sciences and Humanities Research Council of Canada.

Above all we would like to thank Rosemary Jeanes Antze and Jacqueline Solway for their patience, support, and constructive criticism; and our children, Emily and Bridget Antze and Nadia and Simon Lambek, for reminding us of the close connection between memory and the obligations and rewards of family life.

Introduction
Forecasting Memory

Michael Lambek and Paul Antze

It is a poor sort of memory that only works backward.

———Lewis Carroll

History . . . is unfinished in the sense that the future always uses its past in new ways.

———Peter Gay

Imagining Memory

Memory is something we all know intimately. It is a central and unambiguous part of our commonsense world, its presence as indisputable, if unsteady, as the weather. But when we begin to talk about memory, ambiguities and complexities rapidly emerge. How can we grasp memory itself? It is virtually impossible to imagine memory—what it is, how it works, where it lies—without recourse to metaphor.[1] Is memory a storehouse, a computer, a filing system, an encyclopedia, or a landscape, a cathedral, a city? If it is a kind of text or narrative, is our model to be Proust or Joyce, Virginia Woolf or Christa Wolf?

To oversimplify and risk caricature: in cognitive psychology, memory has evolved from a storehouse to the latest technology. Memory is alternately container, contents, information processor, and elaborate architecture, but it is always objective and objectified; the relation to a self, agent, or community that bears memory is omitted from the picture. In psychoanalytic thought, it is access to memory rather than initial input or storage that is problematized. Freud often used an archaeological metaphor: memory lies buried beneath the present or, if we turn the perspective ninety degrees, hidden behind a screen. More actively, memory is conceptualized as a force in conflict with the counter-force of repression and as highly compromised by the encounter. In psychoanalysis, the compromise is often phrased as one between reality and fantasy; memory is the product of their mutual impress upon pliable screens that simultaneously conceal as well as reveal what is behind them. The past does not correspond to the real in any direct, unmediated way since what we remember are memories—screens always already impressed by the fantasies or distortions of a series of successive rememberings. Hence memories, like dreams, are highly condensed symbols of hidden preoccupations.[2]

Although memory is surely a temporal phenomenon, these metaphors tend to transform the temporal into the spatial and are intensely visual. Layers are excavated, veils lifted, screens removed. The position of the viewer is left in question, but there is always a space, a distance, between the spectator and her memory, a space within which the gaze can be focused and the memory recognized as distinct, emergent from the background. This visual metaphor raises questions about the relationship between subjects and their memories and, most consequentially, how the ground between them is to be covered. What happens as memory goes in and out of focus? Can memory be assimilated to the self, and if it can, is it then still memory? Who controls the scene?[3]

A central conceit of this book is to imagine memory as practice, not as the pregiven object of our gaze but as the act of gazing and the objects it generates. Memories are produced out of experience and, in turn, reshape it. This implies that memory is intrinsically linked to identity. However, our approach to identity is less psychological or psychoanalytic than anthropological and historical. The essays that follow examine the cultural means and social institutions through which the practice—or, rather, practices—of memory are mediated. How do these succeed in objectifying memory? How do they construe its authority?

We have been particularly caught by the place of trauma both in memories of the past and in theories about memory. The stories told by both sufferers or survivors and by their witnesses, chroniclers, and commentators—historians, therapists, and a host of other experts—give central place to trauma. Increasingly, memory worth talking about—worth remembering—is memory of trauma. How this has happened and what we are to make of it are central themes of this book.

In contrast to other, more psychologically oriented studies of trauma and memory, our volume attends especially to the cultural shaping of memory, to the roles of trope, idiom, narrative, ritual, discipline, power, and social context in its production and reproduction. Beyond the insistent metaphorization of memory, we have been struck by the spread of talk about memory and especially by the interpenetration of individual and collective discourses: both how history borrows from psychotherapy and vice versa in their respective construals of their subjects, and how the memory of the individual—precisely that which is often taken to epitomize individuality—draws upon collective idioms and mechanisms. Today the commemorating state is likened to the remembering person, just as our idea of the autonomy of personal memory draws upon political imagery.

Many people have noted the increasing salience of memory in the public domain; this book is part of a rapidly developing literature. In a cogent analysis, Richard Terdiman has pointed to a "memory crisis" which he locates not so much in the present as in the nineteenth century, a product of the upheavals in European society at that time. Terdiman (1993) links attempts by founders of sociology like Ferdinand Tönnies to make sense of the transition with the efforts of poets and novelists like Baudelaire and Proust. Their work of retrieval speaks fundamentally to a sense of loss: memory begins when experience itself is definitively past. The ground between the spectator and the object of her gaze begins to lengthen, the connection between them to grow uncertain. Memory bespeaks detachment, or, perhaps, to borrow an evocative phrase from Paul Ricoeur, a dialectic between appropriation and distanciation (1976: 43). Pierre Nora (1989) speaks likewise of a shift from *milieux de mémoire* to *lieux de mémoire*. Memory becomes a "site," a monument visited, rather than a context, a landscape inhabited. The ruins of memory are subject to restoration, and we all become the alienated tourists of our pasts.[4]

In its most extreme form, this increasing dissolution of the social *milieu* (a dissolution that can be understood as a function of the cumulative effects of capitalism) leaves us with only one fixed point of reference, the *lieu* or site provided by our own bodies. Trauma becomes an obvious case in point. Medical discourse has reinforced and reified this state of affairs, individualizing memory, physiologizing it, and rendering it the province of a narrow body of experts. Hence, alongside the increasing isolation of the nuclear family (and, paradoxically, the increasing demands placed upon it to bear the responsibility for social reproduction) is the increasing burden put upon the individual body to serve as the sole site of memory. As index of the past, and hence guarantor of the reality of the present, the body is called upon to provide signs of import.[5] Photographs, personal artifacts, and signs of aging play their part, but they are not particularly compelling. Experts seek evidence of psychic and bodily trauma by means of interrogation, confession, hypnotic regression, lie detector tests, brain scans, physical probing, and similar techniques.

Comparisons with non-European societies are vital in order to reveal the outlines of cultural tropes and social forms that can serve to conceal or highlight memories and legitimate specific versions of the past. Conversely, such comparisons may provide fields of inquiry in which we can demonstrate just how well our tools for unpacking memory do work. But perhaps the most important function of comparison in this volume is to show the degree to which Western ideas about memory—our tools—are products of the rise of scientific disciplines that take memory as their object, and that therefore assert, as Hacking argues in his chapter, that there is an underlying knowledge or truth about memory waiting to be discovered. What has happened over the course of the last century is a shift from talk about memories to expert investigation of Memory; the emergence to discursive prominence of what Hacking (1995)—memorably—refers to as "the very idea of memory." Hence any discussion of memory must consider the institutional forms, the social relations and discursive spaces in which knowledge about memory is produced. Whatever the current controversy over "recovered memories" says about Freud (on this, see p. xxvi–viii), it can only serve to substantiate Foucault's insights regarding the discursive production of subjects. Indeed, whether "recovered memories" are "real" or "true," or not, they illustrate beautifully by way of their subject matter how sex has come to stand for the essence of selfhood. And of all the techniques for its retrieval and inspection, what better than memory?[6]

To the degree that a crisis in memory is simply the flip side of rapid social change, its presence—throughout the last century and increasingly in the present—is indisputable. Terdiman and Nora are right to historicize memory. But the conceptualization of a memory crisis is also a Eurocentric view (Terdiman was, after all, writing primarily about France, and Nora exclusively so) and a romantic one. Many people emigrated to the colonies precisely in order to be able to forget the past, to be free of what they experienced as its burden. And colonial subjects, too, viewed the past from different and varied perspectives, perspectives which themselves have transformed over the course of recent history along with the changing fortunes of postcoloniality. Today we would certainly want to address memory questions from the perspectives of people dislocated in many ways. Hence, to the degree that memory is linked to identity politics, it cannot be reduced to a single macro-historical "crisis." Likewise, any simple before and after picture—an allegory of the loss of an organic, irretrievable innocence of childhood, whether by a disruptive act of violence or simply by the process of maturation—risks serious distortion.[7] It is unlikely that there ever were untroubled, homogenous *milieux de mémoire,* worlds of pure habit, in which everything "goes without saying because it comes without saying" (Bourdieu 1977: 167) or that such *milieux* were not characterized by specific formulations of memory in their own right. Moreover, the European perspective may not fit either the understandings of the life course or the historical experiences of non-European people. The image of the memory crisis could itself be considered as a kind of screen memory, to collectivize Freud's term, one which is significant less for what it reveals than for what it attempts, even inadvertently, to conceal.[8]

In sum, our book is less about memory than about "memory" (after this paragraph no longer written in quotes). That is to say, it is about how "the very idea of memory" comes into play in society and culture and about the uses of "memory" in collective and individual practice. Put another way, it is less about the silent effects of memory than about the invocation of memory, including talk about the silent effects. Thus it raises questions about the possibility of any easy distinction between memory and "memory," between memory as unmediated natural fact or process and the culturally mediated acts, schemata, and stories—the memory work—that comprise our memories, and the way we think about them.

What distinguishes this book from much other recent writing on memory is the attempt to problematize the very subject. We explore the discourses of memory, taking memory as the object of discourse in three senses. First, we are interested in memory as the product of discourses in much the way that Foucault sees sexuality; in the origins of these memory discourses, their social production and reproduction, and the way they operate in private and public life (and, in fact, transcend this distinction). That is to say, we ask how memory itself as a topic is socially and historically constituted. Second, we interrogate the invocation of memory within a number of broader identity discourses (political, historical, ethnic, gender, therapeutic, autobiographical, juridical). Memory is widely called upon today to legitimate identity, indeed, to construct it or reconstruct it (in therapy, in public ritual). We inquire why this is so and compare contemporary North American uses of memory with practices located outside the Western discursive sphere. Third, we are interested in the ways in which the expression of memory is itself discursive. We ask how memory is narratively and dialogically organized and about the relationship of narrative to more embodied or practical forms of remembering.[9] Throughout we examine the invocation of truth claims rather than attempt their evaluation.

Discourse puts the impress of culture on even the most ostensibly private and natural of experiences. We provide a number of case studies in the discursive production or reproduction of memory. Some of these consider the stories individuals have to tell about their lives (Part 1); others examine the talk of the "experts" (Part 2); while yet others look into collective idioms and practices (Part 3). Throughout the book we address arguments concerning the relationship between narrative and experience that lies at the heart of memory, arguments which are evident in discussions of the relationship between memory and both the etiology and healing of trauma. However, our relationship to most of the arguments that beset discussions of memory today, debates that range from the abstract to the minutely concrete, from academic journals to the courtroom, from the street to the couch, is decidedly at an angle. Many of the contributors to this collection find these debates misconstrued, not least because of the participants' certainty that they know what memory is—or indeed that it is something singular to know.

Memory, Narrative Practice, and Identity

Memory serves as both a phenomenological ground of identity (as when we know implicitly who we are and the circumstances that have made us so) and the means for explicit identity construction (as when we search our memories in order to understand ourselves or when we offer particular stories about ourselves in order to make a certain kind of impression). But although we may set up the ideal of an unambiguous, limpid self—there should be no obscurities in our memories—ambiguity is the rule. So while memory should support the dominant view of our identity, the trouble is that it always threatens to undermine it, whether by obvious gaps, by uncertainties, or by the glimpses of a past that no longer seems to be ours. If I am constituted by what I remember, what about all that I do not remember but that I know, because other sources including my common sense tell me, must have been mine? Or what about that which I remember but would prefer to forget? Was that awkward adolescent really me? Can I still be him? Hence the past and its retrieval in memory hold a curious place in our identities, one that simultaneously stabilizes those identities in continuity and threatens to disrupt them. If the past is in one sense determinative of who we are, it provides in another sense inversions of our present state.[10] On the positive side, memory offers a certain scope for the kind of play or freedom that enables us to creatively refashion ourselves, remembering one thing and not another, changing the stories we tell ourselves (and others) about ourselves.

If memory is seen as the continuous traversal of the space between what goes without saying and what cries out to be said; if it is seen as *prac-*

tice, then the distinction between epochs of memory needs to be rethought. Nora's contrast between *milieux* and *lieux de mémoire* comes to figure memory's continuous, dialectical movement in and out of consciousness rather than the distinction between a flat, preconscious and an alienated, exquisitely self-conscious historical time. As memory emerges into consciousness, as it is externalized and increasingly objectified, it always depends on cultural vehicles for its expression. What Nora's argument does suggest, we think, is the need to examine these vehicles. It becomes important to look at the symbols, codes, artifacts, rites, and sites in which memory is embodied and objectified; the coherence or fragmentation of the narratives, rituals, geographies, or even epistemologies (see Bloch's chapter) it relies upon; and the way their authority changes over time (cf. J. Young 1993). What Nora's history points to is the recent reification and commodification of the vehicles for memory, rather than the emergence of distinct vehicles per se.

In forging links of continuity between past and present, between who we are and who we think we are, memory operates most frequently by means of the threads of narrative. Life itself is a creative construction, and there is a point at which a person's life and the stories she tells about it begin to merge. However, stories require interlocutors, and the right to establish authoritative versions never rests with the individual telling the story alone. It shifts from communal institutions and collective memory to the domain of experts and beyond—to market forces and the power of the state.[11]

Our memories are shaped in part by the narrative forms and conventions of our time, place, and position. But as they do not appear to come to us in such a mediated fashion but to be simply what they are, convention is concealed. Our stories have individuated characters; memory is organized around an intrinsic, essential subject, whether an individual I or collective we, as in Québecois narratives of "a people." Stories have beginnings; this idea is imported unnoticed into memory so that contemporary North Americans seek a foundational moment for the establishment of the self. Even the currently popular notion of an early trauma that explains everything has its roots in narrative conventions running back to the myth of the Fall. Moreover, traumas offer a way of inserting a radical, often transformative break in the flow of a life narrative. Here their symbolic role in memory is very much the one suggested by van Gennep (1960) and Turner (1969) concerning the place of violence in rites of passage.

Narrative is chronotopic, its world and the shape of its action constituted by spatio-temporal dimensions particular to a narrative convention. While the chronotope is perhaps more obvious in situating relatively objectified, public memories, like the distribution of monuments in a landscape or the scheduling of commemorative ceremonies, it is surely operative in personal memory as well. To speak of chronotopic conventions seems to be a more useful way to distinguish genres of memory than any strict contrast between "reality" and "fantasy" (but see below). Just as there have been successive and alternative forms of narrative realism in the novel, so there are in narrative memory. These conventions constrain the narrative products, influencing what kinds of actors and events are likely to be the focus of attention and how they are described and connected.[12] This is true not only of contrasting narrative genres produced by different cultures or historical periods, but of the narratives produced by various contemporary professional discourses. For example, the chronotopes of therapy and of juridical evidence are quite distinct. In therapy the client may be told to believe in order to know, to go with the flow of her thoughts. Acceptance here is seen as part of a path forward. However, this assumption creates havoc when it is transposed into the juridical domain with its evidentiary, eye-witness chronotope. We cannot grasp the meaning of memories without attending to their chronotopic frames. Today's "memory crisis" may stem in part from a breakdown of chronotopic conventions that results in the conflation of disparate memory fragments stripped of their original discursive contexts.

In analyzing narrative one can distinguish among author, narrator, character, reader, elicitor, and censor. Acts of memory can likewise be distinguished according to the degree of identity accorded these roles. Does the narrator claim authorship and does she fully identify with the central character, or is she trying to explore and develop the spaces among them? Is the fate of the character understood as fixed, a final resting place for its narrator, or as open-ended? What other cultural and political resources exist for influencing whether the narrative will be one of preemptive closure and permanent inscription or one of continuous creativity?

In other words, there is a dialectical relationship between experience and narrative, between the narrating self and the narrated self. As humans, we draw on our experience to shape narratives about our lives, but equally, our identity and character are shaped by our narratives. People emerge from and as the products of their stories about themselves as much as their stories emerge from their lives. Through acts of memory they strive to render their lives in meaningful terms. This entails connecting the parts into a more or less unified narrative in which they identify with various narrative types—hero, survivor, victim, guilty perpetrator, etc. Danger lies in two directions—both in fragmentation, the failure to produce a narrative of minimal coherence, and in the construction of an excessively determined story in which there is an overidentification with a particular character. People can be confused about who they are, or they can get stuck in a role—or they can use the role to continue the narrative production of their lives. While the choices made may be in large part psychologically determined (i.e. shaped by experience that is somehow prior to the narrative), some culturally provided genres of narrative, some invocations of memory, some subject positions are more enabling or disabling in certain contexts than others. Some narratives remain inchoate (see Kirmayer's chapter), or too dangerous even to imagine.[13]

To speak of memory as narrative is not to imply a set of fixed and bounded texts. We are at once author and reader of our stories, acts which are continuous unless preempted. The meaning of any past event may change as the larger, continuing story lengthens and grows in complexity. As readers we are continuously reexploring the significance of earlier episodes of the story in light of what transpires later, as we are caught up in the hermeneutic spiral of interpretation.[14] Written texts are finite, while narrative memory, in principle, is not. Breaks, endings, decisive moments of closure depend upon the other institutions in which the stories are inserted—ritual transformations and cycles, jural verdicts, therapeutic judgments, and, as Kirmayer notes, the failure of the world to bear witness. Sometimes such contexts are necessary in order to counter internally derived forces of immobility and closure.

By closure, then, we do not mean a simple forgetting. We mean, if anything, the reverse, a preoccupation with a particular fragment of the past, a hypostatization via excessive commemoration (or perhaps enforced silence). As Breuer and Freud famously put it, "hysterics suffer mainly from reminiscences" (1955 [1895]: 7). Or as Freud saw it later, repetition is a pathological form of remembering (1973 [1915–17]: Lecture 27). While the sufferers may not be conscious of the memories, the point is that they have not been lost; hysterics cannot get them out of their system. Such closures are less refusals to continue telling stories than to continue interpreting them. Indeed, sufferers are condemned to reenact their stories until they begin the work of interpretation. With Leys (below, p. 123), we would query any blanket "commitment to the redemptive authority of history"; there is nothing liberating in narrative per se. Merely to transfer the story from embodied symptoms to words is not necessarily either to integrate or to exorcise it. Development may be foreclosed when a particular version is granted complete authority.

Imagined Community, Imagined Self

Memory implies identity, the self caught between its roles as subject and object of memory, the telling and the told. Benedict Anderson has captured this idea in the title of his book, *Imagined Communities*. "Communities," he writes, "are to be distinguished not by their falsity/genuineness, but by the style in which they are imagined"(1991: 6). We have been arguing that this can be applied equally to the self. "Imagined" is not to be confused with "imaginary," but it indicates that selves and communities are not strictly "natural" entities either. Imagining here generates a sense of homogeneity, consistency, and order from unruly, heterogeneous experience; the construction of an identity that is to some degree single, centered, bounded, and located in a regular, directed, temporal trajectory. At least so it has appeared in the West.

If selves and communities are imagined, then the boundary between them is also likely to be mobile and permeable. Although westerners tend to think of their memories as being uniquely theirs, as specifying singularity, this may itself be the product of specific narrative conventions and systematic omissions. Even in the West memory talk is fraught with pronouns that extend beyond the I. Halbwachs begins his book by describing how people appeal to themselves as witnesses. He argues that when someone says, "I don't believe my own eyes," he feels himself two beings (1980: 22). Christa Wolf's approach to memory by means of a complex of shifting pronouns—the narrator speaks as "I" but also addresses herself as "you" and speaks of herself as "she"—is something we can all grasp from our own experiences of remembering (1980).

More generally, the self of memory can be imagined as a player in the larger narratives of a community. However, where conflict prevails, the reception of narrative, as George's chapter demonstrates, may be fraught with tension. Memory becomes a locus of struggle over the boundary between the individual and the collective or between distinct interest groups in which power becomes the operative factor.

Personal memory is always connected to social narrative as is social memory to the personal. The self and the community are the imagined products of a continuous process. The transfers between the individual and the collective are mediated at several points. Thus internalized experiences of selfhood are linked to autobiographic narratives, which are linked to biographies, legal testimonies, and medical case histories, which are linked to forms of therapy and theories of the subject. The same for experiences of nationhood or ethnicity linked to popular narratives and ceremonies, which are linked to newspaper accounts and thence to official histories, museums, boundary disputes, and sponsored ceremonies, which are linked to theories propounded by historians, political scientists, and other experts. The writer of the "simple" life history often unintentionally reproduces the assumptions and biases contained in these links.

The point can be reinforced by a brief look at nonwestern societies. The reflections of Marcel Mauss (1980) on the social origins of the "per-

son" are tremendously important here. Mauss, interested like his uncle
and teacher Durkheim in the evolution of social categories, distinguished
societies whose members were characters, or rather whose members were
supraindividual but reincarnated in the bodies of individuals who bore
them, from those societies whose members were conceptualized as
unique jural and moral persons bearing individuated rights and responsibilities and each quite distinct from the other. In the former case, people are the living embodiment of the past, playing out in the public
domain the drama of collective memory. Hence even to speak of the
"past" is somewhat misleading. It is the dreamtime of Aboriginal Australia,
the past imperfect, continuously reembodied, replayed, relived. As Mauss
argues, in western society there has been a shift away from the repetition
of exemplary occurrences (Connerton 1989: 65) (though see the chapter
here by Kugelmass) and toward a view of social persons as jural individuals. This places tremendous weight upon individuals to seek the sources of
identity and value within themselves, via memory, albeit as shaped by collective narratives and the knowledge of experts.[15]

Memory As an Identity Discourse

Issues of memory are everywhere today. They raise—and are raised by—
epistemological questions regarding history, experience, and truth. They
raise—and are raised by—ontological questions of selfhood and identity.
They are also part of the current fascination in North America with the al-
location of responsibility and the politics of blame. They have become explicit in anthropological theory, where memory is seen as the ground for
cultural reproduction but also as a means for the reification of culture in
various forms of ethnicity, nationalism, and cultural revival and as a
source of resistance to such reifications.[16]

One of our central arguments is that any invocation of memory is part
of an identity discourse and thus that conceptualizations of memory and
of the "self," or "subject," mutually imply one another. We are interested
in how ideas about memory both presuppose and serve to construct certain notions of identity, and in how memory and identity serve to bolster
one another. If this is true at the level of theoretical abstractions, it is
equally true of subjective experience: who people are is closely linked to
what they think about memory, what they remember, and what they can
claim to remember.

It follows from this that current debate over the nature of memory may
be taken as a symptom of crisis over identity. In order to constitute themselves, nations need to discover (or construct) a past, a collective memory.

When their identity is taken for granted, the past is less of an issue. The nineteenth-century memory crisis in France was superseded by a national cult in which formulaic classroom utterances such as "nos ancêtres les gaulois" and pilgrimages, by both political figures and ordinary citizens, to various monuments such as Alésia or the Panthéon became an ordinary, unquestioned part of things (Dietler 1994). That debate over memory indexes an identity crisis is equally true for individuals. When we take our personal identity for granted we are not self-conscious about the past. When identity is not in question, neither is memory.

We add to this the suggestion that accounts of the state or polity and of the individual cannot help but be mutually legitimating allegories of each other. Thus Plato builds his idea of the soul on that of the state and vice versa. Freud also politicizes the mind, speaking of resistance, censorship, parliamentary disorder, and the like. If this is true of great thinkers, at least they use the metaphors consciously; in lesser writers and in the popular imagination these become dead metaphors, all the stronger because they go unnoticed.[17]

As an "imagined community," based on a sense of wholeness, coherence, and continuity, the nation often likens itself to a person, for example as it "awakens from slumber." Every nation must construct a past for itself. In the memory of that past, trauma plays a role, whether suppressed (as in the split between India and Pakistan) or commemorated (as in the Australian depiction of Gallipoli). The metaphoric transfer runs both ways; images of self and personhood also draw on the collective. If there is an "invention of tradition" there may be equally an "invention of biography." The unified, confident, heroic late-nineteenth-century Western European self corresponds, at least in retrospect, with the age of confident, expanding Western European imperialism. Today's fragmented subjects are not unrelated to the complexities of transnational links, cultural pluralism, and the weakening of the state. If individual experience provides idioms and metaphors for understanding collective experience and vice versa, there may be a kind of mutual validation, a reciprocal rendering real, that serves to naturalize what has been imagined. However, this will not be seamless.

The emergence of the illness model of multiple personality disorder illustrates this kind of transposition between identity discourses. Here it is striking how alter personalities are conceptualized as equivalent units to the wholes of which they form parts. Rather than simply seeing identity as amorphous or shifting, sufferers and therapists tend to discern bounded sub-individuals in each new voice that emerges. It becomes apparent that the very idea of "multiple personality" depends, paradoxically, on the idea of a unified, bounded self and is only possible when the whole self itself becomes conceptualized and objectified in such a way. It is quite different from the Maussian perspective on nonwestern societies alluded to above.

There is a close parallel here with the emergent political recognition of ethnic groups within national states. The unitary self is like the European, colonial and postcolonial notions of distinctly demarcated nation states with component ethnic groups as opposed to the shifting, overlapping units found in pre-colonial times. It resembles the ethnically unified nation state (say, early twentieth-century France), while multiple personality disorder is comparable to a state with several reified ethnic groups envisaged in permanent conflict with one another or with the state itself (France today). In either case, identity is realized in a temporal plane; both unified selves and nations legitimate their being by means of memories elaborating a narrative of continuous existence. Contestations by multiples and by ethnic groups make use of the same forms.

Why multiplicity? Precisely because the idea of the unified, bounded, internally consistent "self" is so central to our thinking that the only way to go beyond it is to have multiple persons, each a unity of the same order, rather than accept the idea of an amorphous or poorly bounded whole.[18] Indeed, the very definition of multiple personality has been made to depend on the presence of "two or more distinct personalites . . . each with its own relatively enduring pattern of perceiving, relating to and thinking about the environment and self."[19] Multiplicity is thus over-determined or predetermined by the very idea of the unified identity that it shatters. Much the same holds for the way in which ethnic groups are understood as proto-nations.

The emphasis now by social historians and historical anthropologists on "popular memory" may be linked not only to a Marxist-inspired focus on class and the recovery of subaltern or dissident perspectives, but to aspects of the postmodern condition, including the transcending in importance of the nation by various transnational and regionalizing processes (migration, capital flow, mass media, etc.). Here work on memory enables scholars to transect the old boundaries. Thus the crisis of the individual may come to stand for the crisis of the nation state and the crisis of the state may find its effects most clearly manifested in the individual.[20]

North America is sometimes said to have moved to a postnational condition, a supposed luxury which Third World states cannot yet afford. While transnationalism undoubtedly has its benefits, one of the losses it brings is that of stable community. There are few explicitly bounded forms of social organization beyond the (shrinking) nuclear family and the individual. This loss of the collective may bring new forms of illness. One curious feature of multiple personality is that it ressurects elements of social, political, and family life within the sufferer. Indeed, it could be argued that multiple personality disorder reproduces the family within the individual, singling out not just the "inner child" but also providing it with parenting alters. Here, in other words, the horizon of the social has contracted to the outer bounds of the (now divided) individual.

Therapy is often seen as a triumph over the political.[21] Certainly the rise of popular therapeutic discourse in North America has gone hand in hand with widespread political disengagement. Writing of the codependency and recovered memory movements, Marilyn Ivy describes "a displacement from the possibilities of politics and community in late twentieth-century America into the domain of a privatized imaginary [in which] the child becomes the figure of an absent plenitude that can be reclaimed if only the child can be found or recovered from abuse"(1993: 247). Here historical trauma is displaced by individual drama. Writing about post-traumatic stress disorder among Vietnam War veterans, Allan Young (1995) describes a comparable situation, one in which collective guilt is evaded through the medicalization of individual experience. The overall result has been a shift in moral focus from collective obligations to narratives of individual suffering.

We must not exaggerate this. Sexual abuse and family violence are widespread. Remembering trauma may be personally empowering and sometimes leads to collective organizing. The inscription of trauma narratives may be a necessary, sufficient, and compelling means of establishing recognition. At the same time, such an identity politics can subjugate and immobilize victims in the very act of recognizing their suffering.[22] The reason is that the political gains conferred by a victim identity (e.g. "trauma survivor") are accessible only through expert discourses (in law, medicine, psychiatry) which have their own agendas and are themselves instruments of power. By their very nature such discourses deal in causes rather than meanings, events rather than persons, instances rather than entire lives. Thus, as the case studies in Part 1 make clear, reinscribing personal stories into these public discourses often obscures their richness and moral complexity. There is a vast gulf between the narrative possibilities afforded by notions of personhood, kinship, and morality on the one hand and the dry language of bureaucracy and biopolitics on the other. Where legal and diagnostic categories have become the only legitimate terms in which to remember suffering, then it becomes important to ask what has been forgotten.

Accountability

Memory acts in the present to represent the past. Such representation, as Terdiman (1993) has recently stressed, is extremely complex, no simple retelling but a work of interpretation. Moreover, to say "I remember . . ."

is not to frame a mere description, but to signal a speech act. Memories are acts of commemoration, of testimony, of confession, of accusation. Memories do not merely describe the speaker's relation to the past but place her quite specifically in reference to it. As assertions and performances, they carry moral entailments of various sorts.[23]

The invocation of memory signals association as opposed to dissociation, continuity over discontinuity. Hence it speaks, implicitly and explicitly, to the temporal axis of personhood. This is apparent in the stability of our use of pronouns—the I of the speaker in the present identified with, if not identical to, the I of the actor in the past (similarly, the you of the addressee as object of the memory, and so on). This stability of pronominal reference presupposes continuous identity. Much as we adhere to the causal connection between victimization in the past and pathological symptoms today, so we feel that the man who committed a crime in the past is the same person who ought to be held accountable when his or her identity is discovered today. Indeed, the idea of sameness over time is held even more strongly in the latter case, since in the former causality implies transformation. Readers will think of Heidegger and De Man or, from a more recent period of German history, the effects of the opening of the Stasi files. In the same vein, nations are held to have continuing responsibilities and obligations. Both persons and nations have enduring identities in our memory discourses.[24]

Memory is thus deeply implicated in concepts of personhood and accountability. In anthropological jargon (itself derived from jurisprudence), we may say that persons are corporate with regard to the estate of memory. Turning this around, it is memory and its tokens that provide the substantive grounds for claims to corporateness and continuity.[25]

Clearly, memory is equally implicated in the disavowal of connection and agency. As many theorists have remarked, forgetting is intrinsic to memory. This is one of the most interesting lessons we can gain from Freud and is, of course, also central to Marx's arguments concerning the fetishization of commodities. Indeed, any social constructionist argument must posit the omission or concealment of human agency in the construction of the "real." As Horkheimer and Adorno succinctly remark, "all reification is a forgetting." But if reification is a memory disturbance, some degree of forgetting may be necessary for the construction of identity.[26]

Hence remembering may be a way to challenge the real and a form of therapy in dereifying the self. Conversely, "remembering" may be a highly charged tool to legitimate new forms of reification.

Every society has a system of accountability, given over to human or divine agencies.[27] In contemporary western society the extreme focus on the jural individual (cf. Mauss and note 25 above) places an ever greater weight upon personal memory and accountability. At the same time the very notion of accountability becomes increasingly elusive when applied to the powers that seem to govern our lives, whether these be government bureaucracies or multinational corporations.[28] In everyday life people have great difficulty thinking sociologically (grasping the effects of social forces), perhaps now more so than ever.

It may be said that there is a kind of crisis of accountability today, or at least a time of profound change in what accountability means. Its effects can be seen in such diverse phenomena as the rise in legal suits and the florescence of new forms of dissociation. Much popular debate now turns around claims about recovered memories of sexual abuse, which in "mainstream America" begins to look more and more like what anthropologists mean by witchcraft (as Kenny's paper illustrates) both because of the logic of accusation and because of the view that one person can create and be held accountable for a fundamental flaw in another.[29]

Where abuse has taken place, as in the impoverished eastern Canadian communities described in the chapters by Glynis George and Donna Young, it is instructive to see how successive regimes of power entail their own systems of accountability. It is also compelling to see how local people struggle with dignity against the simple moralistic narratives in which some outsiders have tried to place them.

In the bourgeois mainstream, the search for villains is rampant. Held most accountable of all, perhaps, is Freud.

Remembering Freud

It is impossible to refer to contemporary debates about memory without speaking about Freud. But it is not so easy to do so in a manner that does justice to Freud or to psychoanalytic thought. Indeed, one of the remarkable elements of contemporary discussion is the inadequacy of the pervasive invocations of Freud. Freud's own memory has been ill-served by the debates over memory that invoke him.[30]

Freud's name is particularly associated with the effects of trauma, its repression and recovery. In actual fact, Freud's most subtle appreciations of memory have little to do with trauma per se. The question here is not whether he accepted the reality of childhood trauma or saw it as the product of fantasy. Psychoanalysis, starting with Freud himself, moves very quickly away from the trauma to other questions. Throughout most of his career Freud was less concerned with trauma than with the everyday connectedness of things in daily experience, the ways in which our patterned, repetitive reactions to things or people (as in transference) may never reach consciousness at all. The central issue is not so much a matter of having "forgotten" an original event than of never really seeing what we commemorate in the patterns we repeat. The point of psychoanalytic therapy is not to dig up "repressed memories" but to uncover these patterns and the active part we play now in keeping them alive. Viewed analytically, in fact, early memories are the products of so much condensation (including the condensation of what were once temporally discrete experiences) that they cannot be made to stand for historical facts.[31]

We should not allow the popular misrepresentations of Freud to substitute for Freudian thought itself. We need to ask how contemporary representations of Freud may themselves function like screen memories. Attempts to characterize Freud by means of his earliest writings alone (whether to praise or to bury him) serve only to avoid the moral complexities that psychoanalysis raises. In Freud's earliest work there is a fairly clear distinction between patient-victims and the noxious persons or events that made them ill, together with a certain confidence that the truth of things can be found by retracing them to their beginnings. What is so compelling—and yet so troubling in the later work—is the blurring of these moral distinctions.

Indeed, the whole recent debate about trauma in psychoanalysis can serve to sharpen the problematic issues of truth, history, and representation that circle endlessly around the subject of memory. Memory is, in a sense, a locus of struggle over these epistemological issues. It may be seen as a problematic and perhaps exemplary site for dealing with the complex interlinkage of reality and fantasy in representation and interpretation; the balance between reproduction and representation, or fact and interpretation, or recollection and understanding.[32]

Seen in this light, therapy that is supposed to discover the truth of what "really" happened is a kind of parody of the Enlightenment will to truth. It seeks the kinds of essences Foucault denies. Although such therapy is sometimes justified in Freudian terms and sometimes Freud himself is made accountable for its failings, it can be argued that Freud too denies such essences.

By focusing on decisive events and individual, absolute victims and villains, the recent debate about repression and the recoverability of memory serves to draw attention away from collective forces and issues, and hence away from both the really difficult questions of social etiology and the real, if diffuse, loci of responsibility. A multi-leveled political analysis of violence within the family is necessary, but it need not be understood as opposed to Freudian thought per se. What Freudian thought invites is neither the search for victims and victimizers, nor the disregard for sexual violence and its perpetrators, but the question: why is the labeling and persecution of villains so compelling to so many people?

Abuse stories satisfy the popular imagination because they draw pictures of goodness and evil, mutually exclusive and opposed to one another. This serves to conceal the ambivalence characteristic of each of us, the ways in which people secretly identify with portions of the villain's supposed behavior, perhaps unconsciously projecting their own aggression and desire. Psychoanalysis has always recognized that ambivalence is hard to tolerate—hence the need for projective schemes that demonize other persons or groups. For those who insist that psychotherapy serve the cause of moral clarity, this recognition may be hard to tolerate as well.

When the literalist interpretation of abuse accusations is applied uncritically, it becomes a kind of "assault on fantasy." Fantasy is ambiguous, idiosyncratic, and playful, and it succumbs neither to bureaucratic colonization nor to simplistic moralizing. Hence the products of fantasy can only gain recognition in such contexts when their source as fantasy is denied.[33] By the same token, this viewpoint denies the imaginative element in all remembering. It makes memories into literal records of the past, forgetting that each act of representation is itself an interpretation and that the facts of what "really happened" in childhood are not usually directly accessible.[34]

There is on the one hand an assault on truth by those who deny the holocaust (Vidal-Naquet 1992). There is on the other hand an assault on fantasy by those who take all childhood memories at face value. Reflecting on the depoliticisation of contemporary life, it is probably not coincidental that one has as its subject or protagonist a collectivity and the other an "individual."

Weathering Memory

We recently began a graduate seminar on memory by seeking alternative metaphors. Beyond the seas and landscapes of memory, one of the most striking to emerge was that of weather. [35] Weather brings to mind stability and instability, periods of sunny calm followed by sudden changes in pressure and temperature, the irruption of tempests, the dispersal of curious scudding clouds, the stagnation of humidity—and experts whose lack of control over their science is notorious. It is a vigorous, active metaphor evoking restless movement but also one that prompts us to ask how much of memory lies outside our conscious will. The image of the weathered rock, its surface worn by time, reminds us that forgetting is at least as significant as remembering, and indeed, that one is not possible without the other. The importance of forgetting has held a central place in twentieth-century, especially Freudian, thought. Yet there are at least two ways to understand the significance of amnesia (see Kirmayer's chapter for more). One is to argue that forgetting is inevitable—memory is simply, like the scarred face of the rock, what remains. The other is to say that the past is a treacherous burden, which would crush us if we did not continuously divest ourselves of its weight. Forgetting here is as much an active process as remembering; both require effort and energy. Identity of any kind requires steering a course between holding on and letting go. Identity is not composed of a fixed set of memories but lies in the dialectical, ceaseless activity of remembering and forgetting, assimilating and discarding. Explicit memory is but the self-conscious pole of a process that contains much else.

The pursuit of balance, a theme pervasive in the psychoanalytic literature beginning with the mysterious yet crucial concept of "working through," is necessary and right in collective as in personal life. How do we commemorate the past without becoming servants to it? How do we release the past without losing authenticity? Whether or not memories are formative, how may they become transformative? Beyond the skeptical tendencies evident in many of the following chapters, these remain central questions.

Notes

1. We recognize a notable systematic phenomenological account by Casey (1987) which we admire very much. Casey makes the important point that recollection need not be the only paradigm of memory, though we often operate as though it were. He goes on to distinguish recollection, commemoration, and other forms (129).
2. Some of the key texts in Freud regarding memory include "Childhood Memories and Screen Memories," "The Forgetting of Proper Names," and "The Forgetting of Foreign Words" (in Freud 1965); and "Recollection, Repetition, and Working Through" ([1914] in Freud 1963).
3. The metaphorics of specularity is critically addressed in the chapter by Ruth Leys.
4. Detachment as a modern condition is explored by Taylor (1989). Handler (1988) provides vivid examples of the way the past becomes reassimilated through the gaze of the tourist.
5. For a superb exploration of some of these issues, centering on the role of the "missing person" in consumer culture, see Ivy (1993).
6. A case such as that in Olympia, Washington as reported by Wright (1993, 1994) illustrates how memory has become a contemporary

site of rationalization or "colonization of the life world" (Habermas), especially when combined with the sort of sexual confession described by Foucault. Indeed, the Olympia story illustrates the intertwining of three forms of confessional discourse (not including that of journalism), i.e. those of therapy, the church, and the police. Foucault's study of the history of sexuality might well have been about the discourses of memory: the substance of confession, after all, is memory, and the technique of memory is frequently confession. At the least, both require that "the speaking subject is also the subject of the statement" (Foucault 1978: 61). If sex is a product of discursive focus (inquisition, gaze), so is memory. The anthropologically minded reader of Foucault asks: what is memory (or sex) like in a society that is not burdened with the same kind or weight of institutionalized discursive structures? What is a self before psychology?

7. It is in part surely Freud's challenge to this picture of literal childhood that still invites so much hostility towards him. And indeed, such is the need to shore up a space of organic innocence that its absence can only be imagined in terms of a deliberate and violent despoiling on the part of corrupt adults. It is, likewise, the saliency of a model of innocence that leads to so much heat over accusations of child abuse.

8. The collectivization of the screen memory concept is explored by Battaglia (1993). For the illustration of a (literal) cultural screen memory that considerably elaborates the suspicion expressed in this paragraph, see Santner (1990), especially chapter 3 on the German television series *Heimat*. The Sakalava of Madagascar (see Lambek's chapter) provide an example of people who view their precolonial ancestors as "fierce" (*mashiaka*) by comparison to the present, naive in some respects, but by no means innocent. Ivy (1995) provides a Japanese comparison to the Western European experience, while Werbner (1991) and Malkki (1995) address the memories of traumatized or displaced people in Africa.

9. Casey (1987), Connerton (1989) and De Boeck (1995) provide significant discussions of the embodied qualities of memory. On mimetic memory see Bourdieu (1990) and Taussig (1993).

10. Nora speaks of a distance-memory in which "memory is no longer a retrospective continuity but the illumination of discontinuity." Here "it is no longer genesis that we seek but instead the decipherment of what we are in the light of what we are no longer" (1989:16).

11. George Herbert Mead (1934) elaborates the intersubjective, dialogical production of the self. Berger (1963) discusses the social relevance of

autobiography; the dialectic of internalization, externalization, and objectification developed in Berger and Luckmann (1966) has also influenced our thinking. Terdiman sees memory as representation and likens it to Marxian "labor." His insightful account of the ensuing dialectic between present and past, text and referent, ideal and material (1993: 59 ff) is consistent with the understanding we develop here. See Bateson (1989) on the role of improvisation in the construction of the life course. Fentress and Wickham (1992) and Bloch (1993) emphasize that narrative has to be related to the context of performance. It is also important to remember that not all meaning comes in the form of narrative. People in distress often have *fragmented* narratives or rely on static symbols (Kirmayer n.d.). Memory may be evoked through material forms and by means of the senses. On the politics of silence see Sider and Smith (in press).

12. The idea of chronotope originates with Bakhtin (1981) and is lucidly developed there. On chronotope, see also Lambek's chapter; on landscape, Kirmayer's. On forms of realism the classic work is Auerbach (1953). As examples of alternate "genres" of memory one might perhaps point to reminiscence, nostalgia, and a more forward-oriented yearning.

13. Memory has to work, of course, with external contingent factors, not only where we are born or who our parents are, our gender and class positions, but whom we meet, whether and how we fall ill, and so on. These can play greater or lesser roles in our memories. For a useful overview of the narrative construction of illness see Good (1994). Christa Wolf's *A Model Childhood* (1980) provides a brilliant exploration of some of the issues described here and in the previous paragraph. The book is deliberately deconstructive of prevailing genres, ambiguous as to whether it is novel, biography, autobiography, history, parable, or critique. A shorter, highly evocative piece which illuminates many of our points through the lens of gender and also emphasizes the place of silencing is Kanaaneh (1995).

14. The hermeneutic circle, or spiral, in which the whole can only be understood in terms of its parts, and vice versa, is discussed by authors such as Ricoeur (1976). Lambek (1993, ch. 12) describes the way the meanings of past events are continuously reinterpreted in the light of subsequent ones.

15. Mauss's successor, Maurice Leenhardt, develops an alternative and equally interesting perspective. Describing the Canaque world of New Caledonia, he argues that there is "identity and repetition but not succession." Leenhardt makes the valuable point that the idea of reincarnation is in fact incompatible with such a "mythic" world of

flux and alternation in which both grandfather and grandson are invested with the same ancestral personality (1979: 157). See also Eliade (1959) on corresponding forms of cultural time. As Bloch points out in his chapter, for Lévi-Strauss (1966), what the memories of societies with cyclical time attempt to screen out is precisely history, understood as the uniqueness of events and the irreversability of change. What the memories of *our* societies suppress is the acknowledgement of repetition and social connection. The experience of perdurance (Casey 1987) is limited to specific rituals of commemoration and *lieux de mémoire*. These are, of course, all pairs of ideal types; the facts of any social setting are infinitely more complex and characterized by more internal diversity than the models can capture. The debate between Geertz (1973) and Bloch (1977) on the conceptualization of time in Bali is relevant to the discussion of the "partiality" of the cultural model. See also Taylor (1989) on this point as well as on the "inward" movement of the self over the history of Western thought.

16. On cultural reproduction see Connerton (1989). Recent collections addressing national memory include Boyarin (1994) and Watson (1994).

17. On the allegorical interplay between biological and social theory see Sahlins (1976). On the pervasiveness of metaphor in everyday language, see Lakoff and Johnson (1980); in scientific language, see Martin (1987). We draw on Handler's (1988) brilliant analysis of the ideology of possessive individualism underlying the modern idea of the nation.

18. Note the value judgments that these terms imply! This discourse is also highly gendered, a point which deserves expansion in its own right.

19. The quotation is from the third edition (revised) of the *Diagnostic and Statistical Manual* published by the American Psychiatric Association (APA 1987: 282). The latest edition (*DSM-IV*) replaces "Multiple Personality Disorder" with the term "Dissociative Identity Disorder." However the diagnostic language quoted above remains essentially unchanged.

20. Halbwachs (1980) takes pains to distinguish history from collective memory; interesting discussions of this issue are also to be found in Davis and Starn (1989) and in Nora (1989). On collective memory in historical and anthropological scholarship see Connerton (1989); Fentress and Wickham (1992); Passerini (1987); Tonkin (1992). For subaltern and critical perspectives see Sider and Smith, eds. (forthcoming). On transnationalism see, among others, Hannerz (1992);

Harvey (1989); and the journal *Public Culture*. For a review of the issues surrounding postmodernity and selfhood, see Frosh (1991).

21. See Rieff (1966) for a classic account of how therapy has been displacing religion in North America.

22. As Haaken (1994: 139) argues, the attribution of "victim" or "survivor" in the abuse discourse idealizes the sufferer's purity and hence denies her full moral agency. See also Antze's discussion in chapter 1 of this volume.

23. See Casey (1987) on commemoration; Felman and Laub (1992) on testimony. Speech act theory derives from Austin (1965). On the moral entailments of illocutionary acts see Rappaport (1979). On speech acts in illness and therapy see Shafer (1976), brilliantly anticipated by Janet (1980: 126), as cited by Leys.

24. Consider Locke's formalization of the forensic concept of the person as discussed in Hacking's chapter here. On the Heidegger controversy, see Wolin, ed. (1991). A sensible account of De Man is to be found in Santner (1990). The peculiar consequences of opening the Stasi files are described by Kramer (1992). On the enduring identity of the nation see Anderson (1991).

25. The allusion is to descent theory and to situations such as those in which all members of a group are held accountable for the actions against the member of another group by any one of them. Reciprocity might be seen in a similar fashion. Thus Lévi-Strauss's classic analysis of prescriptive alliance (1969) depicts society constituted through the memory of obligations entered into by its members. This is implicit in his comparison of the exchange of marriage partners to a form of communication. For an analysis of the temporal link between exchange and personhood see Lambek (1990).

26. Horkheimer and Adorno (1972), first used by Adorno in a letter to Benjamin, Feb. 29, 1940 (as cited by Jay 1973: 267). Reification as a memory disturbance is attributed to Lukacs by Terdiman who also makes the point that the very density of experience implies that "reduction is the essential precondition for representation. Loss is what makes our memory of the past possible at all" (193: 22).

27. See especially Douglas (1980) for a general discussion and Fortes (1983) for a particularly significant analysis of a non-Western system of accountability. The notion conjoins political, legal, and psychological dimensions with Weber's ideas regarding theodicy (1963).

28. The change is recognized in some parts of the Third World; "colonial nostalgia" can be understood in terms of the satisfaction in confronting a real agent of one's oppression as opposed to the faceless World Bank and IMF.

29. In comparing contemporary accusations to witchcraft we are of course making connections to the anthropological literature, not debating the reality of specific events. The anthropological issues concern both the ways villainy is imagined and how the cycle of accusations may take place. Like Kenny, we refer to Monica Wilson's famous depiction of witchcraft as "the standardized nightmare of a group" (1982). However there are certainly differences between the African context and the American one; one of the most significant is that African notions of witchcraft are grounded in a deep appreciation of human ambivalence.

30. The literature is enormous. For a penetrating and well-balanced development of several of the issues only touched upon in this section, see Haaken (1994).

31. Transference is, in a sense, the inverse of the commonsense view of memory. It represents an unconscious bringing of the past forward rather than a conscious looking back.

32. This is a central argument in Terdiman (1993).

33. See Obeyesekere (1981) for suggestive discussion on the intolerance of fantasy in the West by comparison to South Asia. However, whereas he argued that the West merely suppresses fantasy, we argue that it is actively distorted by being treated as though it were literal. Acknowledged fantasy, of course, is far from absent in North America, but its production is largely monopolized by the mass media and circulated in commoditized form.

34. As Janice Haaken puts it, "the emotional truth of the past is never reducible to the concrete facticity of events but is always bound up in interpretation, both in the initial experience of events and in their later elaborations and workings-through in memory" (1994: 118). In fact, most anthropologists are accustomed to bracketing the question of the "real" concerning the stories they hear in favor of addressing function and meaning.

35. Our thanks to Paula Pryce.

References

Anderson, Benedict. 1991. *Imagined Communities.* 2nd ed. London: Verso.

Auerbach, Erich. 1953. *Mimesis: The Representation of Reality in Western Literature.* Princeton: Princeton Univ. Press.

Austin, J. L. 1965. *How To Do Things with Words.* New York: Oxford Univ. Press.

Bakhtin, M. M. 1981. *The Dialogic Imagination.* Translated by Caryl Emerson and Michael Holquist. Austin: Univ. of Texas Press.

Bateson, Mary Catherine. 1989. *Composing a Life*. New York: Atlantic Monthly Press.

Battaglia, Debbora. 1993. "At Play in the Fields (and Borders) of the Imaginary: Melanesian Transformations of Forgetting." *Cultural Anthropology* 8 (4): 430–42.

Berger, Peter. 1963. *An Invitation to Sociology*. Garden City, N.Y.: Doubleday.

———, and Thomas Luckmann. *The Social Construction of Reality*. Garden City, N.Y.: Doubleday.

Bloch, Maurice. 1977. "The Past and the Present in the Present." *Man* 12: 278–92.

———. 1993. "Time, Narratives and the Multiplicity of Representations of the Past." *Bulletin of the Institute of Ethnology*. Academica Sinica N. 75.

Bourdieu, Pierre. 1977. *Outline of a Theory of Practice*. Translated by Richard Nice. Cambridge: Cambridge Univ. Press.

———. 1990 [1980]. *The Logic of Practice*. Translated by Richard Nice. Stanford: Stanford Univ. Press.

Boyarin, Jonathan, ed. 1994. *Remapping Memory*. Minneapolis: Univ. of Minnesota Press.

Breuer, Josef, and Sigmund Freud. 1955 [1895]. *Studies on Hysteria*. In *The Standard Edition of the Complete Psychological Works of Sigmund Freud*. Vol. 2. Translated and ed. by James Strachey. London: Hogarth Press, 1953–74.

Casey, Edward. 1987. *Remembering: A Phenomenological Study*. Bloomington: Indiana Univ. Press.

Connerton, Paul. 1989. *How Societies Remember*. New York: Cambridge Univ. Press.

Crapanzano, Vincent. 1980. *Tuhami: Portrait of a Moroccan*. Chicago: Univ. of Chicago Press.

Davis, Natalie Zemon, and Randolph Starn. 1989. "Introduction." *Representations* 26: 1–6.

De Boeck, Filip. 1995. "Bodies of Remembrance: Knowledge, Experience and the Growing of Memory in Luunda Ritual Performance." In *Rites et Ritualisation*. Ed. Georges Thinès and Luc de Heusch. Paris: J. Vrin. pp. 113–38.

Dietler, Michael. 1994. " 'Our Ancestors the Gauls': Archaeology, Ethnic Nationalism, and the Manipulation of Celtic Identity in Modern Europe." *American Anthropologist* 96 (3): 584–605.

Douglas, Mary. 1980. *Evans-Pritchard*. New York: Viking.

Eliade, Mircea. 1959 [1949]. *Cosmos and History*. Translated by Willard Trask. New York: Harper & Row.

Felman, Shoshana, and Dori Laub. 1992. *Testimony: Crises of Witnessing in Literature, Psychoanalysis, and History*. New York: Routledge.

Fentress, James, and Chris Wickham. 1992. *Social Memory.* Oxford: Basil Blackwell.

Fortes, Meyer. 1983. *Oedipus and Job in West African Religion.* Cambridge: Cambridge Univ. Press.

Foucault, Michel. 1978. *History of Sexuality.* Vol. 1. New York: Pantheon.

Freud, Sigmund. 1963. *Therapy and Technique.* New York: Collier.

———. 1965. *The Psychopathology of Everyday Life.* New York: W. W. Norton.

———. 1973 [1915–17]. *Introductory Lectures on Psychoanalysis.* Translated by James Strachey. Harmondsworth, England: Pelican.

Frosh, Steven. 1991. *Identity Crisis: Modernity, Psychoanalysis and the Self.* New York: Routledge.

Geertz, Clifford. 1973. "Person, Time, and Conduct in Bali." In *The Interpretation of Cultures.* New York: Basic Books.

Good, Byron. 1994. *Medicine, Rationality, and Experience.* New York: Cambridge Univ. Press.

Haaken, Janice. 1994. "Sexual Abuse, Recovered Memory, and Therapeutic Practice: A Feminist-Psychoanalytic Perspective." *Social Text* 40: 115–45.

Hacking, Ian. 1995. *Rewriting the Soul.* Princeton: Princeton Univ. Press.

Halbwachs, Maurice. 1980 [1950]. *The Collective Memory.* Translated by F. J. and V. Y. Ditter. New York: Harper.

Handler, Richard. 1988. *Nationalism and the Politics of Culture in Quebec.* Madison: Univ. of Wisconsin Press.

Hannerz, Ulf. 1992. *Cultural Complexity: Studies in the Social Organization of Meaning.* New York: Columbia Univ. Press.

Harvey, David. 1989. *The Condition of Postmodernity.* Oxford: Basil Blackwell.

Horkheimer, Max, and Theodor W. Adorno. 1972. *Dialectic of the Enlightenment.* Translated by John Cumming. New York: Herder and Herder.

Ivy, Marilyn. 1993. "Have You Seen Me? Recovering the Inner Child in Late Twentieth-Century America." *Social Text* 37 (Winter): 227–52.

———. 1995. *Discourses of the Vanishing: Modernity, Phantasm, Japan.* Chicago: Univ. of Chicago Press.

Janet, Pierre. 1980 [1923]. *La Médicine psychologique.* Paris: Flammarion.

Jay, Martin. 1973. *The Dialectical Imagination.* Boston: Little, Brown.

Kanaaneh, Rhoda. 1955. "We'll Talk Later." *Cultural Anthropology* 10 (1): 125–35.

Kirmayer, Laurence. n.d. Paper delivered to the Society of Psychological Anthropology, annual meeting, autumn 1993.

Kramer, Jane. 1992. "Letter from Europe." *The New Yorker,* 25 May: 40–64.

Lakoff, George, and Mark Johnson. 1980. *Metaphors We Live By.* Chicago: Univ. of Chicago Press.

Lambek, Michael. 1990. "Exchange, Time and Person in Mayotte." *American Anthropologist* 92 (3): 647–61.

———. 1993. *Knowledge and Practice in Mayotte.* Toronto: Univ. of Toronto Press.

Leenhardt, Maurice. 1979 [1947]. *Do Kamo: Person and Myth in the Melanesian World.* Translated by Basia Miller Gulati. Chicago: Univ. of Chicago Press.

Lévi-Strauss, Claude. 1969 [1949]. *The Elementary Structures of Kinship.* Translated by Bell and von Sturmer. Boston: Beacon.

———. 1966. *The Savage Mind.* Chicago: Univ. of Chicago Press.

Malkki, Liisa. 1995. *Purity and Exile: Violence, Memory, and National Cosmology among Hutu Refugees in Tanzania.* Chicago: Univ. of Chicago Press.

Martin, Emily. 1987. *The Woman in the Body.* Boston: Beacon.

Mauss, Marcel. 1985. "A Category of the Human Mind: The Notion of Person; the Notion of Self." Translated by W. D. Halls. In *The Category of the Person.* Ed. M. Carrithers, et al. Cambridge: Cambridge Univ. Press.

Mead, George Herbert. 1934. *Mind, Self, and Society.* Ed. Charles Morris. Chicago: Univ. of Chicago Press.

Nora, Pierre. 1989. "Between Memory and History: Les Lieux de Mémoire." *Representations* 26: 7–25.

Obeyesekere, Gananath. 1981. *Medusa's Hair.* Chicago: Univ. of Chicago Press.

Passerini, Luisa. 1987 [1984]. *Fascism in Popular Memory.* Translated by R. Lumley and J. Bloomfield. Cambridge: Cambridge Univ. Press.

Rappaport, Roy. 1979. "The Obvious Aspects of Ritual." In *Ecology, Meaning, and Religion* by R. Rappaport. Richmond, CA: North Atlantic, pp. 173–221.

Ricoeur, Paul. 1976. *Interpretation Theory.* Fort Worth: Texas Christian Univ. Press.

Rieff, Philip. 1966. *The Triumph of the Therapeutic: Uses of Faith After Freud.* New York: Harper & Row.

Sahlins, Marshall. 1976. *The Use and Abuse of Biology.* Ann Arbor: Univ. of Michigan Press.

Santner, Eric. 1990. *Stranded Objects: Mourning, Memory, and Film in Postwar Germany.* Ithaca, N.Y.: Cornell Univ. Press.

Shafer, Roy. 1976. *A New Language for Psychoanalysis.* New Haven: Yale Univ. Press.

Sider, Gerald, and Gavin Smith, eds. In press. *Between History and Histories: The Production of Silences and Commemorations.* Toronto: Univ. of Toronto Press.

Taussig, Michael. 1993. *Mimesis and Alterity.* New York: Routledge.

Taylor, Charles. 1989. *Sources of the Self.* Cambridge: Harvard Univ. Press.

Terdiman, Richard. 1993. *Present Past: Modernity and the Memory Crisis.* Ithaca, N.Y.: Cornell Univ. Press.

Tonkin, Elizabeth. 1992. *Narrating Our Pasts: The Social Construction of Oral History.* Cambridge: Cambridge Univ. Press.

Turner, Victor. 1969. *The Ritual Process.* Chicago: Aldine.

Van Gennep, Arnold. 1960 [1909]. *The Rites of Passage.* London: Routledge.

Vidal-Naquet, Pierre. 1992. *Assassins of Memory: Essays on the Denial of the Holocaust.* New York: Columbia Univ. Press.

Watson, Ruby, ed. 1994. *Memory, History and Opposition Under State Socialism.* Santa Fe: School of American Research Press.

Weber, Max. 1963. *The Sociology of Religion.* Boston: Beacon.

Werbner, Richard. 1991. *Tears of the Dead.* Washington, D.C.: Smithsonian.

Wilson, Monica. 1982 [1951]. "Witch Beliefs and Social Structure." In *Witchcraft and Sorcery.* Ed. Max Marwick. Harmondsworth, England: Penguin, pp. 276–85.

Wolf, Christa. 1980. *A Model Childhood (Kindheitmuster).* Translated by Ursule Molinaro and Hedwig Rappolt. New York: Farrar, Straus, and Giroux.

Wolin, Richard, ed. 1991. *The Heidegger Controversy: A Critical Reader.* New York: Columbia Univ. Press.

Wright, Lawrence. 1993. "Remembering Satan." *The New Yorker,* 17 May: 60–81 and 24 May: 54–76.

———. 1994. *Remembering Satan.* New York: Knopf.

Young, Allan. 1995. *The Harmony of Illusions: Inventing Post-Traumatic Stress Disorder.* Princeton: Princeton Univ. Press.

Young, James. 1993. *The Texture of Memory.* New Haven: Yale Univ. Press.

I. Remembering Trauma, Remaking the Self

We begin with three case studies that examine the narrative presentation of memories by victims of abuse. In contrast to clinical case histories, however, these chapters look beyond the simple question of trauma and its effects to ask about the ways in which memories of suffering are incited, suppressed, or reconstrued by changing circumstances and by the salience of different cultural idioms.

Paul Antze's chapter considers the life story recounted by one of his informants in a support group for people who have been diagnosed with multiple personality disorder. He comes to his material with a question: if multiple personality is not a disease but a cultural idiom, what kind of self-understanding does it afford? He offers a cautious challenge to those who view the multiple's sense of self as inherently inauthentic. Drawing on Paul Ricoeur's concept of narrative identity, Antze begins by examining the "recovered memory narrative" that guides the therapy most multiples receive. While he agrees that such narratives are rightly criticized for their narrowness and interpretive literalism, Antze argues that multiple personality as a cultural idiom offers a broader range of expressive possibilities. As his informant's story suggests, the language of multiplicity can at times articulate moral ambiguity, a complex imaginative engagement with the past, and a sense of self rooted in ethical commitments.

Donna Young's chapter includes a recovered memory story as well, but here it is just one in a triptych of life stories told by three generations of rural New Brunswick women—a grandmother, her daughter, and her granddaughter. Taken together, these stories raise fascinating questions about the relation between narrative text and social context in the personal recollection of suffering. All three women describe the violence and privation they experienced as children growing up in an impoverished rural community. However, their stories differ profoundly in ways that reflect shifts in both power structures and discursive resources over the courses of their lives. The resulting contrasts enable Young to raise her own critical questions about the expressive power of different idioms, and about what is lost when oppression and victimization are recast in the narrow therapeutic language of abuse and recovered memory.

Glynis George considers the idiom of abuse as a focus of controversy in another marginalized community. Her narratives come from two women who grew up in a Francophone fishing village on the shores of western Newfoundland. Here, however, there is no question of "recovered memory"—both women clearly recall the practices they denounce. The dispute is rather about what these events signify and what should be made of them. When George's first informant appears on television to assert that "abuse is part of our culture," she brings down the wrath of her entire community. The ensuing dispute—which breaks down along gender, class, and ethnic lines—shows vividly that the remembering of abuse affects collective as well as personal identities, and that when claims to victimhood are made on more than one level, they can sometimes undermine each other.

1

Telling Stories, Making Selves
Memory and Identity in Multiple Personality Disorder

Paul Antze

Near the end of his recent book on multiple personality and memory, Ian Hacking (1995) raises a curious question. How well, he wonders, can multiples live up to the old delphic injunction "Know thyself?" He is not asking here about the delusions or cognitive impairments imposed by a mental disorder, but rather about the limits of a certain discourse, a certain way of expressing and understanding oneself.

Hacking's interest in multiple personality stems from a larger interest in the phenomenon he calls "making up people" (Hacking 1986). This is his term for what happens when experts in the human sciences create new categories of human beings (the degenerate, the alcoholic, the homosexual) and then new bodies of knowledge about them. Because it is about human beings in social context, he argues, this kind of knowledge can loop back on its subject matter in unpredictable ways, so that it often helps create what it only seemed to describe. The reason is that once new human kinds have been turned loose in society, they take on a life of their own. People begin to inhabit them, invoking them to make sense of their lives or tell others who they are. (Thus a young man in therapy has "insight" into his latent homosexuality, or a drinker checks himself for the telltale signs of alcoholic thinking.) The talk of experts, in other words, can quite literally create new kinds of subjects, new ways of being human, new forms of self-understanding.[1]

For Hacking, the recent multiple personality epidemic is a spectacular case in point. If he is right, then the people we call multiples are very much creatures of a certain time and place. Their condition has been made possible, in a sense, only by specific historical circumstances—by the moral passion and entrepreneurial vigor of some psychiatrists, but also by a variety of social forces that give their theories resonance—feminism, the decline of the family, concerns about child abuse, popular ideas about trauma and memory.

Hacking is at pains to distinguish his view from the usual dismissive objection to multiple personality, that it is some sort of collective delusion based on suggestibility or play-acting. And yet there is an aspect of the phenomenon that he finds troubling. What happens to people who come to live inside this discourse, who use it to make sense of their lives? In a trivial sense they certainly pick up a kind of knowledge about themselves, a knowledge of alter personalities and unsuspected childhood traumas. But what about that deeper kind of self-knowledge enjoined by the delphic oracle? For Hacking, such knowledge is "a virtue in its own right," based in "deeply rooted convictions and sensibilities about what it is to be a fully developed human being" (1995: 264).

Can multiples win this kind of self-knowledge? Can they even pursue it? Having suspended judgment throughout most of his book, Hacking ends by aligning himself with those he calls the "cautious doubters":

> They accept that the patient has produced this version of herself: a narrative that includes dramatic events, a causal story of the formation of alters, and an account of the relationships between alters. That is a self-consciousness; that is a soul. The doubters accept it as a reality. . . . Nevertheless, they fear that multiple personality therapy leads to a false consciousness. Not in the blatant sense that the apparent memories of early abuse are necessarily wrong or distorted—they may be true enough. No, there is a sense that the end product is a thoroughly crafted person, but not a person who serves the ends for which we are persons. Not a person with self-knowledge, but a person who is the worse for having a glib patter that simulates an understanding of herself. (266)

I am not so sure. Recently I concluded a three-year ethnographic study of a small support group for multiples in Toronto.[2] During this period nearly fifty individuals passed through the group, all of them currently under treatment for multiple personality disorder. The group was meant as a supplement to therapy, so conversations dealt mainly with problems in daily living: where to find help in a crisis, how to communicate with alter personalities, what to do if child alters came out at work. Two points struck me with great force.

First, while members shared experiences that most of us would find very strange indeed, they did *share* the experiences. Despite differences in background and educational level, they seemed to understand each other—at least most of the time. Listening each week as they traded advice or sympathy, I couldn't avoid the impression that their condition was something real—as real as any other human experience—and that they had amassed an impressive body of working knowledge about it. This was not self-knowledge in the grand sense of the word, but it was more than glib patter. They were exchanging something that had the look and feel of substantive information.

Secondly, the picture of multiple personality that emerged from their conversations seemed to me both more variegated and less dramatic than the one conveyed by case histories, talk shows, and literary "multographies." Some members lived on welfare and seemed to be constantly in and out of hospitals, while others held responsible positions. Their talk included a good deal of predictable anguish, but also much evidence of creativity and psychological insight. There were more than a few moments of high hilarity. There were clichés aplenty here, to be sure, but I also felt that at times members were wrestling in serious and honest ways with the question, "Who am I?"

While these observations may raise some doubts about Hacking's conclusion, they are consistent with his larger argument about the cultural specificity of multiple personality. Medical anthropologists have studied similar phenomena in a wide array of societies. Twenty years ago these were known as "culture-bound syndromes" (Yap 1969); today they are more often styled as "illness idioms" or "idioms of distress" (Nichter 1981). The change in terms reflects a shift in thinking, based on the recognition that culturally specific illnesses are more than exotic bits of pathology, and that understanding them must begin with a clear sense of their local meanings and uses. Especially where dissociation is involved, these can stray far from the realm of illness per se. The remarkable ethnographies of Michael Lambek (1981) and Janice Boddy (1989) both document forms of possession which result in enduring relationships between host and possessing spirit. Lambek has examined the subtle and often very complex forms of communication (with oneself and others) that such relationships permit, while Boddy has shown how possession offers public opportunities for what she has called "self-articulation" (1989: 232–37; 252–57).

My assumption here is that multiple personality is something of this kind (Antze, 1992). If it is indeed a local idiom of distress akin to other dissociative idioms, then we should not be surprised at the way it enables sufferers to share knowledge about a reality they experience in common.

Such knowledge has its direct counterparts in the possession cults of Sri Lanka, Northern Sudan, and many other parts of the world. It should serve to remind us that the expression of suffering (or indeed anything else) requires a language, and that to use a language is to fill it out and make its objects real. We should also not be surprised that this idiom is appropriated in a variety of ways that could never have been predicted by the experts who first wrote about MPD. An idiom of distress is, like any language, a "form of life" as Wittgenstein put it. Thus it can evolve over time and lend itself to unexpected uses.

Looking at the current wave of multiple personality as an idiom of distress allows us to reformulate Hacking's question in a broader and perhaps more fruitful way, so that it is no longer about what the multiple can do but what the idiom allows. What kinds of expressive and reflective possibilities does it open? What does it foreclose? Questions of this kind cannot be answered in the abstract or by referring only to printed versions of a discourse. We need to see the language as individuals appropriate it in their lives.

One way of doing this is to look at the kinds of stories that people tell about themselves. Elsewhere I have argued that even trivial stories of this kind (a visit to the hair dresser's, a chance encounter on the bus) can be highly revealing when told in groups, where they often serve to translate shared ideas into experiential realities (Antze 1976, 1987, 1992). But asking about self-understanding and its limits calls for a different and more reflective kind of story, one that is usually accessible only through interviews or diaries. Stories of this kind—life stories, as they are sometimes called—mediate even more directly between abstractions and experience. Indeed, one might argue that they are the chief means by which grand cultural discourses like Christianity or psychoanalysis find their way into something resembling self-knowledge.[3]

Indeed, if Paul Ricoeur is right, then our very experience of identity, of being someone in particular, has a tacit narrative structure. In his recent book, *Oneself As Another* (1992), Ricoeur argues that we know ourselves as distinct from others and as continuous over time only through a process he calls *emplotment*, a perpetual weaving and reweaving of past and present events into characters, motives, situations, actions. In effect we are characters in a story that we keep revising as our lives unfold. As Ricoeur points out, this narrative labor has its own dynamic, driven by a perpetual tension "between the demand for concordance and the admission of discordances"—by the need, in other words, to find threads of continuity in the face of "diversity, variability, discontinuity and instability" (140–41). Clearly there are many ways of resolving this tension.

The tension Ricoeur describes surely finds a kind of boundary case among persons diagnosed with Multiple Personality Disorder or (to use the new coinage of DSM-IV) Dissociative Identity Disorder. Both terms suggest a fractured sense of identity: either there are too many selves or one that doesn't hang together. But multiples trying to make narrative sense of their lives face an even graver form of discordance, this one at the level of memory. Many enter therapy with only dim or fragmentary recollections of childhood, yet they seem to be haunted by events from this period that return in other forms, as nightmares, "flashbacks," "body memories." They learn that these experiences hide secrets that hold the key to their recovery. It would be safe to say that for all multiples in therapy today, memory is a central obsession. In fact, while memory is central to anyone's life story, for multiples it is generally the *subject* of the story. This means that if we are to use life stories in attempting to grasp the kind of self-understanding fostered by multiple personality as an illness idiom, we must attend especially to the various ways these invoke memory in framing identity.

This is what I want to do in the pages ahead, drawing on excerpts from a single life story recounted by one of my informants. Before beginning, however, I want to consider some features of the larger discourse she appropriates. Like most multiples today, my informant came to her story with the help of a confessional practice known loosely as "recovered memory therapy." For the past several years this practice has been the focus of a bitter controversy involving feminists, different camps of psychiatrists, and advocates of the "False Memory Syndrome."[4] I don't wish to rehearse the controversy here, save to say that it situates the stories told by multiples in a highly charged field. My interest lies rather with the "master narrative" that guides recovered memory therapy and does so much to shape multiple personality as a cultural idiom.

Remarkably enough, this guiding narrative is itself a story about narrative, memory, and identity. It is in some respects an old story, with clear antecedents in the work of Pierre Janet (1989 [1889]) and the early writings of Freud and Breuer (1955 [1895]). Its modern editions take a variety of forms, ranging from the sophisticated theories of Bessel van der Kolk (1988) and Judith Herman (1992) to the cruder accounts found in many self-help manuals. The core idea is that many common psychiatric disorders (including some severe ones) have their origins in traumas of early childhood—usually sexual abuse. The traumatic events can't be remembered because they have been "repressed" (or more accurately, dissociated) into a series of compartments separate from everyday consciousness. In van der Kolk's terms (1988), they are not "encoded into narrative memory," and yet they are preserved all the better for that. Cut off from any commerce with the rest of mental life, they remain as fresh and painful as the day they happened. In extreme cases they may spawn alter personalities that show themselves only when the patient is an adult. But even if this doesn't happen, they usually find their way into a wide range of symptomatic acts—phobias, compulsions, nightmares. Moreover, they can be "triggered" by objects, words, situations in everyday life that act like hypnotic cues. The abuse survivor may experience sudden attacks of rage or panic or despondency accompanied by odd thoughts or inexplicable bits of behavior. Most abuse therapists believe these reactions offer a pathway to the dissociated traumas themselves. The task of healing is then a matter of helping the survivor to recover and relive these terrible events in a safe therapeutic environment. Once this has happened, the traumas can be reconnected to everyday narrative memory, where they lose their power to do harm.

As it informs therapeutic practice and the counsels of self-help books, this abstract theory can become something more—a template for experience or even a recipe for a kind of self-understanding. In the opening pages of her popular self-help volume, *Repressed Memories* (1992), Renee Fredrickson says this explicitly. "Repressed memories," she tells her readers, "are pieces of your past that have become a mystery. They stalk your unconscious and hamper your life with their aftermath. They will tell you a story if you know how to listen to them, and the story will help you to make sense of your life and your pain" (24). She invites readers to embark on a "journey of discovery and healing," in which "you must piece together mind and body clues to find out what you have forgotten. You will struggle at first to believe what you are remembering, but your healing will take place as you recover your memories."

Symptomatically speaking, this journey can begin almost anywhere. Judith Herman argues that the sequelae of childhood sexual abuse can be extremely varied, so "disguised presentations" are more the rule than the exception. This means that some abuse survivors may appear to be psychotic or borderline, while others look relatively normal. Symptoms can range from phobias and eating disorders to insomnia, drug abuse, or even excessive daydreaming (Herman 1992, 121; Fredrickson 1992, 48–51). In fact, there is no way of ruling out a traumatic cause for *any* set of presenting symptoms.

It is in teaching patients how to understand these symptoms that recovered memory therapy offers a template for experience. As the quotation from Fredrickson suggests, symptoms, feelings, dreams, and other mental productions are important chiefly as clues in a kind of detective story. To know what they mean is to discover the memories hiding behind them. In the words of Gail Fischer-Taylor, a prominent Toronto abuse therapist, "Every symptom has its basis in the survivor's history and is a potential entry point into the unearthing of memories."[5] While this view of symptoms has a vaguely Freudian ring, it is in fact radically different from the one found in psychoanalysis, where all mental productions are taken as complex, highly overdetermined expressions of ongoing fantasies and conflicts. Here the aim is simply to find out what happened.[6] As in a detective story, the connections are made in part by surmise and deduction, but recovered memory therapy gives special authority to direct experience via altered states of consciousness: dreams, "guided reverie," hypnotic regression, "flashbacks," and (for multiples) reports from alter personalities. The assumption is that because traumas have been dissociated, they are most readily accessible in dissociative states.

So far it might seem that the point of recovering traumatic memories is purely instrumental. But there is something more at stake here, a kind of self-knowledge that is charged with moral and political valences. Advocates speak of "the tremendous reward of knowing your own history," of knowing "who you are and where you came from" (Fredrickson 1992: 31). Judith Herman points out that learning about their early abuse enables adult survivors to "become comprehensible to themselves."

> When survivors recognize the origins of their psychological difficulties in an abusive childhood environment, they no longer need attribute them to an inherent defect in the self. Thus the way is opened to the creation of new meaning in experience and a new, unstigmatized identity. (1992: 127)

This last point is an extremely interesting one, because it suggests that the details of the abusive history may be less important for the patient's healing than the *fact* of the abuse itself. The patient has discovered a decisive event in her past that has made her who she is, and that event is a crime, committed when she was a helpless child. Advocates agree that this is a painful discovery, one that brings anger, grieving, and, in many cases, a permanent break with her family. At the same time, once recovered memories have established the trauma as real, she is changed—one might almost say *diagnostically* changed—into a new kind of person: a *survivor*. The word itself suggests strength and a moral affinity to other kinds of survivors—of war, torture, the holocaust.

For Judith Herman this affinity is more than metaphorical. She argues that survivors of all these horrors can be shown to suffer from a common syndrome, which she calls "Complex Post-Traumatic Stress Disorder." Seen in this light, trauma therapy takes on some of the qualities of a political act. The therapist must be prepared to set aside her traditional neutrality, stand with her client against the oppressor, and above all "bear witness" to what was done (1992: 135). By the same token, the client's struggle to recover her history is part of a larger struggle. Remembering is bearing testimony, breaking the conspiracy of silence (181).

To one whole school of critics, this narrative with its crusading overtones is little more than a recipe for false memories and the destruction of families (Crews 1994; Ofshe and Watters 1994). My concern is a different one, and it hearkens back to Hacking's question about self-knowledge for multiples. Imagine someone who gone through recovered memory therapy and made its guiding story her own story, one that makes her life "comprehensible for the first time." What limits does this story impose on her sense of herself as a person, even on the questions she can ask?

In a recent article, Janice Haaken, a feminist psychoanalyst, offers some telling observations on this point. Both recovered memory advocates and their critics, she says, have failed to see that "the emotional truth of the past is never reducible to the concrete facticity of events but is always bound up in interpretation, both in the initial experience of events and in their later elaborations and working through in memory . . ." (1994: 118). Haaken argues that the concrete, historical interpretations favored by trauma therapists are in a sense impoverishing, in that they offer no place for fantasy, imagination, or moral ambiguity. They make the survivor's life comprehensible, perhaps, but at the cost of typecasting her as an innocent victim whose troubles derive entirely from her abuse: this "political construction of the victim" she says, "works against complex truths and honest self-exploration . . ." (123). Worse than that, it leaves the adult survivor, *qua* survivor, as someone without desire or moral agency of her own.

I would add that when memories are taken only as clues to real events, one runs the risk of becoming deaf to their subtler symbolic meanings. Memories visit us unbidden, not simply as records of the past, but as responses to our ongoing needs, hopes, predicaments. From a psychoanalytic standpoint, in fact, much of everyday mental life is informed by a complex metaphorical interchange between past and present. The past is important, not as a series of blind causes that have made us what we are, but as a body of compelling metaphors or prototypes that inform our present experience and behavior. To the extent they are formative, in fact, past events in psychoanalysis are not past at all. They are part of the "timeless unconscious" and thus present here and now—though of course in disguised form. Freud saw the transference as a way of making the unconscious conscious by conjuring it up as "a piece of real life" in therapy, so that one meets it on the same footing with the present.[7] This makes the past into something that, at least in principle, can be reencountered, "worked through," and reappropriated as one continues to live. By contrast, a past composed of frozen events that "tell you who you are" may imprison the client in an equally frozen sense of herself as survivor.[8]

To put it briefly, then, we might say that recovered memory therapy offers clients the benefits of a new identity that exempts them from psychiatric stigma, affirms their oppression, and links their suffering with a larger political struggle—but that it does so at a price. The price is that it inducts them into an illness idiom that excludes fantasy, moral ambiguity, a sense of agency, and the kind of remembering that can offer openings to the future.

My concerns here begin to sound very much like Hacking's contention that multiple personality is a kind of false consciousness—that the multiple is "a thoroughly crafted person," as he puts it, but "not a person with self-knowledge." The difference is that I have been discussing the expressive limits of recovered memory therapy and its guiding narrative, not multiple personality as such. My strictures would certainly apply to multiples who understood themselves exclusively in these terms, but I do not think this is often the case. As Hacking himself has pointed out, today's multiple personality movement is the offspring of a curious marriage between the recovered memory movement, with its close links to the crusade against child abuse, and a more diffuse body of assumptions and expectations rooted in the history of hypnosis and spontaneous trance behavior (Hacking 1992; Kenny 1986; Ellenberger 1970). I would add that in addition to these "vertical" links to earlier dissociative theories and idioms, multiple personality has important "horizontal" affinities to some contemporary psychotherapeutic practices, including psychodrama (Moreno 1945), gestalt therapy (Perls 1969), transactional analysis (Berne 1961), and imaginal dialogues (Watkins 1986). Interestingly enough, advocates of all these techniques see them as ways to foster imaginative engagement with unrecognized dimensions of the self. What I am suggesting, then, is that multiple personality cannot be reduced to recovered memory therapy, and that because its own cultural sources are so diffuse and multiple, its expressive possibilities cannot be determined in advance.

The only way of assessing these possibilities is to look at an actual life story. The above discussion may enable us to do this with a heightened sense of the issues at stake. Certainly the limits of the recovered memory narratives are clear enough. It remains, however, to characterize the difference between stories of this kind and others that reflect a more authentic brand of self-understanding. Here again, I think Paul Ricoeur's work on narrative identity (1992) points the way to an economical and suggestive formulation.

Ricoeur proposes a distinction between two dimensions or aspects of personal identity. On the one hand there is *sameness*, Ricoeur's term for the side of identity that depends on fixed attributes—race, gender, birthplace, but also habits and traits of character. Sameness constitutes identity

11

through permanence in time, but also through similarity with others who share the same attributes (1992: 121). It is implicit whenever we speak of "identifying" with specific persons or groups. It is also clearly implicit in the notion of "identity politics."[9] Ricoeur's term for the other side of identity is *selfhood.* What he has in mind here is the kind of identity implicit in our ability to make commitments or keep promises, to be someone who can be "counted on." But this ability implies something more—an ability to project ourselves forward in time, to say who we will be tomorrow. Identity in this sense of the word is unavoidably an ethical project, but it is also an unfinished one. It depends on "self-constancy," as Ricoeur puts it, on a sense of what matters to us, but this is a sense that remains open to change in an ongoing dialogue between experience and memory (1992: 163–68).

For Ricoeur, the task of narrative self-understanding is to mediate between these two poles of identity, to balance sameness with ethical openness, to anchor selfhood in a personal and social history. Although he doesn't address the issue directly, his work implies that narratives based on either side alone would risk premature closure, replacing the dialectic of self-understanding with blind affiliations or a dry and abstract sense of duty. It is the tension between selfhood and sameness that sustains an open narrative.

Ricoeur's language affords us a way of translating Hacking's question into narrative terms. Instead of asking whether multiples can know themselves, we can now ask in what ways and how "openly" their life stories succeed in framing a narrative identity. In these terms it is easy to categorize the standard recovered memory story as a one-sided narrative of "sameness." Variants on this story are common enough in survivor newsletters and self-help literature, where they often serve polemical ends. However in my experience the stories told privately by multiples tend to be more complex and interesting; this is especially true of the accounts given by those strong enough to pursue careers and other outside interests. Statistically speaking, these stories may not be typical, but they certainly offer a more complete picture of multiple personality as an expressive idiom. The example that follows is a case in point. It includes some of the classic elements of "sameness" found in recovered memory therapy, but there are other currents as well. Some of these imply a more imaginative engagement with the past and suggest an emerging sense of Ricoeurian selfhood.

The woman I shall call Beth is now a pastor in a small Protestant church in eastern Manitoba. At the time she joined the group she was still a divinity student—a slim, quiet woman in her late thirties, given to wearing plaid shirts and faded jeans. Though reserved at first, she found her voice and eventually became one of the group's most active participants— someone who could be counted on to show up every week and talk about herself, but also to listen thoughtfully to others.

Beth had been diagnosed with MPD several months before joining the group. At the time she arrived she said she and her two therapists had contacted nearly forty alter personalities. Like many other "high-functioning" multiples, Beth had always been able to maintain a certain degree of "co-consciousness" with her alters, even when they were in control. She was one of the few participants who would switch regularly during meetings, usually to a wise-cracking child alter named Belinda. However, even these switches seemed governed by an adult sense of appropriateness, since they normally took place only during the early, "social chat" phase of the meetings, or on the rare occasions when someone else produced a child alter.

Beth grew up in a small town in southern Manitoba, the eldest of four children. Her father had suffered a series of mental breakdowns when she was young and so never held a steady job. She remembers her home as "a bad scene—just full of tension and bickering." On finishing high school she moved to a nearby city to begin training as a nurse. Over the next decade she held several nursing positions, including one year as a psychiatric nurse. She also started work toward her B.A. However, she felt drawn toward the church and pastoral counseling. Eventually she took a job as a lay chaplain with a Christian youth organization, which she held for seven years. Her departure from this job coincided roughly with a personal crisis in which she came to recognize her sexual abuse as a child. However, she was not diagnosed as a multiple until more than a year later, by which time she had already begun her divinity studies.

My interviews with Beth took place on two occasions, separated by nearly two years. In the first, shortly after she joined the group, I asked her to tell me how she had come to recognize that she had been abused and to experience herself as someone with "other parts." The second interview took place after she had been ordained and had begun preaching to her first congregation. This time I simply asked her to tell me about how her life had changed since our first interview. The two interviews together yielded about five hours of taped material.

This material conveys a story—a single story, I think—but it is not a linear one. There are false starts, digressions, repetitions. Sometimes the action circles back on itself as recent events turn into portents of an unsuspected past. At one level it describes a kind of mid-life crisis that takes place over a period of about three years. However, because the crisis is experienced through the prism of recovered memories and multiplicity, it becomes a story about her entire life, especially her childhood. It is also in every sense a story about identity.

In what follows I want to consider three narrative strands in this material, as illustrated in three sets of excerpts. In each of these Beth invokes

13

memories in a tacit effort to reframe her identity. But she does so in a three very different ways.

1. Discovery

In telling how she learned that she had been abused as a child, Beth begins not with memories or flashbacks, but with a series of intuitions that grew out of her work as a nurse and counselor. "In the summer of '84," she begins, "I had a nightmare." But then she backs up:

> In the spring of '83 I started seeing a chaplain because I had a couple of students I didn't feel I was counseling appropriately. Maybe he suspected something, because I remember him asking, "What does this trigger?" and I couldn't answer. And then that summer I worked in palliative care the whole time. In the fall I came to the counselor and said, "I've been so in touch with other people's pain all summer, now I really feel in touch with my own." At the end of that conversation I remember him telling me, "Beth, you're an abused child," but I couldn't accept it.
>
> That was fall of '83. In the summer of '84 I was at a cottage with some friends and somebody gave me a book. It was the story of a special ed. teacher who was working with these kids—and I found myself really identified with this special ed. teacher. And then she's talking about this relationship with her lover and I found I could no longer identify with her. And then I found myself identified with one of these little kids that had been abused. Just before going to bed that night I was at a part in the book where the little kid loses it totally and is under a bed and won't come out. That night I had a nightmare, and in the nightmare I admitted I was physically abused. I had never done that before. I was really quite shocked by that. I went back to my counselor and said, "Guess what. . . ."

As she worked with her counselor over the next several months, Beth began to recognize the full extent of her physical abuse. There were no repressed memories involved here, she says: "I never lost memories of the physical abuse. I just had never called it that." She began to withdraw from her family and finally made a decision to change the spelling of her last name. By her own account this "triggered an incredible grieving process," one that continued to deepen over the course of the following year.

As this happened, Beth found herself brooding over other troubling features of her life, including her evident aversion to relationships with men. She had always managed to think of this in religious terms, as being "called to singleness." Now she began to see the actual fear lurking behind this high-minded idea. She also "began to feel there was this wounded child inside me, this kid who could be different ages at different times." These thoughts led her to another realization:

> In the spring of '87 I was walking on the beach praying, and it was as if I had this puzzle and I was trying to put together all these different pieces. I was starting to notice all these different things. . . . As I was praying, I'm not sure what happened, except I realized my sexuality had been abused. I didn't have any memories at that point.

Several points in this narrative segment are striking. Although no repressed memories have appeared as yet, it bears the clear marks of a recovered memory narrative. It begins with symptoms—inappropriate counseling, troubling identifications. Beth's chaplain explains them by proposing that she is a certain kind of person: "Beth, you're an abused child." She rejects this proffered identity, but another, more frightening symptomatic experience compels her to accept it. In doing so she merely redefines what she already knew about her unhappy childhood, but the effect is profound. Now she no longer belongs to her family, but to the company of the abused. She confirms this shift in a little ritual of *disidentification* by changing the spelling of her name. In Ricoeur's terms, it is interesting that so much in this initial change of identity is framed in the language of identification, of sameness. And yet it is Hacking's work that best explains what happens next. Hacking (1991) has shown that the term child abuse has only come lately to bridge the previously unrelated concepts of cruelty to children and incest. Increasingly, the paradigmatic "abused child" is in fact a victim of incest. Thus in seeing herself as an abused child, Beth gains access to other forms of "sameness" implicit it this term. She has been abused, but in how many ways? Does the physical abuse explain all her symptoms? What has she forgotten? Questions like these illustrate what Hacking calls "semantic contagion"(1995: 255–59). They cannot explain Beth's conviction that she was sexually abused, but they show how it is thinkable in the absence of specific memories.

2. Discontinuity

Beth's dark revelation on the beach seemed to set off a long downward spiral into fatigue, paralysis, and depression. During this period, she says, "even God became violent to me." By the following spring she felt she couldn't go on with her job anymore and decided to resign. Her plan was to resume her former occupation as an obstetrical nurse. But three weeks after taking up this new job she was injured in a car accident.

> After the accident it was like I was a different person. I couldn't access the confidence or even the faith I'd had before. . . . Once I'd been injured they told me I'd never be able to work as a nurse again. So the only thing I thought I had was gone. The other thing I thought I had was a good relationship with God, which had now been blown apart. . . . My best friend walked away. So I was really quite alone and quite broken.

She thought of going back to her old job as a lay chaplain, but now she felt a mysterious barrier to that whole part of her life. The work she had done easily there now seemed impossibly difficult.

> I would say to Connie and Dave, the chaplains who were helping me, "I don't understand it, but I can't access the strength I had when I worked for CYC. I don't feel it's even me," I remember saying. "I know I did all these talks. I can still pick up a file and give a talk, but I can't feel it the way I felt it before."

During this period Beth became even more convinced that she had been sexually abused, but she still had no memories. On her chaplain's advice, she began seeing a new therapist who had worked with other abuse victims. After several weeks the therapist pointed out that she seemed to be dissociating in their sessions.

> And somehow everything fell into place at that point. I knew I had the key. Early on Linda [her therapist] had told me, "You've got a message inside you: don't tell, and if we could get to that message we'd get a lot of information." So I went home one day and focused on this "don't tell." And I got this incredible pressure and pain in my vagina, just this incredible pressure. And this voice saying don't tell, this isn't wrong, don't tell. And I could see myself sitting on top of my chest. So I asked, "How old are you?" and I could see I was like nineteen months old. . . .[10]
> Well, that was a flashback. I had triggered a flashback.

The next several weeks brought a whole cascade of these flashbacks, each with its attendant child presenting an abusive scene. The children all had different ages that served them for names ("the eight-year-old"; "the two-year-old"), and once they had appeared, they became part of Beth's life. As might be expected, they often turned up in therapy, but they also started coming out unbidden at other times as well. Beth called this group of alter personalities "the Memory Kids" because each was linked to a specific set of childhood scenes. Over the next several months she and her therapist succeeded in piecing these scenes together into a truly horrific chronicle of sexual abuse at the hands of her father.

Beth's story up to now is a familiar variant on the recovered memory pattern: she finds her repressed memories by way of dissociation and becomes a multiple in the bargain. What happened next, however, could not have been predicted. Just as the story of her abuse was coming into focus, she had another visionary experience:

> I woke up one morning, early early, with this pain in my chest like somebody was pounding on it from the inside. . . . I realized it was somebody pounding like crazy, just a-whompin'. So I asked the other kids if they would stop it. I said, "Whoever's doing that has to stop it," and the Memory Kids said, "Well, it's Marybeth."

A series of these encounters over the next several weeks served to introduce a whole new set of alters whom Beth came to call the "Executive Kids." They were much stronger than the Memory Kids, less fearful, but also harder to control:

> When the Memory Kids came, they needed a lot of nurturing, but they responded really well to that. . . . The Executive Kids didn't respond to that at all. When they first came out they claimed not to know me. . . . Most of them thought I was pretty useless.

The Executive Kids brought a surprising piece of news: *they* were actually the ones who had been in charge of Beth's life during much of her adolescence and adulthood. As she came to know this new group of personalities, a new version of her own history emerged, one that was less autobiography than "serial multography." "What I think now," she says, "is that when I was about ten the abuse just got to be too much for me. So I went under and they started doing things, depending on who had the right skills." This version of events threw a new light on some of the gaps in Beth's memory, her sense of vagueness about entire periods in her life. It also gave her something more important—a way of understanding her long lapse into depression and incapacity:

> What I think is that after the accident we switched again, but this time somehow *I* got jarred loose. That's why I couldn't relate to my

old job—I wasn't the one who did it! Also, I came back in much the same state as when I went under, kind of broken and confused. It was really a difficult time, and just so similar to what I'd grown up with. Losing everything that had promise for me. Being victimized by structures bigger than me through no fault of my own. No support, not sure what the future held and so forth. I think that's why the switch happened—somehow I was just *back*.

There is a revealing ambiguity in this last phrase. "I was just back" could mean "I, the adult, was back in the situation I experienced as a child." Or it could mean, "I, that unhappy child came back from my place of hiding." Clearly it means both. The ambiguity helps us to understand what is at stake in this "realization" and others made possible by the "Executive Kids." Here again dissociation offers Beth a way of drawing on memory to make sense of her life. But this is no longer memory as record of decisive facts; it is memory as *metaphor*. In this respect Beth's experience of the Executive Kids opens up some of the same expressive possibilities as the Freudian notions of transference and the timeless unconscious. As alter personalities these figures allow—in fact compel—Beth to meet and come to terms with each of her former selves, not as a fossil or shadowy construct, but as "a living presence," in Freud's memorable phrase. Here, in other words, the imaginative, theatrical dimension of multiple personality as an expressive idiom offers a way of loosening and compensating for the frozen sense of the past implicit in recovered memory therapy.

3. Difference

The third narrative strand I want to consider is a brief one that appears only in the second interview, where Beth reflects on the experience of being ordained and on her new role as minister. Beth explains that, internally, the most important recent development is that "we finally got to Elizabeth, the one I call the first-born. Linda, my therapist, thinks she's probably the core personality. She's the one who was there before the abuse began." Elizabeth can be "co-present" with Beth, and when she is, the world looks different: "When she's there, I see things in 3-D. When she's not, everything's flat. I'd never seen the colors of a sunset. But how do you know what you don't see? When she first came out, I've had to stop the car because she was so overwhelming."

Elizabeth has the ability to see other people in a more subtly shaded, three dimensional way as well. Seeing the local farmers in her congregation, men she likes and respects, she thinks of her father.

Leonard [Beth's father] grew up on the farm. He loved the farm. Like when I—when Elizabeth looks at these men on our lay leadership board, she sees, like, they're so much like Leonard, in that they're very shy. There's one of them who always comes up and speaks to me, and he's *painfully* shy. I can see the tremendous effort he's making. He's similar to Leonard in that when he's self-conscious he walks kind of slouched over. . . . Leonard would do well in this community if he could have—whatever he couldn't get over.

Elizabeth was telling Linda that she had seen light in Leonard when she was little, and how the light gradually got darker and darker until it was gone. And she was describing how she sees shadows over the light in some of these men, but somehow they can embrace the light, and so they live from the light that's in them. It's like a rim around the moon—the shadow's there but the light prevails. But somehow in Leonard the light went out.

Here for the first time since I have known her, Beth depicts her father in something resembling ordinary human terms. She endows him with qualities (shyness, awkwardness) that she finds endearing in other men. She remembers that he wasn't all bad to begin with and wonders where he went wrong. She is drawing on memory again, dissociated memory, but this time she uses it reflectively, to make a comparison that hints at moral complexity.

Toward the end of this interview Beth begins to ponder her own passage through life in somewhat similar terms. In light of her rotten childhood, she wonders, why didn't she become a criminal or drug addict or something worse? The answer, she thinks, is that "we've always had this dream."

Actually it's Elizabeth's dream. This has been her dream, becoming a minister. But I think we're really fortunate that all the alters have respected the dream? That's been the common thread. I think that's what's kept us from being a juvenile delinquent or alcoholic or getting somehow lost . . . I think it was what kept me alive all those years when I was a kid. That I belonged to God, that I was gonna do something with my life, that I could help other people somehow. I don't remember any adult telling me that.

Here again we see Beth calling on memory to say who she is. But this time instead of seeking a diagnostic sameness, she is trying to explain just what it is that makes her different. Her answer begins to frame an identity that has nothing at all to do with "decisive facts," and that depends instead on a sustaining commitment that joins her past to her future. She continues to understand her life through the idiom of multiple personality, but what she understands begins to look very much like "selfhood" in Ricoeur's sense of the word.

Notes

1. Hacking's notions of "looping" and "making up people" derive in part from the work of both Nelson Goodman (1978) and Michel Foucault (1977; 1980). For a fuller discussion see Hacking (1994).

2. The group was founded by multiples in 1990. After a stormy first year, members made a public appeal for a non-multiple to serve as a volunteer facilitator; I agreed to do so in return for the opportunity to carry out ethnographic research. We worked out a set of guidelines for meetings and agreed that my role would simply be to remind participants of the guidelines where necessary. The only requirement for joining the group was that members be currently under treatment for multiple personality disorder. As it turned out, most participants were referred by their therapists.

   Like most support groups, this one did not draw a random sample of the afflicted; for obvious reasons the severely disturbed either didn't come or quickly drifted away. However, since my interest was chiefly in the culture of multiplicity rather than the pathology of individuals, I do not think this represented a significant source of bias.

3. The use of narrative as a tool of self-understanding has clear antecedents in a Christian confessional literature dating back at least to St. Augustine, who came to identify knowledge of self with knowledge of God's will. For an early and insightful discussion of confessional practices and their mediating role in "systems of self-direction," see Nelson (1965). More recently, Foucault (1978) has noted the ubiquitous role of confession as tool for the "production of truth" about subjects in modern societies, a truth shaped by the discursive practices of law, medicine, psychiatry, and education.

4. See Hacking's chapter in this volume.

5. In a workshop given to other therapists in 1993, Fischer-Taylor described her own discovery that her lifelong mood swings were in fact "feeling flashbacks" triggered by sounds or smells. For example, she explained, she had always felt a strange sense of pain and sadness

when she listened to the piano sonatas of Beethoven, Mozart, and Hayden. Finally she summoned up the courage to explore this with her therapist by recreating the scene when she first heard the music. Phrases came up: "Don't do it. Leave me alone." She shouted them out, she said, "and as I was doing this I started to get the actual visual memories." Her mother played the piano, she said, and she concluded that her father had abused her in the evenings when her mother was practicing these pieces.

6. Interpretively speaking, in fact, recovered memory therapy offers an intriguing parallel to the historical literalism seen in fundamentalist readings of the Bible. Contrast the very different view taken by analysts such as James Hillman, who emphasises the role of the imagination: "[A] trauma is not what happened, but the way we see what happened. A trauma is not a pathological event but a pathologized image, an image that has become intolerable . . ." (Hillman 1983: 47).

7. Clearly there is a fundamental difference between the re-enacting of motifs from early life in transference and the dissociative "abreaction" of traumas in recovered memory therapy. While both might be considered ways of making the past present, the therapeutic point of transference is to provide a way of exposing and reworking metaphoric links between past and present; the therapeutic point of abreaction is to re-experience repressed traumas in their full emotional intensity and then to reconstruct the events themselves in narrative form.

8. In fairness to Judith Herman, it should be said that she recognizes this as a potential hazard. She believes, however, that with good therapy a survivor can free herself of the traumatic past and begin the "re-creation of an ideal self" using her newly liberated capacity for imagination and fantasy. "It takes courage to move out of the constricted stance of the victim," she says. "But just as the survivor must dare to confront her fears, she must also dare to define her wishes" (1992: 202).

9. In fact Ricoeur points out that when national identity is founded exclusively on this kind of sameness, shared traits become solidified and "lend themselves to exploitation by the most harmful ideologies" (1992: 123).

10. I asked Beth how she could tell just by looking that she was nineteen months old. She said she couldn't tell that exactly, but she could "see" that she was alone in the house with her father. "My mother had another baby when I was nineteen months old, and so he had to care for me, because she was in the hospital."

References

Antze, Paul. 1976. "The Role of Ideologies in Peer Psychotherapy Organizations: Some Theoretical Considerations and Three Case Studies." *Journal of Applied Behavioral Science* 12 (3): 323–46.

———. 1987. "Symbolic Action in Alcoholics Anonymous." In *Constructive Drinking: Perspectives on Drink from Anthropology.* Mary Douglas, ed. Cambridge: Cambridge University Press, pp. 149–81.

———. 1992. "Being Multiple Together." Paper presented at Annual Meeting of the Canadian Anthropology Society, Montreal, Quebec.

———. 1992. "Possession Trance and Multiple Personality: Psychiatric Disorders or Idioms of Distress?" *Transcultural Psychiatric Research Review* 24 (4): 319–23.

Berne, Eric. 1961. *Transactional Analysis in Psychotherapy.* New York: Grove Press.

Boddy, Janice. 1988. "Spirits and Selves in Northern Sudan: The Cultural Therapeutics of Possession and Trance." *American Ethnologist* 15 (1): 4–27.

———. 1989. *Wombs and Alien Spirits: Women, Men and the Zar Cult in Northern Sudan.* Madison: University of Wisconsin Press.

Breuer, Josef, and Sigmund Freud. 1955 [1895]. *Studies on Hysteria.* In S. Freud, *The Standard Edition of the Complete Psychological Works of Sigmund Freud.* James Strachey, trans. and ed. London: Hogarth.

Crews, Frederick. 1994. "The Revenge of the Repressed." *New York Review of Books*, November 17 and December 1.

Ellenberger, Henri. 1970. *The Discovery of the Unconscious.* New York: Basic Books.

Foucault, Michel. 1977. *Discipline and Punish.* Alan Sheridan, trans. London: Penguin Books.

———. 1978. *The History of Sexuality. Volume I: An Introduction.* New York: Random House.

———. 1980. *Power/Knowledge.* Colin Gordon, ed. New York: Pantheon Books.

Fredrickson, Renee. 1992. *Repressed Memories: A Journey to Recovery from Sexual Abuse.* New York: Fireside/Parkside Books.

Goodman, Nelson. 1978. *Ways of Worldmaking.* Indianapolis, Ind.: Hackett Publishing.

Haaken, Janice. 1994. "Sexual Abuse, Recovered Memory and Therapeutic Practice." *Social Text* 40: 115–45.

Hacking, Ian. 1986. "Making Up People." In *Reconstructing Individualism: Autonomy, Individuality and the Self in Western Thought.* Thomas C. Heller et al., eds. Stanford: Stanford University Press, pp. 222–36.

————. 1991. "The Making and Molding of Child Abuse." *Critical Inquiry* 17: 253–58.

————. 1992. "Multiple Personality Disorder and Its Hosts." *History of the Human Sciences* 5 (2): 3–31.

————. 1994. "The Looping Effects of Human Kinds." In *Causal Cognition: A Multidisciplinary Approach.* D. Sperber et al., eds. Oxford: Clarendon Press, pp. 351–94.

————. 1995. *Rewriting the Soul: Multiple Personality and the Sciences of Memory.* Princeton, N.J.: Princeton University Press.

Herman, Judith Lewis. 1992. *Trauma and Recovery.* New York: Basic Books.

Hillman, James. 1983. *Healing Fictions.* Barrytown, N.Y.: Station Hill Press.

Janet, Pierre. 1989 [1889]. *L'Automatisme psychologique: Essai de psychologie expérimentale sur les formes inférieures de l'activité humaine.* Paris: Alcan.

Kenny, Michael. 1986. *The Passion of Ansel Bourne.* Washington, D.C.: Smithsonian Institution.

Lambek, Michael. 1981. *Human Spirits: A Cultural Account of Trance in Mayotte.* New York: Cambridge University Press.

Moreno, Jacob. 1945. *Group Therapy.* New York: Beacon House.

Nelson, Benjamin. 1965. "Self-Images and Systems of Spiritual Direction in the History of European Civilization." In *The Quest for Self-Control.* S. Klausner, ed. New York: Free Press.

Nichter, Mark. 1981. "Idioms of Distress: Alternatives in the Expression of Psychosocial Distress." *Culture, Medicine and Psychiatry* 5 (4): 379–408.

Ofshe, Richard, and Ethan Watters. 1994. *Making Monsters: False Memories, Psychotherapy and Sexual Hysteria.* New York: Scribner's.

Perls, Fritz. 1969. *Gestalt Therapy Verbatim.* Moab, Utah: Real People Press.

Ricoeur, Paul. 1992. *Oneself As Another.* Chicago: University of Chicago Press.

van der Kolk, Bessel. 1988. "The Trauma Spectrum: The Interaction of Biological and Social Events in the Genesis of the Trauma Response." *Journal of Traumatic Stress* 1: 273–90.

Watkins, Mary. 1986. *Invisible Guests: The Development of Imaginal Dialogues.* Boston: Sigo Press.

Yap, Pow-Ming. 1969. "The Culture-Bound Reactive Syndromes." In *Mental Health Research in Asia and the Pacific.* W. Caudill and T. Y. Lin, eds. Honolulu: East-West Center Press.

2

Remembering Trouble
Three Lives, Three Stories

Donna J. Young

> Language is like shot silk; so much depends on the angle at
> which it is held.
>
> —John Fowles

My subject is the narrative construction of autobiography in the life stories
of three women, who represent three generations within a single family,
born and bred within an impoverished settlement in rural New Brunswick,
Canada. I will call them Grandmother, Mother, and Daughter, although
the labels conceal far more than they reveal. Implicit in my decision to focus on life stories are certain assumptions about the role of narrative in the
structuring of human experience. First, I assume that even individual au-
tobiographies "depend on being placed within a continuity provided by a
constructed and shared social history in which we locate our Selves and
our individual continuities" (Bruner 1991: 20). I argue that what is at stake
in collecting life stories is not a simple reconstruction of the empirical historical past, nor an indulgent and by turns condescending exploration of
another's subjective, and therefore flawed, understanding of events that
have passed, "but the very historicity of the event in an entirely new dimension" (Felman and Laub 1992: 62). Because there is a creative and formative tension between the ways in which stories are embedded in
historical, political, economic, and ideological worlds *and* the ways in
which narratives create those worlds, the life stories of the women can be
read as a diagnostic of both ideological and discursive shifts that engendered new constructions of narrative identity within new moral orders.

Thus, this exploration of family history over three generations assumes a dialectic tension between *context* and *text*.[1]

Here I have abstracted only anecdotal fragments from the women's life stories that act as a "diagnostic of power," revealing, as they do, "historical shifts in configurations or methods of power" (Abu-Lughod 1992: 41–55). These transformations of power are mirrored in the very forms of textual disclosure and language within which the women couch their tales. The life stories of the first two generations were told to me orally and draw upon similar narrative forms. But the discourses upon which they draw differ considerably.[2] The Grandmother's discursive field is largely religious, while the Mother's discourse is shaped by the language of consumption, highlighting the extent to which their self-understanding and desires are historically contingent. I will focus on their memories of religious retreats, picked up in both narratives, to show how their life stories converge and stray. This is in sharp contrast to the fragmented story of the third generation, which represents an attempt to recover/re-create a life history in the wake of post-traumatic memory loss. Drawn from the pages of a journal that the Daughter created for a team of therapists, it not only has a radically altered narrative form, but draws upon the medical discourse of psychiatry. Still, I will argue that embedded in her story of once repressed and now recovered memories are the remnants of a childhood situated at the crossroads of changing, and utterly incommensurable, cosmologies.

Common threads connecting the three stories are memories of violence and mental illness. In the third generation the violence remembered involves the sexual abuse of children. But to tease this thread of violence from the myriad others used to fashion their life stories would only misrepresent the complexities of their lives and their relationships with each other. It would also lead to the facile conclusion that their states of mental distress are singularly rooted in the sexual abuse of children, as is so often assumed these days, and miss the wider pervasiveness of power and oppression in their lives. The threads with which the women weave the stories that cloak their lives are not transparent. Rather, meaning and significance are to be culled from the very material—the discourse—in which their memories are draped. This is precisely the point of my opening epigraph.

Listening to Grandmother

I first met the Mother and Daughter about ten years ago and count the Daughter among my closest friends. The Daughter literally talked me into doing field work in the settlement where she spent the first eighteen years of her life. And, when I began, she traveled with me to the settlement in northern New Brunswick where her grandmother still lives. I met her Grandmother on that initial trip and have since spent many days rocking and roasting beside the wood stove in her brightly painted lavender kitchen. She has a shy and melancholic nature that on rare occasions erupts into the feistiness for which people of this community are infamous. I recorded her life story on a series of cold and bitter days in December 1992. Although I had dutifully prepared a questionnaire, it was obvious she found my queries disruptive and I soon grew silent. Her story was told only when she was ready, and in richness and cultural meaning it far exceeds anything my dry questions about religious affiliation were likely to elicit. She is a powerful story-teller. Here is an edited slice of her life narrative.[3]

> I was born Catholic. I don't go much anymore. My Mama. Poor Mama used to go to church. If she wasn't sick she didn't miss Church. Especially after they built the Church here. Mama, she didn't drink, she didn't smoke. You know? The women were good then. I remember that. Good living. When I was young both Papa and Mama would go to church. There would be confessions and receivings and in the summer they had what they called retreats.
>
> One summer after I was married we had a big retreat and the Holy Fathers were here for over two weeks. That's what we called them. They were really horrible with the long beards, and the long brown dresses. Yes. The Holy Father would pass our houses and call us to come to hear them preach. First the Holy Father called all the men to come in the afternoon. Then he came for the women at night. Another time he took the older children, then the little children. You know? He didn't want them all together. And then he used to preach. Oh my! He told us all about the sins. He said things that you never heard about; things that couldn't be done.
>
> I remember my poor sister and how she laughed. Yes, she laughed. "You!" he said. "You don't have to laugh there." He said, "Maybe you think I don't know who you are, but I know who you are." He didn't know her from the man in the moon. He was telling us what were sins and he said that it was a sin for women to have sex with the bed post. The bed post! Upon my soul to God. If you had sex with the bed post. How could a woman ever? Can you imagine? But I didn't laugh because they scared me to death.
>
> I remember they called us all into the graveyard at night. This is a long time ago. I had only two children then. "Go into the graveyard and kneel down," they told us. "All of you who have parents lying here, call them." We all kneeled down there, in the graveyard, and we were calling our fathers, mothers, brothers, anyone who was

27

dead. We were scared to death. Not just me. Everybody was scared. I remember my sister and I were crying. It was pitch dark at night.

Then the Father said that all the men that had cut pulp—you know—he said they were stealing and would go to hell. Well! It turned out some fool went to confession and told. Well, I mean, Father also said that it was a sin to smoke and so-and-so there was scared because the Father caught them and got after them. But nothing happened. He was just saying those things. There were a lot of people said it was crazy. And they said if they had another one they wouldn't go.

Now the Priests around here were not like that. They were different. But there were a couple of wicked ones. They had wicked tempers. Strict. There was one: I didn't go around him too much. He would get something cross. That man used to tramp the roads at night to see what was going on. I remember he slapped one of my sister's daughters. She was going out with the man who later became her husband and he caught them. I suppose she was sixteen. He was a wicked priest. When my daughter was young I took her to a movie at the school there and he plainly told me straight up and down: "Why don't you stay home with that kid?" They hurt you so bad. I didn't care for him. She was only two years old. A friend had to take me home. We only got to see a movie once a year and I had to go home.

Mostly every man up here used to work in the woods in the winter. Most times it was just women and children out here. And a few old men. But I never thought to move. I have a lonesome nature. I don't go out much. I used to go to Church and I'd go to house parties and visit my sisters. But I had a nervous breakdown and now I don't go out much.

The settlement that these women grew up in was created under a Free Grants Act in 1879. Land was distributed to indigent French, Irish, and Scottish settlers with the understanding that they would clear the land and farm. However, the land was of poor quality and the settlers soon went to work in the timber trade, legitimately as wage workers, and illegitimately as independent harvesters of timber on the nearby Crown Lands that were leased to large lumber interests. As subsistence farmers, wage workers, and "thieves," the early settlers endeavored to build a community. Almost immediately, taxes were collected to build a school, but their efforts to find and to keep a teacher were feeble. In the depression years of the 1920s and 1930s it became impossible to make a living wage in the woods, and the local school was closed more than it was opened.

This paved the way for the Catholic church to make inroads into the settlement in the 1940s. The Acadian sisters and clergy that went to work in the settlement shared with the settlers a vision of independent farming settlements, fueled in part by Acadian nationalism.[4] Perhaps the frustrated hopes of the Grandmother's parents found redemption in a revived Catholicism. The settlement became a Parish in 1941, and Les Filles de Jesus established a convent and school in 1944. Whereas the Grandmother had briefly attended the secular school, her children were sent to the Convent School, although none would make it past grade five.

Through acts of charity and mission building the Catholic church came to be the dominant political and cultural force in the settlement in the years following the depression. Increasingly the local priest became the spokesperson for the community, mediating between government officials and local people. Political patronage and church politics were briefly entwined. The Sisters designed the school's curriculum and daily administered instruction and discipline in both English and French. They toiled to provide the children with a proper Acadian *formation*, despite their poverty and confused lineage. Exercising power through doctrine and charity, clergy were by turns revered and feared. There are stories of both kindness and abuse.

Yet the hegemony of the church was never complete and the people of the settlement refused to embrace an Acadian identity. In the 1960s when the school was again made secular, this time under the banner of "equal opportunity," they chose to *become* English. No doubt the seeds of resistance to the authority of the church over matters of identity and livelihood were rooted in that period of early settlement when Catholicism resided in the folk practices of the lay Irish and French settlers and their survival demanded numerous strategies, legitimate and otherwise.

What is most evident in Grandmother's tales of the retreat are her feelings of resentment towards a church that was morally intrusive and judgmental. While community members were more easily dismissive of the clergy's condemnation of the illegal economic pursuits upon which their livelihood depended, they internalized a sense of shame that was at times unbearable on matters of family and sexuality. Having been publicly slandered and humiliated by the priest who questioned her parenting abilities when she took her daughter to a movie, Grandmother's sense of social isolation (at home with a large family while her husband was at work in the woods) could only be alleviated by leaving her children at home alone. The priest's moral outrage and his imposition of family rearing practices as they developed in the post–World War Two era belongs to a new moral economy from which the grandmother is excluded. I believe these economic and cultural developments led to, or at least solidified,

the notion that the people who lived in the settlement were both culturally backward and economically dysfunctional and it is in this period that
their fate as an under-class was sealed.

Listening to Mother

In Mother's life story there is a brief passage which carries a trace of
Grandmother's life and times. The passage focuses on a childhood memory of a cruel beating Grandmother gave to Mother. Mother then links
this memory to that of a beating she inflicts upon her eldest son. But the
relationship between these two memories would wrongly be interpreted
as simple evidence that violence begets violence. Both Mother and
Daughter are adamant that their mothers were not physically abusive. The
brutal thrashings are memorable because they are exceptional and because they make vivid rage borne of frustration and exclusion. The stories
give the interiority of shame, and a rebellious spirit that refuses that
shame, material presence.

> Ah, Moma. I deserved it, mind you. There was a retreat going on.
> And the kids weren't allowed to go to the retreat. But the women
> had to go. I don't know why and I don't know what they did. But I
> wanted to find out what they did. So I followed her. She brought me
> home. I followed her again. She hired a friend—she had to pay
> him—and he drove us both home and she gave me a beating. Not a
> . . . you know, a beating. She went back. I followed her again. So this
> time she got her brother to take us home and I got it. She cut a
> switch. And she hit me with that switch till there was nothing left to
> it. Then she beat me with both her hands till she couldn't hit any-
> more, that her hands were too tired. And when she finished I
> jumped up and I danced up and down on that floor and I said, "I'll
> go again, I'll go again, you go and I'll follow you again for spite." And
> I cried and cried till I fell asleep. I was about five and you can ask her
> the story today and she will tell you because she remembers it. And
> she always says that when I said, "I'll go again . . ." they could have
> killed me. I would not, I would not take an order from anybody.
>
> I was always stubborn. They say that my grandfather was that
> stubborn. So I don't know if I got it there, or if it was just bred into
> me because they left me mostly on my own. I always did what I
> wanted and I always got what I wanted, one way or another. The first
> time that I didn't get what I wanted, I was married and I had a baby,
> and I was pregnant with the second one, and I cried. I hid and I

cried. I don't know what I wanted but I remember the feeling. No, it was just some little thing, I don't know, it was nothing big, I think it was a new dress or something that I wanted for Christmas. I showed it to my husband in the catalogue. I was only fourteen and I thought that he would buy it for me. He sort of babied me too, and, you know, let me pretty well do what I wanted, which was wrong I suppose. But then, I wouldn't have taken an order either. Anyways, I remember he said no, I remember that, and I remember the feeling: I felt my heart, in here, as if I was that full, that I was going to choke, and the feeling that I had because I couldn't get what I wanted. And remember I was married and had a baby of my own, and that was the first time, you know, that I remember. Because I had always got what I wanted.

Like me, my first child was spoiled. He thought that he was going to do what he wanted when he wanted. One day I was outside and I was washing out dirty diapers. And I had two of them on diapers. And my son said, "I want ten cents to get an ice-cream." I said, "Wait till Mommy's finished." Because that meant taking my hands out of the diapers, which I hated doing anyway, going in and washing them two or three times to get the smell and everything off of them, giving him the ten cents and then going back and putting my hands in it. And you know, once my hands were in it, I wanted to finish. But he yelled, "I want it, and I want it now!" And I heard everything coming down in the house. And I went in and here he was, naked as a jay bird, he had the chairs all knocked down in the house and he was in the process of knocking down the table. I went out and I broke myself a switch and I walked back in. I said, "You want to dance? Here, dance with this." And I come at him with a switch. Never, ever, ever took another fit. He was five years old. Never took another one.

He conned me and. . . . You know, he had that ability.

He'd say, "My God Mom, you look tired. I'll do the dishes for you." I'd say, "Ah, he's looking for something." But he found a way to get around everybody. And he was the same—I mean, he died at fifteen years old and I don't think that child could say at any one time, "There was something I wanted and I didn't get it." He had a skidoo to drive in the winter, he had a bicycle. The only jeans he liked were GWGs and he always had. . . . I think I gave away 13 pair when he was killed.[5] He played hockey, he had the best skates, he had all the hockey equipment he wanted. He had drums, he had a banjo, he had an electric guitar, he had an amplifier. You name it, he had it. He had it all. Anything he wanted, he had. He had the ability to. . . . And I mean we weren't rich, by any means.

31

Indeed, they were anything but rich. This litany of consumption belongs to an entirely different era from that of the Grandmother. Whereas the grandmother's sense of inclusion/exclusion was dependent on her ability to participate in a community life that was largely centered on the church, and her sense of failure as a wife and mother was engendered by Catholic morality, the mother's sense of inclusion depended upon her ability to consume in the burgeoning market place, a market place from which she is, from the outset, largely excluded. She recalls her first years of marriage:

It was Christmas Eve—my second son was a baby. He had been born the twenty-first of November. We had a terrible winter of snow that winter. I didn't have a can of milk, I had nothing. I mean nothing. He come out of the woods. I can see him yet. He got out of the car with a case of beer and he come into the house and he had two dollars. He had been in the woods for I don't know how long and they'd got paid at Christmas. He had got five dollars. That was his pay. Well I mean they talked about it. He had it thrown in his face at elections: "You're wife and kids were starving while you were laying under the trees sleeping." You know?

For the first time I went to the welfare. Christmas Eve. Moma came with me. 1961. Welfare had just come out. And it was a man there in the rule. And we went in his house and we sat in the kitchen and Moma told him. I mean me, me being 16, and I sat there. You know. Now Moma told him, "You know she's got nothing and she just has a new born baby. She has one that's 18 months old and a new born of a month old. And she has absolutely nothing. And she needs something." And he said, "Ah, wait there a minute. It's Christmas Eve, but I'm not . . . I need to do some research and get some information, I just don't give out orders like that." Moma told him I wanted an order for groceries because we had nothing. So anyways, the man's wife—not a word—she got up, she went upstairs and she came down with two suitcases. He said to her, "Where are you going to?" She said, "I'm leaving." He said, "You're what?" She said, "You there! It's Christmas Eve." She said, "There's a baby with two babies and you have the face to say you have to do information!" She said, "Look at them." You know . . . I was near to tears. She said, "You're not fit for anybody to stay with, I'm leaving." He said, "Hold it, hold it, hold it." He pulled out the paper and he wrote out an order for groceries for $75.

So that's what happened then. And I mean, that was the first time I ever, in my life . . . I called it begging. I found it awful hard. Like often, then—after that I mean—I've often had to go through times.

Because, as I said, my husband made big money when he worked. He could go and get a job anywhere. But he was a job jumper. He'd work some place two months and then he'd leave. Three months, and he'd leave. The woods, forget it. Anytime he went to a job in the woods, I mean forget it. I remember once, that's the time I tried to commit suicide. . . .

I will not delve into the tale of the suicide attempt except to say that, like the Grandmother's tale of "the nerves," it marks a time of desperation that signals both an act of resistance against the forces that confined her and a tragic resignation to her lot in life. If her idea of the good mother depended on her ability to provide her children with the consumer goods she herself had so desperately desired—to the point of feeling that she was suffocating—then she too had failed as a mother. The overwhelming sense of her exclusion from that world often led to rage. Once angered, Mother has a harsh and bitter tongue that can strike terror into the souls of the most impervious.

From the sixties onward the people in the settlement were increasingly dependent upon welfare programs, either through unemployment benefits or through social assistance. Households drew upon wage labor, unemployment benefits, and social assistance to make a living. The settlement went from being a ward of the church to being a ward of the state; making a living involved working the welfare system to their advantage. But a terrible price was paid, for increasingly they were scrutinized and labeled, by the courts, doctors, and government officials. If the priests had called them sinners and scandals, they could at least be forgiven and saved. Now they were labeled sick and degenerate. They became the objects of community psychiatric studies and the people became parts of case loads. Daughter's formative years correspond with this phase of the settlement's history.

It was Mother's early pregnancy that had, in her view, trapped her in a relationship with an easy-come, easy-go spendthrift. When Daughter was ten, her parents separated and Mother moved in with a man with whom she had had a clandestine relationship for years. To the dismay of her family, Daughter has no memory of that winter she and her siblings lived alone with their father. The following spring Father left the family and Mother returned with her lover, thus exposing the entire family to horrendous physical and emotional brutality. In retrospect, Mother explains herself succinctly, "Now with him there, there was always enough wood put in for the winter." Read dialogically, Daughter's nostalgic memories of late autumn mornings when Mother would load her small children into the truck and head for the woods to get a load of wood in for the winter

33

are as discordant as her judgment that her mother abandoned her children to fulfill fervent sexual needs. Yet, this rival and inharmonious etiological explanation heralds a new and altered vocabulary of desire.

Reading Daughter's Journal

In retrospect it is probably fitting that my initiation to fieldwork roughly corresponded with Daughter's to therapy. To my dismay I spent most of my first few weeks in the settlement aiding her quest to track down dream fragments. On our very first trip she was eager that I meet the local priest, which I was, of course, happy to do. Within moments of our arrival she began to ask the priest about a house out on the coast that had been kept by a religious order for religious retreats. The priest told us the house had been destroyed years ago and the property sold. He kindly gave us directions to the property and encouraged us to visit the woman who presently lived there. Her business completed, Daughter thanked the priest for taking the time to talk to *me*, and we departed.

It was obvious my friend was in a distressed state of mind. She revealed that she had been having nightmares about such a house on the coast. I volunteered to take her there if she thought it would help. As we drove to the coastal property, which is several miles from the settlement, I had the sense that I was traveling away from my research project (at that point still firmly rooted in the prosaic) to probe the mysteries of the otherworldly, a task better suited to spirit mediums than to anthropologists. Still, as we drew close to the apparent scene of her nightmare, Daughter began to tremble and cower beside me and I could not ignore the embodiment of her daytime encounter with what she calls her "nighttime life." Later, safely removed from the scene, she confessed to a sudden and vivid recollection of an event at low tide, on the night of a full moon, when worshippers of Satan met to engage in sexual escapades with children and to sacrifice newborn babies.

I began to suspect my key informant an unreliable witness. By her own account she suffered complete memory loss at the age of fifteen, although memory loss seems an inadequate definition for the state of mind she describes in her journal. She writes:

> I started to have daytime night terrors. I felt my body go into a physical sensation and everything felt weird and I'd panic. Often I thought I was dreaming, that's how out of touch with reality I felt. But when reality leaked in I was terrified. . . . Other times my vision would go black. It would start outside and tunnel in. This was accompanied by a physical sensation. My hearing became very sensi-

tive as well. The worst was the memory. It was the same as I experience now, except now it lasts only seconds or a minute. I feel as
though I'm stripped of everything known. . . . I drifted in and
out—though mostly out—of remembering—realizing about the
world. Most times I couldn't remember who I was. But I remembered always that this was my mind shutting off. I became an observer in my own hell.

With considerable skill Daughter would sabotage my best-laid plans to
use her subsequent visits to further my research. Frequently, she would
borrow my car on the pretense of running errands and return hours
later distraught at her numerous encounters with people she had deliberately sought out in search for clues that would unravel the significance
of her night terrors. Stranded, I spent such days cooling my heels and
awaiting her return. But my anger would dissipate at the sight of her distress. It became obvious that my role was to serve as a bridge between the
two worlds her life uncomfortably straddles. She explains it to her therapist thus:

Whenever I visit the settlement I become another person. I feel as
if I'm on another planet. My emotions, personality, everything becomes different. I have difficulty connecting the two realities of my
life here and there. It is as if they are different worlds. . . .

I asked Daughter to sit down and tell me her life story as had her
Grandmother and Mother. But she protested that she had already done
this work for her therapists and instead gave me her journal. The journal,
written at different times for four therapists, reveals a great deal about the
Daughter's relationship to both worlds: the poverty stricken settlement in
rural New Brunswick in which she came of age; and the urban Maritime
city in which she now lives and works.

Daughter was originally encouraged into therapy, as a form of "marriage counseling," by her female partner. Typically, Daughter sat through
these counseling sessions frightened and withdrawn, but on one occasion
she became provoked and flew into a fit of rage. Within a week one of the
counselors phoned to encourage her to seek individual therapy. The therapist later explained that she had never in her life witnessed such a radical change from passive to aggressive behavior. (Although, had the
therapist grown up where Daughter did, she would have found such lulls
and eruptions of temperament to be rather common.)

Over the course of therapy the journal entries shift radically from the
world in which Daughter presently struggles to one previously repressed.

In time, previously repressed memories are incorporated as facts into the reports she writes under headings such as "family members," "my night-time life," "significant people," "background/upbringing," "the settlement," "violence," "who I am." The contrasts between the journal entries of 1991 and 1992 are striking:

Excerpt: Spring 1991.

> For several weeks I have felt very despondent, to say the least. I've felt like a complete failure in life. My nights are spent visiting torture chambers and my days are filled with harsh realities: that I'm not able to live and accomplish the way normal people do.
>
> At night I struggle for my sanity and my life. Daytime is a struggle to prove I'm worthy of an advanced education. But I'm not always able to prove myself in the only terms they will accept. I desperately needed a qualifying course and was doing very well until the professor humiliated me in front of the class. I haven't been back since. He was as cruel as my mother.
>
> More than anything, I want to use my intelligence in either engineering or scientific research. But I'm failing. . . .

Excerpt: Spring 1992.

> I guess you could say that I am here to save my life. The only reason I want to find out what happened is because I feel it is the key to ending these night-terrors and my "nighttime life.". . . . In 1987 I began to experience hypnagogic hallucinations upon waking. Often, I would recognize the image for only a split-second, but during that split second, my recognition of it caused me to feel the same extreme fear/insanity I feel in night terrors.
>
> In the winter of 1990, I had an hallucination of a cross. This forced me to acknowledge 1) the existence of satanic ritual abuse and 2) the possibility that this happened to me. After this I experienced nightmares and memory flashes which revolved around a scene of satanic ritual. . . . My dreams were like clues. Every month or so they'd give me a little bit more information. I figured out about "the Brother's house" and the beach from my dreams. I'd always see the beach at low tide under a full moon. Often the clues, answers were given to me by my oldest brother, who's now deceased. My brother represents the truth to me, and I trust him completely, so when he'd tell me something in my dreams, it was something true and actual. He doesn't appear often, but when he does he sup-

plies me with information. What my brother told me about in actual dreams turned out to be actual events I had forgotten about.

I believe that I am using my memory of my brother as a way to safely reveal my painful secrets to my consciousness. I think I've transferred all the secrets to him and am allowing him to reveal the information to me when I am ready. . . .

I researched all kinds of books and articles on neuroscience, particularly night-terrors, eye-sight and hallucinations. I discovered that what I experience are hypnagogic hallucinations. It makes sense to me now . . . It is my understanding that an area in the occipital lobes (visual cortex) takes signals received from the eyes and "forms" what we see, then sends those images to our consciousness (thought, recognition, and acknowledgment) to be acknowledged. So it seems to me that what happens when you have hypnagogic hallucinations is that the occipital lobes must also be picking up visual signals from elsewhere. I think that the occipital lobes are getting signals from the temporal lobes where memories are stored. In memory loss or blocking out, the memories have not disappeared, it is the *accessing* of memories which has stopped. . . .

I do think "splitting" is a major form of coping. We all split in varying degrees. But I don't like the analogy of being two different people. I think that your consciousness probably decides to ignore the existence of certain stored feelings and memories which cause trauma to other areas if accessed. . . . In dreams, creating another person who has access to these memories and feelings is a common way to deal with this. . . .

In therapy for almost a year, Daughter was referred to an expert in the field of post-traumatic memory loss and ritual abuse. The second excerpt is taken from Daughter's initial lengthy letter to the expert therapist and demonstrates her growing competency in the psychoanalytic discourse of repression and dissociation. Placed within the context of Daughter's frustrated ambitions to be a scientist, I find the tenor of these excerpts sadly revealing. Daughter splits before our very eyes: one Self, would-be medical researcher, detached and objective, offering for dissection her other Self as patient. Denied entry into the world of the educated middle class as an equal, Daughter trades her ravaged psyche as currency for acceptance into a class to which she aspires.

What I find sad about my friend's attempt to write her life is how abysmally it fails. Rarely does she describe an event by placing herself squarely in the action of the unfolding story. One almost wonders if she was ever there at all. And yet, in contrast to Grandmother and Mother, her stories inevitably begin by evoking memory. Pierre Nora correctly notes that "we should be aware of the difference between true memory, which has taken refuge in gestures and habits, in skills passed down by unspoken traditions, in the body's inherent self knowledge, in unstudied reflexes and ingrained memories, and memory transformed by its passage through history, which is nearly the opposite: voluntary and deliberate, experienced as a duty, no longer spontaneous; psychological, individual, and subjective; but never social, collective, or all encompassing" (Nora 1989: 13). Although obdurate in her convictions about the truth of others and their pasts, Daughter is unable to construct a life story, to wrest her story away from her interlocutors, as her Grandmother and Mother were able to do with me. Most striking is the voice of the detached observer she assumes in describing life in the settlement. It is the voice of an outsider, or, perhaps more to the point, a would-be outsider:

> You know, I was born into the settlement, and if I could have existed there like them and been happy it would have been okay. But I hated it, never belonged there, and didn't belong with those people. I belong with educated people. I don't like the term "educated people" but it's the only way I can describe where I feel I belong in a social context.

Her journal is laced with flashes of memory, nightmares, and hastily drawn pictures of gruesome knives dripping with blood, bearded demons, and religious iconography. Daughter's therapists became increasingly convinced that her night terrors and memory loss were the consequence of childhood sexual abuse and Satanic ritual abuse. During the course of therapy Daughter did recall an incident of childhood sexual abuse at the hands of a neighbor which was later confirmed to be true by her Mother. But the leap of faith required to assert all recovered memories of the same kind, and therefore *true*, is staggering. Further, the literality of the therapist's interpretation of her nightmares and memory flashes denies, and so erases, the historical and cultural context within which Daughter's imagination and language unfurled.

Daughter grew up in a place where God and Satan battled for turf. Daughter remembers her mother proclaiming Satan stronger than God (the misery of her life provided ample proof) and Grandmother gave me a very convincing description of Satan: "Now Satan, he's not what you think. No, no. He doesn't have horns and hooves and all that. No, no. Satan is a very good looking man, with the black hair and the dark eyes." Grandmother and Mother deeply resented the Church and its power, but their rejection of the Church did not take the form of disbelief. In accepting, and sometimes reveling in, their position as sinners, Grandmother and Mother resisted the power of the Church, albeit on the Church's terms.

Daughter, like her mother, began school at the Convent. There she received encouragement from the Sisters, who recognized her quick intelligence and understood the impoverished and unstable conditions of her life. As a child, Daughter, who had learned fear and loathing of the Church at her Mother's knee, felt deeply conflicted by the care and affection the Sisters lavished on her. To this day she makes a radical distinction between the Church (in the parlance of the settlement, wicked) and the Sisters (saintly).

At school, Daughter was taunted by the other children who called her the Warlock Whoremaster's bastard. The "Warlock Whoremaster" was her Mother's lover and he bore an uncanny resemblance to Grandmother's Satan. While Daughter was still in the primary grades, the convent was converted to a secular public school and the language of instruction switched from predominately French to English. Daughter's family was French speaking; the Warlock Whoremaster, English. Mother, well aware of the advantages the English-speaking people of New Brunswick historically enjoyed, believed it in the best interest of her children to school in English. Daughter writes to her therapists:

> I don't believe in the devil now. But then, did I ever. I spoke to the devil in English. I don't know why that seems so significant to me, but it seems to be. To me, the devil's power was brought up in English.

When it came time to attend high school Daughter was bussed, with the other children of the settlement, to the nearest town. She recalls:

> The emotion I felt most, growing up, was shame. . . . If I stayed late for an activity in high school, the bus would take all the kids [from the surrounding communities] home at once. Sometimes the students would ask the bus driver to go to the settlement first so they could see what it looked like. I was horrified by this. I didn't want people to know I lived in the settlement, especially which house was mine. I'd get off of the bus about a half a mile from home in front of an okay looking house. After all, we didn't have a bathroom, my bedroom was two pieces of press wood nailed to a couple of beams that didn't reach the ceiling, and there were no doors anywhere in the house. . . . You could see the outside through the cracks. In winter time, I used to stare at the nails that were in the boards cause they were white with frost.

39

> I was also ashamed about the things I was never taught that I learned were standard in other homes. . . . General hygiene, social skills, everything I learned was preceded by the humiliating realization that I was doing something almost barbaric.

As she approached adolescence Daughter was increasingly absent from school, and by grade ten, the year she "lost her memory," she did not attend at all.

Conditions in Daughter's home had steadily deteriorated. Having lost one brother in a tragic accident, her other brother was forced out of the home because of the Warlock Whoremaster's jealous rage (he accused the boy of sleeping with his mother). At fourteen, like his father and his grandfather before him, he went into the woods to work. Daughter spent most of her energy avoiding the sexual advances of the Warlock Whoremaster. At fifteen (the year of her memory loss), she maintained enough presence of mind to know that her Mother's lover was dangerous, even if she could not remember who the Warlock Whoremaster was. Further, she had the wherewithal to realize her memory lapses should be concealed from the strangers in her midst. It seems the luxury of complete dissociation was one she could not afford.

The following spring she formed a close and healing friendship with another girl in the settlement who had been molested by her stepfather. Together they plotted her friend's departure from the settlement. Soon after that her Mother and younger sister made their own dramatic escape from the Warlock Whoremaster and the settlement. Daughter went to live with Grandmother so that she could finish high school, but the scars of the lost years were too deep and she soon left to join her Mother in the city. There she wrote and passed high school equivalency exams. As she puts it, "I was the first person in my ancestry to finish high school." But this remarkable feat meant little in the urban center to which she moved, nor was it enough to open the doors to the institutions of higher learning that she soon realized were the only ticket out of a world she despised. A world despised, but one she could not expunge from her Self.

Excerpt: Letter to D. Young, 1993.

> You know, Donna, I know that I have a lot of determination sometimes, but you know what? I'm really very, very afraid. I don't know if I can do anything anymore. Can I succeed at anything? I'm beginning to think that I can't which is scary because without my education, I don't want to live.
>
> God Donna. Sometimes I get so depressed. Life just isn't fair. By the way, have you heard about the natives blocking the highways in

NB because the provincial government decided to make them pay tax? The government was forced to back down. The way I feel now I'd have sent tanks into the reserves and blown them all away. You don't want to pay your share? BOOM! (Vicious, aren't I) But when you consider the poverty I came from, how hard I struggled, and that I'm still nowhere but can't get financial aid to get my education, and that I still owe hundreds of dollars in taxes, I am filled with rage. And they can get their fucking twenty-first century education paid for! Yet natives and the rich don't pay taxes. I am furious. I am disgusted. Okay, I'm sure you disagree with me, but that's how I feel. Extremely disgusted. Fuck them.

My friend knows me well, and I do feel exceedingly uncomfortable with the vehemence and direction of her rage. Like her Grandmother and Mother before her, she strikes out at those who in many ways share her predicament. But I will not disparage the rage.

Listening to Life Story Narratives

> Discourse is not simply that which expresses struggles or systems of domination, but that for which, and by which, one struggles; it is the power one is trying to seize.
> —Michel Foucault

In listening to Grandmother, Mother, and Daughter I began to "understand not merely subjective truth, but the very historicity" (Felman and Laub 1992: 62) of the events that marked their lives. Especially when listening to Grandmother I began to *hear* a particular resonance receding in time, certainly removed from the shores of facticity that too often preoccupied my thoughts in the field. Yet the women's narratives, seemingly incommensurate, are of the same historical moment; they co-exist not only in time but within the same family. Hastily drawn abstractions charting a dominant discourse at a particular moment would make no sense of this *fact* nor of the internalized contradictions wrought by social change. I have tried to tie the women's life stories to changing historical circumstances that demonstrate the particular ways in which dominant discursive fields (religious and secular) intersect with, and give form to, constructions of the self.

Within this century, massive economic, social, and cultural change swept through the rural communities of New Brunswick, leaving many distraught. As idioms of distress, to use Mark Nichter's apt expression

41

(1981; Kenny 1986: 9–12; Antze, this volume), the Grandmother's nervous breakdown, the Mother's suicide attempt, and the Daughter's night-terrors and memory loss all attest to the cruel social conditions that create within people desires that are not met. While the unspeakable—unspeakable because it is so pervasive it appears to contour every desire—shifts from generation to generation, the frustration of those desires in each generation gives way to life story narratives that powerfully reveal an inchoate sense of oppression. It becomes evident that the structures of both power and desire are historically bound together in the women's tales and that redemption is always historically mediated.

What is startling in the Daughter's narrative is the disjuncture between individual and family memory. My friend's historical narrative is only tenuously connected to a remembered time and place where there was/is oppression and suffering. But, and I find this odd, it has not prevented her from making the most adamant truth claims about the lives of others. Daughter has little patience for my sympathetic understanding of the women who in many regards refused the subject positions of Mother and Grandmother, subject positions created and recreated for them in an economic and moral order from which they were excluded. Her pain is simply too great.

Listening again to the recorded stories of Grandmother and Mother I began to understand that although I could more carefully document the settlement's past than could many community members, I might fail to understand the local character of human existence at particular points in history. And it is this insight I would like to share with my friend who is driven to uncover the motley facts of her case history.

Daughter's desire to find a key that can unlock her story is as much framed by historical and cultural discourse as were the desires of her forebears. Her therapists, and countless books on childhood and ritual abuse written for a public with an enormous appetite for salacious stories, convinced her that within her recovered memories, her Self, lay a horrible truth. But will the story thus revealed be hers? I believe Grandmother and Mother found an element of redemption in their stories by naming oppression with a language that embraced their historical realities; the discourse of trauma and repression has not afforded my friend such comfort.

Notes

1. Felman and Laub argue that the "demand for the *contextualization of the text* itself needs to be complemented, simultaneously, by the less familiar but yet necessary work of *textualization of the context*; and how this

shuttle movement . . . the very *tension between textualization and contextualization*—might yield new avenues of insight, both into the texts at stake and into their context—the political, historical, and biographical realities with which the texts are dynamically involved and within which their particular creative possibilities are themselves inscribed" (1992: xv). Canning adopts Sonya Rose's succinct notion of a "double vision of text and context" to "embed the discourses of social reform in a specific historical context" in Weimar Germany (1994: 380, 382).

2. Terdiman (1985) defines discourse as a "complex of signs and practices which organize social existence and social reproduction. In their structured, material persistence, discourses are what give differential substance to membership in a social group or class or formation, which mediate an internal sense of belonging, an outward sense of otherness" (1985: 54). To this I would add that discourse gives differential substance to membership in different generations.

3. I have removed identifying markers and deleted the rhythmical repetitions of short clauses at the ends of sentences that are part of the oral presentation. For instance, a more accurate representation of a sentence from the first paragraph would be: "The women were good then." Pause. "Yes, the women were good then." Clipping her prose thus, I have butchered the memory of the voice I carry in my head. But this voice is already lost in print.

4. Acadians were the first European settlers of lands which today form Nova Scotia, New Brunswick, Prince Edward Island, and a part of the State of Maine. According to Naomi Griffiths:

> By the mid-eighteenth century the Acadians were very definitely a separate people. They were accustomed to living on their lands according to traditions of political action which they developed during the seventeenth century, when English influence upon their society was as important as French authority (1974: 67).

Thus, when war broke out again between the British and the French in 1755, both sides perceived the Acadians as French allies. Although the Acadians promised to remain neutral, they were expelled by the British and dispersed throughout the Thirteen Colonies. Acadians were allowed to return to the region in 1764; by the turn of the century, an estimated 8,000 had resettled on marginal lands along the coastal areas of Nova Scotia, Prince Edward Island, and northeastern New Brunswick. For a discussion of the link between the Catholic church and Acadian nationalism see Léon Thériault (1982).

5. On Thanksgiving weekend in 1975 her oldest son was killed in a car accident. He and his friends were heading for the bootleggers on returning from a dance in the wee hours of the morning. Cresting a

knoll they met a car parked in the right-hand lane. Speeding, they swerved to the left lane only to collide with a pulp truck, without lights or tailgate reflectors, sitting in the left lane. Three boys in the front seat of the car were killed. People in all three vehicles were intoxicated.

References

Abu-Lughod, Lila. 1992. "The Romance of Resistance: Tracing Transformations of Power Through Bedouin Women." *American Ethnologist* 17: 41–55.

Bruner, Jerome. 1991. "The Narrative Construction of Reality." *Critical Inquiry* 18 (Autumn): 1–21.

Canning, Kathleen. 1994. "Feminist History after the Linguistic Turn: Historicizing Discourse and Experience." *SIGNS* (Winter): 368–402.

Felman, Shoshana, and Dori Laub, M.D. 1992. *Testimony.* New York: Routledge.

Griffiths, Naomi. 1974. "Acadians in Exile: The Experiences of the Acadians in the British Seaports." *Acadiensis* IV: 1 (Autumn): 67–84).

Kenny, Michael G. 1986. *The Passion of Ansel Bourne.* Washington, D.C.: Smithsonian Institution Press.

Nichter, Mark. 1981. "Idioms of Distress." *Culture, Medicine and Psychiatry* 5: 5–24.

Nora, Pierre. 1989. "Between Memory and History: *Les Lieux de Mémoire.*" *Representations* 26 (Spring): 7–25.

Terdiman, Richard. 1985. *Discourse/Counter-Discourse.* Ithaca, N.Y.: Cornell University Press.

Thériault, Léon. 1902. "The Acadianization of the Catholic Church in Acadia." In *The Acadians of the Maritimes.* Jean Daigle, ed. Moncton, N.B.: Centre d'Etudes Acadiennes, 1902: 271–339.

3

Contested Meanings and Controversial Memories
Narratives of Sexual Abuse in Western Newfoundland

Glynis George

> In the day, I gets flashbacks—I remember certain things—
> they come to me again. Like, when certain things happen, or
> I see things. Especially when a man talks to me in a certain
> way, when I'm down home, a certain voice. When somebody
> comes from behind me and presses up against me. I can't take
> it. I gotta run
>
> ——Rhonda, aged 32

In the spring of 1992 a television documentary addressed the problem of
child sexual abuse in Western Newfoundland after a man from the region
was convicted of sexually abusing twenty neighborhood children. The
program, which was shown across the country, highlighted the economically depressed context in which the case took place and featured moving
accounts from two area women. One woman, her image obscured, recounted a personal experience of childhood incest and the sexual abuse
of her son by the convicted man. The second woman, Mary, not only recounted the incest experienced by her children, but described assorted
abuses as pervading her entire community of White Brook, one of the few
Francophone communities in the area. On TV Mary stated that 90 percent of the people in White Brook had experienced abuse. In fact, she
declared, "*Abuse in our community is a way of life; it is a part of our culture.*"[1]

Such public confessions by traumatized citizens are commonplace in media accounts of current social problems. The focus on individual experiences of child sexual abuse satiates tastes for public drama, implicating a cast of characters whose apparent goodness and evil simplify complex relations and cultural ambivalence towards the institutions of family and state. The "experience" of abuse, once voiced, is packaged within discursive layers which legitimate or query the veracity and meaning of these personal claims. Current preoccupation with repressed memory, the politics of psychotherapy and the meaning, prevalence and cause of child sexual abuse underscores the singularity of our curiosity and displaces the everyday exploitations of our maturing and gendered bodies.[2] Moreover, the current tendency within academic, political and popular debate to problematise "experience" and to interrogate memory, renders the "raw" experience of sexual abuse elusive, yet welcomes its graphic representation.[3]

This paper explores the personal narratives of two women whose experiences of sexual abuse are never forgotten but are mediated within shifting discursive arenas and social relations of gender and family. It considers the ways in which women absorb and transform the overlapping discourses surrounding abuse to reconstitute the subject positions assigned to them within the discursive domain. In so doing, I argue, they reinterpret life experiences, reshape their identities, and change the course and meaning of their lives (Canning 1994). At the same time, other local actors invoke the discourse of sexual abuse to produce shared meanings and meaningful differences that bear directly on longtime conflicts, relations of power, and collective identities. The effect is to simplify complex historical processes in ways that oppose rather than integrate multiple experiences of exploitation. Local debates following the televised documentary illustrate this process vividly.

Culture and Marginality

White Brook is a Francophone outport situated on the shores of western Newfoundland, 40 kilometers from the nearest town. Although a pulp and paper mill and government services in town provide some economic stability and employment for area residents, underemployment prevails in White Brook and other outlying rural communities. Moreover, White Brook and nearby Francophone outports are particularly marginalized by social disparities, local constructions of difference, and a history of coercive assimilation through the English-speaking Catholic school system. A Francophone heritage, rooted in nineteenth-century settlement, persists through a local French dialect, an Acadian music tradition, and kinship ties. Only in the last twenty years have Francophone residents sought to reclaim their past through French language education and the formation of community-based Francophone organizations.

The problem of sexual abuse is not peculiar to White Brook. The issue gained local prominence in the late 1980's through the conviction of three area priests and several other male residents, the grass-roots activism of a local Women's Council, and the widely publicized trial and conviction of members of the Christian Brothers order at the Mount Cashel orphanage in St. John's. Media debates that followed the documentary revealed several different public positions on child sexual abuse, reflecting different local political identities shaped by class, gender, and ethnic relations (Valverde 1991).

Media Debates

Following the television documentary, Mary's neighbors in White Brook wrote letters to challenge her claims and protest the marginalization of their community through its depiction as an impoverished place. Mary was accused of "disgracing" her home and "spreading vicious lies" about a community that possessed "high morals" and "strongly Catholic" values. One resident wrote,

> The CBC tore us down worse than anybody could. They put us down as a poverty area dependent on the fishery, unemployment, and welfare, but right now in Newfoundland that's happening everywhere, not just here.

Residents interpreted Mary's use of the word "culture" as a condemnation of their Francophone community culture and challenged the terms in which this culture was now being defined and depicted on television. As one wrote, "The Secretary of State is giving us money to preserve and promote our culture, which is a culture of what—sexual abuse?"

A local political leader/journalist from a nearby community responded in his weekly column. He narrowed the scope of the problem to child sexual abuse and sought to distance it from this region in particular. He also identified himself explicitly with rural working-class men. "I live in this area and I don't abuse children," he began. He proceeded to condemn the Women's Council, Mary's "exaggerations," and the absence of scientific evidence to support her claims. He concluded:

> People from this area grow the tobacco in PEI, man the fish plants in Nova Scotia, and the dry dock in New Brunswick. We cut logs in Cape Breton, and bake bread in arctic mining camps. Against all

odds, we have struggled to preserve our families and our homes. When someone accuses us of abusing our children, it is the last straw.

In contrast, the local Women's Council, whose membership includes women in town and in the rural communities, offered Mary their public support. Drawing on feminist interpretations of culture, their spokesperson linked child sex abuse with all forms of abuse of women and children. She suggested that Mary had identified a problem shared by all communities in the area. She also invoked the feminist notion of "disclosure" in calling on other victims of abuse to break their silence.

It is culturally acceptable in society in general for women and children to be victims of abuse. Its acceptable in a culture that has so little value for women and children. Incest in our culture is not taboo—to speak about it is taboo.

The interpretations of sexual abuse implied in these positions are rooted in historically constituted cultural processes through which local identities of collective victims are constructed. It is interesting that each speaker seeks to reposition the issue of sexual abuse with respect to a particular understanding of culture. The reason, I think, is that their interpretations are informed by different political identities which emerge from discrete collective histories of exploitation rooted in structures of class, gender, and ethnicity.[4]

White Brook residents defend their shared Francophone culture, which offers to them a state-sanctioned identity, financial resources, and social dignity. The journalist reacts to the association of sexual abuse with a particular culture, that of the rural working class family unit which is marginalized through the national political economy. Local feminists shift the focus from a particular culture in order to emphasize the systemic and thus pervasive nature of female and child abuse. In sum, speakers erect distinct categories of "victims" and in so doing oppose groups of people to each other in relation to the problem of sexual abuse. However, while the issue of sexual abuse is mediated at the public level through these "chains of association and displacement" (Nava 1988), the political boundaries that surface are hardly maintained in everyday life or the personal memories of individual women.

Women's Life Stories and Narratives of Abuse

I collected numerous life stories of women throughout this region during fourteen months of fieldwork beginning in May 1992.[5] These narratives convey social ties, shared experiences, and feminine identities that bridge publicly constituted boundaries and thus challenge the fixity of these political categories. They also include many stories of abuse, most of them told without any prompting on my part.[6]

Specifically, these narratives reveal that traumas are hardly confined to experiences in childhood; rather, women experience numerous personal crises throughout their lives, which they do not necessarily connect to any singular traumatic experience. These narratives describe many forms of pain and suffering, including rape, domestic violence, child sexual abuse, neglect, underemployment, and addictions, which are experienced through women's roles as daughters, mothers, sisters, workers, and wives. They implicitly challenge the singular focus of the debate on childhood sexual abuse, pointing instead to the wider context of exploitation involving boys, girls, women, and men which cuts across life cycles and blurs boundaries of complicity and coercion in everyday social relationships (Haaken 1994).

Mary and Rhonda

What follows are partial life stories of Mary and Rhonda, two women whose experiences bridge the political boundaries erected in local debates over sexual abuse. Their experiences are recounted not in a coherent chronology but in an open-ended outpouring of mixed metaphors, multiple explanations, and unfinished stories that center them as eye-witnesses, actors, and victims. For this paper, I focus on narratives on abuse to demonstrate how women draw on the discourse of abuse to interpret their experiences and reshape their identities to facilitate changes in their lives. Both women raised families in White Brook, and their accounts of adult and child sexual abuse are woven through everyday relations of family and community. While their narratives convey a shared experience as daughters of fishermen and wives of waged workers, their accounts are distinguished by differing narrative contexts and the different positions from which they currently speak.[7]

I met Mary, aged 42, after community pressure in the wake of her television appearance had compelled her to leave White Brook. Although "abused" as a child herself, her focus on the issue stems from her position as mother and adult observer in the community. When I met Rhonda, who is 32, she was under severe stress. She had recently left a home for battered women and had begun counseling to deal with years of child sexual abuse. She was also attempting to rid herself of a six-year prescription drug dependency. Her story emerged from our everyday discussions and from insights and anxieties that came with new understandings of her past and her relationships with family and community members.

Each of these narratives invokes the discourse of sexual abuse and extends its meaning to describe relations of power that pervade community life. While both these women focus on relations of family and community, their experiences are not simply rooted in the longtime practices of an isolated community culture. Rather, they are structured within a context of power in which dominant discourses of gender, sexuality, church, and state are reproduced locally.

Mary

Mary is one of 13 siblings from a family who have lived as fishers in White Brook for several generations. Eleven years ago, Mary discovered through her doctor that her four year old daughter had contracted gonorrhea. Sexual abuse was suspected and Social Services almost took her daughter away. Shortly thereafter the child's grandfather was charged and served two months in jail. Mary's experiences in the court, the community, and within her immediate family precipitated her intense interest in the issue of abuse and impelled her to seek information on the subject from grassroots counseling and resource services. She explains how the issue of sexual abuse became important to her, and how it transformed her attitude towards state services and community norms.

> I have to go back 11 years. That's where it began for me. It began before that, it began as a child, being raised into the community. The abuse was there then—if we're talking about sex abuse—it was there then. Growing up into the community, we were allowed (to go) certain places and not certain places. We didn't understand why. I'm talking about my family and as I grew up. It was part of something that you saw and it was accepted 'cause you didn't know the difference. I'm talking from the knowledge that I have today.
>
> Then I had children of my own and that brings me to 11 years ago where my children were sexually abused. It became a very strong issue for me. I was supposed to give up my child because of that. She was very young. It was then I decided I had to talk and I approached the Dept. of Social Services, the RCMP and I gave them the story of my life as I saw it in an abusive situation in the area where I come from. I had to educate myself to help them. And it was a family thing, so it was really, really, really hard to do. And then, I thought that because I gave them the information, they would do something about it.

Mary's awareness of sexual abuse is rooted in her intimate knowledge of residents, and the lived experience of poverty and religious hierarchy which pervades community life.

> Now even some of the men confess it to me. I say, you have to start your acceptance, you have to go into your mind, and see, were you abused? One man told me he didn't need to go into his mind for that—it was all there and let me tell you, it wasn't no sunshine! His rectum was all torn up even as a child. And now he says he can't help himself, he just goes into a trance and does the same thing to others.
> We got people home who's 60, who can remember being abused by the priest. You can see the connection between the church and the abuser in the community. One man, he's a real hard case, he was a real pirate. He told me when he was an altar boy his father beat him black and blue for telling what the priest tried to do! The church was as big an abuser as the parents.
> (Are there many offenders?) Yes, mostly men, but women too— if we're talking about all abuses—but with sexual abuse, its mostly men. And their victims are children whose parents are on social assistance. There's no such thing as an allowance for a child. OK? The only way a child can get an allowance is to go away and let their body be mauled by a man. Now, older women do it too. If they want to go to the bingo, they'll go to this place and get laid then they go up to the bingo. That's fine. To me, you got your age. But when you see a man and a crowd of little girls around him and coming out of his house and going to the store and buying all kinds of candy, knowing those people are all on social assistance and their parents can't give them any money, you can't put a blind eye to it.
> I made it plain (for TV) that if I talk about sexual abuse, I'm clearing the innocent. But if I'm talking about abuse, I'm involved too. I made it plain that I'm guilty too. A child is a person. Its nothing for a parent to smack a child across the face. Now, I'm not saying that I never did smack my children, cause I'd be lying to you. I reared up my first child giving her smacks. And then I did a program and learned what I was doing wrong. Its so easy to let that hand go and smack and then you get complete silence.

It is her awareness of the broader context of power and her concern to transform and redefine social norms that prompted her participation in the documentary.

I saw the problem getting worse. Like, it was coming more out into the open. In the community. And little children would actually imitate what they were doing with their father, with their uncle. Like I was the witch cause I found something wrong with it. And I realized it was useless going to Social Services and the RCMP. Here, the system made you feel dirty. Social Services made you feel dirty.

When I went on TV, I had support, but not from this area. How the kids were treated? How my child was treated by the system? She was completely abused over and over, OK? So I decided I would get it to the public eye, where I knew I would have support, that I as a person living in the community, who brought the abuser to court. I had proof. He got jail. But in the community, they didn't see my daughter as the victim, they saw him as the victim. He came back to the community—no problem for him. Now they won't accept us, just him. We weren't supposed to bring this to the public eye.

In "bringing out a memory," Mary attempts to legitimate and redefine collective memory to include experiences of "abuse." In so doing, residents become implicated as complicit and potentially guilty within a legal framework and changing definitions of normative behavior.

Some women came to me after I spoke and said, "you have no right to speak for us." The women, they're hiding. They don't have a choice. Survival. The parents always rule. And its the mother who has the most influence out there. But its the father who's the boss. You know what I mean? These mothers are the best actresses in the world. You wouldn't believe it, they're perfect my dear, everything is perfect!

But, when I spoke out, my phone was unreal, the calls I got from women all over the area, not just my community. They wanted to put in place something that would help them. They didn't want to put people to jail. And that's not my idea either. They said, "Don't ask us to go to Social Services. Don't ask us to go to the RCMP." What they needed was a support group. And we need people from the outside, who's going to help no matter who you are—let you be a cop's wife, let you be on social assistance, let you be the biggest bag on earth! Somebody to help you as a human being, no matter for your status.

Since I spoke out I've been talking to some women from my community, and we were talking about the people who are abusers and you know, how better to bring out a memory than to reminisce. And I'd say, "did you visit that house?" And then, the realization that it was wrong!

Rhonda

Such memories trouble Rhonda, who both condemns Mary's TV appearance and accepts her claims. Rhonda has just left a violent husband and family members, who scorn her "foolish" behavior. She has not forgotten experiences of sexual abuse. But lately, the way Rhonda tells it, memories come often, in various forms. They appear, unsolicited, in frequent nightmares and daytime flashbacks. At the same time, she consciously invokes details of her past through counseling and conversation with sympathetic listeners.

Rhonda draws on the discourse of abuse to reinterpret sexual practices that pervade her life. She repeats the key words, of "abuse," "rape," and "healing," which mark shifts in her own knowledge and understanding. It is more difficult to convey, in text, the long glances, downward gazes, and frequent pauses. Because we were together frequently for a few weeks, I recount her story as it unfolded in our everyday conversation.

"Home" as Rhonda puts it, is neither "all good nor all bad," nor are its residents. The community is a place where the intimacy of family relations and neighborly visits are both reassuring and unwanted, friendly yet prying. Neighbors arrive unannounced and news of family conflicts passes quickly from house to house. Drunken holidays generate endless argument and conflict, which can erupt at family gatherings. In describing her home to me, Rhonda began to talk about her family and her reasons for leaving White Brook.

> They aren't all bad home. But it was just getting to be too much. I wanted a good life for my children. I didn't know life was any different. I didn't know you could do other things. Now I'm seeing things so different. . . . I used to hit my kids—that's what they did in my family. Now I'm learning to talk to them more. And I worry about John (her son) cause he's always getting into fights and the boys would be out after him all summer long.

Rhonda then expressed concern for her adolescent daughter, which prompted her to talk more extensively about sex and her discovery of the word "abuse."

> You know, I never knew of the word "abuse." There was no pamphlets home, no information. I never heard of the word rape—I didn't know it was rape. It was just—bad. I never knew that you could say no. Some of them home don't think anything of sex. You just go along. I was like that too. I never said anything to nobody. It

wasn't talked about. But everyone knew it was going on. It's just something you have to live through. Sex is just living to them. Its life!

One day, during lunch, I joined Rhonda for a cup of tea and she began to tell me about her day. In so doing, she revealed her own experience of sexual abuse. That morning the social worker had dropped by to inform her that her brother was suspected of sexually abusing his daughter. The social worker wanted both Rhonda and her sister to formally state that their brother had abused them as children, and Rhonda was anxious to help. She deliberated aloud as if to finalize her decision.

I decided I have to say something. The way I see it, it started with Mary and she went one step, and that may have got her nowhere, but then, now there's me. And I'm here. And if I speak up, then maybe somebody will come forward, cause its got to stop. Its got to stop. I'm going to tell my sister to help.

I'm not going to worry about my family anymore. Mom, she just says to leave it alone, its in the past, its done. (Pause) He abused me and my sister, and my sister got it much worse than me. But she won't go public with it. She'll admit it to me, but she won't go public.

We talked extensively about her family and Rhonda's ambivalence towards leaving them. Of her eight siblings, she is closest to her middle brother, a wood cutter.

I haven't told my brother yet, maybe at Christmas. But all they like to do at Christmas is drink. Maybe we'll solve it then! (She laughs) Christmas is always supposed to make things better, but it never does. And I'll be alone this Christmas. Just me and the kids. That's OK, I don't mind. (Silence) But it hurts. I wouldn't have said that before. It hurts. I wouldn't have said anything. But now I can. (Silence)

You know, if I was talking this way home, they'd look at me like I was crazy. And if I'd met you five years ago, and you were to mention abuse, I'd say you were foolish. And if you was to come to where I live, they'd just put you out.

Rhonda hinted that she was also sexually abused by others.

I never heard the word abuse. I didn't know what it meant. (Pause) And now, I knows. I know it can mean many things. There was just rape—but for me, it was just, you were in the wrong place at the wrong time. I thought it was just my fault. . . . You know, when you go in a place and it happens. (Pause) They starts tearing off your clothes. I hated it! There's some places I wouldn't go without a rope or a belt tied to me pants. And then, I goes home, and I was told I was just stupid for being in the wrong place.

The notion of abuse allows Rhonda to consider related infringements on the body and thus to identify with her husband's experience.

I'm just beginning to see that there are other things out there. My husband, he was physically abused by his parents. He got a lacing all the time and I don't know what that's like. But I knows sexual abuse. We share that. He's in counseling now. But sometimes he looks at me like I've changed so much—he can't understand what's happened to me. I've changed a lot.

The next day, Rhonda urged me to sit down and have some tea. She had returned from a counseling session that had put her in an upbeat mood. Perhaps this is what prompted her to continue her story, this time, by focusing on her addiction. It was after the birth of her second child that Rhonda began to get "the baby blues," and lose sexual interest in her husband. Rhonda now realizes that her husband's frequent outbursts of swearing, put-downs, and physical violence, directed towards herself and her son, may have increased her depression. At the time however, her family told her it was "just nerves," and she went to a doctor who prescribed drugs which she has taken for the past 6 years.

I started with two pills. And then, I was up to 12 pills a day and I couldn't do nothing—they were to calm me. I could sleep 24 hours. I couldn't do my housework. I tried to quit them but I kept getting sick. It was like I had the flu and I felt sick to my stomach and the doctor gave me more pills. I went to that doctor 'cause I was depressed and I told him, I though it might be in my head, and he burst out laughing. I felt so foolish!

But all the time I was just wanting someone to talk to. For six years I tried to find someone to talk to. I called Social Services twice, but they couldn't help. (she whispers so her son won't hear) Then, I tried to commit suicide. That's what it took.

Then I got counseling. I wouldn't be here now if it weren't for counseling. I calls it my medicine, that's what talking is.

Rhonda did not remain so upbeat once she came closer to openly accusing her brother of child sexual abuse. She was concerned that he would serve a short time in jail, receive little counseling, and threaten her upon his release. A few days later, she had "nightmares" and "a panic attack" so severe that she was taken to hospital. The following day, however, she was able to talk about this experience and consider the possible cause of her nightmares.

> I gave everyone some fright the other morning, didn't I? I was even worse in the hospital. They were going to call in the psychiatrist. When I heard that, I got even worse. (She laughs) Oh I hates Dr.——
> ——! I cried even louder then.
> I had two bad days this week. Everything come at once. (Pause) It starts with a nightmare—its like my past coming back and like I'm reliving it. I got to tell myself its in the past. But then, I can't breath and my heart starts beating so fast.

I asked Rhonda whether she always had nightmares.

> Ever since I remember I've had nightmares. Well, they started when I was about 15. I can't really remember before that. Well, I remember some things. But, now it comes back to me. It's like I'm living two lives. In the day, I'm doing my housework, I'm living. Then, at night, I gets nightmares.
> (Are the nightmares things that happened to you?) No, not exactly. Its not so simple. They're just things like what happened to me. In the day, I gets flashbacks—I remember certain things—they come to me again. Especially when a man talks to me in a certain way, when I'm down home, a certain voice. I gets a flashback. Like, when somebody comes from behind me (she demonstrates, pushing against the wall) and presses up against me. I can't take it. Or when a man holds me too tight. I got to get away. Or when I'm in a room and there's too big a crowd. It's also drunks. I can't take them. I got to learn to be near them, but its so hard.

It is the *feeling* of memories that resurface through touches, smells, and voices which affect Rhonda so profoundly, but defy precise, discursive description.

A few days before my departure Rhonda came to see me. She was very depressed. She sat down on the rocking chair beside me and began rubbing her "sore stomach." Rhonda asked if I "knew about" the drugs she was taking and the effects on her body. Perhaps I could explain the cause of her anxiety? She was very upset, and straining to speak without crying. Her sister had phoned to say she would not go for counseling. This upset Rhonda, as did her sister's lack of interest in her well-being and that of her children. The ambivalence returned about leaving her family to live in town, where she had no friends.

> My mother only visited me once. Nobody calls. After next week, you won't be here no more. I don't want many friends. Just a few friends—just somebody who can be my family. I was on the verge of a panic attack all day. So I took a long walk to calm down. (Pause) But I gets a tight head and my stomach, its so sore, and I can't sit still. So I try walking—I don't know what to do.
>   Sometimes I wonder if its a disease I got. I wonder if it comes from my family, if we all got it. I wonder, is it the stress that makes my head so tight? Is it the drugs? Do you think its the Prozac? Sometimes I think it gets worse before my period. I gets a tight head. I get goose bumps all over and my body jumps as if its upset and nervous.

When conversation turned to mutual friends, Rhonda reflected on changes in her character.

> Like I told my sister-in-law, today, "Nobody deserves to be hit or talked badly to when their husband is drunk!" Now, that's my brother who's hitting her and even though he's my brother, he has no right to do that. I wouldn't have thought that before. I would have thought, "Oh, she probably deserved that." I don't think that anymore.
>   I sees myself now—how weak I was. Now I sees other women who are weak. Men can pick 'em out! Men, home, don't know you can say no. You say it once and they don't hear it—they just keep going. My husband raped me more than once. (Pause) But he wouldn't call it rape. He didn't know it was wrong. (Silence)
>   I says "no" (to sex) and he's there, putting me down on the bed, accusing me of losing my feelings for him, that I love someone else. I tried to explain to him the other day, that it's wrong, that he can't do that. And my sister, she don't understand that you have a right to say no. She sees it as normal. It's crazy isn't it? They're horrible, aren't they? (She looks at me) I knows what you're thinking. Its wrong—they're bad, and I knows it!

We talked more extensively about Mary's television appearance, and Rhonda expressed her ambivalence.

When she went on TV, I just said to myself, "oh, that's Mary!" She made things worse. It's the way she said it—she said it was our culture—she made us feel like we were the only ones, and by doing that, she included everybody, even me. But I didn't do anything sexual. It happened *to* me.

But in a way it was good for me. I started thinking of all the things that happened to me and I didn't want it for my children. I wanted a better life for them. And then I started thinking about how I grew up and how bad my life had been and how things were with my husband.

I used to think it was my fault. Just for being there. And my family—they blame me. They blame me. Everyone blame me—for the way I am—for the way I were. I was always so cross and contrary. But they knew. It was just living to them. It's the way things are.

Memory and the Context of Power

The narratives of Rhonda and Mary reveal how sexual abuse is lived, interpreted, and extended to comprise emotional, physical, and sexual practices that impinge on the "practiced" body and the self (Bordo 1989; Brock 1991). Moreover, they highlight the importance of broadening analyses of sexual abuse to acknowledge ambivalence and embrace a "broad configuration of relations," which include ties of power, family, and community (Haaken 1994:120). Loyalty and anger towards family members and struggles to maintain yet sever familial and social ties comprise the lived experience that both informs sexual abuse and the construction of women's social identities.

In recounting their lives, Rhonda and Mary center themselves as victims and agents of past experience and refashion their identities in the repeated retelling of their lives. Months have passed since my last talk with Rhonda, who is now settled in town and in much better spirits. Such news is a pleasant reminder that her personal transformation, suspended in text, is nonetheless an ongoing process. The discourse of abuse helps Rhonda to effect changes in her identity as mother, sister, and daughter. It clarifies the meaning of ambiguous memories and ambivalent emotions that might facilitate her transformation (Ferguson 1991; Herman 1992).

The subversive character of narratives of abuse is underscored in a context where social pressures encourage women who have not forgotten to "let it pass." Indeed, the performance of femininity in this setting has been, until recently, an act of forgetting, of eliding the expression of self and experience with others, within the family unit (Greene 1991). The expression of personal memories is structured by cultural relations of power that privilege the reproduction of certain social memories over others (Lourie 1988). Social conflict emerges when personal memories begin to contest collective understandings, public representations, and social practices.

The Politics of Memory

Like Rhonda, Mary draws on the discourse of abuse to characterize many relations of power, of which child sexual abuse is only a part. It is this context of power, "the way things are" in Rhonda's words, that Mary labels "culture," as in a particular way of life.However, Mary harnesses the discourse of abuse to redefine the local culture of White Brook, which has, in the last 20 years, transformed itself into a distinct, Francophone culture. It is Mary's public redefinition of Francophone culture that effects dramatic change in White Brook.

After the television documentary, residents of White Brook demonstrated against Mary in their community. They demanded her resignation from the board of the local Francophone Association and forced its closure. Furthermore, numerous residents boycotted the annual celebration of St. Jean Baptiste Day. Six months after the documentary, the community center in White Brook, which was owned and operated by the Francophone Association, was burned to the ground. Many residents linked the burning directly to events surrounding the documentary. Mary has her own interpretation of these events.

> They figures I would shut my mouth and everything would quiet down if they got rid of the French center, 'cause all my volunteer time was given over there. Everything we work with, the women's group, everything was done through that center. All our progress. If we can't get the French center back on its feet, we've lost. Because its there we had the facilities to contact people. I knows, me, as a volunteer, we'd have seminars on crafts and behind it we had another motive—to get the women together and get their support.

The community center was a social space that embodied the construction of a new Francophone culture, one that recognized relations of power among neighbors, between genders, and within families. Mary and others brought resource people to the center who provided education on assorted topics including parenting and abuse. Tragically, the destruction of this social space also meant the loss of their recorded history, some two hundred tapes of songs, stories, and family histories.

59

Conclusion

The television documentary gave province-wide exposure to local instances of abuse and served to deepen the moral crisis that had emerged from the convictions of Christian Brothers at Mount Cashel. Provincial ministers were compelled to respond to local activists who had long lobbied for a sexual abuse counseling service for the region. Rhonda was able to access this service and recognizes that she benefited in some way from Mary's TV appearance.

It is tempting to erect cultural boundaries around the life experiences of Mary and Rhonda, to distinguish a rural, Francophone culture from the lives of nearby English-speaking Newfoundlanders, who themselves are marginalized as earthy folk and "have-nots" in national myths (Kelly 1993; Overton 1988). In this way we might mark the transformations of a socially embedded folk culture. To do so, however, would be to reinforce local stereotypes in which townspeople distinguish themselves as implicitly superior to their rural neighbors. It would also mean reducing a complex history to a reified set of behaviors and cultural traits. It would assign blame for these traits to the local Francophone culture while overlooking the constitution of social subjects within a wider hegemonic context.

The stories told by these women reveal their cultural connection to a broader social universe, the Canadian welfare state, whose mechanisms of power in the welfare bureaucracy, the labor market, the judiciary, and the medical profession structure their experiences of sexual abuse. For residents of White Brook, culture is both "the ways things are," a history of lived experiences, and a bounded unit with political meanings rooted in the shared history of Francophone experience and marginalization. It is also a source of government funding, social resources, and identity that, since the early 1970's, residents have proudly reclaimed (Handler 1988). Perhaps the conflicting meaning of culture itself in popular discourse fueled the destructive response to Mary's allegations about abuse in White Brook.

Post-structuralists draw our attention to cultural processes which generate new fields of meaning for the negotiation of truth claims in contemporary political arenas (Ferguson 1991). A culture that is politically constructed through state mechanisms and the discourse of marginalization may develop a collective identity of victimhood that collides directly with claims to victimhood inside the culture itself (Valverde 1991). To give voice to one, through a politics of identity, may be in the current political climate to delegitimize the claims of another. To imply that victims may also abuse ruptures the fixity of contemporary political categories. It exposes the ambiguity of shared experience and the pervasiveness of power as both productive and constraining.

Notes

1. All names and places in this paper have been changed.
2. This paper is a preliminary exploration. Elsewhere, I examine the relationship between the discourse of abouse, survivor discourse in particular, and personal narratives (George 1996). On sexual abuse and survivor discourse see: Haaken (1994); Ivy (1993); Brock (1991); Gordon (1986); Hacking (1991); Alcoff & Gray (1993); Kelly (1988); MacLeod and Soraga (1988); MacIntosh (1988); and Nava (1988).
3. On the impact of post-structuralism on experience, see: Scott (1992); Swindells and Jardine (1990); and Alcoff (1988). The particular confluence of discourses on sexuality and the body may foster the proliferation of explicit descriptions of sexual abuse whether real or imagined. This seems to be rooted in and reinforced by divergent and contradictory social trends and is found in popular accounts, self-help books (Fredrickson (1991); Herman (1992), and in pornography and erotica.
4. On the crystallization of historical relations of power and exploitation into political identities, see: Valverde (1991); Sewell (1980); Mouffe (1992); Smith (1989); and Swindells and Jardine (1990).
5. Funding for research, conducted from May 1992 to June 1993, was provided by the Social Sciences and Humanities Research Council of Canada. I would like to thank Stuart B. Philpott, Michael Lambek, Pauline Aucoin, Gavin Smith, and Claudia Vicencio for helpful comments on the written draft.
6. These include 55 taped and 15 hand-recorded narratives as well as informal accounts. Initial interviews were open-ended, while those that followed were more focused. In most cases, stories of abuse and life crises emerged through the narrative. Anthropologists are not trained counsellors; I often had to judge whether my questions or further probing were welcome. This emphasised to me the importance of allowing informants to direct the flow of the discussion, although the emotional outcome of narrating an event was often a surprise to them as well. See also Bauer (1993); and Jacobs, (1993).
7. The translation of lengthy narratives into text is the subject of much debate. Feminist critiques and post-structural insights do not however, solve the problem that, regardless of the need to "give voice," practical concerns of space and clarity compel the author to edit. I am aware that the following narratives in particular may "do violence" to the women's voices. They are structured by my argument and spliced to highlight key themes. At the same time, I maintain the distinct forms of both discussions—one taped, the other an ongoing conversation. My own words

61

are scarce, in part because these women had a lot to say and needed or wanted little direction. I have maintained the flow of my conversations with Rhonda, unfolding the themes chronologically, as they were conveyed in our many discussions. However, both conversations dealt extensively with topics other than abuse. On narratives as critical and creative practice see: Behar (1992); Heilbrun (1988); Ochberg (1992); Reissman (1992); Steedman (1986); and Swindells (1989).

References

Alcoff, Linda. 1988. "Cultural Feminism Versus Post-Structuralism: The Identity Crisis in Feminist Theory." *Signs: Journal of Culture and Society* 13 (3): 405–436.

———, and Laura Gray. 1993. "Survivor Discourse: Transgression or Recuperation?" *Signs: Journal of Culture and Society* 18 (2): 260–290.

Bauer, Janet. 1993. "Ma'ssoum's Tale: The Personal and Political Transformations of a Young Iranian Feminist and her Ethnographer." *Feminist Studies* 19 (3): 519–548.

Behar, Ruth. 1992. "A Life Story to Take across the Border: Notes on an Exchange." In *Storied Lives: The Cultural Politics of Self-Understanding.* George C. Rosenwald and Richard L. Ochberg, eds. New Haven: Yale University Press.

Bordo, Susan. 1989. "The Body and the Reproduction of Femininity: A Feminist Appropriation of Foucault." In *Gender/Body/Knowledge: Feminist Reconstructions of Being and Knowing.* Alison Jaggar and Susan Bordo, eds. New Brunswick: Rutgers University Press.

Brock, Debi. 1991 "Talkin' Bout a Revelation: Feminist Popular Discourse on Sexual Abuse." *Canadian Woman Studies* (Fall) 12 (11): 12–15.

Canning, Kathleen. 1994. "Feminist History after the Linguistic Turn: Historicising Discourse and Experience." *Signs: Journal of Culture and Society* 19 (2): 368–404.

Gordon, Linda. 1986. "Feminism and Social Control: the Case of Child Abuse and Neglect." In *What is Feminism?* Juliet Mitchell and Ann Oakley, eds. Oxford: Basil Blackwell.

Ferguson, Kathy. 1991. "Interpretation and Genealogy in Feminism." *Signs: Journal of Culture and Society* 16 (2): 322–339.

Frederickson, Renee. 1991. *Repressed Memories: A Journey To Recovery from Sexual Abuse.* New York: Fireside.

George, Glynis. 1996. "Grass Roots Feminist Practice and the Politics of Culture in Bay St. George Newfoundland." PhD. dissertation, Department of Anthropology, University of Toronto.

Greene, Gayle. 1991. "Feminist Fiction and the Uses of Memory." *Signs: Journal of Women in Culture and Society* 6 (2): 290–321.

Haaken, Janice. 1994. "Sexual Abuse, Recovered Memory, and Therapeutic Practice." *Social Text* 40: 115–145.

Hacking, Ian. 1991. "The Making and Molding of Child Abuse." *Critical Inquiry* 17: 253–288.

Handler, Richard. 1988. *Nationalism and the Politics of Culture in Quebec.* Madison, Wisconsin: University of Wisconsin Press.

Heilbrun, Carolyn. 1988. *Writing a Woman's Life.* New York: W. W. Norton and Co.

Herman, Judith. 1992. *Trauma and Recovery.* New York: Basic Books.

Ivy, Marilyn. 1993. "Have You Seen Me? Recovering the Inner Child in Late Twentieth Century America." *Social Text* 37: 227–252.

Jacobs, Janet. 1993. "Victimised Daughters: Sexual Violence and the Empathetic Female Self." *Signs: Journal of Women in Culture and Society* 19 (1): 126–145.

Kelly, Liz. 1988. "What's in a Name: Defining Abuse." *Feminist Review* 8 (January): 66–73.

Kelly, Ursula. 1993. *Marketing Place: Cultural Politics, Regionalism and Reading.* Halifax: Fernwood Publishers.

Lourie, Margaret. 1987. "Introduction: Women and Memory." *Michigan Quarterly Review* 26: 1–8.

MacLeod, Mary and Ester Saraga. 1988. "Challenging the Orthodoxy: Towards a Feminist Theory and Practice." *Feminist Review* 28: 16–55.

McIntosh, Mary. 1988. "Introduction to An Issue: Family Secrets as Public Drama." *Feminist Review* 28: 6–15.

Mouffe, Chantal. 1992. "Feminism, Citizenship and Radical Democratic Politics." In *Feminists Theorize the Political,* Joan Scott and Judith Butler, eds. New York: Routledge.

Nava, Mica. 1988. "Cleveland and the Press: Outrage and Anxiety in the Reporting of Child Sexual Abuse." *Feminist Review* 28: 103–121.

Ochberg, Richard. 1992. "Introduction." In *Storied Lives: The Cultural Politics of Self-Understanding.* George C. Rosenwald and Richard Ochberg, eds. New Haven: Yale University Press.

Overton, Jim. 1988. "A Newfoundland Culture." *Journal of Canadian Studies* 23: 6–15.

Parr, Joy. 1990. *The Gender of Breadwinners.* Toronto: University of Toronto Press.

Reissman, Catherine Kohler. 1992. "Making Sense of Marital Violence: One Woman's Narrative." In *Storied Lives: The Cultural Politics of Self-Understanding,* George C. Rosenwald and Richard Ochberg, eds. New Haven: Yale University Press.

Scott, Joan W. 1992. "Experience" In *Feminists Theorize the Political.* Joan Scott and Judith Butler, eds. New York: Routledge.

Sewell, William. 1980. *Work and Revolution in France: The Language of Labor From the Old Regime to 1848.* New York: Cambridge University Press.

Smith, Gavin. 1989. *Livelihood and Resistance: Peasants and the Politics of Land in Peru.* Berkeley: University of California Press.

Steedman, Carolyn. 1986. *Landscape for a Good Woman: A Story of Two Lives.* London: Virago Press.

Stimpson, Catharine. 1987. "The Future of Memory: A Summary." *Michigan Quarterly Review* 26: 259–265.

Swindells, Julia. 1989. "Liberating the Subject? Autobiography and Women's History: A Reading of the Diaries of Hannah Cullwick." *Interpreting Women's Lives.* Personal Narratives Group, eds. Bloomington: Indiana University Press.

———, and Jardine, Lisa. 1990. *What's Left?: Women in Culture and the Labor Movement.* New York: Routledge.

Valverde, Mariana. 1991. "As If Subjects Existed: Analysing Social Discourses." *Canadian Review of Sociology and Anthropology* 23 (2): 173–187.

Weedon, Chris. 1987. *Feminist Practice and Post-Structural Theory.* Oxford: Basil Blackwell.

II. The Medicalization of Memory

Just as the case studies in Part 1 sought to place traumatic memories in their local discursive contexts, the chapters that follow situate today's traumatic memory discourses within a larger historical context. Where did we get the idea that, as Hacking puts it, "what has been forgotten is what forms our character"? How did "trauma"—once a medical word for physical wounds—find its way into our everyday psychological talk? What accounts for our belief that we can be healed by reliving what has hurt us? As our authors show, the answers to these questions take us back a hundred years and more, to the work of experts founding what they thought to be sciences of memory.

Ian Hacking traces this development to its beginnings in the late nineteenth century. His aim is to show just how we have come by the assumption that memory itself is knowable, and why this knowledge has become so politically charged. Invoking Foucault's notions of "anatomo-politics" and "bio-politics," he proposes that the sciences of memory have established a third realm of power mediated by expert knowledge—a "memoro-politics," in which claims about memory have come to take the moral and political place once occupied by claims about the soul.

According to Hacking, memory in Western thought has always been close to notions of identity and soul. Until recently, however, the connection was positive and unproblematic—as, for example, in Locke's equation of identity with remembered biography. The decisive break came in the 1870s with Theodule Ribot's work linking traumatic amnesia with an emerging science of memory. Elaborated by Charcot and then by Janet and Freud, this idea led to an even stranger notion: that people are shaped in central ways by what they have forgotten. This belief is central to memoro-politics, and it is ubiquitous today.

While Hacking sketches the rise of memoro-politics in bold strokes on a very large canvas, Allan Young and Ruth Leys consider two of its aspects in much finer detail. Young traces the complex path taken by the notion of trauma as it migrated from medicine into psychiatry and thus from body into mind. The vestiges of this migration are still with us, he argues, and they have done much to shape current psychiatric thinking about post-traumatic stress disorder. He shows that trauma actually has two meanings in psychiatry today, each with its own history. At one level traumatic memories are simply painful images, emotions, sensations, and words, "located in psychological space," as Young puts it. But psychiatry recognizes another, cruder form of traumatic memory as well, this one rooted in neuroanatomy, physiology, and evolutionary history. This latter, bodily version of traumatic memory still bears the traces of old ideas about fear as "remembered pain" and pathology as a survival mechanism gone awry. As such, Young argues, it underwrites a second kind of trauma narrative with its own implicit values. In practice this narrative serves both to legitimate and to reconstrue trauma narratives framed in moral/psychological terms.

Leys examines another rich vein in the history of trauma, this one located very firmly in psychological space. Her subject is a fascinating debate that took place in the early decades of this century concerning hypnosis and the abreaction of traumatic memories. While this debate anticipates aspects of the current repressed memory controversy, Leys shows that it has more important lessons to teach. These bear especially on the problems and paradoxes that arise when cathartic therapies for trauma are theorized in terms of long-standing Western assumptions about subjectivity.

At first the issues look simple enough. During World War I psychologists routinely used hypnosis to cure shell-shocked soldiers. How did it work? To some it was a clear case of liberating pent-up emotions through a cathartic reliving of the repressed trauma. To others the important point was not the catharsis but the restoration of memory. As Leys shows, however, the two views reflected two very different views of the subject under treatment. Was he a passive recipient of medical interventions or a moral agent who collaborated in his cure? Both answers ended in difficulties—moral and political ones in the first case, conceptual in the second. Hovering behind these, she argues, there was a profound ambivalence about hypnosis and the nature of emotional memory, an ambivalence running through the work of nearly every psychologist who addressed the subject—from Charcot, Janet, and William James to Freud and Ferenczi. In one way or another all these writers were grappling with a possibility that today's trauma therapists fail to recognize—namely that "emotional memories" may not be memories at all.

4

Memory Sciences, Memory Politics

Ian Hacking

It has become commonplace to speak of a politics of this or that or almost anything. What once had shock value has now become banal. It is thus not much of a metaphor to speak of a politics of memory. At the time of revising this essay, the most vivid political confrontation over memory has two easily recognizable sides. On the one hand are the allies of the False Memory Syndrome Foundation. On the other hand is a popular front of therapists who practice age regression, who treat Dissociative Identity Disorder (the new name given, in 1994, to Multiple Personality Disorder), or, more broadly, who diagnose a great deal of adult unhappiness and illness as the product of early and repeated child abuse.

The False Memory Syndrome Foundation was founded early in 1992, in Philadelphia, and has been winning vocal adherents ever since. It is a banding together of parents whose adult children, during therapy, recall hideous scenes of familial child abuse. Its mission: to tell the world that patients in psychotherapy can come to remember horrible events of childhood that never happened. Distressed thirty-somethings believe that they were horribly abused by parents or relatives long ago. But, urges the Foundation, many of the resulting accusations and subsequent family chaos result not from past evils but from false memories engendered by ideologically committed therapists.

The Foundation divides its swelling ranks into "Families" (the parents who feel betrayed), "Professionals" (many of whom are clinicians who hold that all too much therapeutic practice suggests repressed memories to clients), and "Retractors" (people who have, in the course of therapy, accused their family, but who now realize that their recovered memories are simply false). The Foundation has won an immense amount of media publicity. Therapists have been successfully sued by their clients for malpractice. Many more suits are in the courts. Both the memory expert Elizabeth Loftus and the sociologist Richard Ofshe have teamed up with journalists to publish powerful books denouncing even the possibility of repressed memory (Loftus and Ketcham 1994, Ofshe and Watters 1994).

Meanwhile their opponents, who had previously had two decades of intense and almost unchallenged growth, denounce the false memory organizations as support groups for child molesters. A great many radical feminists remain firmly committed to this side of the debate. There are public demonstrations, and mass demonstrations of support in Washington. There are vigorous attempts on both sides to influence law-makers: a politics of memory, in short.

Essential to this confrontation is the received opinion that childhood trauma, typically sexual abuse which memory suppresses and forgets, is a cause of uncontrollable deviance. That was for some time regarded as proven. The recent rash of multiple personalities furnishes one of many examples. Practitioners of all levels (M.D.s, Ph.D. psychologists, social workers) who diagnose or recognize multiple personality disorder take for granted that the disorder was caused by early sexual abuse. I have elsewhere sketched the rise of child abuse as a major social and political issue (Hacking 1991, 1992a), and then shown how the abuse etiology of multiple personality became established (Hacking 1992b). Early and repeated sexual abuse is one type of psychological trauma that has riveted our attention. Here I hope to show how forgotten psychic trauma has changed the very idea of the spiritual self, the soul. It was that change that made easy the official doctrine about multiple personality.

The doctrine of forgetting has now been fiercely challenged. Loftus titles her book *The Myth of Repressed Memory*. She agrees that there are sexual assaults on children (though she is dubious about some very high estimates of the prevalence of such abuse). But it is a scientifically demonstrable fact, she asserts, that adults do not forget such events. Lenore Terr (1994) says it is a scientific fact that there are two types of trauma, repeated and once-only. We do recall once-only events, but to escape from repeated trauma we repress it, turn it into a secret even from ourselves. Van der Kolk (1993) states that Loftus studies only memory encoded in propositions, but there is another type of memory, engraved in visual scenes or felt in our bodies. It is buried; we recover it in strange flashbacks, a phenomenon at the frontier of scientific research.

A battle, then, is engaged, a battle fought over the bodies of young women with psychological problems. It is no metaphor to speak of politics here. The politics is, however, of a particular sort. It involves a power struggle built around knowledge, or claims to knowledge. It takes for granted that a certain sort of knowledge is possible. Individual factual claims are batted back and forth, claims about this patient, that therapist, combined with larger views about vice and virtue. Underlying these competing claims to what we might call surface knowledge there is a depth knowledge; that is, a knowledge that there are facts out there about memory, truth-or-falsehoods to get a fix on. There would not be politics of this sort, if there were not that assumption that there is a knowledge about memory to be gained by science.

My talk of depth and surface knowledges obviously imitates Michel Foucault's expressions, *savoir*—what I call depth knowledge—and *connaissance*—surface knowledge (Foucault 1972). My idea that the politics arises from and is built around a kind of knowledge likewise owes much to Foucault. But one might see things in reverse, as the politics making prominent what would otherwise be items from obscure sciences of memory. That is perhaps an implication of Judith Herman's *Trauma and Recovery* (1992), a superb exploitation of the politics of memory. It is self-conscious about the role of politics: "Three times over the past century, a particular form of psychological trauma has surfaced into public consciousness. Each time the investigation of that trauma has flourished in affiliation with a political movement" (p. 9). Yet I shall argue that although the sciences and the politics mutually interact, it is the underlying depth knowledge, that there are certain sorts of truths about memory and forgetting, that makes the politics possible.

The politization of memory can be analyzed at many different levels. I am not claiming that depth knowledge is the only story. I do insist that it has served as an essential backdrop to other events. For a full understanding of the political phenomena one must attend to the immediate circumstances and current situation. Many interests are in play, and the casual observer can distinguish several centers of power or subversion that seem central. Many wings of feminism, with their emphasis on survivors of incest and other forms of family violence, find the recollection of past evil to be a crucial source of empowerment. Sects of Protestant fundamentalism impressed by tales of satanic ritual abuse, and of programming by diabolical cults, rely on the restoration of buried memory. Many people are hostile to both of these important social groupings, the feminists and the fundamentalists. The False Memory Syndrome Foundation is a political action group that crystallizes the fear and loathing of several larger publics towards these forces. Few people are attracted to both militant feminism and militant fundamentalism, because they have entirely different class allegiances, interests, and geographical distributions. Hence it is remarkable how subgroups within them agree on the basic knowledge about recovered memories. All of these diverse forces play out their conflict on top of that depth knowledge that is my focus here. They all suppose that there is knowledge of memory and one only has to get it right.

Forgetting

One feature of the modern sensibility is dazzling in its implausibility: the idea that what has been forgotten is what forms our character, our personality, our soul. To grasp this we need to reflect on how knowledge about memory became possible late in the nineteenth century. What were the new sciences of memory trying to do? I claim that they emerged as surrogate sciences of the soul, empirical sciences, positive sciences that would provide new kinds of knowledge in terms of which to cure, help, and control the one aspect of human beings that had hitherto been resistant to positivist science. If we address only the surface facts about memory, the politicization of memory will seem only a curious accident. But if we think of how the very idea of such facts came into being, the battles may seem almost inevitable.

There are several sciences of memory. Despite our deep commitment to the unity of science, there is virtually no overlap between them. Think of (i) the neurological studies of the location of different types of memory which began with Broca (1861); (ii) the psychodynamics of memory, which even Freud-haters can never entirely separate from Freud's work; (iii) the experimental studies of recall that originated in the laboratory of Ebbinghaus (1885). All three are nineteenth-century sciences. Only neurology has been deeply affected by the high technology advances of the twentieth century: we really can do things to brains of which nineteenth-century neurologists could only dream. Yet the psychodynamics of memory is the only knowledge, of the three that I have mentioned, that has profoundly influenced Western culture. Certainly the location of distinct memory functions, in distinct parts of the brain, has confirmed a materialist approach to memory. Broca's program is in excellent state at this very moment, yet its reach into our deepest concerns has been limited to confirming that there are real facts about memory to discover. Likewise Ebbinghaus's laboratory research, which began in 1779, continues in a thousand departments of experimental psychology today. It has given us certain phrases of common speech—who does not know of short and long term memory? Yet its chief function, from a larger point of view, may be to shore up the depth knowledge, that there is a body of facts about memory to be known.

Raising Consciousness

Before proceeding I have to state clearly that the public recognition of child abuse, starting with battered baby syndrome in 1962, and encompassing incest by 1975, has been one of the most important American consciousness raising activities of the past thirty years. Arguably it is *the* most important, for it has led to awareness of many other features of current life, starting with other kinds of family violence. Even the important phrase "battered women" seems to have been patterned after "battered baby syndrome." There are many passions out there, and much fear. But I insist on not being misunderstood. An essay such as this is inevitably distanced from real events. The relative calm that results is not to be taken to imply any downgrading of the child abuse movement. My distance is not to be confused, for example, with sympathy for the False Memory Syndrome Foundation, many of whose machinations I deplore. Its leaders tend to say "O, yes, child abuse is simply terrible, *but . . .*" and then move on to allegedly false accusations. No "buts," please.

Michel Foucault's Poles

Readers of Michel Foucault's first volume about sexuality will know that I pattern "memoro-politics" on his anatomo-politics and bio-politics. These were his names for "two poles of development linked together by a whole intermediary cluster of relations," two forms of power over life that (he claimed) started in the 17th century.

> One of these poles—the first to be formed, it seems,—centered on the body as a machine: its disciplining, the optimization of its capabilities, the extortion of its forces [etc.], all this was ensured by the procedures of power that characterized the *disciplines*: an *anatomo-politics of the human body*. The second, formed somewhat later, focused on the species body, the body imbued with the mechanics of life and serving as the basis of the biological processes: propagation [etc.]. Their supervision was effected through an entire series of interventions and *regulatory controls: a bio-politics of the population* (1980: 139).

Foucault wrote of "an explosion of numerous and diverse techniques for achieving the subjugation of bodies and the control of populations, marking the beginning of an era of 'bio-power.' " When Foucault speaks of power he does not mean power exercised from above by the sovereign,

71

even if self-sustaining bureaucracies have a lot to do with its practice. You and I are part of its exercise. The word "power," in Foucault, is *pouvoir*, not *puissance*. His title *Power/Knowledge* (1980) is a translation of *Pouvoir/Savoir*. We could call that "depth power/depth knowledge."

Foucault spoke of "two poles of development linked together by a whole cluster of relations." On the next page he speaks of two initially distinct directions for the development of bio-power during the eighteenth century (discipline and demography). The metaphor of poles and intermediary relations hardly gets at the complexities, yet I have found it useful to adapt it. What I call memoro-politics is a third extreme point from which (to continue the metaphor of mapping and surveying) we can triangulate recent knowledge. But I can't talk about three poles (for there's only North and South) unless I make a gross pun. I grow my runner beans—pole beans—on a tripod made of three poles. The lush growth at the top, as the beans planted around each pole tangle with the others, is the richest image of Foucault's "cluster of intermediary relations."

The Soul

Anatamo-politics *of the human body*; bio-politics *of the population*, writes Foucault: what is memoro-politics a politics of? Of the self, the "subject" or the human mind? Or of those substantivized personal pronouns, *ego, me*? I prefer to say a memoro-politics of the human soul, not a popular word nowadays. Philosophers of my stripe speak of the soul not to suggest something transcendental or eternal, but to invoke character, reflective choice, self-understanding, values that include honesty to others and one-self, and several types of freedom and responsibility. Those are intellectual conceits, powerful but abstract. Love, passion, envy, tedium, regret, and quiet contentment are the stuff of the soul. The gentle soul cares for others not from duty but from affection and affinity. The soul nevertheless remains self-centered because it means that we do have a center. This is not to say that the soul is eternal, or that the soul is a fixed point that somehow explains character. The soul (as I understand it) stands for whatever strange mix of things is, at some time, imaged as inner—a thought not contradicted by Wittgenstein's dictum, that the body is the best picture of the soul.

These ideas of the soul are in no way universal. But they do permeate the European background from which memoro-politics emerged. Other peoples don't have anything like this idea. They do not talk about the soul. Good for them. They don't have memoro-politics either. Within various bits and pieces of what is called the Western tradition conceptions of the soul have certainly been used to maintain a great many hierarchies, and have played a central role in power plays (Comaroff 1994). The soul has been a way of internalizing the social order, of putting into myself those very virtues and cruelties that enable my society to survive. This functionalist view of the soul, as what maintains public order, does not unnerve me. The centrality of the soul in my tradition is well illustrated by the fact that one can so quickly place it by allusions to either Plato or Aristotle. Most of our other ideas and sentiments—both in and on either side of what is now called modernity—ride more cheerfully with one camp or the other, but the soul mingles gladly with Platonists and Aristotelians, with sophists and Sapphists, even if it is dubious about latter-day Christian accretions.

Memoro-politics is a power struggle founded upon a depth knowledge. That came into being fairly late in the nineteenth century as a way to study the soul. The depth knowledge was the knowledge that there are underlying truths about memory. The surface knowledge is constituted by the several sciences of memory that came into being at that time. One among the many reasons that we are now so uncomfortable speaking about the soul is that the sciences of memory have become surrogates for the soul. We prefer all sorts of abstract nonsense nouns—the self, the subject—to what does make sense, the soul.

Psychology as Physiology: Anatomo-Politics

What discipline aims at knowledge of the soul? We'd expect it to be psychology, the science of mind. A cynic, doubting that psychology has taught us much, might still inquire, what has psychology done to the soul? Perhaps it made the soul bodily, physiological. That is an implicit theme of Danziger (1991), a history of psychology from the time that Wundt established the psychology laboratory.

His ambitious title, *Constructing the Subject,* implies a story about how the "subject" of experimental psychology came into being as an object of study, with attributes that can be measured. But his book is not a history of what everyone means by "psychology." Instead he tells us about experimental psychology as developed in universities. That science certainly spreads far beyond scholarly research; its measures of skill, intelligence, personal relationships, or child-parent bonding, are the stock in trade of corporate personnel departments, prisons, and maternity wards. But these measurements did begin in the psychology laboratory. They have a valid field of application in the larger world because they determine what is to be measured and counted as knowledge about the larger world.

The psychology laboratory began with Wundt and with Fechner. Fechner started with psychophysics, with investigations into the relationships between body and mind, but Fechner was notoriously his own, odd, man. Wundt was the organizer *par excellence* who inaugurated the institutional frame of experimental psychology. One of Danziger's most important lessons is in his opening pages. Every new science needs an old model against which it can be legitimated. Psychology chose physiology, even down to the fine detail of laboratory design and organization. Thus it patterned itself on the study of the body. Its domain and its model, in terms of Foucault's poles, was anatomy. The power of the physiological model continues in experimental psychology to this day. Behaviorism, cognitive science, neurophilosophy, neurology, localized brain function, mood altering drugs, or biochemical theories of mental maladies: these are all branches of physiology. I offered: psychology invented a surrogate for the soul. But that is wrong. Most laboratory psychology is about the body, and provides the knowledge that determines the exercise of anatomo-power, seen at its most extreme when disorderly minds are to be controlled by electro-shock or chemicals. That is the first way that we got a fix on the soul: through physiology, through the body.

From the Body to Populations: Bio-Politics

The second point for triangulating the soul is located at the level not of the body but of the population, the collection, the classification and enumeration of kinds of people. Here we have the politics of the species, of the human race as species to be categorized into its varieties—I use the word as did the horticulturalists, seedsmen, and stock-breeders of old. The census takers and counters of every sort flood our panorama of humanity with new kinds of person (Hacking 1983, Desrosières 1993). Counting, enumerating, and classifying may seem some distance from the soul, but I repeat that I am triangulating. Those who enumerate must classify, and they constantly create new varieties, new descriptions, new ways to be a person. All human action is action under a description, and new classifications literally create new kinds of things to do. But there is a further feature of the enumerators: they are able to determine what is "normal," our most striking example of a concept which is both descriptive ("that's the average") and evaluative ("that's how one ought to be. Normal = healthy"). But what is normal? The entire apparatus of laboratory psychology is there to tell us. Danziger shows that although experimental psychology began as physiology, it increasingly became a statistical science. Individuals were grouped into classes for which norms could be determined.

Truly statistical psychology began with Hermann Ebbinghaus in 1879. Memory was to be investigated by ability to recall a series of nonsense syllables. Then one was to construct a statistical analysis of the ability to recall. Ebbinghaus began work on himself, a typical human being, but his behavior was to be understood only through statistical scrutiny. His approach became standard, integrated with learning theory. Whole cohorts of research psychologists have devoted their entire careers to what I see as the program of Ebbinghaus. But from afar we notice that it was precisely in the study of memory that laboratory psychology was transferred from the body to populations, from anatamo- to bio-, from the individual event to statistics.

Transfers between Poles: The Case of Trauma

With "anatomo-" and "bio-," Foucault directed our attention to the body and kinds of people. I am proposing a third pole, memory. But I have to make two more observations. One is a stark reminder less of the intertwining of material from each pole, than of straightforward transfer from one pole to another. I've mentioned how the normal and the pathological—concepts of medicine, physiology, and the organs of the body—were transferred to the species, collectivities, kinds of people. Normalcy, which is the cardinal meta-concept of bio-politics, was lifted straight from physiology. I call normalcy a meta-concept because no thing or person is simply "normal" or "abnormal." They are normal in some group of respects or other, as the age at which a child first walks, or the age at which an older person first begins have trouble recalling proper names.

Another transfer is close to hand. As I sharpen my focus on memoro-politics, I shall increasingly attend to memories of trauma, cruel and painful experiences that corrupt or destroy one's sense of oneself. But just as "normal" comes from medical pathology, so "trauma" means wound (a cut, lesion, or break in the body produced by an outside force or agent). The word "trauma" was not a word of common English when it was in the hands of surgeons treating mutilated soldiers; it was one of those fancy words that lay people don't use, and often do not even understand. But now "traumatic experience" and all the rest are standard English. From that it might seem as if my distinction between three "poles" just collapses. I think not. These profound transfers, of "normality" or "trauma," always occur at the level of metaphor, which becomes dead metaphor. No one now looking at technical uses of the expression "normal distribution" (i.e. the Gaussian, bell-shaped, probability curve) ever thinks of pathology or diseased (as opposed to healthy) organs of the body, although that is where our modern idea of the normal comes from

(Canguilhem 1980, Hacking 1990, chapt. 19). Likewise, I have found that few people outside of the medical profession easily recall that "trauma" meant a physical wound, a cut or break.

Trauma means wound, and it entered the psychology of the soul via anatomy, as what we now call whiplash injury, or the old "railway spine." Engines went off the rails, steam boilers blew up, cuttings caved in, at a rate per mile that would now seem impossible to us. There were insurance companies, as speculative as steam boilers, and eager litigants (Schivelbush 1986, Trimble 1981). There arose the category of the hysterical male who had been injured in a railway accident, and was thereafter unable to do useful work, though you could not quite see what ailed him. The anatomo-politics of railway spine made it possible to have a really horrible event that worked in mysterious ways. The physical theory of memory, of unremovable brain traces of events that had been experienced, worked at the level of the body. But now we had bad events that could work on the soul. Instead of the remembering being what affected us, it was the forgotten. That strange transmutation was helped by an anatomical theory of memory, that everything that happened was preserved in some little spot of the brain. If it were forgotten, it was still there, and hence could act in potent ways. The transfer of trauma from the physical to the psychological was effected by 1885, when a French medical thesis on trauma could routinely have a chapter on *traumatisme morale* (Rouillard 1885). That was the year that Freud came to Paris to study under Charcot.

Freud

Freud has gone out of fashion, and now some historians of psychoanalysis scurry like old-time undertakers to the scene of the most recent exposure, hoping to drum up some trade for the burial business. Such pettiness tries to ignore the fact that Freud transformed Western consciousness more surely than the atomic bomb or the welfare state. His famous inventions, such as the Oedipus complex, are familiar enough, but we often ignore more fundamental aspects of his work. He cemented the idea of psychic trauma. It is a curious fact that many of the clinicians now most deeply involved in memoro-politics hate Freud. Therapy by the recall of forgotten memory of real abuse is their stock in trade, but the father of the idea must be slain. "Freud did to the unconscious mind with his theories what New York City does to the ocean with its garbage" (Ross 1989: 181). That is from one of the two text-books on multiple personality disorder. The author is a past president of the International Society for the Study of Multiple Personality and Dissociation.

There is an easy explanation for this loathing. Memory therapy for the recovery of scenes of child abuse is central to the treatment of multiple personality, which itself needs the very idea of child abuse to furnish its aetiological theories. Memory therapists cannot forgive Freud for his abandoning, in 1897, of the child assault (seduction) theory that he had so enthusiastically advanced in 1893. Yet Freud has a curious role in much writing on trauma, since he symbolizes the importation of repressed memory into the Western mind. It was he who made all of us aware of how forgotten trauma could act upon us.

War

The body, the species, and the memory vie with each other for control of the soul, like the bean plants at the top of the apex, each twisting for the other's light, trying to put the other in the shade. Physiology, in the forms of the different types of anatomo-psychology, got there before Freud, whether in Wundt's laboratory or with localizing neurosurgeons after the Franco-Prussian war. Both needed the 1914–18 War. Intelligence testers defined techniques to sort a cohort of American conscripts, one of the most successful mobilizations of science of all time. The brain surgeons did their work on the field or when the boys came home. Memory was driven by war away from the mind. Perhaps the Freudians, some of whom opted out or were kept out of the mobilization, kept memoro-politics going. Those who were involved in treating shell-shocked soldiers, such as Ferenczi or Abraham, thought deeply about the causes of hysterical symptoms. It was not in lost events of childhood, but in terror of battle and its surroundings. That terror might be repressed, remembered, or distorted (Leys 1994). There was more than a change in the psychotrauma that produced the neurosis. There was also a change in emotional tone. The patients of the *Studies in Hysteria* by Breuer and Freud had, in the end, felt guilty about their childhood sexual experiences. In war there was no room for guilt. There was only fear. And here we get the seeds of the transition to a more recent conception of the effect of sex in childhood. We are not to think of it as guilt but as fear. We are victims. There are perpetrators who have terrified us.

Despite the deep worries about shell-shock, expressed not only by Freud's colleagues on the German side but also by W. H. R. Rivers in England, shell-shock was most commonly treated in a non-dynamic way. In France, a powerful influence was the renegade neurologist, Babinski. Once Charcot's favored student for the study of hysteria, he took control of the medical administration of shell-shocked soldiers. Where the soldiers had all the symptoms of hysteria or at least traumatic neurosis, Babinski completed the dissipation of hysteria as even a possible diagnosis. Hypnotism and suggestion were rejected. It took a couple more wars to reinstate the old ideas, and make the forgotten battlefield the cause of mental illness.

That did not happen for medical or psychiatric reasons. The past works only when there are procedures for making it work. That needs money and careers. One of the most efficient uses of memoro-politics is due to the U. S. Veterans Administration. We had to wait for the Vietnam War for memoro-politics to take its revenge, as the VA hospitals cultivated Post-Traumatic Stress Disorder. It is very rewarding for drop-out vets of the Vietnam War to pass very strictly administered tests for Post-Traumatic Stress Disorder. It is very desirable for the United States, which has to be more imaginative than other countries in providing bases for social welfare.

Allan Young (1995) has shown how this disorder has been cultivated, and the virtues that it serves. The traditional veterans associations, the American Legion and the Veterans of Foreign Wars, at first opposed this complaint, for the vets of former wars did not have it. Or, less agreeable to say, the old vets became drunk, disorderly, and dead. At first the VA itself was totally opposed to PTSD. But then it created career niches for whole units of psychiatrists and psychologists. They turned trauma outside-in. Their mission was not so much to help the combat veteran with ghastly memories. On the contrary, the vet who is unable to get on with his life, but who can *not* remember what made him that way, is the victim to be helped. In many cases a man obtained treatment and a special pension only if he could not, except in therapy, remember what had happened to him. And if he still could not remember, he could get even more help. The men who remembered very well the god-awful things that happened were sometimes less able to benefit under this program, because PTSD was made to essentially involve not remembering but forgetting. Don't misunderstand me. I am not a critic of the VA and its use of PTSD. Nations notoriously like to forget the detritus of their former wars. If this is the way to help old soldiers, I'm all for it. This is the way that bureaucratic doctors can find beds or pensions for male wrecks that the limited American social net is unable to catch in any other way. I am here concerned only to comment on the way in which PTSD is part of the politics of memory—based on a supposed knowledge.

Before Science

Now let us stand back and develop Foucault's ideas of anatomo- and biopolitics. His readers have rightly much emphasized that both were concerned with discipline, with the organization of people and the state. But there is the further and more complex part of his doctrine, about the integral part played by knowledge in making possible this impersonal power. If we are to extend his analysis to memoro-politics, we should go back and look at the sciences of memory. My first and obvious observation, is that the sciences of memory have not been with us always. They emerge in the nineteenth century.

I don't mean that we began to think about memory only late in the nineteenth century. I claim that before that time there was no conception of a scientific knowledge about memory. We are concerned with a generation or so, the last quarter of the century; direct and self-conscious ancestors do not go back much before 1800. That was when the depth knowledge, that there are facts about memory, came into being. Why did it come into being then? Because the sciences of memory could serve as the public forum for something of which science could not openly speak. There could be no science of the soul. So there became a science of memory.

Memoria Technica

First I should corroborate my assertion that the sciences of memory were truly new. Here we have a fortunate contrast between art and science. No art was more carefully studied, from Plato until the Enlightenment, than the Art of Memory, or, perhaps we had better say, the art of memorizing. Because of Michel Foucault's careful talk of technologies of the self, his imitators love to use the word "technology" for things that are not technologies. The word is supposed to invoke power and knowledge; its use is thought to be daring. In fact it is often boring. But we can instructively talk about technologies of the memory. I mean the Art of Memory, *De arte memorativa, memoria technica,* mnemonics.

Plato and Aristotle refer often to this art, particularly to a form of it that is translated as "placing." It has been called an architectural mnemonics (Carruthers 1990: 71). In the mind one forms the image of a three-dimensional space, a well furbished house, or even an entire city. Would you remember that printing was invented in 1436? Then place a book in the 36th memory place in the fourth room of the first house in town. Cicero thought that such techniques, which survived long after the invention of printing, were of the highest importance, above all to the orator. Many people have read Frances Yates's wonderful book *The Art of Memory* (1966). Her study, along with Rossi (1960), was sensational when published because almost everyone had forgotten about this art.

Three things will be noticed. First, the Art of Memory had a central role in both the ancient world and the Renaissance. Expertise conferred great stature; it was, in truth, a political asset. Doctors of the Church, who relied on the Art of Memory, were regarded as more reliable than the imperfect copies of manuscripts scattered across Europe. Gutenberg changed all that. Mnemonics will always be with us, but they are little more than parlor tricks today. This technology of memory, *memoria technica*, entirely antedates the desire to know about memory that came into being in the nineteenth century.

Secondly, the Art of Memory is truly a *techne*, a knowing how, and not a knowing that. It was not *scientia*, not knowledge about an entity, the memory. It was not knowledge about memory at all, but knowledge of how to improve it. Third, the Art of Memory was altogether outer-directed. It was at most incidentally concerned with one's own experiences. It aimed at nearly instant recall of any set of desired facts. One was to arrange external material in a vivid picture in one's mind, to which one has direct access. There is some truth in the thought that what we call computer memory, and its numerous technologies, are the lineal descendant of the Art of Memory.

The Forensic Self

The Art of Memory did not fade away, only to be immediately replaced by sciences of memory. There were new descriptions of memory aplenty. Hume famously taught that the principal difference between memory images and ideas and perceptual images and ideas is that perceptions are always more "vivid" than memories. Locke knew better. Could there be a more powerful description of that 1980s phenomenon of recovered memory, the flashback, than this:

> The Mind very often sets it self on work in search of some hidden *Idea*, and turns, as it were, the Eye of the Soul upon it; though sometimes too they start up in our Minds of their own accord, and offer themselves to the Understanding; and very often are rouzed and tumbled out of their dark Cells into open Day-light, by turbulent and tempestuous Passion; our affections bringing *Ideas* to our Memory, which had otherwise lain quiet and unregarded. (*Essay*, II.x.7; Locke 1700[1975], 152–153).

Memory played a cardinal role in Locke's celebrated discussion of personal identity. He was struggling with the pull of the two poles, body and memory. He made "man" a concept based in part on bodily continuity. He made "person" what he called a forensic concept, having to do with

80

memory and responsibility. Mary Douglas argues, in a way that I find compelling, that Locke's notion of the person as forensic and as linked by chains of memory and responsibility, is a characteristic of what she calls the enterprise culture. It involves a very different conception of selfhood than she found in African communities with which she has worked (Douglas, 1992). Locke's forensic person was a new figure who arose from evolving practices of law, property and trade. Yet Locke was nevertheless only moving memory around on the epistemological board. The Socratic fable of recollection—anamnesis—was a central figment of the Platonic theory of knowledge. Locke, the arch-enemy of innate ideas, moved memory from the black square of Platonism into the white square of empiricism, from innate ideas to the association of ideas. In Plato's *Meno*, all real knowledge, starting with geometry, was made a matter of self-knowledge modeled on recollection and techniques of recall, which include geometrical proof that enables one to see what was always there, deep dark down. In Locke's *Essay*, memory defined what it is to be a person. Locke wanted to be as unplatonic as could be. He elevated memory into the bright light of what every good man knows, and needs no tutor to recall. The moves made with memory in the *Essay* are different in kind from Plato's moves, but notice how the pawn of memory remains the same, and has an equally central status for the philosophy.

Memories of Deviance

From Locke's exceptional point of view, the person is constituted not by a biography but by a remembered biography. We have had told "lives"— as in Plutarch's lives, the lives of the saints, Aubrey's *Brief Lives*, for as long as we have had a remembered past. But those have been the lives of the exceptional. The typical *Life* of a typical saint enjoins us against enthusiasm, the tale is told "more for our admiration than our emulation." Augustine, Petrarch, Rousseau: might not each of us have confessed to such a life? No. Those are not ordinary folk. Where shall we locate the idea that everyone has a biography, even, or especially, the lowest of the low?

The pictures of biography are of course everywhere. A human life becomes conceived of as a story. A nation is thought of as its history. A species becomes an evolutionary object. A soul is a pilgrimage through life. A planet is thought of as Gaia. There are well known suggestions about how the biography, the dossier, the medical or legal record, became the life of the deviant, the law breaker, the mad person. If we are to look for the beginning of these dossiers, they and their role are described with surprising precision by their inventors. For example, in England Thomas

81

Plint (1851) said, in so many words, that once the criminals had been identified by their biographies, society would finally be able to protect itself. Yet even there my three poles intertwine. For a biography is not enough. We need to know which body goes with which life. Identification—the hooking of a narrative on to a person in the dock—was in part effected by new technologies of anatomy, Bertillon's ear-prints or Galton's fingerprints. You needed these to be sure which story fit which person.

Likewise medical case histories, although used in the nosologies of the eighteenth century do not flourish until the mid-nineteenth century. Part of the project, as Jan Goodstein (1988) puts it in the title of her book, was *To Console and Classify*. But it was also to provide the life story of the patient. At first, what the patient said was no more to be trusted than what the criminal said. But just after Plint was telling London how to write the life stories of criminals, Briquet (1859) in Paris was telling how to write the life stories of hysterical women. And he was telling how these women had so often experienced terrible things early in life, often from a father. Briquet's textbook on hysteria was the classic mid-century work. In retrospect we can go back to it and see a doctor horrified by what his female patients were telling him about their past.

Why did memoro-politics emerge in the nineteenth century? Is it because the systematic recording of the lives of truly uninteresting people began in the mid-century, with the lives of criminals being recorded, lives of men who usually lied about their past? Is that it, plus the telling of the lives of the mildly deranged? Could that be what so transformed modern mores, our present conception of who we are and what made us? Certainly such events are not irrelevant, but they are not central either. Briquet's book seems not to have been read in our way, in terms of abuse, during his lifetime. Moreover there was no question of *forgotten* trauma. Briquet's patients knew all too well what had happened to them. Plint's criminals may have lied, but it was never suggested that they forgot. Forgetting may have been set up by new genres of biography, the medical case and the criminal record, and the recording of memories of deviant people. But it required something else to put forgetting in place: the sciences of memory.

Ribot: An Ideal Type of the New Sciences of Memory

I have mentioned three new kinds of sciences of memory. One is neurological, a science of the body and its parts. One is statistical, not only a branch of laboratory psychology, but also arguably the first, bottom, and foundational branch. The third is the study of pathological memory, such as is evidenced in dissociation as well as in the result of trauma, be it phys-ical or psychological. This third science of memory comes closest to the soul. If you look in Baldwin's classic *Dictionary of Philosophy and Psychology* (1901) under memory, you will find that the article on *Memory, (defects of)* chiefly focuses on *amnesia* (which also has a separate essay, and that *defects of* article is twice as long as the regular *Memory* article that surveys the phi-losophy and psychology of memory from Plato to the (then) present. The word "amnesia," or rather *amnésie*, seems to be first used in the translation of Sauvages' nosography (1771). That is not significant; it emerged dur-ing a time of neologisms as medical textbooks were translated to the ver-nacular. It does matter that amnesia names a medical disorder, a potential object of knowledge. The early attempts to localize various sorts of mem-ory were based almost entirely on lesions. That is, when a person had an abnormality of memory, and a wound or tumor, then the aspect of mem-ory that was unusual was associated with the place in the brain that was damaged. If there were no visible organic disorder, then after death the cadaver would be subject to rigorous autopsy, in order to determine what part of the brain was unusual. Thus was phrenology internalized.

I shall not here attempt to sketch a history of the sciences of memory and their corollary, the knowledge of forgetting, during the nineteenth century. One excellent source is Michael Roth's essay, "Remembering For-getting" (1989). Roth introduces one of the great memory experts, Théo-dule Ribot, and his book, *Les Maladies de la mémoire* (1881). That book is based on lectures given in Paris in the very year, 1879, that Ebbinghaus was establishing his memory laboratory. Ribot was the first professor of psychology at the Collège de France. His successor, Pierre Janet, said the chair was created precisely because of the fascination with the first mod-ern multiple personality, Félida X.

Ribot has a fitting place in any history of the sciences of memory dur-ing the nineteenth century. For me he is exemplary because he is so clear about both his philosophical motivation and his conception of what a knowledge of memory ought to be. He was an early member of the French positivist school of psychology. He opposed all ideas of a tran-scendental self, of a soul, of a metaphysical subject. Of "the old school," he wrote, "they accuse us of filching their *moi*." I have said that the new sci-ences of memory proposed not to attack religious or philosophical ideas of the soul directly, but to provide a surrogate for the one aspect of a hu-man being that seemed resistant to science. There is no speculation about that in the case of Ribot. He said that was exactly what he was doing.

The new multiple personalities were splendid. For if a person could have two personalities, each connected by a continuous or normal chain of memories, aside from amnesic gaps, and if at least one personality was ignorant of the other, then there were two persons, "two souls in one body." The old Lockeian conception of memory as the basis of the person was wonderfully confirmed. It is however another, if related, aspect of Ribot's soul-surrogate that I wish to emphasize here. Here are a few of his sentences. First, the positive picture of what memory "is":

> Memory is a biological fact. A rich and extensive memory is not a collection of impressions, but an accumulation of dynamical associations, very stable and very responsive to proper stimuli. The brain is like a laboratory full of movement, where thousands of operations are going on at once. Unconscious cerebration, not being subject to restrictions of time, operating, so to speak, only in space, may act in several directions at the same moment. Consciousness is the narrow gate through which a very small part of all this work is able to reach us (38–39).

Second, the negative picture of what clinical forgetting "is." Ribot discovered a law of regression:

1. In cases of general dissolution of the memory, loss of recollections follows an invariable path: recent events, ideas in general, feelings, and acts.
2. In the best known cases of partial dissolution, (forgetfulness of signs) loss of recollection follows an invariable path: proper names, common nouns, adjectives and verbs, interjections, gestures.
3. In each of these classes the destructive process is identical. It is a regression from the complex to the simple, from the voluntary to the automatic, from the least organized to the best organized.

His remaining points confirm *the law of regression* (his italics) in those rare cases of recovery, and, more remarkably, that the law explains

> the extraordinary revivification of certain recollections when the mind turns backward to conditions of existence that had apparently disappeared forever.

Pierre Janet seems to have invented the French word *dissociation* that now plays so large a part in the discussion of dissociative disorders (e.g. Janet 1887). But it seems clear that Ribot had all but the exact word, "dissociation." The idea as conceived by both men was a matter of regression, of de-associating, or to use another word of Janet's, *désagregation*. There was a fragmenting at the level of what Ribot was calling the unconscious (*inconscient*), in the reverse order to which associations had been formed. But if there were a flashback (as the clinicians now say) to an early stage of formation, then there would be that powerful "revivification" of which Ribot and Locke speak so movingly.

I do not conclude in this way to encourage you to read the obscure Ribot as some sort of wonderful precursor of more recent ideas. I use Ribot as an ideal type of the beginning of the many sciences of memory. These sciences had as their aim the takeover of the soul, the last refuge of a person from all prior science. The laboratory science of memory, in the style of Ebbinghaus, had to content itself with statistical studies of recall. The brain, according to Ribot, was a "laboratory" itself, or so he said in one of my quotations above. I have been much interested in the ways in which the medical wound, trauma, became the psychic wound. I mentioned above the familiar story of railway spine and male hysteria. Notice that for Ribot there is remarkably little difference between railway shock and psychological shock. The shock or hurt may create a break—a lesion—in associations which need not demand a strictly physical lesion. Or else a lesion is postulated, imagined, in that laboratory of the brain.

Thus we may say that at the time of Ribot the space had been made clear for the following: (i) Sciences of memory. (ii) These sciences as transforming our conception of the soul, of providing a surrogate for the soul, or of "filching the *moi*." (iii) But whereas in Locke it was positive memory that constituted the idea of a person, in the time of Ribot one understood the memory that would teach us about the unhappy soul in terms of forgetting. (iv) Systematic forgetting was to be explained in terms of lesions, not necessarily physical. These became items of knowledge enunciated in numerous ways both by the famous and by those who are known only by scholars. The way to have information about and control over individuals was to operate at the surface level of facts about what those individuals forget. Old campaigns and new ones—that provoked by the False Memory Syndrome Foundation, for example—can be conducted at this level only because of the emergence of a structure of possible knowledge of memory and forgetting during that critical period.

Notes

The present paper is a shortened and much altered version of my "Memoro-politics, Trauma and the Soul," *History of the Human Sciences* 7 (2) (1992): 29–52.

References

Briquet, P. 1859. *Traité clinique et thérapeutique de l'hystérie.* Paris: Baillière.

Broca, P. 1861 "Perte de la parole, ramollisement chronique et destruction partielle du lobe antérieur gauche du cerveau." *Bulletin de la Société d'Anthropologie* 2: 235–237.

Canguilhem, G. 1943, 1966/1978. *On the Normal and the Pathological.* Trans. C. R. Fawcett. Reidel: Dordrecht.

Carruthers, M. J. 1990. *The Book of Memory: A Study of Memory in Medieval Culture.* Cambridge: Cambridge University Press.

Comaroff, J. 1994. "Aristotle Re-membered." In J. Chandler, A. I. Davidson and H. Harootunian, eds. *Questions of Evidence: Proof, Practice, and Persuasion across the Disciplines.* Chicago: University of Chicago Press, 463–469.

Danziger, K. 1991. *Constructing the Subject.* Cambridge: Cambridge University Press.

Desrosières, A. 1993. *La Politique des grands nombres.* Paris: Découverte.

Douglas, M. 1992. "The Person in an Enterprise Culture." In S. H. Heap and A. Ross, eds. *Understanding the Enterprise Culture: Themes in the Work of Mary Douglas.* Edinburgh: Edinburgh University Press.

Ebbinghaus, H. (1885/1964). *Memory.* Trans. H. A. Ruger and C. E. Bussenius. New York: Dover.

Foucault, M. 1972. *The Archaeology of Knowledge.* New York: Harper and Row.

———. 1980. *A History of Sexuality.* Vol. I. *An Introduction.* New York: Vintage.

———. 1980. *Power/Knowledge.* Brighton: The Harvester Press.

Goodstein, J. 1988. *To Console and Classify: The French Psychiatric Profession in the Nineteenth Century.* Chicago: University of Chicago Press.

Hacking, I. 1983. "Biopower and the Avalanche of Numbers." *Humanities and Society* 5: 279–95.

———. 1990. *The Taming of Chance.* Cambridge: Cambridge University Press.

———. 1991. "The Making and Molding of Child Abuse." *Critical Inquiry* 17: 253–288.

———. 1992a. "Multiple Personality Disorder and Its Hosts." *History of the Human Sciences* 5: 3–33.

———. 1992b. "World-Making by Kind-Making: Child Abuse for Example." In M. Douglas and D. Hull, eds. *How Classification Works: Nelson Goodman among the Social Sciences.* Edinburgh: Edinburgh University Press.

Herman, J. L. 1992. *Trauma and Recovery.* New York: Basic Books.

Leys, R. 1994. "Traumatic Cures: Shell Shock, Janet, and the Question of Memory." *Critical Inquiry* 20: 623–662.

Locke, J. (1700/1975). *An Essay concerning Human Understanding.* Oxford: Clarendon Press.

Loftus, E. and K. Ketcham. 1994. *The Myth of Repressed Memories: False Memories and Allegations of Sexual Abuse.* New York: St. Martin's Press.

Ofshe, R. and E. Watters. 1994. *Making Monsters: False Memories, Psychotherapy and Sexual Hysteria.* New York: Charles Scribners' Sons.

Plint, T. 1851. *Crime in England: Its Relation, Character and Extent, as Developed from 1801 to 1848.* London: Charles Gilpin.

Ribot, T. 1881. *Les Maladies de la mémoire.* Paris: Baillière.

Ross, C. A. 1989. *Multiple Personality Disorder: Diagnosis, Clinical Features, and Treatment.* New York: Wiley.

Rossi, P. 1960. *Clavis Univeralis. Arti Mnemoniche e logica combinatoria de Lulle a Leibniz.* Milan: Ricardi.

Rouillard, A.-M.-P. 1885. *Essai sur les amnésies principalement au point de vue étiologique.* Paris: Le Clerc.

Ryle, G. 1949. *The Concept of Mind.* London: Hutchinson.

Sauvages, F. Boissière. de la C. (1768/1771). *Nosologie methodique.* Vol. 1. Paris: Hérissent et fils, 157.

Schivelbush, W. 1986. *The Railway Journey.* Los Angeles: University of California.

Terr, L. 1994. *Unchained Memories: True Stories of Traumatic Memories, Lost and Found.* New York: Basic Books.

Trimble, M. R. 1981. *Post-Traumatic Neurosis: From Railway Spine to the Whiplash.* New York: Wiley.

van der Kolk, B. 1993. "The Intrusive Past: The Flexibility of Memory and the Engraving of Trauma." Tape XIII–860–93A. Alexandria, Va.: Audio Transcripts Ltd.

Yates, F. 1966. *The Art of Memory.* London: Routledge and Kegan Paul.

Young, A. (1995). *The Harmony of Illusions: An Ethnography of Post-Traumatic Stress Syndrome.* Princeton, NJ: Princeton University Press.

5

Bodily Memory and Traumatic Memory

Allan Young

Halfway through his account of memoro-politics (this volume, chapter 4), Ian Hacking reaches a defining moment: the point at which the word "trauma," until now limited to bodily damage, was extended or transferred to include invisible injuries inflicted on the mind, self, or soul. From this point forward, the varieties of "cruel and painful experiences that corrupt or destroy one's sense of oneself" have a common name, "trauma."

What does it mean to say that a transfer was effected between body and mind? Was it simply a matter of a word? The most common answer found in the psychiatric literature is that the two senses of "trauma" are connected by analogy. A well-understood phenomenon, the physical effects of violence inflicted on the body, is employed to conceptualize (analogize) a less well-understood and less visible phenomenon, namely what happens to the mind when it is assaulted. In the following pages, I want to argue that this answer is unsatisfactory for two reasons: First, the initial transfer was between kinds of bodily mechanisms (surgical shock and nervous shock) rather than between different orders of events (bodily and mental traumas). Second, the historical relation between these bodily mechanisms is genealogical rather than analogical.

The answer to this question—What actually was transferred?—is of more than passing interest, since it will determine how we understand the signature feature of psychogenic trauma, its special kind of memory (Young 1995). Connection by analogy would produce a single kind of traumatic memory, consisting of images, emotions, sensations, and words located in psychological space. Genealogy yields an additional, simpler kind of memory, rooted in neuroanatomy, physiology, and evolutionary history. And it is this latter memory, its origins, and its incorporation into psychiatric thinking and practice that are the subject of this article.

Surgical Shock and Nervous Shock

The earliest medical reports concerning the phenomenon that we now call traumatic stress are found in nineteenth-century accounts of victims of railway accidents. The authors of these accounts are generally surgeons employed by railway companies. The companies believe that they are the targets of people seeking compensation for spurious disabilities, and the physician's job is to distinguish the fakes from functional disorders, that is, cases in which the disability seems authentic enough even though its physical basis is unknown.

That a functional disorder might be precipitated by a railway accident is indicated by a phenomenon with which the surgeons are already familiar. Two patients are admitted with similar medical problems and in similar states of health; one recovers following his operation, the second succumbs. In extreme cases, a patient dies even before the cutting begins. These surgical cases are linked to railway cases by a syndrome—weak and fluttering pulse, cold sweat, relaxed sphincter muscles, shallow breathing, deep depression, incoherent speech, etc.—that follows an experience of extreme fear or fright (fear plus surprise). Four organ systems are implicated: circulatory, respiratory, nervous, diagestive. Which one is determinative? The syncope—a sudden drop in blood pressure followed by loss of consciousness—is the syndrome's typical feature. Since the action of the heart is controlled by the nerves, the syndrome must be mediated by the nervous system. The diagnosis: fear or fright, of a magnitude comparable to to a physical blow, delivers a "shock through the medium of the brain . . . such as to suspend the faculties of sense and volition, and to act directly upon the heart as a powerful sedative producing [a loss of circulation and] a prostration of the nervous system. . ." (Morris 1867:20–21, also 9–11, 17, 19; Erichsen 1859: 106).

This much was clear by the end of the nineteenth century: fear (or fright) and physical injury to the nervous system might sometimes produce similar bodily effects. These are two species of shock, each operating through a pathoanatomical pathway. Are the pathways parallel or congruent? Opinions differed.

The matter rests here until the end of the century, when George W. Crile, an American surgeon-physiologist, proposes to connect fear to physical injury and nervous shock to surgical shock by introducing two additional elements into the equation: pain and bodily memory. Crile writes that pain announces itself in two ways. There is dumb pain: the intrinsically unpleasant experience that sensate organisms instinctively strive to avoid; pure negativity, no subtext. But pain can also be a supremely important kind of bodily knowledge, a signal that locates injury and that is a portent of mortality. Non-human organisms do not fear injury *per se*, rather they must *learn* to fear the events that cause injury. And what they learn to fear is the pain that accompanies injury. It is precisely because pain is unpleasant, that it is also a gift. Without the knowledge of pain, the organism and its species would be free to pursue their own destruction.

The organism fears pain and it fears the things that will bring it pain. Thus fear is constituted from two things: a bodily state and a memory. These memories are acquired ontogenetically, through the organism's own experience with pain, and they are also acquired phylogenetically, through inherited fears. This conclusion, that fear is the memory of pain, is not original with Crile. Darwin made a similar suggestion in *The Expression of Emotions in Man and Animals* (1872), and the source of Darwin's idea is Herbert Spencer, whose account of fear is given in *The Principles of Psychology* (1855: 594–600).

Spencer is the missing link in the genealogy of traumatic memory.[1] What are the origins of fear? How do organisms know what things they must fear? The answer seems obvious: fear is an instinct and the organism's ability to recognize elemental dangers is likewise instinctive. For Spencer, however, the answer begs the question, since one is led to ask: What is "instinct" and what are *its* origins? For many of his contemporaries, that question was simply unnecessary, since instinct was assumed to be the starting point for explaining behavior and not the object of explanations. That Spencer felt otherwise was the consequence of his particular brand of positivism.

Spencer had started with a localizationist view of the brain. Like Gall and other phrenologists, he divided the cortex into regions, each the site of a mental faculty, among which fear could be included (Clarke and Jacyna 1987: 220–234, 238–244; R. Young 1990: 173, 180–181). In *The Principles of Psychology*, he shifted to an associationist position: percepts and simple concepts agglutinate into complex ideas and cognitive-affective structures when they are linked through resemblance (analogy), contiguity (in time, space), causality, and sensation (pain and pleasure). Like David Hume, he rejects the innateness of human knowledge and any suggestion that the repository of knowledge, the "self," is more than a fiction based on personal memories. But there is also an important difference between Spencer and Hume. Hume's position is that the self is a fiction constructed on personal memories: "Had we no memory, we never shou'd have any notion of causation, nor consequently of that chain of causes and effects, which constitute our self or person" (Hume 1964: 542). This proposition is not good enough for Spencer because it fails to explain two truths. First, there is knowledge that is universal but cannot be traced to an individual's own experiences or instruction. The infant's "instinctive" fear of snakes is an instance of such knowledge. Second: "If, at birth, there exists nothing but a passive receptivity of impressions, why is not a horse as educable as a Man? Should it be said that language makes the difference, then why do not the cat and the dog, reared in the same household, arrive at equal degrees and kinds of intelligence?" (Spencer 1880:468).

Spencer answers his questions by introducing an evolutionary premiss, in the guise of phylogenetic memory:

> [T]here are established in the structure of the nervous system ab-
> solute internal relations—relations that are potentially present be-
> fore birth in the shape of definite nervous connexions; that are
> antecedent to, and independent of, individual experiences; and
> that are automatically disclosed along with the first cognitions. . . .
> But these pre-determined internal relations, though independent
> of the experiences of the individual, are not independent of expe-
> riences in general: they have been determined by the experiences
> of preceding organisms. (Spencer 1880:470).

Each phylogenetic memory begins as an individual experience. To say that an experience is remembered means that it has left a neurological trace. These traces (which include memorized action patterns) tend to fade over time unless they are periodically recalled and/or reenacted, in which case a trace evolves into a permanent neural pathway. Pathways grow progressively deeper as the organically registered experiences of multiple generations are accumulated. In time, such pathways permit impulses to move unimpeded so that no cognitive effort is required to move from initial perception to completed response. On reaching this point, a phylogenetic memory is equivalent to what is called an instinct (Spencer 1880: 450–451).

One might argue that a phylogenetic memory is not really a memory, since it does not enter consciousness. However, the same objection might be raised concerning pathogenic secrets described by Ribot, Charcot, Janet, Breuer, Freud, and others (fixed ideas, repressed memories, and so on). In fact, the phylogenetic memory *does* enter consciousness: not through cognitive effort it is true, but at the moment of reenactment.

What is special about this conscious memory is that, at the moment of remembrance and reenactment, it collapses time, fusing the ancestral past and the experienced present.

Spencer's phylogenetic memory is indebted to Haeckel's notion of epigensis, the idea that a species' evolutionary history is recapitulated in the embryological development of its individual members. Spencer's theory is subsequently elaborated by the British neurologist John Hughlings Jackson, who pictures the nervous system as an accretion of layers. Consciousness and active memories lie at the topmost level; more recently acquired ancestral memories, still requiring cognitive effort, make up the next layers; and the lower levels consist of the most ancient and "instinctive" memories (Smith 1982a: 76, 78–79; Young 1990: 178, 182–183, 186–187).

The rediscovery of Mendel's genetic experiments at the turn of the century signaled the end of Lamarckian theories and the ascendance of Darwinian mechanisms: chance, mutation, and natural selection. The decline of use-inheritance was not immediate: Pavlov entertained the possibility of hereditary transmission of conditioned reflexes into the 1920s (Pavlov 1927: 285); German and French researchers kept the door open to Lamarckianism for two more decades; and Freud continued to base the sexual etiology of the psychoneuroses on a phylogenetic (Oedipal) memory of the sort described by Spencer (Kitcher 1992: 67–74, 104–109, 174–190; Sulloway 1983: chapt. 4). However, there is no necessary link between phylogenetic memory and Lamarckian premises, and one can argue that simple kinds of phylogenetic memory might be inherited just as easily through Darwinian mechanisms. And this is how Crile and Cannon think of fear. Fear looks to the past (memory of pain) and likewise to the future, to actions (fight or flight) that allow the organism to avoid pain, injury, and death. Here again, the key idea—that fear and its opposite, anger, are dual expressions of one physiological phenomenon—originates with Spencer (1855: 596; for similar observations, see Darwin 1872: 74, 77). What makes Cannon's account of fear different from Spencer's is that it moves elements of phylogenetic memory out of the brain and into the sympathetic nervous system and its functional extension, the adrenal glands.

Cannon represents fear and anger as phases of physiological mobilization within an internal environment (the organism) that is perpetually striving to adjust itself, through the regulative actions of the sympathetic nervous system and the endocrines, to changes and challenges originating in the external environment (Cannon 1914: 275; also Cannon 1929: chapters 12, 14). It would seem that Cannon, like Spencer and unlike Erichsen and Page, is depathologizing fear, shifting its traumatic associations to the field of evolutionary biology and redefining its neurophysiology as a transient state of adaptive arousal. One has to follow him only one step further to see that this is not the whole story. A dramatic account of how a survival mechanism, physiological mobilization triggered by fear and anger, can be transformed into its opposite, a pathogenic process, is found in Cannon's article titled " 'Voodoo' Death," published at the end of his career. According to Cannon, episodes of successful sorcery (voodoo death) go through a sequence: a curse is laid on in public, the victim is isolated by his community, and then the community converges on the wretched man "in order to subject him to the fateful rite of mourning." Over the course of these events, the victim is filled with "powerless misery." Spurred by fear and anger, he is physically primed to either escape or attack the source of danger, but is unable to follow either course. "If these powerful emotions prevail, and the bodily forces are fully mobilized for action, and if this state of extreme perturbation continues in uncontrolled possession of the organism for a considerable period, without the occurrence of action, dire results [including death] may ensue" (Cannon 1942: 176).

Cannon's ideas about the pathophysiology of voodoo death are based on research conducted on decorticated cats earlier in his career. In the experiments, Cannon severed connections between the cerebral cortex and the remainder of the nervous system, producing a state of excessive activity of the sympathic-adrenal system that was allowed to continue unabated. Cannon called this state "sham rage" and claimed that it replicates the states of intense fear and anger that occur naturally in whole animals. After several hours of sham rage, the decorticated cat's blood pressure gradually dropped, to the point where its heart stopped beating. This process is Cannon's solution to the mystery of voodoo death and it likewise explains the nervous shock syndrome described by Erichsen and Page. Victims "die from a true state of shock, in the surgical sense—a shock induced by prolonged and intense emotion." Although the hocus pocus of voodoo death is foreign to civilized societies, similar processes occur there too. Cannon mentions cases of World War I soldiers who fell into shock following "wounds . . . so trivial that they could not be reasonably regarded as the cause of the shock state" (Cannon 1942: 179).

Cannon's idea of voodoo death is rooted in a universal biology, but it is a remarkably circumscribed phenomenon, found mainly among primitive peoples, "bewildered strangers in a hostile world. Instead of knowledge they have a fertile and unrestricted imagination, which fills their environment with all manner of evil spirits capable of affecting their lives disastrously" (Cannon 1942: 175). Further, in his account fear is inescapable and its effects unrelenting. What happens though when exposure to traumatic shock is intermittent? Cannon (like Crile) calls this phenomenon "summation"—a process during which the physical effects of multiple exposures accumulate and eventually lead to the progressive destabilization associated with voodoo death. Animal experiments conducted by Pavlov at about the same time pointed to a radically different possibility: during periods between exposures, the organism returns to homeostasis, but a state different from the *status quo ante*. In other words, recurrent trauma produces a transformation rather than summation.

This is a critical moment in the genealogy of the traumatic memory. In Cannon's experiments, a distance had been preserved between the victim and the source of its pain and fear. The Pavlovians collapsed this space and interiorized the source of pain. In a classic conditioning experiment, an animal is exposed to a source of inescapable pain, such as electric shock. The animal is repeatedly reexposed to the shock and each time it produces pain and physiological arousal. At the same time, it is aware of stimuli in its immediate environment that co-occur with the source of its pain but are incidental to it. The victim learns to associate these phenomena with the shock and they acquire a mnemonic power: whenever he encounters them, he is forced to remember and relive his distress and arousal.[2] In time, the scope of the conditioned response is extended, through association, to objects and events located outside the original place of pain. Escape is now impossible: each reexposure revives the victim's pathogenic memory and the potency of the conditioned stimuli.

A properly conditioned victim has several ways of responding to its pathogenic memory. Pavlovians focused on two reactions: some victims develop routines (phobias) allowing them to avoid noxious stimuli, and other victims simply give up (learned helplessness). There is a third possibility, let us call it *neo*-Pavlovian, since it emerges later, in connection with post-traumatic stress disorder. The basic idea is that victims of traumatic memory seek out circumstances that replicate their etiological events. This scenario is based on anecdotal and experimental evidence suggesting that endorphins (endogenous opioids) are released into a victim's bloodstream during moments of traumatic shock. This would be an adaptive response during fight-or-flight emergencies, since endorphins would produce a state in which the individual is undistracted and undeterred by pain. In cases of post-traumatic stress disorder (PTSD), endorphins would produce a tranquilizing effect by reducing the feelings of anxiety, depression, and inadequacy that often accompany this syndrome. Over time, such people would become *addicted* both to their endorphins and to the memories that release these chemicals. When intervals between exposures grow too long, people can be expected to experience the symptoms of opiate withdrawal (which are, coincidentally, also criterial features of the PTSD diagnostic classification): anxiety, irritability, explosive outbursts, insomnia, emotional lability, hyperalterness. These symptoms would exacerbate the on-going distress intrinsic to this disorder and pain would build to the point where the individual is induced to self-dose with his endorphins. And this would be accomplished by reexposing himself to situations that mimic his original traumatogenic event (van der Kolk et al. 1985; Pitman et al. 1990).

Spencer, Crile, and Cannon script an evolutionary narrative in which the inability to feel pain is represented as a dangerous kind of ignorance. The body is said to remember its pain, and "fear" is the name given to this memory. Fear, like pain, is transmuted into an evolutionary gift, enabling the organism to anticipate threats and to avoid its destruction. The account is positive and reassuring, signalling the beneficent wisdom of a higher pragmatism. Pain and fear have been normalized, turned into memories with which the individual can now make his way in the world. With the neo-Pavlovians, the meaning of memory is turned inside out, and transformed into a recognizably modern phenomenon: an affliction through which pain and fear colonize and degrade the sufferer's life-world.

Post-Traumatic Stress Disorder

The traumatic memory is given a home in the official psychiatric nosology in 1980, in the third edition of *The Diagnostic and Statistical Manual of Mental Disorders of the American Psychiatric Association (DSM-III)*. At this point the memory becomes synonymous with post-traumatic stress disorder and it is provided with a formal definition: the remembrance of an event that is outside the range of usual human experience and that would cause marked distress to nearly anyone. Traumatic memory is represented in a syndrome whose criterial features include (A) intrusive memories and re-experiences of the traumatic event, (B) symptomatic efforts to avoid circumstances that might trigger memories and reexperiences, (C) emotional numbing (a means of damping the emotional effects of feature (A), and (D) autonomic arousal, evidenced as irritability, a tendency to explosive violence, hypervigilance, etc.

Let us identify the two forms of traumatic memories. There is a *mental memory*: the mind's record of the patient's own traumatic experience. This memory may contain information that the mind conceals from itself or other persons (Ellenberger's "pathogenic secret"), but secrets are not a necessary feature. And there is a *bodily memory*, which is discussed in the preceding pages of this article. *DSM-III* is not explicit about the two memories, but makes the distinction nevertheless.

The content of the mental memory is inscribed on features (A), (B), and (C). Without these inscriptions, the PTSD classification would lose its distinctiveness, and cases would be indistinguishable from combinations of other, long-established mental disorders: depression, anxiety disorder, panic disorder. Thus avoidance behavior (B) becomes "avoidance behavior," rather than simple phobia, only after it is connected *symbolically* to the individual's traumatic experience. For example, a Vietnam War veteran diagnosed with PTSD claims that he avoids shopping malls and other public spaces where he might encounter Asian children because they remind him of the Vietnamese children who are part of his mental memory of his traumatic experience. Without these details, his behavior looks like agoraphobia.

Feature (D)—autonomic arousal, evidenced as irritability, a tendency to explosive violence, hypervigilance, etc.—signals the bodily memory of trauma. Unlike the mental memory, it is uncomplicated and there are no biographical inscriptions, since it recollects an evolutionary story that the patient shares with all human beings.

Despite its simplicity and universality, the bodily memory signaled in (D) is part of the memoro-politics described by Hacking. To understand this, one must recognize the particularity of PTSD, the fact that it is a *disease of time* in the etiological sense. That is, the pathology consists of the past invading the present in reexperiences and reenactments, and of the person's efforts to defend himself from the consequences. In other words, the traumatic experience/memory is the cause of post-traumatic symptoms. This seems both obvious and straightforward. Actually it is not, since psychiatry knows an alternative way to interpret the same combination of symptoms, *including the mental memory and its insciptions*. Before I describe this alternative, we need to make a distinction, one also employed by diagnosticians, between PTSD cases that are acute (lasting less than six months) and whose onset occurs very soon after the traumatic experience, and PTSD cases that are chronic, whose onset may begin many years after the etiological event, and that are generally accompanied by other psychiatric diagnoses, especially depression and anxiety disorders. The vast majority of currently diagnosed cases of PTSD fall into the second (chronic) category, and the alternative interpretation of traumatic time applies mainly to them.

I state this alternative baldly, without nuance, to keep my account concise: chronic cases of PTSD can be explained just as plausibly if we supposed that time is moving in the opposite direction, that is, from the present (symptoms) back to the past (event). In this scenario, diagnosable depression and anxiety disorders precede the onset of PTSD symptomatology (rather than following or simply co-occuring), and individuals re-

discover and rework their memories of past events as a means of accounting for their present distress. (Empirical findings from Scotland and Australia support this interpretation: Alexander and Wells 1991; McFarlane
1986, 1988, 1989, 1993). Individuals "choose" PTSD for this purpose, to
reorganize their life-worlds, because it is a widely known and ready-made
construct, it is sanctioned by the highest medical authority, it is said to
originate in external circumstances rather than personal flaws or weakness, and (in some situations) it earns compensation. In short, these cases
of PTSD would be instances of what Hacking calls the "looping effect"
characterizing certain psychiatric classifications. (For a more complete account, see Young 1995: chapts. 4 and 5).

Given the plausibility of this interpretation, why do the great majority
of psychiatric therapists and researchers find this interpretation only mar-
ginally interesting? (My question is ethnographic and not an implied criticism of these therapists and researchers.) There are many ways in which
psychiatric workers might want to respond to this question, but there is
one answer that would be (for them) especially persuasive. Here we return to feature (D)—autonomic arousal—and, more to the point, the
bodily memory that this feature signals. Although we tend to think of
PTSD and traumatic memory in terms of mental memory (the disorder's
typical feature), remember that the bodily memory is firmly attached to
trauma from its historical beginnings: an unbroken genealogy going from
Spencer's *Principles of Psychology* (1855), to Freud's account of the war neuroses in *Beyond the Pleasure Principle* (1919), to Kardiner's *The Traumatic
Neuroses of War* (1941), to *DSM-III* (1980), and now *DSM-IV* (1994). And remember also that the bodily memory's particularity is that it gets traumatic time to run unequivocally in one direction, from trauma to
syndromal effects. Mental memory, at home in the brain's cortex, is notoriously reviseable and permits time to move in two directions; bodily
memory, locked into the limbic and sympathetic systems, is reviseable
only through evolutionary mechanisms.

This is the point at which I see bodily memory entering memoro-politics. At this point and one other that I can mention only in passing. Memoro-politics is about representations of the self or, as Hacking might have
it, the soul. We know ourselves and others through various self-represen-
tations, one of which is Locke's "forensic self": an intentional agent accountable for its past actions. The forensic self (as we live it in the West,
where it is connected to ideas about free will) is inescapably also a "self-
narrated self." That is to say, the self exists not only in its accountability to
others for its actions in the past, but because it *"owns and imputes to itself
past actions, just upon the same ground and for the same reason as it does
the present"* (Locke 1959:467; my emphasis). The self knows its continu-

ity by gluing together, into a loose-knit biography, its memories of its intentional behavior.

The reviseable mental memory installs one narrative. PTSD enables it to connect heaps of heterogeneous, stigmatizing, and self-defacing memories into a unitary and satisfying account and self-representation. But only up to a point, for war-related PTSD often brings memories and acts in which the individual is not a victim of terror and atrocity, but a perpetrator—circumstances in which self-defacement seems irreparable. Beneath this mental memory, the bodily memory installs a second narrative and also a second system of accounting—one whose elements are reduced to fear, anger, and pain; whose highest value is defined as survival rather than virtue; and whose bio-logic may, in the right hands, challenge the mental memory's moral logic (Young 1995: chapt. 6).

Notes

1. Most of Spencer's ideas about phylogenetic memories of pain can be traced to Jean-Baptiste Lamarck's *Zoological Philosophy* (1809). According to Lamarck, bodily movement is precipitated by the movement of the fluid ("animalised" electricity) in the nerves. "[W]hen this action has been several times repeated . . . the fluid cuts out a route which becomes specially easy for it to traverse, and . . . acquires a readiness to follow this route in preference to others" (Lamarck 1984: 317–318, 349–350). Likewise memory: "ideas which we have formed through the medium of sensations, and those that we have acquired later by means of thought, consist of specific images or outlines graven or impressed more or less deeply on some part of our organ of intelligence. These ideas are recalled by memory, whenever our nervous fluid, aroused by our inner feeling [including the instinctive need to avoid pain], comes in contact with their images or outlines. The nervous fluid then transmits the effects to our inner feelings and we immediately become conscious of these ideas . . ." (Lamarck 1984:393). "Now every change that is wrought in an organ through a habit of frequently using it, is subsequently preserved by reproduction. . . . Such change is thus handed on to all succeeding individuals in the same environment, without their having to acquire it in the same way that it was actually created" (Lamarck 1984: 124, 334, 338, 352).

2. The ideas behind "conditioning" are based on associationist premises. This is the thread that connects Pavlov and Cannon to Spencer and Lamarck, and to enlightenment empiricists like Locke and Hume. The structure of conditioning is already anticipated in David Hartley's

1746 monograph on perception, motion, and the generation of ideas. According to Hartley, perception of external objects produces vibrations in the "medullary particles" of the (receptor) nerves. The vibrations are communicated, via a "subtle fluid," to the brain, where a corresponding set of vibrations is produced. Vibrations that are repeatedly experienced leave behind vestiges or images of themselves ("usually called simple ideas of sensations"). Once a set of sensations (A, B, C, D) has been experienced in association a sufficient number of times, it acquires "a power over the corresponding ideas" in the brain (a, b, c, d). From this point on, when any one of these sensations is experienced, it is can excite the corresponding set of ideas in the mind: so that the experience of A precipitates a, b, c, d (Hartley 1959: 3, 4, 22).

References

Alexander, D. A., and A. Wells. 1991. "Reactions of Police-Officers to Body-Handling After a Major Disaster: A Before-and-After Comparison." *British Journal of Psychiatry* 159: 547–555.

Cannon, Walter B. 1914. "The Interrelations of Emotions as Suggested by Recent Physiological Researchers." *American Journal of Psychiatry* 25: 256–181.

———. 1929. *Bodily Changes in Pain, Hunger, Fear and Pain.* Boston: Charles T. Branford.

———. 1942. " 'Voodoo' Death." *American Anthropologist* 44: 169–181.

Clarke, Edwin and L. S. Jacyna. 1987. *Nineteenth-Century Origins of Neuroscientific Concepts.* Berkeley: Univ. of California Press.

Crile, George W. 1899. *An Experimental Research Into Surgical Shock.* Philadelphia: Lippincott.

———. 1910. "Phylogenetic Association in Relation to Certain Medical Problems." *Boston Medical and Surgical Journal* 163: 893–904.

———. 1915. *The Origin and Nature of the Emotions.* Philadelphia: W. B. Saunders.

Darwin, Charles. 1965 [1872]. *The Expression of the Emotions in Man and Animals.* Chicago: Univ. of Chicago Press.

Ellenberger, Henri F. 1993a [1966]. "The Pathogenic Secret and Its Therapeutics." In Mark Micale, ed. *Beyond the Unconscious: Essays of Henri F. Ellenberger in the History of Psychiatry.* Princeton: Princeton Univ. Press, 341–359.

Erichsen, John E. 1866. *On railway and other injuries of the nervous system.* London: Walton and Maberly.

———. 1872. *The Science And Art Of Surgery.* Sixth edition. London: Longmans, Green.

———. 1883. *On Concussion of the Spine, Nervous Shock and Other Obscure Injuries to the Nervous System, In Their Clinical and Medico-Legal Aspects.* New York: William Wood.

Freud, Sigmund. 1955 [1920]. *Beyond The Pleasure Principle.* In *Standard Edition of the Complete Psychological Works of Sigmund Freud.* Vol. 18. London: Hogarth Press, 3–143.

Hartley, David. 1959 [1746]. *Various Conjectures on the Perception, Motion, and Generation of Ideas.* Trans. Robert E. A. Palmer. Los Angeles: William Andrews Clark Memorial Library, Univ. of California.

Hume, David. 1964. *A Treatise of Human Nature.* Vol. 1. Aalen: Scientia Verlag.

Jordan, Edward Furneaux. 1880. *Surgical Inquiries; Including the Hastings Essay on Shock, the Treatment of Surgical Inflammations, and Clinical Lectures.* London: J. and A. Churchill.

Lamarck, Jean-Baptiste. 1984 [1809]. *Zoological Philsophy: An Exposition with Regard to the Natural History of Animals.* Trans. Hugh Elliot. Chicago: Univ. of Chicago Press.

Locke, John. 1959 [1700]. *An Essay Concerning Human Understanding.* Vol. 1. Oxford: Oxford Univ. Press.

Kardiner, Abram. 1941. *The Traumatic Neuroses of War.* Washington, D.C.: National Research Council.

Kitcher, Patricia. 1992. *Freud's Dream: A Complete Interdisciplinary Theory Of Mind.* Cambridge Mass.: MIT Press.

McFarlane, Alexander C. 1986. "Post-traumatic Morbidity of a Disaster: A Study of Cases Presenting for Psychiatric Treatment." *Journal of Nervous and Mental Disease* 174: 4–14.

———. 1988. "Relationship Between Psychiatric Impairment and a Natural Disaster: The Role of Distress." *Psychological Medicine* 18: 129–139.

———. 1989. "The Aetiology of Post-Traumatic Morbidity: Predisposing, Precipitating and Perpetuating Factors." *British Journal of Psychiatry* 154: 221–228.

———. 1993. "Synthesis of Research and Clinical Studies: The Australia Bushfire Disaster." In *International Handbook of Traumatic Stress Syndromes.* Ed. John P. Wilson and Beverley Raphael. New York: Plenum Press, 421–429.

Morris, Edwin. 1867. *A Practical Treatise on Shock After Surgical Operations and Injuries, With Special Reference to Shock Caused by Railway Accidents.* London: Robert Hardwicke.

Page, Herbert W. 1883. *Injuries of the Spine and Spinal Cord Without Apparent Mechanical Lesion, and Nervous Shock, in Their Surgical and Medico-Legal Aspects.* London: J. and A. Churchill.

Pavlov, Ivan P. 1927. *Conditioned Reflexes: An Account of the Physiological Activity of the Cerebral Cortex.* London: Oxford Univ. Press.

Pitman, Roger K., B. A. van der Kolk, S. P. Orr, and M. S. Greenberg. 1990. "Naloxone-Reversible Analgesic Response to Combat-Related Stimuli in Post-traumatic Stress Disorder." *Archives of General Psychiatry* 47: 541–544.

Smith, Roger. 1992. *Inhibition: History and Meaning in the Sciences of Mind and Brain.* Berkeley: Univ. of California Press.

Spencer, Herbert. 1855. *The Principles Of Psychology.* London: Longman, Brown, Green, and Longmans.

———. 1880. *The Principles Of Psychology.* Second edition. London: Longman, Brown, Green, and Longmans.

Sulloway, Frank. 1983. *Freud, Biologist of the Mind.* New York: Basic Books.

van der Kolk, B., M. Greenberg, H. Boyd, and J. Krystal. 1985. "Inescapable Shock, Neurotransmitters, and Addiction to Trauma: Toward a Psychobiology of Post Traumatic Stress." *Biological Psychiatry* 20: 314–325.

Young, Allan. 1995. *The Harmony of Illusions: Inventing Post-Traumatic Stress Disorder.* Princeton: Princeton University Press.

6

Traumatic Cures
Shell Shock, Janet, and the
Question of Memory

Ruth Leys

Shell Shock and Medical Catharsis in World War I

When soldiers began to break down on a large scale during the First
World War and when it became evident to some physicians that, in the absence of physical lesions, their wounds were psychological rather than organic in nature, hypnotic suggestion proved to be a remarkably effective
treatment.[1] The use of hypnosis to deal with the war neuroses marked a
return to a therapy that, since the time of its flourishing under Charcot's
leadership more than twenty years earlier, had been largely abandoned by
the medical profession. More precisely, practitioners returned to Breuer
and Freud's early method of treatment of hysteria by hypnotic catharsis or
"abreaction," a method whose abandonment by Freud around 1896 had
been the decisive gesture by which he had sought to differentiate the "discipline" of psychoanalysis from the "enigma" of suggestion. The revival of
hypnosis to cure what was understood as a virtual epidemic of male hysteria during the war was attended by a revival of the many doubts and objections that have repeatedly accompanied the use of hypnosis as a
technology of the subject in the West. The nature of those doubts and objections is complex, but I believe they can all be seen to revolve around a
single question: *How does hypnosis cure?*[2]

In London in the spring of 1920 that question was the topic of a brief
but, I will argue, highly significant debate between three well-known doc-

tors who had played significant roles as psychotherapists during the war.[3] The discussion was led by William Brown, who had seen nearly three thousand cases of war neuroses in France and Britain. Following Breuer and Freud, Brown argued that the characteristic signs of "shell-shock"— mutism, loss of sight or hearing, spasmodic convulsions or trembling of the limbs, anesthesia, exhaustion, sleeplessness, depression, and terrifying, repetitive nightmares, symptoms hitherto associated chiefly (although not exclusively) with female hysteria—were all bodily expressions of obstructed or "repressed" emotions. Brown reasoned that when a soldier was confronted with the need to maintain self-control and army discipline in front-line conditions of unremitting physical and psychological stress, he was likely to respond to any significant trauma by breaking down. Unable to discharge his powerful emotions directly, through action or speech, he unconsciously "materialized" them by converting them into physical or bodily symptoms. Most striking of all, the patient would not remember anything about the horrifying events that lay at the origin of his pitiable state. *Dissociation* or *amnesia* was therefore the hallmark of the war neuroses (Brown 1918). "*Hysterics suffer mainly from reminiscences*" (Breuer and Freud 1955 [1895]: 7). The famous Breuer-Freud formula, according to which hysterics suffered from repressed traumatic memories, served Brown as the basis for a hypnotic therapy designed to restore the victim's memory through the trance-like repetition and abreaction of the shattering event. Brown reported:

> It has been found again and again in the case of shell-shock patients, especially those seen in the field, that they suffer from loss of memory of the incidents immediately following upon the shell-shock and that, if [through the use of light hypnosis] these memories are brought back again afterwards with emotional vividness—hallucinatory vividness, I might say—the other symptoms which they were showing tend to disappear . . . [T]he facts seem to indicate that emotion has been pent up in these patients, under strain of attempted self-control, and that the liberation of such pent-up emotion (known as "abreaction") produces a resolution of the functional symptoms. Another obvious factor, of course, is the re-synthesis of the mind of the patient—the amnesia has been abolished, and the patient has once more full sway over his recent memories (Brown 1920: 16–17).

For Brown the efficacy of hypnosis depended crucially—though as we shall see, not exclusively—on the emotional catharsis involved. What appeared to him to be fundamental was that in the hypnotic or trance state the traumatic event was "reproduced" or "relived" with all the affective intensity of the original experience. Only in this way, he thought, could the pent-up emotion be successfully abreacted: "The essential thing seems to be the revival of the emotion accompanying the memory" (1920: 16). Breuer and Freud had also emphasized the importance of emotional discharge in the cathartic treatment. "Recollection without affect almost invariably produces no result," they had observed. "The psychical process which originally took place must be repeated as vividly as possible; it must be brought back to its *status nascendi* and then given verbal utterance" (1955 [1895]: 6). At military centers just behind the French front line, Brown had obtained such emotional relivings without difficulty. But in cases of longer standing back home in Britain, where the symptoms had had a chance to become more "fixed," he had found it much less easy to obtain the same results. Brown stated that one of his patients, who had suffered from hysterical deafness and loss of speech, had recovered his memories under hypnosis on several occasions but had not regained his voice and hearing until, one night, he had experienced an extremely intense dream and had suddenly tumbled out of bed with his speech and hearing restored. "In the case of deaf-mutes treated in the field such failure never occurred," he observed. "The explanation seems to be that, in this case, I did not produce the emotional revival with sufficient vividness" (Brown 1920: 16).

But C. S. Myers and William McDougall, the other participants in the debate, rejected Brown's emphasis on the emotions in hypnotic abreaction. They maintained that what produced the relief of symptoms was not the affective catharsis but the cognitive dimensions of the cure. Implicitly embracing the traditional distinction between the lower emotional appetites and the higher functions of rational control, they emphasized not the affective reliving but the conscious reintegration of the dissociated or "repressed" memory into the patient's history. "[I]t is the recall of the repressed scene, not the "working out" of the "bottled up emotional energy" . . . which is responsible for the cure," argued Myers (Brown 1920: 21). "[T]he essential therapeutic step is the relief of the dissociation," McDougall agreed. "[T]he emotional discharge is not necessary to this, though it may play some part" (Brown 1920: 25). McDougall pointed out that in an earlier discussion of his procedure, Brown had insisted to the patient, while the latter was still under hypnosis, that on waking he would remember the scenes that he had just relived. Without such a precaution, the patient on being roused from the trance state characteristically forgot again everything that had just occurred. "In this procedure [Brown] seems to have recognised practically that the emotional excitement was not in itself the curative process," McDougall noted, "but that at the most it was contributory only to the essential step in the process of cure, namely the relief of amnesia or dissociation" (Brown 1920: 25). (As will become clear, this did not wholly misrepresent Brown's ideas.) McDougall conceded that the revival of emotion was important as an aid to securing the complete relief of the traumatic experience, both directly, by giving force and vivacity to the recollection, and indirectly, by overcoming the continued tendency to repress or forget the unpleasant memories. But the essential thing in treatment was the reappearance of the traumatic memory in the clear light of consciousness. Indeed, McDougall claimed that it was possible to obtain the recovery of the repressed traumatic event without emotional excitement of any appreciable kind (Brown 1920: 25–26).

What is the significance of the debate between Brown and his colleagues? I submit that theirs was not simply a disagreement about a minor point of therapeutic technique. Nor, in spite of McDougall's interest in the topic, was theirs essentially a dispute about the cerebral mechanisms that might underlie the symptoms of the war neuroses. Far more basic issues were at stake. For the force of Myers's and McDougall's denial of the importance of emotional abreaction was to insist that what mattered in the hypnotic cure was to enable the traumatized soldier to win a certain knowledge of, or relation to, himself by recovering the memory of the traumatic experience. The idea was to help the subject achieve an intellectual reintegration or resynthesis of the forgotten memory so that he could overcome his dissociated, fractured state and accede to a coherent narrative of his past life. For this a certain degree of the patient's participation was required. Put more generally, it is as if two competing accounts of the role or position of the subject in medicine opposed one another in the debate. The first account imagined that the collaboration of the subject was an inseparable part of the cure, while the second account imagined that, as in the case of drug therapy or surgery—dominant modes of medical therapy in the West—the collaboration of the subject was irrelevant to treatment. For the psychotherapists of the war neuroses the key question was this: did hypnosis heal the patient by soliciting the subject's participation? Or did a suggestive therapeutics achieve its effects by encouraging the patient's docile "subjection" to the "coercive" or authoritative command of the hypnotist that bypassed the consent and as it were the collaboration of the self?[4] If we rephrase those positions in the light of Foucault's work on discipline and knowledge, we might say that the first account emphasized the active role of a subject understood as constituted through categories of consent and refusal, while the second imagined a subject—but does the term make sense in this context?—who somehow escapes both alternatives.[5]

Now a revealing feature of the 1920 debate in this regard was the fear that, in the absence of cognitive insight, the hypnotic reliving of the trauma might be positively harmful to the patient by reinforcing an emotional dependence on the physician that was incompatible with psychic autonomy and self-control (Brown 1920: 24–25). This was also the message of psychotherapist Paul-Charles Dubois, whose influential attacks on hypnosis, starting in 1905, had helped precipitate the rapid decline of hypnotic therapy in the prewar years. Eerily anticipating the equation between the therapeutic value of self-control and the requirement of military discipline that was characteristic of medical discourse in World War I, Dubois had written:

> The object of treatment ought to be to make the patient *master of himself*; the means to this end is *the education of the will*, or, more exactly, *of the reason* . . . . There exists between neurotic patients of every stamp and delinquents and criminals more connection than one would think. The neurotics, like the delinquents, are *antisocial* . . . . The delinquents are, in our eyes, the unworthy soldiers who must be punished with discipline, even shot down. Neurotic people are stragglers from the army. We are a little less severe with them. They show more or less their inability to march; they are lame, that is plain. But we do not like them much; we are ready to throw in their faces reproaches of laziness, of simulation, or lack of energy. We do not know whether to believe in their hurts and put them in the infirmary, or to handle them roughly and send them back to the ranks.
>
> We are already involved in a problem of liberty and of responsibility, and it is the absence of a clear solution which makes us hesitate which course to follow (Dubois 1908).[6]

Dubois's widely heeded response to that uncertainty had been to demand the abandonment of hypnotic "manipulation" in favor of a moral rehabilitation of the patient based on "rational persuasion." Adamantly rejecting what he defined as the hypnotist's exploitation of the patient's childish and "effeminate" passivity and automatic obedience, he had urged physicians instead to increase the soldier's virile self-discipline and autonomy by strengthening his rational and critical powers. "It is our moral stamina which gives us strength to resist these debilitating influences [or suggestions]," he had maintained (Dubois 1908: 116).[7] Even Pierre Janet's scathing condemnation of Dubois's position—his proposal that hypnosis should be considered no different from medical technologies such as drug therapy or surgery, the efficacy of which did not depend on the patient's insight or awareness—could not prevent the reorientation of psychotherapy towards moralization and "rational" analysis that occurred at this time.[8]

All this suggests that for hypnosis to be installed successfully at the core of a medical therapeutics during the First World War it had to be re-theorized as exemplifying not the hierarchical, "coercive" model but the consensual or participatory model of treatment. And in fact Brown himself interpreted hypnotic suggestion along these lines. If, for Brown, emotional catharsis had a legitimate place in the treatment of the war neuroses, this was precisely because it avoided the abjection and mechanical automaticity of "direct suggestion." In hypnotic catharsis, Brown had earlier explained, "the patient goes through his original terrifying experiences again, his memories recurring with hallucinatory vividness. It is this which brings about the return of his powers of speech, and not direct suggestion, as in the ordinary method of hypnosis." Catharsis was thus imagined as "free from the defects" attaching to the "ordinary" use of hypnotic suggestion (Brown 1918: 198).[9] As a means toward helping the patient achieve self-mastery and self-knowledge, the emphasis in Brown's treatment fell squarely on the recovery and re-synthesis of the forgotten memory:

> Remembering that [the patient's] disability is due to a form of dis-
> sociation and that in some cases hypnotism accentuates this dissoci-
> ation, I always suggest at the end of the hypnotic sleep that he will
> remember clearly all that has happened to him in this sleep. More
> than this, I wake him very gradually, talking to him all the time and
> getting him to answer, passing backwards and forwards from the
> events of his sleep to the events in the ward, the personalities of the
> sister, orderly, doctor, and patients—i.e., all the time re-associating
> or re-synthesising the train of his memories and interests. [Brown
> 1918: 198–199].

Hypnotic catharsis was theorized not as an apparatus of behavioral manipulation but as a "supplementary aid" to a medical treatment designed to "discipline" the subject by getting him to accept a certain version of his history and identity. Brown conceded:

> [P]sychologically we are forced to recognise the great therapeutic
> effect produced by the intellect in the analytic review of past mem-
> ories, especially in the analytic treatment of what have been called
> "anxiety states," where the patient is helped and encouraged to look
> at past events from a more impersonal point of view, and so to ob-
> tain a deeper insight into their mutual relations and intrinsic values.
> The method, which might be called the method of *autognosis* [that
> is, self-knowledge], does produce a readjustment of emotional val-

ues among the patient's past memories. These memories are scrutinized from the point of view of the patient's developed personality—or rather of his ideal of personality so far as it becomes revealed
in the course of the analysis—and the relative autonomy that some
of them had previously enjoyed by virtue of their over-emphasis is
withdrawn from them. The progress is from a state of relative dissociation to a state of mental harmony and unity. The "abreaction" of
excessive emotion here is no merely mechanical process, but is controlled at every step by the principle of relativity and intellectual ad-
justment (Brown 1920: 19).[10]

In other words, the disagreement between Brown and the others, basic as
it seemed at the time, emerges in retrospect as a matter of emphasis, not
of fundamentally opposed viewpoints.

It is significant in this regard that, in order to avoid the perceived
dangers of hypnosis, Brown advocated limiting its use to a "very small
minority of cases," namely the major hysterias, and preferably to only
one treatment (Brown 1918: 199).[11] As he was the first to recognize, it
was owing to the brevity of hypnotic treatment that there were no diagnoses of multiple personality in the war—a fact of considerable interest
given the previous success of the multiple personality diagnosis in Europe and the United States (Hacking 1992). In 1926, the psychoanalytically oriented physician Bernard Hart, in a Presidential address to the
British Psychological Society on "Dissociation," commented on the "remarkable absence" of cases of double personality in the literature of psychoanalysis. In the discussion that followed, Freud's disciple, Ernest
Jones, attributed such a lack to the Freudian rejection of hypnotic methods that he, Jones, regarded as especially likely to produce the weakening and dissociation of the ego characteristic of multiple personality.
Brown was inclined to agree, pointing out that although functional nervous diseases had been produced in the thousands during the war, "no
well-marked cases of multiple personality were reported or observed."
He ascribed this to the absence of prolonged hypnotic treatment: "Cases
of extensive amnesia, fugues, etc., were numerous; but the first aim of
the army doctors in the battle areas was to remove these amnesias and
re-associate the patients as quickly as possible, so that the latter might be
either returned to the line or sent down to the base with the minimum
of delay. Some of these cases might have lent themselves to uninten-
tional hypnotic "training," under less urgent and peremptory conditions of hospital treatment, and thus have added to the literature of
multiple personality; but this was not to be" (Hart 1926, Part IV: 255,
257–260). Brown's observations can help us understand multiple per-

sonality as a historical-social construct. During World War I, in a context which saw a modest revival of Freud's cathartic treatment, the fear of suggestibility and automaticity in the male—the demand for the revirilization of the demoralized soldier—limited the deployment of hypnotic suggestion in such a way as to contain the emergence of the more florid symptoms hitherto associated with the diagnosis of "multiple personality." That factor, in combination with Joseph Babinski's assault on the entire hysteria diagnosis and the general neurological-organicist orientation of the psychiatric profession, ensured that the shell-shocked soldier might be regarded as a malingerer or treated as a case of male hysteria, but he would never be seen as an example of multiple personality.[12]

Nevertheless, the war neuroses brought into prominence once again the very phenomenon of dissociation or splitting that had been considered the defining characteristic of female hysteria and female multiplicity. "The war neurosis, like the peace neurosis, is the expression of a splitting of the personality," Ernst Simmel wrote (1918: 33). The rediscovery of splitting as the essential feature of shell-shock reopened the debate, inaugurated by Freud, over the role of sexuality in the production of hysteria. Since for Brown, Myers, and many other physicians the notion of sexual conflict seemed inapplicable to the traumas of the war, the threat of annihilation—the feeling of utter helplessness when confronted with almost certain death—rather than sexual repression came to be regarded as the cause of hysteria. Indeed, repression itself was called into question as the mechanism of hysteria, with the result that psychotherapists returned to Breuer and Freud's concept that in the traumatic neuroses a "hypnoid" or psychical splitting of the ego occurred prior to, or independently of, any mechanism of repression.[13] Furthermore, with the new emphasis on the trauma of death came a return to a thematics of maternal identification and maternal trauma that I have already located at the center of discussions of multiple personality at the turn of the century.[14] (We shall see that Janet's case of the dissociated and traumatized Irène, to be discussed in the next section, fits this model.) Not only was the mother, conceived as the mesmerizing "object" of the suggestible child's first passionate identificatory tie, scapegoated as the source of her son's "feminine" hysteria and lack of virile courage in actual battle.[15] More significantly, the war neuroses came to be thematized—notably by Freud's colleague, Sandor Ferenczi, and by Freud himself—as a repetition of the child's earliest reaction to the threatened loss or disappearance of the maternal figure. In short, the hysterical splitting associated with the traumatic neuroses of both war and peace emerged as the sign of a prior, impossible mourning for and incorporation of the lost mother.

Affect, Memory, and Representation

Can hysteria so defined be cured? Here I want to emphasize that Brown's advocacy of hypnotic abreaction as a technique for recovering traumatic memories involved the claim that emotion always "involves a reference, vague or explicit, towards some object" (Brown 1920: 17), which is to say that the emotions belonged to a system of representations. That is what made it possible for emotions to persist in the mind with the same continuity and verisimilitude as the images on a movie reel to which Brown compared them, just as the experiences or objects to which the emotions were attached were completely preserved in the memory. And that is why, when emotions were repressed or dissociated, they had not disappeared but were lodged in the unconscious in the form of forgotten recollections. For Brown, it is because the affects participate in the same representational system as other experiences that they can be recalled or "reproduced" under hypnosis with all the intensity of the original experience. He observes:

> Hypnotic experiments in the revival of early memories of childhood seem to confirm one in the view that the emotional tone of the individual experiences is retained in the mind in the same way in which those experiences themselves are retained, so that, although the mind becomes more and more complex in various ways in course of time, and various experiences, that later on leave their traces in memory, interact, as it were, with one another and produce more complex mental formations, there is at least a continuous thread of actual experience being deposited in memory from moment to moment, like the successive photographic views on a cinematograph ribbon, and these early memories can be revived in the exact form in which they were originally laid down as the mind passed beyond them to new experiences. (1920: 17)

Brown's idea that the subject is incapable of forgetting anything—that even if conscious access to such memories is blocked we unconsciously retain a complete record of every single event or experience that has ever happened to us, however insignificant—testifies to the extraordinary importance traditionally attached to memory as—along with volition—*the* defining mark of personal identity. But what if emotional memories were not what they were assumed to be? What if the (often temporary yet) "undeniable successes" of hypnosis in the treatment of the war neuroses depended not on the revival of emotions that had been previously experienced and were now re-presented to the subject as past, but on the

111

repetition of the emotional experience *in the present*, with all the energy of the initial "event" (Ferenczi and Rank 1956 [1924]: 61)? What if, accordingly, the passionate "relivings" or "reproductions" or "repetitions" characteristic of the cathartic cure could not be used to retrieve emotional memories, for the simple reason that the memories in question did not exist? More broadly, what if the emotions defied a certain kind of representational economy?

It is greatly to Brown's credit that he realized that the question of emotional memory, far from being "entirely unreal" as McDougall believed (Brown 1920: 24, n. 1), went to the heart of the issue of suggestion and the nature of the hypnotic cure. Moreover, he was also aware that it was a question that in the prewar years had excited the curiosity of many of the best psychologists of the day, with results that did not always support his own position. Brown drew attention to two contributions of particular interest, those of the Swiss psychologist, Edouard Claparède, and of Sigmund Freud.

Claparède, in a remarkable contribution of 1911, had rejected the theory of emotional memory or "affective representation" (1911: 363), which subtended Brown's analysis. It will help us get our bearings here if we recall that the controversy over emotional memory was part of a wider turn-of-the-century debate over the epistemological foundations of psychology, and that one consequence of that debate was a general shift away from an atomistic, sensationalist psychology to a more intentionalist or functional-pragmatic approach that called into question the general role of sensation and the image, or representation, in psychic life. Hovering about these prewar developments, and influencing them in ways that have yet to be determined, was the talismanic figure of Henri Bergson. We will not let Sartre's brilliantly articulated phenomenological critique of Bergson, Claparède, and others prevent us from acknowledging the historical interest of their work in revising the interpretation of the place of the image and representation in mental life.[16] Although what has chiefly attracted the attention of historians is the debate over "imageless" thought, the role of the image in emotion was also a major topic of interest and discussion.[17] A key figure here was William James, discussed by both Brown and Claparède, who had denied the existence of emotional memory. When we think of a past feeling, James had argued, what surges up in our consciousness is not the *memory* of that feeling, but a *new* feeling experienced actually, *in the present*. "*The revivability in memory of the emotions*, like that of all the feelings of the lower senses, is very small," James writes in a passage cited by Claparède. "We can remember that we underwent grief or rapture, but not just how the grief or rapture felt. This difficult *ideal* revivability is, however, more than compensated in the case of the emotions by a very easy *actual* revivability. That is, we can produce, not remembrances of the old grief or rapture, but new griefs and raptures, by summoning up a lively thought of their exciting cause. The cause is now only an idea, but this idea produces the same organic irradiations, or almost the same, which were produced by its original, so that the emotion is again a reality. We have "recaptured" it" (James 1981 [1890]: 1087–1088). With respect to the hypnotic treatment of the shell-shock victim, we might put it that, according to James's theory of emotion, it is because the organic conditions of the original experience have been brought back so vividly to the traumatized soldier that they again produce the emotion of fear—but the emotion is an actual, present feeling caused by the visceral sensations aroused during the hypnosis.

Claparède extends James's argument. Specifically, he sets out to discover what he himself experiences when he tries to remember a past emotion. Claparède reports that when he attempts to project an emotion into the past—the sadness he experiences at the thought of his dead parents (significantly, an example of mourning)—either he continues to feel the emotion actually, *in the present*, and hence not as past, or he ceases to experience the emotion altogether and instead merely represents himself to himself as a kind of depersonalized or dead "mannequin-self" whom he sees objectively, at a distance, without any emotion, as if he were a spectator of himself. "For me," he writes, "it is impossible to *feel* an emotion as *past*" (1911: 367). He observes: "Thus I know that I was sad, but I have no consciousness of any state of sadness. In order for these non-affective images of sadness to renew their original meaning and their life, I am obliged to retranslate them into affective terms; but then I relapse into a emotional states in the present, which is to say that it is my present self that is sad, and no longer only my past self" (367). An emotional state and projection into the past are "incompatible facts," Claparède states, for "emotion . . . is always conscious," is always only experienced in the present. In a fascinating passage he adds:

> As soon as I project the past moment far from the present moment which fills myself, then it is as a simple spectator, so to speak, that I consider these past memories—which is to say that if I represent myself there to myself, I see myself *from outside*, in the same way that I represent other individuals to myself. My past self is thus, psychologically, distinct from my present self, but it is . . . an emptied and objectivized self, which I continue to feel at a distance from my true self which lives in the present. And if, from being a simple spectator, I try to become an actor, if I try to identify myself with this second self [*image-sosie*], then I draw it back to the present in order to reincarnate it;

113

but it attracts with it the ambient images, and then I have the impression of again enjoying in the present the scene that has passed (368).

He concludes:

This tendency to experience in the present a previously experienced scene is especially likely to occur when I seek to represent to myself a past emotion: the emotion can only be experienced as a state of myself. It can only be known from within, and not from outside. If I attribute it to my phantom-self [or double] (which is only seen from outside) then in that very moment I see it vanish from my present consciousness. *One cannot be a spectator of one's feelings; one feels them, or one does not feel them; one cannot imagine them [image them, represent them] without stripping them of their affective essence* (368–369; emphasis added)[18]

As a description of what might be called the "phenomenology of affect" this could hardly be bettered. In his modest yet elegant way, Claparède appears to break with an entire metaphysics of representation according to which—in a genealogy that goes back to the dominant interpretation of Descartes—the certitude of the *Cogito* is conceived as the spectatorial or specular certitude of the self-observing *subject* or onlooker who *sees or represents* himself to himself, as if in a mirror or on a stage. On the contrary, Claparède, in his critique of the concept of emotional memory or affective representation, abandons the metaphorics of specularity and spectatorship on which such an ontology of the subject crucially depends.[19] Indeed there is a sense in which he breaks even more decisively with that ontology than Freud himself. This becomes clear when we consider the other text on emotional memory, besides Claparède's, to which Brown in his paper on the traumatic neuroses of the war also draws attention—Freud's great metapsychological essay of 1915 on the unconscious. It is one of Brown's achievements that he should have pointed to the precise moment in Freud's difficult and disconcerting text where he seems to posit the absolute irreducibility between affect and representation on which Claparède also insists. This is the moment where Freud appears to acknowledge that if there is such a thing as an unconscious idea or representation—since, for Freud, even in the unconscious the drive (or instinct) is known only through its representations—*affect itself* manifests the drive directly, without any intermediary or representation. In the passage cited by Brown, Freud writes:

An instinct can never become an object of consciousness—only the idea [*Vorstellung*] that represents the instinct can. Even in the unconscious, moreover, an instinct cannot be represented otherwise than by an idea. If the instinct did not attach itself to an idea or manifest itself as an affective state, we could know nothing about it . . . We should expect the answer to the question about unconscious feelings, emotions and affects to be just as easily given. It is surely of the essence of an emotion that we should be aware of it i.e., that it should become known to consciousness. Thus the possibility of the attribute of unconsciousness would be completely excluded as far as emotions, feelings and affects are concerned [Freud's words here are strikingly close to Claparède's similar claim]. But in psycho-analytic practice we are accustomed to speak of unconscious love, hate, anger, etc., and find it impossible to avoid even the strange conjunction, "unconscious consciousness of guilt," or a paradoxical "unconscious anxiety." Is there more meaning in the use of these terms than there is in speaking of "unconscious instincts"? The two cases are in fact not on all fours. In the first place, it may happen that an affective or emotional impulse is perceived but misconstrued. Owing to the repression of its proper representative it has been forced to become connected with another idea, and is now regarded by consciousness as a manifestation of that idea. Yet its affect was never unconscious; all that happened was that its *idea* had undergone repression . . . . *Strictly speaking . . . there are no unconscious affects as there are unconscious ideas* . . . . The whole difference arises from the fact that ideas are cathexes—basically of memory-traces—whilst affects and emotions correspond to the processes of discharge, the final manifestations of which are perceived as feelings. In the present state of our knowledge of affects and emotions we cannot express this difference more clearly.[20]

Brown remarks of this passage that "Freud finds great difficulty in coming to a conclusion on the nature of "unconscious affects" as contrasted with "unconscious ideas," and recognises that the problem of the former is different from that of the latter" (Brown 1920: 33). Of the same problematic of affect in Freud's 1915 text, Mikkel Borch-Jacobsen has recently commented:

It is no accident if Freud writes . . . "even in the unconscious, moreover, an instinct cannot be represented (*repräsentiert sein*) otherwise than by a *Vorstellung* [an idea]," despite immediately adding, as through remorse, that the drive would remain unknowable if it "did not attach itself to an idea or *manifest itself as an affective state.*" In reality, it is only the *Vorstellung* that *reprasentiert* the drive, for the good reason that the affect, for its part, *presents* it immediately, without the slightest mediation. This is attested to by the fact . . . that affect, by Freud's own admission, cannot possibly be unconscious, as if it would short-circuit every distance and every exteriority between the drive and the psyche (between "body" and "soul"). Affect either is or is not . . . . Contrary to the *Vorstellung*, which can be and yet not appear, the affect *is* only in appearing, exists only as manifest . . . . That is why, according to Freud, there cannot be, in all rigor, any "unconscious affects." And so, in speaking of "unconscious anxiety" or, still more paradoxically, of an "unconscious consciousness of guilt" (*unbewusstes Schuldbewusstein*), the psychoanalyst would only mean that the representation to which the affect was initially attached has succumbed to repression. But the affect itself would never cease to impose itself on consciousness. In other words, the affect may well be "suppressed" ("inhibited," "blocked," reduced to the state of a "rudiment"), but it can by no means be *repressed*.[21]

Indeed it would be possible to show that, in his writings of the 1920s on the transference and the second topography, Freud simultaneously conceives affect as that which is always and only experienced *in* consciousness and as that which absolutely *resists* coming into consciousness: paradoxically, Freud appears to undo the very distinction between consciousness and unconsciousness which he elsewhere appears to enforce. "[T]he affect," Borch-Jacobsen has observed in this connection, "far from being a second psychic *Repräsentanz* of the drive . . . is much rather its very manifestation. That affect always be "conscious" means, in effect, that the psyche can never "distance" it, never flee it (repress it) like an exterior reality, never ob-pose itself to it in the light of the *Vor-stellung*, and thus neither can it ever dissimulate it from itself. In short, this signifies that the opposition of consciousness and the unconscious is not applicable to affect" (1993: 139).[22] So that—always according to the same logic—the transference, or emotional tie to the analyst, far from dissimulating a prior, repressed Oedipal, or pre-Oedipal memory or representation, as Freud continues to argue, rests on an affect that, as Freud also states, can only be experienced in the immediacy of an acting in the present that is unrepresentable to the subject and that, like the unconscious or primary process itself, knows no time, no negation, and no degrees of certainty (Freud 1953–77 [1915]: 186–87). Most paradoxically of all, it is hypnosis that, again according to Freud, best exemplifies the peculiar workings of the unconscious defined in those terms. Strangely, Freud treats hypnosis as the paradigm of the emotional transference to or identification with the other at the very moment he seeks to exclude hypnosis from the psychoanalytic project.[23]

All this suggests that what is problematic in the use of hypnosis to cure the war neuroses is precisely the attempt to recover past traumatic experiences in the form of emotional representations that can be brought back into the subject's consciousness, for the passionate relivings or "reproductions" characteristic of hypnotic abreaction precede the distinction between "self" and "other" on which the possibility of self-representation and hence recollection depends. The same is true of psychoanalysis, defined as the reconstitution of the subject's history through the recovery and analysis of the patient's repressed memories or fantasies, because the existence of such affective memories or affective representations is what Freud calls into question. In sum, there is no "subject" of suggestion in the sense of a subject who can see or distance himself from his emotional experience by re-presenting that experience to himself as other to himself: that appears to be the lesson of Claparède's and Freud's astonishing dissection of the emotions.

But that is a conclusion that Freud also resists, as do Brown and his colleagues. They remain committed to the view that what "disciplines" or cures patients is that they can be made to distance themselves from their traumatic emotional experiences by *re-presenting* them to themselves as other to themselves in the form of recollected "repressed" or "dissociated" experiences. Accordingly, they demand that the emotional acting out of the hypnotic catharsis be converted into re-presentation and self-narration—that the patient's speech and behavior under hypnosis be interpreted not as a "reproduction" of the traumatic scene in the mode of a "blind" emotional acting in the *present* but as a narrative in full consciousness of that lived experience as *past*.

Yet a scrutiny of the case-histories of the traumatic neuroses suggests that this is a demand that cannot readily be met. The subject in deep hypnosis is not a spectator of the (real or fantasized) emotional scene but is completely caught up *in* it, as Claparède claimed. And if, as Borch-Jacobsen has argued, speech or verbalization often accompanies those scenes, it does so not in the form of a discourse in which the patient narrates the truth of his past to himself or another (the physician or analyst), but in the mode of an intensely animated miming of the traumatic "event" that occurs in the absence of self-observation and self-representation.[24] As Brown himself states, the shell-shocked soldier "immediately begins to twist and turn on the couch and shouts in a terror-stricken voice. He talks as he talked at the time when the shock occurred to him. He really does live again through the experiences of that awful time. Sometimes he speaks as if in dialogue, punctuated by intervals of silence corresponding to remarks of his [hallucinated] interlocutor, like a person speaking at the telephone. At other times he indulges in imprecations and soliloquy . . . .

117

In every case he speaks and acts as if he were again under the influence of the terrifying emotion (Brown 1918: 198, his emphasis). Still more drastically, the emotional acting out of the trauma in the trance state occurs in a profound absence from, or forgetfulness of, the self: the dissociated patient suffers his passion "beyond" himself—beyond memory and self-representation—literally fainting away in the hypnotic enactment. In Brown's paraphrase: " 'It is not I who feel, it is not I who suffer, it is not I who speak . . . . I am dead' " (Brown 1921).[25]

That is why it was difficult for the physician to obtain information concerning the traumatic scene while the traumatized soldier was in the regressed state and why patients often became confused to the point of swooning when they were asked to narrate their experiences in the past tense. "In some cases [the shell-shocked soldier] is able to reply to my questions and give an account of his experiences," Brown relates. "In others he cannot do so, but continues to writhe and talk as if he were still in the throes of the actual experience" (1918: 198). Sometimes, patients responded to the demand for self-narration by alternating between the past and present tense. "One subject . . . whispered to me. "Did you see that one? . . . It went up on top,' " Myers reports. " 'What now?" I asked, "What did you say?" "I was talking to my mate," was the reply. To my question "What were you saying?" he answered "get rifles." He could be made to realise he was in hospital, but explained his inconsistent behavior by the remark: "Can't help it. I see 'em and hear 'em (the shells).' " " "[His thoughts] repeatedly fly to the trenches," Myers notes of another patient. "For a few minutes his attention could be gained, then his answers became absurd; the question "How old are you?" for example receiving the reply, "It passed my right ear." He would often ask me to speak louder when on the point of lapsing into thoughts of trench life. In another case the alternation of states was so marked that on being unduly pressed for his thoughts when in a stuporous condition he assumed an attitude of hostility, rushing about the room with an imaginary rifle in his hands." (Myers 1916: 67–68). Breuer and Freud had made similar observations about their female patients. "In the afternoons she would fall into a somnolent state which lasted till about an hour after sunset," Breuer had stated of Anna O. "She would then wake up and complain that something was tormenting her—or rather, she would keep repeating in the impersonal form "tormenting, tormenting." For alongside of the development of the contractures there appeared a deep-going functional disorganization of speech . . . . It was also noticed how, during her *absences* [or unconscious states] in day-time she was obviously creating some situation or episode to which she gave a clue with a few muttered words. . . . When she was like this it was not always easy to get her to talk, even in her hypnosis" (Breuer and Freud 1955 [1895]: 24—30). "The words in which she described the terrifying subject-matter of her experience were pronounced with difficulty and between gasps," Freud had reported of Emmy von N., adding of the case of Elizabeth von R. that the details of a certain episode "only emerged with hesitation and left several riddles unsolved" (Breuer and Freud 1955 [1895]: 53, 151).

Moreover, as Freud was the first to observe, patients lacked conviction as to the reality of the reconstructed traumatic scenes. "[S]ometimes, finally, as the climax of its achievement in the way of reproductive thinking [a brilliant formulation]," he observes of his "pressure" technique in *Studies on Hysteria*, "it causes thoughts to emerge which the patient will never recognize as his own, which he never *remembers*, although he admits that the context calls for them inexorably, and while he becomes convinced that it is precisely these ideas that are leading to the conclusion of the analysis and the removal of his symptoms" (272). To which he adds in a stunning admission of the inherent irretrievability of the traumatic "event":

> The ideas which are derived from the greatest depth and which form the nucleus of the pathogenic organization are also those which are acknowledged as memories by the patient with greatest difficulty. Even when everything is finished and the patients have been overborne by the force of logic and have been convinced by the therapeutic effect accompanying the emergence of precisely these ideas—when, I say, the patients themselves accept the fact that they thought this or that, they often add: "But I can't *remember* having thought it." It is easy to come to terms with them by telling them that the thoughts were *unconscious*. But how is this state of affairs to be fitted into our own psychological views? Are we to disregard this withholding of recognition on the part of patients, when, now that the work is finished, there is no longer any motive for their doing so? Or are we to suppose that we are really dealing with thoughts which never came about, which merely had a *possibility* of existing, so that the treatment would lie in the accomplishment of a psychical act which did not take place at the time? It is clearly impossible to say anything about this—that is, about the state which the pathogenic material was in before analysis—until we have arrived at a thorough clarification of our basic psychological views, especially on the nature of consciousness (300).

The problem of the patient's lack of confidence in the reality of the memory of the trauma—the victim's inability to remember, and hence testify with conviction to, the facticity of the reconstructed event—will haunt not only psychoanalysis but the entire modern discourse of the trauma.[26] "[T]here is one feature of the modern that is dazzling in its implausibility: that the forgotten is the formative," Ian Hacking has said (chap. 4, this volume).[27] One can see the force of this. But the entire impetus of my argument is to suggest that, at the limit, it is precisely what *cannot* be remembered that is decisive for the subject—and for psychoanalysis. Indeed it may be, as I have proposed elsewhere, that the trauma cannot be lifted from the unconscious because that trauma has never been "in" the unconscious in the form of repressed or dissociated representations.[28] If Brown, Myers, and McDougall gloss over the failure of memory in the cathartic cure—that is, the failure of memory defined as self-narration and self-representation—Freud, on abandoning hypnosis, interprets that failure as an expression of the patient's *resistance* to recollection and narration. Such a strikingly original solution opens up an entire dynamics of unconscious desire and repressed representations and dramatically shifts attention away from the affective reliving of the cathartic cure to the question of corporeal signification and linguistic meaning; but it is a solution that will eventually unravel at the level of practice in the problem of traumatic repetition and at the level of theory in the aporias of Freud's second topgraphy. In short, as Freud himself becomes increasingly aware, nothing is less certain than whether the cathartic "reproduction" or "repetition compulsion" can be converted into conscious recollection, nothing more ambiguous than the nature and mechanism of what he calls "working through."[29]

The Persistence of Janet

If I mention Janet at this juncture it is partly because, recognizing in one of Janet's early cures a method analogous to theirs, Breuer and Freud place Janet at the origin of the cathartic cure (an ambiguous gesture, as we shall see).[30] But it is also because Janet has been hailed by Herman, van der Kolk, van der Hart and other recent theorists of the trauma as a pioneer in developing a fully formulated mnemo-technology for the treatment of the trauma victim. In particular, returning to Janet's long-neglected meditations on the nature of memory and narration, Herman and others have praised Janet for distinguishing between two kinds of memory—"traumatic memory," which merely and unconsciously *repeats* the past, and "narrative memory," which *narrates the past as past*—and for validating the idea that the goal of therapy is to convert "traumatic memory" into "narrative memory" by getting the patient to recount her history. "In the second stage of recovery, the survivor tells the story of the trauma," Herman writes. "She tells it completely, in depth and in detail. This work of reconstruction actually transforms the traumatic memory, so that it can be integrated into the survivor's life story. Janet described normal memory as "the action of telling a story." Traumatic memory, by contrast, is wordless and

static . . . . The ultimate goal . . . is to put the story . . . into words" (Herman 1992: 175, 177).[31]

But such an appropriation of Janet on the part of Herman and others involves repudiating that aspect of his psychotherapy that seeks to make the patient *forget*. Take for example Janet's famous cure of Marie (the case cited by Breuer and Freud). Marie was a nineteen-year-old girl whom Janet saw at Le Havre early on in his career when she was hospitalized for hysterical convulsive crises and a delirium that, Janet soon established, always coincided with the arrival of her menstrual periods, periods that, after about 20 hours, would then abruptly cease. During her delirium, Marie sometimes "uttered cries of terror, speaking incessantly of blood and fire and fleeing in order to escape the flames; sometimes she played like a child, spoke to her mother, climbed on the stove or the furniture, and disturbed everything in the room," he wrote in his first description of the case in 1889. The end of each hysterical crisis was accompanied by the vomiting of blood. Marie was completely amnesiac for what had transpired. In between her attacks she suffered from small contractions of the muscles of the arms and chest, various anesthesias, and a hysterical blindness of her left eye.

Positing a connection between the origin of Marie's hysterical symptoms and the onset of her menstrual periods, Janet hypnotized her in order to "bring back" the apparently forgotten memories. Based on Marie's dramatic reenactments in the trance state, Janet was "able to recover the exact memory of a scene which had never been known except very incompletely." Owing to the shame she had felt when, aged thirteen, she had experienced her first menstrual period, Marie had succeeded in interrupting the flow of blood by plunging into a large tub of cold water. The shock had produced shivering, a delirium for several days, and a complete cessation of her periods; when five years later these had recommenced, they had produced the symptoms which had led to her hospitalization. Janet continued: "Now, if one compares the sudden cessation [of bleeding], the shivering, the pains which she describes today in the awake state, with the account [*le récit*] which she gives in somnambulism and which, besides, was confirmed indirectly, one arrives at this conclusion: Every month the [hallucinated] scene of the cold bath is repeated, leads to the same cessation of her periods and to a delirium which, it is true, is

121

much stronger than before, to the point that a supplementary hemorrhage takes place via the stomach. But, in her normal consciousness, she knows nothing of all this." (Janet 1989 [1889]: 410–412).

Janet's "supposition" concerning Marie's originary trauma, "true or false" as he expresses it (1989 [1889]: 412), served as the basis for her cure. "I could only succeed in effacing this [fixed] idea by a unique method. It was necessary to take her back by suggestion to the age of thirteen, to put her back again into the initial circumstances of the delirium, and thus to convince her that her period had lasted for three days and had not been interrupted by any unfortunate incident. Now, once this was done, the next menstrual period arrived on time and lasted for three days, without leading to any pain, convulsion or delirium." He treated Marie's remaining symptoms, including her hysterical blindness, as well as other cases of dissociation by the same method (412–413).[32]

In other words, according to Janet's first account of the case, and contrary to the ingrained beliefs of many of his commentators (Janet 1989 [1889]: 7) Marie was cured not by the recovery of memory but by *the excision of her imputed or reconstructed trauma*. In 1880 the novelist Edward Bellamy imagined an invention for the extirpation of thought processes. "I deem it only a question of time," Dr. Gustav Heidenhoff says to Henry, who loves a woman driven almost to suicide by a guilty sexual past that she cannot forget, "when science shall have so accurately located the various departments of thought and mastered the laws of their processes, that, whether by galvanism or some better process, the mental physician will be able to extract a specific recollection from the memory as readily as a dentist pulls a tooth, and as finally, so far as the prevention of any future twinges in that quarter are concerned. Macbeth's question, "Canst thou not minister to a mind diseased; pluck from the memory a rooted sorrow; raze out the written troubles of the brain?" was a puzzler to the sixteenth century doctor, but he of the twentieth, yes, perhaps of the nineteenth, will be able to answer it affirmatively." (Bellamy 1969 [1880]: 101). In 1894 Janet himself remarked that one of the most valuable discoveries of pathological psychology would be a sure means of *helping us to forget* (1990 [1898]: 404). The same year he criticized Breuer and Freud's account of the cathartic cure on the grounds that what mattered in the treatment of the neuroses was not the "confession" of the traumatic memory but its elimination (1990 [1898]: 163).[33] Nor did the ethical implications of such "modern exorcism" or "psychological surgery" (1976 [1919] 1: 678) trouble him. As he observed of a cure strikingly similar to that of Bellamy's fictional scenario, that of a hysterical husband whose guilt over his infidelity had driven him into hysteria: "The memory of his fault was transformed in all sorts of ways thanks to hallucinated suggestions. Finally even the wife of Achille, evoked by hallucination at an appropriate moment, came to give a complete pardon to this husband who was more unfortunate than guilty" (1990 [1898]: 404).

But it is precisely that aspect of Janet's legacy that Herman disowns: "Janet sometimes attempted in his work with hysterical patients to erase traumatic memories or even to alter their content with the aid of hypnosis," she observes. "Similarly, the early "abreactive" treatment of combat veterans attempted essentially to get rid of traumatic memories. This image of catharsis, or exorcism, is also an implicit fantasy in many traumatized people who seek treatment. It is understandable for both patient and therapist to wish for a magic transformation, a purging of the evil of the trauma. Psychotherapy, however, does not get rid of the trauma. The goal of recounting the trauma story is integration, not exorcism. In the process of reconstruction, the trauma does undergo a transformation, but only in the sense of becoming more present and more real. The fundamental premise of the psychotherapeutic work is a belief in the restorative power of truth-telling" (Herman 1992: 181). What appears to motivate Herman's attitude here is a powerfully entrenched, if undertheorized, commitment to the redemptive authority of history—even if that commitment is tempered by an awareness of the difficulty of historical reconstruction. For Herman and for the modern "recovery movement" generally, even if the victim of trauma *could* be cured without obtaining historical insight into the origins of her distress, such a cure would not be morally acceptable. Rather, she must be helped to speak the horrifying truth of her past—to "speak of the unspeakable" (175)—because telling that truth to herself and others has not merely a personal therapeutic but a public or collective value as well. It is because personal testimony concerning the past is inherently political and collective that the narration of the remembered trauma is so important. "In the telling, the trauma becomes a testimony," Herman writes, adding: "Testimony has both a private dimension, which is confessional and spiritual, and a public aspect, which is political and judicial. The use of the word *testimony* links both meanings, giving a new and larger dimension to the patient's individual experience" (181). Or as she also states: "Remembering and telling the truth about terrible events are prerequisites both for the restoration of the social order and for the healing of individual victims" (1992: 1).[34]

Recently, a few critics have begun to analyze the stakes in assuming that the determination and recuperation of the historical past has an inherent ethico-political value.[35] But what I want to focus on here is the influence exerted by an apparently similar commitment to the importance of historical reconstruction on Janet's representation of his own contribution to psychotherapeutics. As a consequence of a growing emphasis on recollection and narration in psychotherapy, mediated in part by his famous rivalry with (but also implicit dependence on) Freud's model of the "talking cure," Janet comes to distort his own record.[36] He doesn't want to forget that he was the first to propose a technique for the cure of patients by getting them to remember their traumas. But precisely because he doesn't want to forget his priority, he forgets what that discovery was.

In fact from the start Janet's attitude toward memory appears ambivalent. On the hand, he believes that memory is overvalued. " 'One must know how to forget,' " he is fond of quoting Taine as saying, and of remarking that: "One must not be surprised at this forgetfulness, it is necessary that it should be so. How could it be that our own minds, our poor attention, could fix itself constantly on the innumerable perceptions which register in us? We must, as has often been said, forget in order to learn. Forgetting is very often a virtue for individuals and for a people" (Janet 1990 [1898]: 421).[37] On the other hand, memory—continuous, narratable memory—increasingly comes to have a privileged status in his texts as that which makes us distinctly human. Thus at the almost the same moment Janet discovers the therapeutic value of erasing memory, he begins to suggest that, in order to be cured, patients must be helped to dissolve their amnesia by telling the story of the traumatic event. As it does for Brown and his colleagues, the task of psychotherapeutics becomes one of getting the patient to "*say* 'I remember' " (Janet 1990: [1898]: 137; emphasis added). For Janet in this mode, memory proper is more than dramatic repetition or miming: it involves the capacity to distance oneself from oneself by representing one's experiences to oneself and others in the form of a narrated history. In a statement of 1919 that has recently been cited by van der Kolk and others, Janet observes:

> *Memory*, like belief, like all psychological phenomena, is an action; essentially, it *is the action of telling a story*. Almost always we are concerned here with a linguistic operation . . . . The teller must not only know how to [narrate the event], but must also know how to associate the happening with the other events of his life, how to put it in its place in that life-history which each of us is perpetually building up and which for each of us is an essential element of his personality. A situation has not been satisfactorily liquidated, has not been fully assimilated, until we have achieved, not merely an outward reaction through our movements, but also an inward reaction through the words we address to ourselves, through the organisation of the recital of the event to others and to ourselves, and through the putting of this recital in its place as one of the chapters in our personal history" (Janet 1976 [1919] I: 661–662).

Strictly speaking, Janet adds, "one who retains a fixed idea of a happening cannot be said to have a "memory" of the happening. It is only for convenience that we speak of it as a "traumatic memory." The subject is often incapable of making with regard to the event the recital which we speak of as a memory; and yet he remains confronted by a difficult situation in which he has not been able to play a satisfactory part, one to which his adaptation had been imperfect" (663).

Janet calls this act of narration "presentification," an operation of self-observation and self-representation that he imagines as an act of internal policing or self-surveillance by which at any moment we are compelled to attend to and communicate our present experiences to ourselves and above all to others—for memory is preeminently a social phenomenon—and to situate and organize those experiences in their proper time and place. "Presentification" thus depends on our ability to constitute the present *as present* and to connect the stories we tell about ourselves with present reality and our actual experiences. Janet conceives "narrative memory" in economic terms as an act of abbreviation that—unlike "traumatic memory," which is rigidly tied to the specific traumatic situation, takes place without regard for an audience, and by virtue of its inflexible acting out takes a considerable length of time—can be performed in only a few minutes and, depending on the social context, in a variety ways. For Janet, it is precisely because language is conceived as intrinsically portable—as representing an absent present—that "narrative memory" can be detached from the occasioning event in this manner. The act of "presentification" is one that animals, primitive people, young children, and hysterics are characteristically unable to perform—animals, because they are incapable of self-knowledge and self-representation, and primitive people, young children, and hysterics because, owing to their undeveloped or degenerate or weakened mental condition, they lack the mental synthesis necessary for paying attention to present reality and hence for locating their narratives in an appropriate temporal order. From this perspective, as Janet makes clear, the animated acting out or "reliving" characteristic of the trauma patient, for all its inclusion of verbalization (Herman seems clearly wrong to describe traumatic repetition as "wordless"), does not constitute such a narration, precisely because it occurs in the absence of self-representation (Janet 1928).[38]

Janet's favorite example of the *failure* of "presentification" is the case of Irène, a young woman who was traumatized by the death of her mother (a case of maternal mourning, as I've already noted). Unable to realize the fact of her loss, Irène instead reenacts the scene of death in a somnambulistic repetition that is completely unavailable to subsequent recall. "[Irène] has not built up a recital concerning the event, a story capable of

125

being reproduced independently of the event in response to a question," Janet observes. "She is still incapable of associating the amnesia of her mother's death with her own history. Her amnesia is but one aspect of her defective powers of adaptation, of her failure to assimilate the event . . . [I]n her crises she readopts the precise attitude which she had when caring for her mother in the death agony. This attitude is not that of a memory which enables a recital to be made independently of the event; it is that of hallucination, a reproduction of the action, directly linked to the event" (Janet 1976 [1919]: 662–663).

Janet seems to imply that Irène was cured when she became capable of transforming the traumatic memory of her mother's death into narrative representation. But a careful reading of the text from which the above quotation is taken reveals that something far more interesting and complex is going on. For in this text Janet singles out not the case of Irène but that of *Marie* as exemplifying the cure of hysteria by the recollection and narration of the forgotten trauma. Emphasizing his priority over Breuer and Freud, Janet revises his earlier account of the case of Marie by suggesting that she was cured *not by the excision but by the recollection and narration of the traumatic memory*. Without referring to his attempts to hypnotically *eliminate* memories in that case, Janet observes:

> In my early studies concerning traumatic memories (1889–1892), I drew attention to a remarkable fact, namely that in many cases the searching out of past happenings, the giving an account [*l'expression*] by the subject of the difficulties he had met with and the sufferings he had endured in connexion with these happenings, would bring about a signal and speedy transformation in the morbid condition, and would cause a very surprising cure. *Marie's case was typical* . . . . In the somnambulist state, this young woman told me what she had never dared to confess [*dire*] to anyone. At puberty she had been disgusted by menstruation, and had dreaded its onset. When the flow began, wishing to check it, she got into a cold bath. After she had made this disclosure, her fits of hysterics ceased, and normal menstruation was restored . . . . In these earlier writings, I drew the inference . . . that the memory was morbific because dissociated . . . the morbid symptoms disappeared when the memory again became part of the synthesis that makes up individuality. I was glad to find, some years later, that Breuer and Freud had repeated these experiments, and that they accepted my conclusions without modification. In their first work on hysteria, these authorities said that they had noticed how the hysterical symptoms disappeared one after another, disappeared for good, when it had been possible to

bring the exciting cause into the full light of day, and to reawaken
the affective state which had accompanied it (Janet 1976 [1919]:
672–674].

In other words, Janet seems to transform a cure based on the excision of
memory into a therapy based on the patient's conscious insight and recollection. And yet in another section of the same book, to which in the
passage just quoted the translators (but not Janet) refer the reader, Janet
writes of Marie: "Finally, it was found possible, by modifying the memory
in various ways [*en modifiant le souvenir par divers procédés*], to bring about
the disappearance or the modification of the corresponding symptom"
(591)—a formulation that, in the light of my earlier analysis of his original description of the case, strongly suggests that Marie's traumatic memory was altered or replaced by others, and in that sense eliminated. But
what, then, of the melancholic Irène—the focus of the recovery movement's interest in Janet—who failed to mourn her mother by failing to remember that her mother was dead? How was *she* cured?

In this text as in later writings, Janet's attempts to describe and explain
the therapeutic process are extraordinarily convoluted, as if the task of
characterizing the nature of the cure—of defining what Freud calls "working through"—defies systematic articulation. More precisely, his texts are
marked by displacements and slippages such that every gesture toward
stabilizing an account of his various psychotherapeutic methods (for he
recognizes the need for many different approaches) necessitates repeated
gestures of supplementation. So that far from belonging unproblemati-
cally to the category of cure by narration—indeed chiasmatically crossing
the case of Marie—Irène's case turns out to depend not entirely or exactly
on rememorization and in the absence of hypnosis but on an additional
procedure or set of procedures that Janet calls both "assimilation" and
"liquidation" and that appears to have much in common with—no surprise here—hypnotic suggestion. "Irène's case is of special interest because her absurd behaviour was so out of place in the circumstances, and
because of the lacunae in her interior assimilation which found expression in her amnesia," Janet writes in the same text of 1919. "After much
labour I was able to make her reconstruct the verbal memory of her
mother's death [nuances in original are lost in the English translation: *je
suis arrivé à lui faire retrouver ou plutôt à lui faire construire le discours-souvenir
de la mort de sa mère*]. From the moment I succeeded in doing this, she
could talk about the mother's death without succumbing to crises or being afflicted with hallucinations; the assimilated happening had ceased to
be traumatic" (1976 [1919] I: 680–681). But in citing this same passage,
van der Kolk and other modern trauma theorists (van der Hart, Brown,

and van der Kolk 1989: 388) fail to acknowledge that Janet's claim leaves a certain remainder. For he immediately adds:

> Doubtless so complex a phenomenon cannot be wholly explained by such an interpretation. Assimilation constitutes no more than one element in a whole series of modified varieties of behavior which I shall deal with in the sequel under the name of "excitation." Irène, under the influence of the work which I made her do, threw off her depression, "stimulated" herself, and became capable of bringing about the necessary liquidation . . . . Irène was cured because she succeeded in performing a number of actions of acceptation, of resignation, of rememorisation, of setting her memories in order, and so on; in a word, she was able to complete the assimilation of the event (Janet 1976 [1919]: 681).[39]

Under Janet's authoritative "influence" Irène was "excited" to give up her melancholic attachment to her dead mother and adapt to the needs of the present. And in general the process of cure in Janet does not necessarily depend on the recovery and narration of memory. As he writes in 1923:

> The well-known expressions one repeats without cease, "to act, forget, pardon, renounce, resign oneself to the inevitable, to submit," seem always to designate simple acts of consciousness . . . . In reality these expressions designate an ensemble of real actions, actions that one must perform, other actions that one must suppress, new attitudes to adopt, and it is all these actions which liquidate the situation and make one resigned to it. A woman is very gravely ill since the rupture with her lover, you will say this is because she cannot resign herself; no doubt, this absence of resignation consists of a series of actions which she continues to make and which it is necessary for her to cease making. *To forget the past is in reality to change behavior in the present. When she achieves this new behavior, it matters little whether she still retains the verbal memory of her adventure, she is cured of her neuropathological disorders* (Janet 1980 [1923]: 126; my emphasis).

A process of *both* "assimilation and liquidation," then, requiring a "discharge" or "demobilization" of psychic energies that Janet links to Freud's method of cathartic abreaction and that in relation to the cure of Irène he describes in the following terms:

> I have already often remarked that it is necessary to employ the most eloquent imprecations and to use all the resources of rhetoric

in order to make a patient change a shirt or drink a glass of water. This is what I especially emphasized in my earliest researches. "The treatment which I imposed on the patient is not only a suggestion, but moreover an excitation. In psychological treatments, one has not always distinguished between the role of suggestion and the role of excitation which tries to increase the mental level. I demand attention and effort on the part of Irène, I demand clearer and clearer consciousness of her feelings, everything that helps to augment the nervous and mental tension, to obtain, if you will, the functioning of the higher centers. Very often I have observed with her as with so many other patients that the truly useful séances were those where I was able to make her emotional. It is often necessary to reproach her, to discover where she has remained suggestible, to support her morally in all sort of ways to raise her up and to make her recover memories and actions." All the reeducation of neuropaths of which there is much talk today are subject to the same law, whether it's a matter of gymnastics, the education of movements, the excitation of the sensibility, the search for memories, it is always necessary that the influence of the superintendent awakens attention and effort, excites emotion and produces a larger tension. When the higher functioning is obtained, the subject feels a modification of his consciousness that translates into an increase in perception and activity (Janet 1980 [1923]: 129–130).

If Janet's notion of "assimilation" appears terminologically analogous to the recovery movement's notion of "integration" based on the recovery and narration of memory, it is nevertheless the case that for Janet narrated recollection is insufficient for the cure: a supplementary action is required, one that involves a process of "liquidation" that terminologically sounds suspiciously like "exorcism" or forgetting. Moreover "liquidation" doesn't just supplement "assimilation"; the mutual entanglement of the two operations is so intense that the entire chapter in which Janet in 1919 expounds his understanding of the therapeutic process is called "Treatment by Liquidation"— not "Assimilation." Perhaps most important, the supplementary procedures necessary for Irène's cure manifestly involve the physician's deliberate manipulation of the patient by processes that Janet himself understands as involving suggestion (1976 [1919]: 145). In Janet's mnemo-technology, hypnotic suggestion is discovered to be not external to the process of cure but internal to its effectiveness. In sum, Janet's extensive writings bear witness to the impossibility of sustaining theoretically or practically the opposition between forgetting and remembering upon which so much of the edifice of modern psychotherapeutic thought has been made to depend.

***

In 1920, the "daemonic" compulsion to repeat painful experiences—a phenomenon long familiar to psychoanalysts as the "fixation" to the trauma in the case of female hysterics (Freud 1953–74 [1920]: 13), but appearing during World War I as the revelation of a "new and remarkable fact" (20) now that it was seen to apply to a large number of males—led Freud to posit the existence of death instincts that lay "beyond" pleasure and that seemed to pose a virtually insuperable obstacle to remembering. If Freud never completely abandons his belief in the curative power of recollection, this is not the case for one major school of his successors— the linguistic-rhetorical school of Lacan and his followers—for whom the failure of memory in the trauma exemplifies the need for a structural or formal version of psychoanalysis, conceived (or reconceived) as a discipline that on the one hand invests patient narratives with decisive significance but on the other hand maintains that those narratives are characteristically, perhaps inherently, discrepant with the (themselves often unknowable) "facts" of the case. As Lacan emphasized, in the Wolf Man case of 1918 Freud himself attempted to resolve the tension between forgetting and remembering by proposing such a structural treatment of the problem of psychoanalytic narrative. Put more strongly, psychoanalysis as Lacan and the Lacanians define it is committed to the project of formalizing memory by eliciting and analyzing narratives whose fidelity to individual experience is no longer of central importance.[40]

More provocatively, it might be argued that Janet's psychotherapeutic work also may be understood as committed to such a project. As we have seen, what mattered according to Janet in the treatment of hysteria was that, through the use of techniques of "liquidation" and "assimilation," the patient acquired the ability to produce an account of herself that conformed to certain requirements of temporal ordering but that did not necessarily entail a process of self-recognition. The distinction between forgetting and remembering thus virtually collapsed in the demand that, whether or not she remembered the traumatic "event," the patient became capable of developing a coherent narrative of her life the importance of which lay not so much in its adequation to personal experience as in its bearing on her present and future actions. Viewed in this perspective, Janet's well-known disagreement with Freud over the sexual content of psychoanalysis seems less significant than their agreement that, if narration cures, it does so not because it infallibly gives the patient access to a primordially personal truth but because it makes possible a form of self-understanding even in the absence of empirical verification. In short, what I earlier described as Janet's ambivalence with respect to the problem of memory emerges as more apparent than real. For his seemingly

conflicting claims that memory is overvalued and that memory is fundamental turn out to resolve themselves into the non-contradictory propositions that memory conceived as truth-telling is overestimated but that
memory conceived as narration is crucial.

But this account of the convergence between the views of Janet, Freud,
and Lacan overlooks certain significant differences. In the first place, notions of speech and narration by no means play an indispensable role in
Janet's assessment of the totality of the methods of psychotherapy. In
Janet's writings the opposition between remembering and forgetting dis-
solves in the requirement that the patient learn to make an appropriate
"adaptation" to the past, present, and future, but narrative self-understanding is not always essential for such adaptation and other forms of ad-
justment may serve the purposes of cure. For Janet, the physician's
rhetorical and suggestive skills are directed at improving the traumatized
subject's mental synthesis by producing modifications in conduct and behavior, modifications that do not necessarily depend on acts of conscious
self-representation and self-enunciation. (For Lacan, of course, psychoanalysis has nothing to do with what is ordinarily meant—or what Janet
presumably meant—by adaptation.)

Moreover, my discussion of the role of rhetoric and suggestion in
Janet's work implies a second difference between his view of psychical
treatment and the views of Freud and Lacan. Throughout his career
Janet defended the use of hypnosis in psychotherapy and regarded the
emotional rapport between physician and patient as fundamentally suggestive. Such an interpretation of the relationship between patient and
physician was alien to Freud and especially to Lacan who, developing
various themes in Freud's thought, configured psychoanalysis as a
rhetorical enterprise, but one from which the persuasive arts of hypnotic suggestion were strictly excluded. But recent deconstructive and
other readings of the Freudian corpus have shown that the problem of
suggestion in psychoanalysis cannot be disposed of so easily.[41] On the
contrary, that problem resurfaced in Freud's texts of the 1920s at precisely those junctures where it appeared that the best way to understand
the nature of the identificatory bond between the ego and the other was
by comparing that bond to the unconscious hypnotic rapport between
subject and physician—even if that comparison threatened to unsettle
the dynamics of repressed emotional and desiring representations on
which the very identity of psychoanalysis—like that of Lacan's subsequent "return to Freud"—ultimately depended. More than anyone else,
it was Freud's disciple and colleague Sandor Ferenczi who, through his
revival of catharsis and Freud's theory of trauma, during the same years
made those issues a matter of urgent debate. For this, he was considered

131

a traitor to the psychoanalytic cause. It took another major war—World War II—for the value of hypnotic catharsis in the treatment of the traumatic neuroses to be rediscovered. But the history of trauma is a history of forgetting, as the delayed reaction to the trauma of the Holocaust also serves to "remind" us. And it is not at all obvious even today, when the trauma of sexual abuse, the diagnosis of hysterical splitting, and the deployment of hypnosis for the recovery of memories are commonplaces of psychotherapy, that we have grasped the scandalous nature of the traumatic cure.

Notes

1. The present essay is a shorter version of a paper that appeared in *Critical Inquiry* 20 (Summer 1994): 623–662. Earlier drafts were presented to Ian Hacking's seminar on dissociation at the University of Toronto, March 1993; the "History of the Human Sciences" section of the Committee on the Conceptual Foundations of Science at the University of Chicago, April 1993; and the Women's Studies seminar at Johns Hopkins University, November 1993. I thank Lorraine Daston, Ian Hacking, Kirstie McClure, Mary Poovey, Robert Richards, and the other participants of those seminars for their observations. I am also grateful to Walter Benn Michaels for his input at an early stage of the project, to Frances Ferguson for stimulating discussion of the issue of memory and narration explored here, and to Michael Fried for helpful comments on various drafts.

2. In a large literature on the history of the concept and treatment of "shell-shock," see especially Fischer-Homberger (1975); Stone (1985); Bogacz (1989); and Fendtner (1993).

3. The three doctors were William Brown, Charles S. Myers, and William McDougall. Brown delivered a paper—"The Revival of Emotional Memories and Its Therapeutic Value"—at a meeting of the medical section of the British Psychological Society on 18 Feb. 1920. Myers and McDougall responded, and Brown's rejoinder closed the meeting. The proceedings were published under the title of Brown's paper in *The British Journal of Medical Psycholgy* (Brown 1920).

4. Although Myers, McDougall, Brown, and many others believed that hypnosis involved the imposition of the physician's coercive will onto an essentially passive subject, I would argue that the hypnotic rapport involves rather an inmixing of "activity" and "passivity" or a mimetic "invention" of the subject that tends to exceed the dual relationship between the hypnotist-analyst and the patient.

5. If for Foucault power, discipline, and knowledge line up together, they do so by presupposing the production of a subject capable of consent and resistance. In a key text he writes: "[W]hat defines a relationship of power is that it is a mode of action which does not act directly or immediately on others. Instead it acts upon their actions . . . . A relationship of violence acts upon a body or upon things . . . . On the other hand a power relationship can only be articulated on the basis of two elements which are each indispensable if it is really to be a power relationship: that the "other" (the one over whom power is exercised) be thoroughly recognized and maintained to the very end as a person who acts . . . . Power is exercised only over free subjects, and only insofar as they are free" (Foucault 1982: 220–21). For Foucault, power and freedom are thus mutually constitutive, as has been emphasized by Mark Maslan (1988).

6. The extent to which those in charge of Austrian military hospitals were guilty of abusing shell-shock patients by the deployment of "disciplinary" techniques of punishment was the subject of hearings in 1920 at which Freud gave testimony. See Eissler (1986). For recent treatments of the conflation between the requirements of military discipline and medical therapy in the treatment of the traumatic neuroses in World War I, see Showalter (1985); Stone (1986); and Barker (1992), for a discussion of the treatment of the poet Siegfried Sassoon.

7. For objections to hypnosis similar to those expressed by Dubois see Binet (1910: 193); and Dejerine and Gauckler (1913). Suggestion was characteristically defined as "the process by which ideas are introduced into the mind of a subject without being subjected to his critical judgment. The effect of any suggestion depends on its evading the critical judgement of reason" (Hadfield 1920: 63). By contrast, persuasion was defined as "a form of treatment which appeals to the conscious reason and enforces its claims on logical grounds" (82). Ominously, however, for those who—like Dubois—wanted to maintain an absolute distinction between these two processes, Hadfield went on to remark that "in actual practice the success of persuasion depends on suggestion, especially that derived from the authority of the physician and the expectancy of the patient" (ibid.). In effect, Hadfield—like Brown and so many others—attempted to distinguish between "good" suggestion, which helped strengthen the patient's will and freedom, and "bad" suggestion, which weakened psychic autonomy. Suggestion thus conformed to the structure of the *pharmakon* (or *supplement*) in Derrida's sense of those terms, as that which is simultaneously remedy and poison. It is worth noting in this regard

that the term "shell shock," introduced by Myers and others early in the war, was officially banned in 1917 on the grounds that it helped spread, by contagion or "suggestion," the very symptoms whose cure *by* suggestion was the goal of psychotherapeutic treatment. (See Myers (1940: 12–13, 92–97).

8. For Janet's criticisms of Dubois and the turn to rational persuasion see Janet (1976) [1919]. "Influenced by the prevailing fashion," Janet sarcastically remarks of a certain Dr. Levy who had converted to Dubois's rational therapeutics, "he now tells us that hypnotism has fallen into disfavour "because it is regarded as a special nervous condition." He, too, wants the patient to participate in the work of the cure, which is, of course, to be "rational." The patient must learn to discipline himself morally and physically. In a word, the whole of Levy's therapeutic system depends upon "rational education and re-education'" (113). In response to this Janet quotes from an article by Max Eastman: " 'It is difficult to see why it is any more a suspension of judgment to let a physician you have decided to trust lodge a helpful idea in your mind, than to let him lodge an ominous-looking capsule in your body' " (337). To Janet's conception of hypnotic treatment as a medical technology no different from drug therapy or surgery we might oppose Freud's conviction that hypnosis cannot function as a medical technology precisely because its effects are incalculable. "The chief deficiency of hypnotic therapy," he observes in 1891, "is that it cannot be dosed. The degree of hypnosis does not depend on the physician's procedure but on the chance reaction of the patient" (Freud, 1955 [1891]: 111). By contrast, Freud will come to regard psychoanalysis as *more* technological than hypnosis precisely because, in the form of the management of the transference and the lifting of resistances, its procedures can within limits be controlled by the physician. It is in this sense of technological control that psychoanalysis can be compared to surgery, Freud argues, even going so far as to acknowledge the role that the physician's "suggestions" may play in the success of the psychotherapeutic operation. See Freud, (1953–74 [1910]: 146); (1953–74 [1912]: 115); and (1953–74 [1915–17]: 446–52).

9. By the "ordinary" method of hypnosis Brown (1919) meant Hyppolite Bernheim's method of direction suggestion in which the physician verbally suggested to the hypnotized patient that the symptoms (or their cause) would vanish.

10. For similar descriptions of the task of hypnotic therapy see Brown (1923a: 10); Myers (1940: 68); Rivers, (1917: 914); and Ernst Simmel's discussion of catharsis in S. Ferenczi, et al (1921: 30, 33).

11. See also Brown (1923a: 34–35) and (1923b: 170).

12. For a contemporary critique of Babinski's views on hysteria by one of the chief architects of the multiple personality diagnosis see Prince (1920: 312–24).

13. For British post-war discussions of the distinction between splitting and repression see Rivers (1922); and McDougall (1926), esp. chapt. 12. I am glad to draw attention here to the convergence between my emphasis on the relationship between splitting and death in discourses on hysteria and dissociation and the work of Juliet Mitchell (1993) who, on somewhat different grounds, has recently raised important questions about the link between hysteria, splitting, and the death drive.

14. For an interpretation of hysterical splitting as involving a melancholic identification with or mimetic incorporation of the maternal figure, see Leys (1992: 189–94).

15. For mother-fixation as a cause of the war neuroses, see for example Nicoll (1920: 101); Miller (1920: 115–28); Simmel (1918: 31). For general discussions of the gender aspects of the war experience, see Showalter (1985) and Higgonnet (1987).

16. See Sartre, (1972), where he argues that despite the new orientation and new terminology, Bergson and others retained the concept of the image in its classical empiricist and materialist guise.

17. See Humphrey (1963); Mandler and Mandler (1964); and Lindenfeld (1980: 220–64).

18. Among those mentioned by Claparède as supporting the idea of emotional memory are Ribot, Pillon, Pieron, Dugas, Paulhan, Dauriac, Baldwin, Bain, Fouillée, and Patini; among those he mentions as opposing the idea of emotional memory are James, Titchener, Höffding, and Mauxion. At the end of his essay Claparède recognizes the psychologist Alfred Binet's role in launching a general critique of the mental image in psychology. In this connection see especially Binet (1911: 1–47), cited with approval by Claparède (1928). In that essay, Claparède is still asking: "Does a true affective memory exist? (Or do affective memories constitute an *actual* revival of feelings and emotions?)" (125).

19. More generally, what is at stake here is not the rejection of the image or representation as such, but the rejection of a particular interpretation of the image or representation as always involving a "representative theatricality," implying a specular distance between the subject and object, ego and alter ego. On this topic see especially Henry (1985); Borch-Jacobsen (1988, 1991, 1993); and Gasché (1986).

20. Sigmund Freud, (1953–74 [1915]: 177–78), emphasis added; Brown's source for Freud's text was Freud (1953–74 [1906]: 22).

21. Borch-Jacobsen points out in this connection that Freud never uses the expression "affective representative" (1993: 197, n. 26).

22. Borch-Jacobsen goes on to point out that this does not mean that the unconscious is thereby reabsorbed into consciousness as pure manifestation, presence, or auto-affection, as the phenomenologist Henry maintains, but that—following Freud's own arguments of *The Ego and the Id* and other writings—"the unconscious invades consciousness itself; indeed, here everything depends on that infinitesmal yet decisive difference of accent between a *conscious* unconscious and an *unconsciousness* of consciousness" (1993: 142).

23. Here I am summarizing a complex argument, brilliantly elaborated by Borch-Jacobsen in *The Freudian Subject* (1988) and other texts.

24. On these points see Borch-Jacobsen's essays in *The Emotional Tie* (1993), especially "Hypnosis in Psychoanalysis," in which he emphasizes the fundamental ambiguity, in *Studies on Hysteria* and other texts by Breuer and Freud, between the re-experiencing of a traumatic event in the trance state and the recollection and narration of that event in clear consciousness, and the ways in which Freud resolved that ambiguity for psychoanalysis by deciding in favor of recollection and narration.

25. It might appear that the claim that hypnotic experience is not a specular process of self-observation is contradicted by the "hidden observer" phenomenon of age regression and other hypnotic experiences. Thus Breuer reports of Anna O. that "even when she was in a very bad condition—a clear-sighted and calm observer sat, as she put it, in a corner of her brain and looked on at all the mad business" (Breuer and Freud in Freud 1955 [1895]: 46); and in another passage that "Many intelligent patients admit that their conscious ego was quite lucid during the [hysterical] attack and looked on with curiosity and surprise at the mad things they did and said" (228). Similarly, Freud states that Emmy von N. "kept a critical eye upon my work in her hypnotic consciousness" (62, n. 1). Binet and others made similar observations. Breuer qualifies Anna O.'s claim by attributing it in part to her retrospective sense of guilt for all the trouble she has caused and to her feeling that, from the perspective of her reunified personality, she could have prevented it, noting of her in this connection that "this normal [or specular] thinking which persisted during the secondary state must have fluctuated enormously in its amount and must very often have been completely absent" (46). It is also likely that the "hidden observer" phenomenon is a function of the demand characteristics of hypnotic age regression experiments and of contextal cues. Of special interest in this connection is the use of induction

procedures in which hypnotized witnesses in criminal cases are asked to recall memories by "zooming" in on them as if the witnesses were a TV camera. This is a technique that yields confabulation and false memories with considerable regularity, yet the "recollections" are accompanied by a sense of great subjective conviction as to their veracity on the part of the hypnotized subject and are rarely questioned by the police. For a valuable review of the contradictory data on this topic, see Perry (1988).

26. "They have an "unstory" to tell, that which, according to Blanchot, "escapes quotation and which memory does not recall—forgetfulness as thought,' " writes Lawrence Langer of the victims of the Holocaust. " 'That which, in other words, cannot be forgotten because it has always already fallen outside of memory' " (Langer 1991: 39). Langer adds, in terms that invoke the acting out of the cathartic repetition, that: "The witness does not *tell* the story; he reenacts it. The brusque economy of his narrative, the motions of his arms, as if placing the actors on the stage (and then playing all the roles himself), the brief, staccato sentence, with connectives often omitted, all conspire to reduce the value of verbal effect and to remind us how often terms like "heroic" and "dignified" become orphans in this obscure universe . . . . Witnesses in the testimonies do not search for the historicity of the experience, nor do they try to recapture the dynamic flow of events. They are concerned less with the past than with a sense of the past that is in the present" (27, 40).

27. Compare Hacking (1991).

28. See the section devoted to "The Subject of Trauma" in Leys (1992) where, on the basis of a reinterpretation of Freud's concept of identification, I argue that the trauma is never present to the subject in the form of affective representations that could in principle be remembered. Rather, trauma can be be defined as the mimetic affection or identificatory dissociation of the "subject" that occurs outside of, or prior to, the representational-spectatorial economy of repressed representations or the "subject-object" distinction on which recollection depends. Cathy Caruth has also emphasized that the traumatic symptom cannot be understood in terms of repression, interpreting the "enigmatic core" of the trauma in terms of the inherent latency or belatedness of the traumatic event (Caruth 1991).

29. (Freud 1953–74 [1914]. "Remembering, Repeating, and Working Through."). In this remarkably complex paper, written at the same time as the Wolfman case and apparently in reference to its theoretical and therapeutic difficulties, Freud in a highly significant gesture identifies hypnotic catharsis with the "simple" or "ideal" form of re-

membering, that is with self-representation and self-narration, and psychoanalysis with the compulsion to repeat (*zwange zur wiederholung*) or the tendency to act out (*agieren*) in the absence of any awareness of the repetition: "the patient does not *say* that he remembers that he used to be defiant and critical towards his parents" authority; instead, he behaves that way to the doctor. He does not remember how he came to a helpless and hopeless deadlock in his infantile sexual researches; but he produces a mass of confused dreams and associations, and complains that he cannot succeed in anything and asserts that he is fated never to carry through what he undertakes" (150; emphasis added). On this basis Freud compares the process of "working through" (*durcharbeiten*) the resistances, by which the repetition of repressed affects and representations are to be converted into recollection, with hypnotic abreaction: "This working-through . . . is a part of the work which effects the greatest changes in the patient and which distinguishes analytic treatment from any kind of treatment by suggestion. From a theoretical point of view one may correlate it with the "abreacting" of the quota of affect strangulated by repression—an abreaction without which hypnotic treatment remained ineffective" (155–56). But on the basis of Freud's discussion of affect in "The Unconscious" and other texts we may need to ask: do the affects belong to the scheme of repressed representations posited here? If not, what is the nature and mechanism of "working through"?

30. "In Janet's interesting study on mental automatism (1889) [a reference to Janet's classic text, *L'Automatisme psychologique*], there is an account of the cure of a hysterical girl by a method analogous to ours" (Freud and Breuer [1895] in Freud 1953–74, I: 7, n. 1).

31. For similar appeals to Janet's work, see van der Kolk and van der Hart, (1989; 1991); van der Hart and Horst (1989); van der Hart, Brown, and van der Kolk (1989); and Putnam, (1989).

32. See also Janet's "L'Amnésie Continue" [1893], "Histoire d'une idée fixe" [1894], and "Un Cas de possession et l'exorcisme moderne" [1895] in Janet (1990 [1898]: 156–212, 375–406).

33. Here as elsewhere Janet adds that more than simple suggestion is necessary to cure hysteria and goes on to describe the various methods he uses to remove or "rub out" (*enlever*) or efface (*effacer*) or otherwise transform the patient's traumatic "memories." These methods include the method of "decomposition" and "substitution" by which the traumatic memories are broken down into their component parts—into specific images, words, or even parts of words—and hypnotic suggestion is then deployed, in a lengthy treatment process, to

substitute neutral or positive experiences for each of the traumatic component elements.

34. Even as they emphasize the therapeutic importance of transforming traumatic memories into narrated memories, van der Kolk and his colleagues recognize the difficulty of achieving such a transformation in severe or chronic cases of trauma and indeed acknowledge that the restoration of memories alone doesn't necessarily cure (van der Hart, Brown, and van der Kolk 1989: 380). Moreover, they grant that Janet treated some patients not by converting traumatic memories into narration but by hypnotically "exorcising" the past—for example, by using the trance state to substitute pleasant memories for painful ones (van der Kolk and van der Hart 1991: 450). These authors even observe that Janet's famous patient, Marie, was cured in this way (van der Hart, Brown, and van der Kolk 1989: 388). But, apparently uneasy with the idea of altering or playing with history, these authors appear to equate Janet's hypnotic manipulation of memory with the patient's voluntary control of the past: "Many patients who are victimized by rape and other forms of violence are helped by imagining having all the power they want and applying it to the perpetrator. Memory is everything. Once flexibility is introduced, the traumatic memory starts losing its power over current experience. By imagining these alternate scenarios many patients are able to soften the intrusive power of the original, unmitigated horror" (van der Kolk and van der Hart 1991: 450).

35. For vigorous arguments against the widespread belief that there is an intrinsic relationship between history and ethics, arguments bearing for the most part on the question of collective rather than individual memory, see Knapp (1989) and Michaels (1992, 1993, 1994). For reflections on the moral dilemmas associated with the often unrealizable demand that veterans of the Vietnam War and other wars be made to remember as a requirement of the treatment strategies for "Posttraumatic Stress Disorder" (PTSD), see Young (1995). My thanks to Ian Hacking for drawing Young's work to my attention, and to Allan Young for allowing me to read his manuscripts.

36. For Janet's well-known rivalry with Freud, see especially Perry and Laurence, (1984).

37. " 'It would seem . . . that the identity of the self rests entirely on memory,' " observes Theodule Ribot in his *Maladies de la mémoire* [1888], cited by Michael S. Roth in his valuable "Remembering Forgetting: *Maladies de la mémoire* in Nineteenth-Century France," (1989:54). At the same time, as Roth has shown, for physicians and philosophers at the turn of the century too much memory, or hyper-

mnesia, was as potentially dangerous to health as too little memory, or amnesia. We are reminded here of William James's remark that "if we remembered everything, we should on most occasions be as ill off as if we remembered nothing" (James 1983 [1890]: 640). For an interesting discussion of Proust's theory of involuntary memory as an example of hypermnesia see Terdiman (1993: 185–239).

38. As Janet makes explicit, for him narrative replaces the role previously given to the mental image in theories of memory proposed in the past and, in a revised form, by Bergson. Janet's views on memory may thus be seen to participate in the general reaction against the role of the mental image in psychology to which Claparède's critique of affective representation also belongs, even as Janet appears to side with those who, unlike Claparède, continue to believe in the existence of affective memories or representations. Janet's discussion of the widely debated phenomenon of "déjà vue" or "false recognition" bears on this topic: he attributes the phenomenon not to any confusion between perceptual images on the one hand and memory images on the other, as had previously been argued, but to the hysterical absence of the capacity to attend to or represent—that is, to narrate—the present. Recently, Monique David-Ménard has used the term "presentification" in a sense opposite to that of Janet—not for the process of self-representation to which Janet attaches the term but for the hysterical acting in the present that occurs precisely in the absence of self-representation and symbolization (David-Ménard 1989: 110).

39. If in this text Janet claims that Irène recovered, her cure can't have been a simple matter, for in 1926, apparently referring to the same case, he observed that "patients act out *indefinitely* the scene of rape or the scene of the death of their mother *for years after the event.*" (Janet 1975 [1926] II: 322, 334; emphasis added).

40. "[T]he dimension proper to analysis is the reintegration by the subject of his history right up to the furthermost perceptible limits, that is to say into a dimension that goes well beyond the limits of the individual," Lacan observes in 1954. "[T]he fact that the subject relives, comes to remember, in the intuitive sense of the word, the formative events of his existence, is not in itself so very important. What matters is what he reconstructs of it . . . [T]he stress is always placed more on the side of reconstruction than on that of reliving, in the sense that we have grown used to calling *affective.* The precise reliving—that the subject remembers something as truly belonging to him, as having been truly lived through, with which he communicates, and which he adopts—we have the most explicit indication in Freud's writings that that is not what is essential. What is essential is reconstruction . . . I

would say—when all is said and done, it is less a matter of remembering than of rewriting history" (Lacan 1988: 12–14). For helpful analyses of Freud as a pivotal figure in the modern critique of memory conceived as that which restores the past to full presence, see especially Krell (1990); Lukacher (1986); and Forrester (1990).

41. In addition to texts already cited, see Roustang (1983, 1990) and Chertok and Stengers (1992).

References

Barker, Pat. 1992. *Regeneration*. New York.

Bellamy, Edward. 1969 [1880]. *Doctor Heidenhoff's Process*. New York.

Binet, Alfred. 1910. *Les idées modernes sur les enfants*. Paris.

———. 1911. "Que'est-ce qu'une emotion? Qu'est-ce qu'un acte intellectuelle." *L'année psychologique* 17: 1–47.

Bogacz, Ted. 1989. "War Neurosis and Cultural Change in England, 1914–22: The Work of the War office Committee of Enquiry into 'Shell-Shock.' " *Journal of Contemporary History* 24, 227–56.

Borch-Jacobsen, Mikkel. 1988. *The Freudian Subject*. Trans. by Catherine Porter. Stanford, California.

———. 1991. *Lacan: The Absolute Master*. Trans. by Douglas Brick. Stanford, California.

———. 1993. *The Emotional Tie: Psychoanalysis, Mimesis and Affect*. Stanford, California.

Breuer, Josef and Sigmund Freud. 1955 [1895]. *Studies on Hysteria*. In S. Freud, *The Standard Edition of the Complete Psychological Works of Sigmund Freud*. Vol. 2. Trans. and ed. by James Strachey. London.

Brown, William. 1918. "The Treatment of Cases of Shell Shock in an Advanced Neurological Center." *Lancet* 2: 197–200.

———. 1919. "Hypnosis, Suggestion, and Dissociation." *British Medical Journal*, 14 June: 734–36.

———. 1920. "The Revival of Emotional Memories and Its Therapeutic Value." *British Journal of Medical Psychology* 1: 16–33.

———. 1921. *Psychology and Psychotherapy*. London.

———. 1923a. *Talks on Psychotherapy*. London.

———. 1923b. *Suggestion and Mental Analysis*. London.

Caruth, Cathy. 1991. "Psychoanalysis, Culture, and Trauma," *American Imago* 48: 1–12.

Chertok, Léon and Isabelle Stengers. 1992. *A Critique of Psychoanalytic Reason: Hypnosis as a Scientific Problem from Lavoisier to Lacan*. Trans. by Martha Noel Evans. Stanford.

Claparède, Edouard. 1911. "La question de la 'mémoire' affective." *Archives de psychologie* 10: 361–77.

———. 1928. "Feelings and Emotions." In *Feelings and Emotions: The Wittenberg Symposium.* Ed. Martin L. Reymert. Worcester, Mass.

David-Ménard, Monique. 1989. *Hysteria from Freud to Lacan: Body and Language in Psychoanalysis.* Trans. by Catherine Porter, with a foreword by Ned Lukacher. Ithaca.

Dejerine, J. and E. Gauckler. 1913. *The Psychoneuroses and Their Treatment by Psychotherapy.* Trans. by Smith Ely Jelliffe. Philadelphia and London.

Dubois, Paul. 1908. *The Psychic Treatment of Nervous Disorders.* Trans. by Smith Ely Jelliffe and William A. White. New York.

Eissler, K. R. 1986. *Freud as an Expert Witness: The Discussion of War Neuroses between Freud and Wagner-Jauregg.* Trans. by Christine Trollope. Madison, Conn.

Fendtner, Chris. 1993. " 'Minds the Dead Have Ravished': Shell Shock, History and the Ecology of Disease Systems." *History of Science* 31: 377–420.

Ferenczi, Sandor and Otto Rank. 1956 [1924]. *Sex in Psycho-Analysis and The Development of Psychoanalysis.* New York.

Ferenczi, Sandor, et al. 1921. *Psychoanalysis and the War Neuroses.* London.

Fischer-Homberger, Esther. 1975. *Die traumatische Neurose. Vom Somatischen zur Sozialen Leiden.* Bern.

Forrester, John. 1990. *The Seductions of Psychoanalysis: Freud, Lacan and Derrida.* Cambridge, England.

Foucault, Michel. 1982. "Afterword: The Subject and Power." In Herbert L. Dreyfus and Paul Rabinow, *Michel Foucault: Beyond Structuralism and Hermeneutics.* Chicago.

Freud, Sigmund. 1906–22 [1915]. Das Unbewusste. *Sammlung Kleiner Schriften zur Neurosenlehre.* 5 vols. Vienna. Vol. 4: 309.

———. 1953–74. *The Standard Edition of the Complete Psychological Works of Sigmund Freud.* Trans. and ed. by James Strachey. London.

———. 1953–74 [1891]. "Hypnosis." *Standard Edition,* Vol. 1.

———. 1953–74 [1910]. "The Future Prospects of Psychoanalytic Therapy." *Standard Edition.* Vol. 11.

———. 1953–74 [1912]. "Recommendations to Physicians Concerning Psychoanalysis." *Standard Edition.* Vol. 12.

———. 1953–74 [1914]. "Remembering, Repeating, and Working Through." *Standard Edition.* Vol. 12.

———. 1953–74 [1915]. "The Unconscious." *Standard Edition.* Vol. 14.

———. 1953–74 [1915–17]. *Introductory Lectures on Psychoanalysis. Standard Edition.* Vol. 16.

———. 1953–74 [1920]. *Beyond the Pleasure Principle.* Standard Edition. Vol. 18.

Gasché, Rodolphe. 1986. *The Tain of the Mirror: Derrida and the Philosophy of Reflection*. Cambridge.

Hacking, Ian. 1991. "Two Souls in One Body." *Critical Inquiry* 17: 838–67.

———. 1992. "Multiple Personality Disorder and Its Hosts." *History of the Human Sciences* 5 (2): 3–31.

Hadfield, J. A. 1920. "Treatment by Suggestion and Persuasion." In *Functional Nerve Disease*. Ed. by H. Crichton Miller. London.

Hart, Bernard. 1926. "The Conception of Dissociation." Presidential Address to the Medical Section of the British Psychological Society, Dec. 15, 1926, with discussion by Ernest Jones, T. W. Mitchell, William Brown, and Edward Glover. *British Journal of Medical Psychology* 6: 241–63.

Henry, Michel. 1985. *Généalogie de la psychanalyse*. Paris.

Herman, Judith Lewis. 1992. *Trauma and Recovery*. New York.

Higgonnet, Margaret, et al., eds. 1987. *Behind the Lines: Gender and the Two World Wars*. New Haven.

Humphrey, George. 1963. *Thinking*. New York.

James, William. 1981 [1890]. *Principles of Psychology*. Ed. by F. Burkhardt, F. Bowers, and I. K. Skrupskelis (3 vols). Cambridge.

Janet, Pierre. 1928. *L'Évolution de la mémoire et de la notion du temps*. Paris.

———. 1975 [1926]. *De l'angoisse à l'éxtase*. Paris.

———. 1976 [1919]. *Psychological Healing. A Historical and Clinical Study*. 2 vols. Trans. by Eden and Cedar Paul. New York.

———. 1989 [1889]. *L'Automatisme psycholoqique. Essai de psychologie expérimentale sur les formes inférieures de l'activité humaine*. Paris.

———. 1980 [1923]. *La médicine psychologique*. Paris.

———. 1990 [1898]. *Névroses et idées fixes. I: Études expérimentales sur les troubles de la volonté, de l'attention, de la mémoire, sur les émotions, les idées obsédants et leur traitement*. Reprint of the 4th edition. Paris.

Knapp, Steven. 1989. "Collective Memory and the Actual Past." *Representations* 26: 123–48.

Krell, David Farrell. 1990. *Of Memory, Reminscence, and Writing: On the Verge*. Bloomington and Indianapolis.

Lacan, Jacques. 1988. *Freud's Papers on Technique, 1953–1954*. Ed. by Jacques-Alain Miller, trans. by John Forrester. New York.

Langer, Lawrence. 1991. *Holocaust Testimonies: The Ruins of Memory*. New Haven.

Leys, Ruth. 1992 "The Real Miss Beauchamp: Gender and the Subject of Imitation." In *Feminists Theorize the Political*. Ed. by Judith Butler and Joan Scott. New York.

Lindenfeld, David F. 1980. *The Transformation of Positivism: Alexius Meinong and European Thought, 1880–1920*. Berkeley, California.

Lukacher, Ned. 1986. *Primal Scenes: Literature, Philosophy, and Psychoanalysis.* Ithaca and London.
Mandler, Jean Matter and George Mandler, eds. 1964. *Thinking: From Association to Gestalt.* New York.
Maslan, Mark. 1988. "Foucault and Pragmatism." *Raritan* 7 (3): 94–114.
McDougall, William. 1926. *Outline of Abnormal Psychology.* New York.
Michaels, Walter Benn. 1992. "Race into Culture: A Critical Genealogy of Cultural Identity." *Critical Inquiry* 18: 679–80.
———. 1993. "The Victims of Historicism." *Modern Language Quarterly* 54 (1): 111–20.
———. 1994. "The No-Drop Rule." *Critical Inquiry* 20 (Summer 1994): 758–69.
Miller, H. Crichton. 1920. "The Mother Complex." In *Functional Nerve Disease: An Epitome of War Experience for the Practitioner.* Ed. by H. Crichton Miller. London.
Mitchell, Juliet. 1993. "Psychoanalysis and Hysteria." Paper presented to the School of Criticism and Theory, Dartmouth College, July 1993.
Myers, C. S. 1916. "Contributions to the Study of Shell Shock." *Lancet* 1 (January 8): 65–69.
Myers, C. S. 1940. *Shellshock in France.* London.
Nicoll, Maurice. 1920. "Regression." In *Functional Nerve Disease: An Epitome of War Experience for the Practitioner.* Ed. by H. Crichton Miller. London.
Perry, Campbell W., et al. 1988. "Hypnotic Age Regression Techniques in the Elicitation of Memories: Applied Uses and Abuses." In *Hypnosis and Memory.* Ed. by Helen M. Pettinati. New York.
——— and Jean-Roch Laurence. 1984. "Mental Processes Outside Awareness: The Contributions of Freud and Janet." In *The Unconscious Reconsidered.* Ed. by K. S. Bowers and D. Meichenbaum. New York.
Prince, Morton. 1920. "Babinski's Theory of Hysteria." *Journal of Abnormal Psychology* 14: 312–24.
Putnam, Frank W.. 1989. "Pierre Janet and Modern Views of Dissociation." *Journal of Traumatic Stress* 2 (4): 413–29.
Rivers, W. H. R. 1917. "Freud's Psychology of the Unconscious." *Lancet* 1, 16 June: 912–14.
———. 1922. *Instinct and the Unconscious: A Contribution to a Biological Theory of the Psycho-Neuroses.* Cambridge.
Roth, Michael S. 1989. "Remembering Forgetting: *Maladies de la memoire* in Nineteenth-Century France." *Representations* 26: 49–68.
Roustang, François. 1983. *Psychoanalysis Never Lets Go.* Trans. by Ned Luckacher. Baltimore.
———. 1990. *L'Influence.* Paris.

Sartre, Jean-Paul. 1972. *Imagination: A Psychological Critique.* Trans. Forrest Williams. Ann Arbor, Michigan.

Showalter, Elaine. 1985. "Male Hysteria: W. H. Rivers and the Lessons of Shellshock." In *The Female Malady: Women, Madness, and English Culture, 1830–1985.* New York: 76–91.

Simmel, Ernst. 1921. "Symposium Held at the Fifth International Psycho-Analytical Congress at Budapest, September 1918," in *Psycho-Analysis and the War Neuroses.* London.

Stone, Martin. 1985. "Shellshock and the Psychologists." In *The Anatomy of Madness: Essays in the History of Psychiatry.* Vol. 2. Ed. by W. F. Bynum, Roy Porter, Michael Shepherd. London and New York.

Terdiman, Richard. 1993. *Present Past: Modernity and the Memory Crisis.* Ithaca and London.

van der Hart, Onno, Paul Brown, and Bessel A. van der Kolk. 1989. "Pierre Janet's Treatment of Post-traumatic Stress." *Journal of Traumatic Stress* 2 (4): 379–95.

——— and R. Horst. 1989. "The Dissociation Theory of Pierre Janet." *Journal of Traumatic Stress* 2 (4): 397–412.

van der Kolk, Bessel A. and Onno van der Hart, 1991. "The Intrusive Past: The Flexibility of Memory and the Engraving of Trauma." *American Imago* 48 (4): 425–54.

——— and Onno van der Hart. 1989. "Pierre Janet and the Breakdown of Adaptation in Psychological Trauma." *American Journal of Psychiatry* 146: 1330–1342.

Young, Allan. 1995. *The Harmony of Illusions: Inventing Post-Traumatic Stress Disorder.* Princeton, N.J.

III. Culture As Memorial Practice

The remaining chapters turn away from the memories recounted by individuals and the theories of memory debated by experts to examine the way memory is shaped by different cultural contexts. Arguing both that culture and practice must always address the past in some way, and that our memory of the past is always culturally mediated, the contributors explore a variety of cultural representations of the past, models of memory, and commemorative practices, as well as the diverse social and historical contexts of memory production.

Both Michael Kenny and Laurence Kirmayer address cultural models for explaining the relationship between traumatic events and subsequent distress. Where Hacking argued that the sciences of memory have created a distinctive break with alternate ways of thinking about the soul, the thrust of Kenny's paper is to show similarities between contemporary psychiatric disease categories and patterns of diagnosis and the models of explanation developed in non-Western societies. Specifically, he describes the similarities in the social process through which illness, and in particular the general feeling of deep malaise or "bad destiny," is explained in terms of past events. What are the limits of my responsibility for a spoiled life? Kenny shows that the therapeutic responses to such a question must address the boundaries of the self. The models under consideration all serve to shift responsibility for the source of the problem outside the sufferer and often outside the body of concerned citizens and experts who make the diagnosis. This displacement of responsibility and guilt may help produce new and unstigmatized identities. However it is based on a retrospective attribution of causality that must at times be hypothetical. Hence it is no wonder, as Kenny makes clear, that there is a good deal of disagreement in the psychiatric community when proponents of a post-traumatic stress model attempt to absorb more and more disease categories.

Kenny compares psychiatric models with explicit "folk" ones that similarly ascribe causality to forgotten events, whereas Kirmayer examines the largely implict cultural and social factors which help generate the distinctive patterns of memory that become reified in psychiatric nosology. Of all the contributors to the book, Kirmayer, as a psychiatrist, is perhaps most directly concerned with how personal memory actually works and with the consequences of the diverse ways in which people remember traumatic events. After a masterful review of the experimental literature, Kirmayer challenges the argument recently popularized by Judith Herman (and described also by Kenny) that the psychological effects of trauma are everywhere somehow alike. In trying to understand the evident differences between recent accounts by survivors of childhood abuse and the testimony of witnesses to the Holocaust, Kirmayer turns to the role of cultural constructs and narratives, to the social expectations for registration, rehearsal, and recollection, and to the contexts of retelling.

Most important in the chapter is Kirmayer's formulation of the concept of the *landscape of memory,*which attempts to convey the metaphorically organized but nonetheless real shape of acts of remembering, especially the sense of distance and the effort required to stabilize and later recall socially and affectively charged events. He thus addresses both the role of imagination in memory and the lived contexts in which the experience of remembering and the struggle with the past occur.

All of the papers so far have addressed the consequences of firsthand acquaintance with trauma. But how should the second generation remember it? Like Kirmayer, Jack Kugelmass is concerned with memory of the Holocaust, but here less in the consciousness of individual survivors than in the public domain of their successors. Where Kirmayer examines the cultural and social factors enhancing or inhibiting internal memory, Kugelmass documents a historical change in the public space occupied by the Holocaust within North American Jewish life. Like Terdiman (1993), Kugelmass is concerned with how and why memory becomes a social preoccupation and with its effects on cultural production.

After an initial period following World War II of relative silence over the Holocaust and its implications, as well as over the legacy of eastern Europe, North American Jews have in recent years demonstrated a new engagement with remembering. Kugelmass distinguishes two strands, namely commemorative pilgrimages to the sites of the death camps and the attempts by genealogists to recover the prewar lives of their families. In interpreting the pilgrimages as a form of secular ritual, Kugelmass introduces to the volume the importance of cultural performance in (re)connecting to the past as well as to other people. Developing the link between individual memory projects and larger mythic frames of death and redemption, he both demonstrates that the removal of a sense of guilt or defilement requires a good deal more than the simple displacement onto others and warns that a reconstruction of the past in mythic terms robs history of its critical power to disturb.

In opposition to recent assessments of a "post-historical" age, Kugelmass argues for the continuing relevance of historical consciousness. Why do some societies appear to be more interested in their past than others? This large question is one of the central themes in Maurice Bloch's chapter. Bloch moves the discussion from social factors to more basic epistemological ones. Beginning with Lévi-Strauss's distinction between external and internal history (descended from his better known discussion of "cold" and hot" societies) and drawing upon Coleman's delineation of the distinction between Plato's and Aristotle's views on memory, Bloch develops a characteristically elegant cultural typology which he fleshes out by means of ethnographic comparison. He argues that different cultures constitute the relationship of the person to history in very different ways and that peoples' views of themselves in history have strong implications for the form and content of their actual engagement with history, and in particular with the kind of interest they will have in long term memory and the shape they will give it. Indeed, he concludes that human beings have no generalized need to remember the past.

Bloch notes as well an "elective affinity" between these positions and local theories of kinship and the body. This is highly suggestive in light of the fact that the current debate about trauma in North America so often locates its source in bodily transgessions within the nuclear family. Bloch, however, addresses his arguments to cognitive rather than clinical psychologists, attempting to show the inadequacy of their supposedly abstract rather than culturally shaped and committed actor. Yet, as Bloch is at pains to point out, he sees this as only one side of the picture. To understand the full force of his position the reader needs to turn to his papers examining the naïveté of anthropologists and historians with regard to the claims of the cognitivist psychologists.

Lambek provides brief excerpts from his ethnographic work on spirit possession in Mayotte and northwest Madagascar. While no more than suggestive in their present form, they demonstrate a context in which questions of individual memory are developed by means of a public idiom and conversely the memory burdens of individuals contribute to the reproduction of that idiom and its ability to continue to commemorate the past. Not coincidentally, in light of the discussion in chapters by Antze, Kenny, and Kirmayer, this takes place by means of dissociation.

If Bloch contrasts Platonic and Aristotelian views of memory and discovers their analogues in distinct ethnographic examples, Lambek appears to side firmly with the Aristotelian model, claiming that it provides a better account of remembering than do pervasive, popular North American discourses that objectify memories and hence, paradoxically, detemporalize what is intrinsically a temporal process. Like Kirmayer, he criticizes popular ideas about memory as veridical recall. He also wants to develop a more inter-subjective picture of memory, one which might replace the current focus on blame and victimhood with moral questions of consensuality, dignity, and concern for others. In describing remembering as a form of moral practice, Lambek takes up a theme that is present to one degree or another in all the papers in this section and, indeed, throughout the volume. The integral relationship between memory and moral order that Kirmayer discovers as a historical lesson of the Holocaust and perhaps of any experience of trauma, Lambek sees as true of autobiographical and historical memory more generally, even in nontraumatic contexts.

7

Trauma, Time, Illness, and Culture
An Anthropological Approach to
Traumatic Memory

Michael G. Kenny

"Witchcraft explains unfortunate events." So reads one of the most influential and widely quoted observations in the history of anthropology. It is the central proposition of E.E. Evans-Pritchard's *Witchcraft, Oracles and Magic Among the Azande* (1937), a work which at last made witchcraft beliefs comprehensible as something other than mere superstition. Evans-Pritchard lived among the Azande of the southwest Anglo-Egyptian Sudan (now the Sudan Republic), and discovered that "witchcraft" dominated Zande thinking about evil. It seemingly explained anything bad that could befall a person: illness, poor luck in hunting, marital discord, difficulties with a superior—all could be attributed to malign human agency. As the anthropologist put it, "the concept of witchcraft provides a *natural philosophy* by which the relations between men and unfortunate events are explained and a ready and stereotyped means of reacting to such events. Witchcraft beliefs also embrace a system of values which regulate human conduct" (1937: 63).

Evans-Pritchard claimed that these witchcraft beliefs are indeed a "natural philosophy," a system of explanation with an irrefutable internal logic. The theory embraces elements of what we would call "natural law," but adds to them a moral dimension which explains not just *what* happened but what personal agency was behind it. The Zande, it turned out, are rather unwilling to attribute events to fate or accident. Witches are seen as intervening in natural processes so as to ensure that someone is in

151

the right place just at the right time for misfortune to occur. The motivation for this witchcraft resides in the everyday enmities and tensions of village life: the witch is a neighbor, a spouse, an enemy who nurses grievances and has the mystical power to act on them. In turn witches can be detected by diviners who manipulate oracles that confirm which of a possible list of suspects is the actual witch.

But, if witchcraft explains unfortunate events, what exactly is to count as an "event'? Here Evans-Pritchard may have exceeded himself somewhat in his embracing claim that witchcraft explains *all* Zande misfortune (Gillies 1976; Laurence 1993: 69–70). Perhaps not all misfortunes need explaining—the death of an elderly person for example, or of infants who are prone to die young anyway. Then there are misfortunes which are not strictly speaking events at all: such as long-term patterns of wrongness, each element of which may not deserve much attention per se, but which in sum may come retrospectively to be seen as something other than mere coincidence.

I speak of the circumstances of an unfortunate *life*, not just of isolated misfortunes that might in the Zande way be attributed piecemeal to witchcraft. What to do if the wrongness seems to permeate everything, even one's very self? At this point a deeper interpretation may be called for; western psychiatry, and more specifically the theory of "traumatic memory," claims the ability to provide it. This theory arose out of nineteenth-century European neurology, and took its best-known form in Freudian psychoanalysis. It is a historical mode of interpretation in which the psychic residue of past trauma is held to be at the root of present distress. Trauma theories are found elsewhere in the world. My purpose here is to examine in cultural context how such notions serve to explain and deal with misfortune. I begin with certain western "mental disorders" that have been attributed to the effects of unpleasant events, and then move on to less familiar conditions from outside the bio-medical mainstream.

§

The mental disorders officially recognized in the United States, and increasingly by the rest of the world, are described in *The Diagnostic and Statistical Manual* of the American Psychiatric Association (currently in its fourth edition: *DSM-IV*; 1994). Consider some of the *DSM* psychiatric "disorders" that the research literature attributes to past and sometimes forgotten trauma: Borderline Personality Disorder—evident in a long-term pattern of dysfunctional and unstable social relationships; Dissociative Identity Disorder (formerly called Multiple Personality Disorder)—an involuntary and somewhat uncanny alternation of personal identities accompanied by amnesic episodes; Post Traumatic Stress Disorder (PTSD)—manifest in a wide variety of symptoms including in some cases obsessive reliving of the traumatic experience, in others inability to re-member it at all. There are many other possible symptoms of one or an-other of these three: depression, voices in the head, eating disturbances, mood swings, sleep difficulties, sexual problems. . . . The list goes on, and there is considerable overlap with other recognized diagnoses, such that victims may display "symptomatic forms that mimic virtually every cate-gory of psychiatric disorder" (Herman 1992: 114; see Lindy et al. 1984; Davidson and Foa 1991: 352).

Theories of traumatic memory posit the existence of a dissociated mental realm that contains and to an extent seals off recollections of things too painful to bear, often recollections of sexual abuse in child-hood. These memories are external to the self in so far as they are beyond the reach of normal waking consciousness. Yet—so the theory goes—the effects of such memories may leak through in the form of the problems identified by late-nineteenth-century clinicians as the symptoms of "hys-teria," and which some now see as the symptoms of the various *DSM* dis-orders mentioned above. The relation between symptom and its past cause is frequently judged to be "symbolic" in nature, the symptom being a transformed representation of past events that demands interpretive de-coding as an essential aspect of the therapeutic process: hallucinatory ex-periences and dreams may be flashbacks to the scene of a crime; inexplicable phobias may be associated with things that were present when the traumatic memories were first laid down. It is necessary to re-cover memory of those events so as abreact the passion—the guilt, the rage—associated with them.

Pierre Janet, Freud's contemporary and critic, coined the term "trau-matic memory." He maintained that in weakly organized nervous systems sudden shock can cause partial disintegration of a person's capacity to synthesize impressions into a conscious whole. Such persons are incom-plete, fragmented beings, and in extreme cases may present themselves as genuine "multiple" personalities. Memories of traumatic events live on outside of consciousness, separated from it but still accessible via appro-priate therapy. Such a memory is inimical to health because it is "apart from the personality, because it belongs to a group of phenomena over which the conscious will of the subject has no longer any control" (Janet 1925: 40). The therapeutic goal is to assimilate this material *within* the personality, to make it part of oneself. The therapeutic process is aimed at freeing the victim from the dead weight of the past.

This bringing of "pathogenic reminiscences" to light is the functional equivalent of identifying a witch. In so far as these memories are of trau-matic abuse at the hands of an actual person, to recover the memory is also to name the culprit. Therapists who deal in this currency are therefore the functional equivalent of Zande diviners and oracles, the process in which they are involved a social process with social implications. It is a process which entails the construction of a story or "narrative"—a return to the scene of the crime in which the formerly dissociated material now finds a place in consciousness. As Janet said, "memory is an action: essentially it is the action of telling a story" (van der Kolk & van der Hart 1989: 1534). Sometimes it is a story that leads to legal action against the newly exposed perpetrators.

Because of this forensic context, the imagery of "witchhunting" permeates current debates about the reality of so-called "False Memory Syndrome": pseudo-memories thought to be confabulated in therapy, often with the aid of hypnosis. Skeptics claim that allegations of incest and sexual abuse made on the basis of recovered memories are no better than the highly subjective and even at the time rapidly discredited "spectral evidence" used in the Salem witch-trials of 1692 (e.g. Gardner 1991). However, my aim in invoking the idea of witchcraft has a different point. Here I am not so much interested in abstract "truth" about the past as in the social process through which illness is explained in historical terms.

Both Zande witchcraft and western traumatic memory therapy deploy a theory of causation within a framework of moral judgments. For the Zande the witch is a person who sought to do ill but, since witchcraft can operate "unconsciously" as a projection of unacknowledged enmity, may not necessarily have been aware of it. Hence there is a gray area in Zande jurisprudence between causal determinism and moral agency that allows for great flexibility in judging the rights and wrongs of particular cases. There are shades of culpability and guilt. Traumatic memories are concealed in another unconscious realm, not this time a sump of illicit desire, but a self-constructed fortress protecting the victim against realization of things too terrible to bear. The patient is innocent, no matter how deviant or pathological the behavior. It is the perpetrator who is guilty, but even here there may be moral ambiguities. It is supposed that those who abuse were often abused themselves in a pattern continuing generation after generation until the chain is broken.

When viewed as a cultural construct, it is apparent that the "unconscious" and its equivalents can be filled up with what others project into it. Having been identified by an oracle, an accused witch may confess to unconscious witchcraft. A trauma patient may uncover evidence for crimes that never occurred. In the limiting case, accused perpetrators and witches may confess to crimes they never committed and yet have become fully convinced that they did. In still other cases, fully remembered traumas may be credited with psychological effects that they have only acquired by retrospective application of newly-minted theory. One possible consequence is that responsibility for a disrupted life is deflected away from oneself and onto persons and past events over which one had no control. The unconscious is a supple idiom, and the boundary between what is a part of oneself and what is not subject to redefinition via cultural processes that amount to "rewriting the soul"—redefining human nature (Hacking 1995; Kenny 1986).

In what follows I will examine the social process of diagnosis and treatment of "traumatic memories" by contrasting current North American psychotherapeutic ideas about trauma with similar notions in other cultural settings. My first example will be Latin American *susto* ("fright illness") as compared to the *DSM* category of Post Traumatic Stress Disorder. My second is that of West African notions of "Destiny" set against the *DSM* label of Borderline Personality Disorder. The central issue for us is the way in which an interpretive link is established between present and past; a secondary concern is the way in which such interpretation serves to delineate and define the boundaries of the self.

§

In his *Confessions* St. Augustine wrote of the mysteries of memory, of "the abyss of human consciousness" known only to God (1991: 179). He sought to recover his first memories, his entry into the moral life, and found it a difficult task. Of his infancy he said that "I do not wish to reckon this as part of the life that I live in this world; for it is lost in the darkness of my forgetfulness, and is on the same level as the life I lived in my mother's womb" (10). Some would now say that even those earliest days have left a record in the form of pre-linguistic bodily or perceptual memory that affects the entire course of one's life. If this record is one of trauma, then the search for an explanation of life's difficulties must go back to its earliest days and—if one subscribes to reincarnation and past-life regression—even before them.

Though the conditions I will now discuss are held to be initiated by traumatic or startling experiences, they posit a variable relationship between trauma and symptom. The appearance of symptoms may be more or less immediate, as with some forms of PTSD, or may appear only later as with *susto* and "delayed onset" PTSD. But in all cases the nature of the causal connection is a matter of interpretation, a theoretically motivated endeavor with existential consequences.

Susto is widely distributed in Central and South America, and in its classical form is precipitated by fright leading to soul-loss and generalized debility (Gillin 1948). PTSD is explained psycho-physiologically, and may include reference to Janet's concept of traumatic memory. The following are the DSM criteria for its onset:

. . . the development of characteristic symptoms following exposure to an extreme traumatic stressor involving direct personal experience of an event that involves actual or threatened death or serious injury, or other threat to one's physical integrity; or witnessing an event that involves death, injury, or a threat to the physical integrity of another person; or learning about unexpected or violent death, serious harm, or threat of death or injury experienced by a family member or other close associate (APA 1994: 424).

The symptoms of PTSD are as heterogeneous as their cause: obsessive reliving of the event, dreams thereof, flashbacks, efforts to avoid circumstances reminding one of the traumatic event, inability to remember an important aspect of the trauma. Sometimes the distress may be triggered by cues "that symbolize or resemble an aspect of the traumatic event." There are also generalized social and emotional problems associated with this disorder (but also with others): restricted affect, feelings of estrangement, vague foreboding, sleep problems, irritability, and exaggerated startle response.

PTSD and *susto* are constructs built upon local cultural understandings about the nature of the self or soul that, in an appropriate context, make diagnosis of one or the other reasonable, though not inevitable. Each is predicated on the notion that the connection between body and soul may be unhinged by frightening events. Each has a cultural history and a unique cultural relevance, though only with PTSD is it possible to see all of this clearly because of the recency of its emergence as a psychiatric concept.

§

Susto is a serious and potentially life-threatening affliction. Among its symptoms are "restlessness in sleep, listlessness, loss of appetite, weight loss, loss of energy and strength, depression, introversion, paleness, lethargy, and sometimes fever, diarrhea, and vomiting" (Ortiz de Montellano 1990: 221–222). However, these various signs can also be taken as indications of "innumerable" other disorders ranging from hookworm infestation to clinical depression (Crandon 1983: 158; Gillin 1948: 398). *Susto* therefore "involves no single defining set of symptoms" and to this extent resembles PTSD (Logan 1993: 192; see Good & Good 1982). The interpretive power of the concept lies in its flexibility, and the key to this diagnosis is vaguely defined distress in the context of the total life-situation of the patient.

A diagnosis of *susto* matches many possible experiences and situations, a wide variety of cultural contexts from Mexico to the Andes to New York City, a variety of physical or mental illnesses as we conceive them, with varying degrees of supernatural involvement. The common thread in all of this is that the soul is the essence of life and vitality, and that fright can destabilize or weaken it, or even decouple it from the body before death, though death must eventually follow its loss (see Scheper-Hughes 1992: 187–215). Expert advice must be sought out, since without such help it cannot be definitively known what caused the soul to depart or even for sure that it did so, given alternatives such as witchcraft or physical ailment. And so one resorts to the diviner.

The process of divination is retrospective in nature: if it is determined that the presenting symptoms are indeed those of soul-loss, then it must also be decided just which frightening event caused to soul to depart. This is important because the soul should be sought where it was first lost, the site of the fright that led to its departure and where it might again be found and enticed back. But there often is a significant temporal gap between trauma and symptom: the greater the distance from the trauma, the more of life's intervening difficulties can be explained by reference to their cause. "These signs and symptoms do not occur immediately. A man does not perceive the wandering off of his "shadow" at the very moment it is happening. Little by little he feels the consequences of his fright, and, if there is no cure, the evil progresses until death comes" (Lopez Austin 1988: 226).

A particularly chilling instance of such a diagnosis—in this case *pro*spective—is reported from a shanty town in Brazil, where a mother may conclude on the basis of certain signs that her languishing infant has experienced such a severe *susto* that the child is unlikely to live and therefore not worth the care that, from an outsider's perspective, might have saved it (Scheper-Hughes: 340–399).

That is out of the child's hands. Adults are in a position to intervene in the determination of their own fates, but even so a diagnosis of *susto* requires social confirmation. Much work on this disorder has therefore focused not on what *susto* actually *is* in bio-medical terms—since it can be many things, some not strictly speaking "medical" at all—but rather on how, among the available possibilities, *susto* becomes the diagnosis of choice in particular instances. One generalized feature of this condition is withdrawal from normal social intercourse, which an influential study finds to be the end result of a number of difficulties the victim has had in living up to social expectations (Rubel et al 1984). *Susto* is a message, a social role, an appeal to others to be seen differently, a decision by others that the afflicted *should* be regarded as ill and therefore as not fully responsible (O'Nell & Selby 1968: 97; Crandon 164).

The experience taken to be responsible for the *susto* may have happened just a short time ago, in which case the correlation of frightening

157

event with onset of symptoms is relatively straightforward. But it may also have happened a very long time ago, even when the victim was in the womb: the mother's fright being transmitted to the developing soul of her unborn child. The fright may have happened at *any* time in the past, and because of this "the causal episode is cut loose, so that one may seek his fright at large. This virtually assures that some kind of episode will be available to everybody, but more than that it gives enough latitude for the *asustado* to find a kind of episode that fits his overall personal fiction" (Uzzell 1974: 373). The task is to determine which fright is behind the problem—"some past event that will provide etiological support for a diagnosis of susto"—and when "this telescopic discovery of primary causes" is accomplished, rituals are performed to reintegrate the victim into family and community, a kind of rite of passage back to normal life (Rubel: 42; Signorini 1982: 32).

The following two examples, the first from Guatemala, the second from southern Mexico, illustrate the flexibility of the idea:

A Pokomam Indian woman was in a depressed state of mind, suffered from pains in the stomach, loss of appetite, diarrhea, and occasional fever. A curer was called in and elicited from the woman a long history of personal difficulties. The diagnosis was *susto,* and the precipitating event taken to be a quarrel with her husband that had erupted when the couple passed by a spot where the man had been deceived by a "loose woman." A well-attended curing ceremonial was undertaken in which the "evil winds" within the woman were charmed into eggs that were then taken to the spot where the *susto* occurred. The curer then invoked the local spirits to help him recover the lost soul (adapted from Gillin: 391–392).

A Chinantec man was at first uncertain about the nature of his condition. He felt a "burning in his heart" and was diagnosed by a physician with "liver problems." He then suffered a bout of diarrhea and his condition deteriorated. Ten years previously a son had been killed in a battle over land with a neighboring village, following which the father became sad and lost interest in life. His remaining son was a drunk and the source of much trouble including an episode in which the father was incarcerated because of the son's refusal to pay a fine. Most lately he was frightened by someone shooting randomly near him in the pasture, and came to attribute his malaise to these three *sustos* in combination. A healer was called in who performed a ritual and after that the victim felt much better and went back to work (adapted from Rubel: 39–40).

Trauma may be the explanation for *susto*, but scarcely is its *cause*: the diagnosis is a retrospective interpretation arrived at with specialist assistance, and is more the product of a theory than of an actual experience. Soul loss is an apt metaphor for loss of ability to sustain a viable life. What then of PTSD?

§

Post-Traumatic Stress Disorder may be an old phenomenon but it is a new diagnosis, first appearing in the Third Edition of the *Diagnostic and Statistical Manual* in 1980. The process through which that came about is well known. It was seen that many psychiatric disorders and readjustment problems were occurring among the veterans of the Vietnam War. Groups of committed U.S. veterans and their psychiatric allies therefore advanced the PTSD concept and persuaded the American Psychiatric Association to include it in the DSM (Scott 1990; Young 1995).

The pathologies attributed to wartime PTSD are diverse in nature: alcoholism, drug use, crime, spousal abuse, depression, alienation, nihilism—in addition to the more specific (but also diverse) symptomatic criteria listed in the DSM. The veterans subject to these difficulties are depicted as victims of the situation evoked in the first Rambo film—brave fighters in a lost war adrift in a civilian society which fails to honor them, damaged souls lost in time, tied to each other but to no one else.

"Post-Vietnam Syndrome confronts us with the unconsummated grief of soldiers—impacted grief, in which an encapsulated, never-ending past deprives the present of meaning" (Scott: 301). The past must therefore be exorcised, the grieving process completed, the bio-psychological effects of trauma reversed or controlled. Hence it is not simply a matter of a transient war neurosis, but of treating a comprehensive alteration in life-situation induced by the residue of acknowledged or covert traumatic memories.

This is a murky affair. Not all traumas are the same; not all people respond to similar traumas in similar ways; the *meaning* of seemingly traumatic events, and therefore response to them, may depend on social circumstances and culture (Summerfield 1993). The concept of PTSD has expanded its range to include traumas of other kinds. Like soul-loss, PTSD turns out to have considerable metaphorical power: behind deviance and debility there may be the still harsher reality of sexual and political oppression. The personal thus becomes political and a diagnosis of PTSD motivated by other than purely medical concerns.

With this disorder there is a variable time between putative cause, the emergence of symptoms, and final diagnosis and treatment (APA: 425). As I write, specialists in psychological trauma are attempting to help the survivors of the recent Oklahoma City bombing. Elsewhere other experts, using other methods, are attempting to help the victims of traumas which may have happened ten, twenty, or thirty years ago, and yet only recently brought to light or finally seen for what they were. Like *susto*, PTSD is a flexible idiom.

It is also a diagnosis closely related to the Dissociative Disorders, themselves attributed to trauma in childhood, but found—some would say unnaturally—in a different DSM category, the Anxiety Disorders (see Davidson & Foa 1991: 349–250; Spiegel & Cardena 1991). A central trend in modern research on this subject has been an attempt to establish a neuro-physiological basis for all trauma-induced dissociated memories. The presumption is that the effects of past trauma may be diverse in their manifestations yet unitary in their cause (see van der Kolk 1994 for an overview). In a self-consciously political effort to transform the conceptual structure of modern psychiatry, the symptoms of many different psychiatric disorders are being assimilated to a trauma model purporting to explain their origins (see Kenny 1995). What began in Vietnam, and with an abused young woman known as *Sybil* who proved to be a multiple personality, has in recent years become part of a more general psychotherapeutic social movement.

As war-induced PTSD has diverse and diffuse effects, so it is with child abuse. One authority finds that there are so many possible effects that "we must organize our thinking about childhood trauma or we run the risk of never seeing the condition at all" (Terr 1991: 10). This may be difficult because "post-traumatic symptoms are so persistent and so wide-ranging, they may be mistaken for enduring characteristics of the victim's personality" (Herman 1992: 37). The symptoms are protean, heterogeneous, and frequently mis-diagnosed as the signs of other disorders. Multiple Personality (Dissociative Identity Disorder) is particularly notorious in this regard, years of misguided therapy often supposedly elapsing before "correct" diagnosis by properly trained specialists.

It is believed that traumatic memories are stored in such a way that they retain their primordial emotional power long after the experiences which generated them; if the trauma was repetitive, then memory of it may be driven underground (see Terr 1991, 1994). "It is as if time stops at the moment of trauma" (Herman: 37). The therapeutic goal is to set time moving again by bringing traumatic memories—which often are experienced as obscure physical symptoms, nightmares, flashbacks, or strange compulsions and phobias—within the orbit of conscious life by recreating "the narrative flow of history."

Doing so can be both horrifying and cleansing; to know what actually happened so long ago, often at the hands of relatives, demands a reinterpretation of one's life course. "The goal of treating PTSD is to help people live in the present, without feeling or behaving according to irrelevant demands belonging to the past. Psychologically, this means that traumatic experiences need to be located in time and place and differentiated from current reality" (van der Kolk: 261).

What is found on such excursions into the unconscious past, and how it comes to be incorporated into one's fully conscious personal narrative, is at the heart of the recovered memory controversy. It is not my purpose to explore that problem here. But I will point out the parallel with this therapeutic process and the rituals involved in alleviating the consequences of *susto*. The dissociated realm of the traumatic unconscious is a metaphorical space into which the patient is accompanied by the therapist. The dissociated memory is akin to a long-lost part of the soul floating somewhere in real space where, with the aid of the diviner, it can be tracked down and recaptured.

As with *susto*, the journey back to this place is driven by a theory about what may await there. As with *susto* the therapeutic process is a kind of rite of passage aimed at reconstruction of the present life of the victim. Whatever else may be said about the reality of recovered memories, a meaningful change is wrought in the client via the therapeutic process itself. The present and past are conjoined by learning how to tell a story which links them together in a new and morally significant way. The story takes shape with the telling; heretofore meaningless and troubling behaviors and experiences are stitched together with memories—some that have always been remembered, some recovered lately—and so one acquires a new past. Symptoms are regarded as symbols or encapsulated representations of actual events, and as time goes on they become the basis of fully discursive memories in which their meaning is at last made clear.

Not all of this may be provable in a forensic sense, but neither is the story necessarily a complete fabrication or artifact. However, it most certainly *is* a new interpretation, a new history: "The process of uncovering one's history does not depend on a single memory. New memories must be gradually blended with old ones and alternative explanations weighted until a *coherent* and largely verifiable account is constructed" (Herman and Harvey 1993: 5). A survivor said that, once the reality of the abuse was finally acknowledged, "my life suddenly made sense. Once I had a framework to fit new memories into, my recovery time got much faster" (Bass and Davis 1988: 80–81). A Canadian novelist, who discovered late in life that she was an abuse victim suffering from Multiple Personality Disorder, put it this way: "When finally I began excavation, I brought these pieces to the surface in random order, to be fitted into patterns and dated" (Fraser 1987: 218).

161

A similar process has been described by medical anthropologist, Allan Young, on the basis of observations in a psychoanalytically oriented U.S. Veteran's Administration PTSD unit. The patients treated by this unit ended up there because of deep disturbances in their post-war lives. The therapeutic ethos of the unit focused on linking present misfortune to past origin:

> In order to recover, each patient must satisfactorily recall his etio-logical event and then disclose it, in detail, to his therapists and fel-low patients in the course of psychotherapy sessions. this narrative is the Rosetta stone of his disorder. The postwar life of the typical pa-tient is suffused by misfortune and failure: barroom brawls, domes-tic violence, unsuccessful marriages, erratic employment, impulsive relocations, and so on. A properly decoded narrative delineates the pattern beneath the chaos (Young 1993: 111; see Young 1995).

And so a narrative takes shape which, as Young says, "gives these men an honorable collective history" (Young n.d.: 19). The past is brought in line with present perceptions about its significance, such that—as Freud put it—the illness becomes "intelligible." But, as I have mentioned before, there is often more than one way to interpret a given illness episode or ex-istential situation. Which interpretation will win out, and why? The follow-ing example from the Pacific Northwest illustrates that problem, and also the nature of the PTSD diagnosis as it has come to be commonly applied:

> A 34 year-old Kwakiutl man was beginning to make a name as a carver and had recently returned to his reserve community after a long stay in the city. He was about to assume a high-ranking title among his people, and a friend said that it was "as though the an-cestral spirit inside him was waking up." However, he had become suspicious of plots against him, and thought the whitening of his beard to be a sign he was transforming into an eagle. Family and friends referred him involuntarily to regional mental health ser-vices where he spent a short time as an in-patient. Upon release he disappeared and was found in a garage where he had been setting small fires, and whose owner he stabbed on discovery. The police found him running naked with a knife in a nearby forest, and on at-tacking one of their dogs and threatening them, an officer shot him dead. The inquest revealed that his original psychiatric diagnosis was of "complex" PTSD, supposedly provoked on return home by arousal of memories of his childhood with alcoholic and sexually abusive caretakers. Others thought that perhaps his behavior was

due to an old head injury. Still others believed that he was trying to complete his transformation, something whites could not understand. A consulting psychiatrist testified that, given his psychotic behavior, he had been released far too soon (adapted from *Vancouver* [B.C.] *Sun,* June 6 & 12, 1995).

PTSD is currently in favor as an explanation for many of the pathologies of Canadian Native life, and has emerged in a politicized context critical of white racism, the reservation system, and Indian Residential Schools. "Complex" Post Traumatic Stress Disorder is an unofficial diagnosis specifically applicable to persons with a "history of chronic trauma." The disorder is held to be capable of wearing a "multiplicity of disguises" (Herman: 123, 127). Of course, that is also true of *susto,* and a central feature of the present case is the hypothetical nature of the connection between a psychotic episode and the arousal of memories from a long ago dismal childhood.

For a final example of this kind of reasoning I turn to a comparison of Borderline Personality Disorder with evil Pre-Natal Destiny.

§

If a woman entered therapy displaying the pattern of disturbance characterizing male victims of wartime PTSD, she might well be diagnosed as suffering from Borderline Personality Disorder, which the *DSM* characterizes as "a pervasive pattern of instability of interpersonal relationships, self-image, and affects, and marked impulsivity that begins by early adulthood and is present in a variety of contexts" (APA: 650). Seventy-five percent of reported borderline cases are female, a disproportion found with even greater prominence in the reporting of Dissociative Identity Disorder.

This gender-biased imbalance is attributed to the fact that women are more likely than men to be sexually abused. However, the over-representation of women in the reporting of Borderline Personality Disorder and Multiple Personality may also reflect deeply embedded cultural factors concerning the psychological significance of gender. It has also been suggested that BPD is heavily overdiagnosed because "so many patients can be shoehorned into its capacious definition"—that this diagnosis has become "the virus of psychiatry," applied when the patient "has vague, general symptoms indicating instability of any kind" (Morrison 1995: 479; Simmons 1992: 222).

Until lately, a diagnosis of Borderline Personality Disorder—"the negative catch-all of psychiatric diagnoses" (Simmons: 219)—has been regarded as highly stigmatic, an equivalent to the pejorative diagnosis of "hysteric" in the late nineteenth century—histrionic, demanding, intractable, irritating, and usually female. This unpleasant melange some-times evokes in therapists what are quaintly termed "hostile countertrans-ference reactions." Being regarded as both annoying and hopeless is not likely to encourage the patient.

Like PTSD, Borderline only became a formally recognized diagnosis with the publication of *DSM-III* in 1980. The concept has a curious history reflective of conceptual shifts within North American psychiatry. As origi-nally applied it referred to the "borderland" between neurosis and psy-chosis, to the psychiatric walking wounded outside the asylum walls (Showalter 1985: 105-106). Later it came to refer to the kind of perva-sively unstable individual at the center of the current *DSM* definition, per-sons "whose disturbed ego and social functioning affected every area of their lives" (Mack 1975: 11). Interpretation was at first predominantly psy-choanalytic in nature, with a focus on inadequacies of ego-development resulting in unstable personal relationships paralleled by "markedly and persistently unstable self-image or sense of self." More lately the trauma theory has invaded this frontier, and may well claim it.

However it is explained, Borderline Personality Disorder is a manifestly *bad* destiny. There are parallel concepts in other societies, one such be-ing the personified idea of Prenatal Destiny widely found in what are now Nigeria, Benin, and Ghana. Unlike *susto* and PTSD, the notion of Destiny is not related to trauma, but to choices made before birth that are ascer-tainable only by expert diviners deploying complex analytical tools. The root of the difficulty is internal discord resulting from an incompatibility between the parts of one's soul: between one's conscious self and one's Destiny (see Horton 1961: 113). Once again, the present is explained in terms of the past, and in this case the pre-natal past.

The classical statement of the consequences of an evil destiny is that of British anthropologist Meyer Fortes on the basis of his research in north-ern Ghana:

> Before it is born a child is "with Heaven," not in any literal sense but in the symbolical sense of being in process of creation. At that time it declares its wishes . . . . It may declare that it does not wish to have parents or a spouse or children or farm or livestock. This means that it rejects ordinary human living though it cannot avoid being born. This is its Evil Prenatal Destiny. The victims of Prenatal Destiny are a selected type. They are out on a limb, or potentially so, in the social structure . . . having apparently incurable physical or psychological defects that put them in danger of leaving no chil-dren and of thus eventually becoming socially forgotten. In these circumstances the notion of Prenatal Destiny serves as a legitimate

alibi. It relieves the sufferer's kin, and therefore society at large, of responsibility and guilt for his troubles and, indeed, exonerates him in his own eyes. For he is not aware that he is the victim of his Prenatal Destiny until this is revealed by a diviner (Fortes 1983: 17–18).

Destiny corresponds to idiosyncratic experience and the arbitrariness of fate. "A person's destiny determines, within limits, whether he will be lucky or unlucky, rich or poor, kind or cruel, wise or foolish, popular or unpopular." It "serves to identify the fact of irremediable failure in the development of the individual to full social capacity" (Fortes 1983: 38; Bascom 1969: 116). This need not lead to fatalism. There is the possibility of altering or renouncing Destiny itself. At the least therapy aims to improve the terms of association, reconciling conscious desire with the unknown forces thwarting it: "the onus . . . is shifted on to the supernatural plane and the individual's feelings of helplessness and depression are made tolerable" (Fortes: 35).

Which brings me back to Borderline Personality Disorder. Like bad Prenatal Destiny, BPD contaminates the pattern of a whole life, and seen in this light has a family resemblance to the trauma-induced syndromes in general. Hypothetically therefore, Borderline Personality Disorder could be a variant of PTSD, which arises because of events in early childhood. The current literature has been tending strongly in this direction. One of the effects of doing so has been to make the diagnosis more hopeful and, as with the now "honorable" status of wartime PTSD, far less stigmatic (Gunderson and Sabo 1993: 19). It is far better to be a victim of traumatic child abuse than a troublesome pain in the neck, just as it is better to suffer from wartime PTSD than to be a drunk, a vagrant, a psychopath, or a crook: "thus the way is opened to the creation of new meaning in experience and a new, unstigmatized identity" (Herman: 127). The reinterpretation of life alters life itself: "the validation of the trauma is a precondition for restoration of an integrated self-identity and the capacity for appropriate relationships with others" (Herman et al. 1989: 494; see Saunders and Arnold 1993: 199).

The causal nexus between trauma and disorder thus becomes the focal point of therapy and, as with the treatment of PTSD, emphasis is on the reintegration of traumatic memories into the structure of the ego. Because the trauma in most cases is only known retrospectively, there are methodological problems in establishing a straightforward etiology in particular cases; the fact that "borderline patients are highly suggestible as to the causes of their psychopathology" probably does not help (Ogata et al. 1990: 1012). Yet confidence is high that the trauma model will help to deal with this most intractable of neuroses, that behind "all the multiplicity of disguises" disorders of this kind can assume, there lies the reality of a "complex post-traumatic syndrome."

Trauma specialists focus on a child-abuse etiology for BPD and, in so far as they are also inclined toward the concept of traumatic dissociation, they entertain the possibility of unrecovered traumatic memories. The most radical claim is that the Borderline condition is not a Personality Disorder at all, where it is currently situated, but in fact is a Dissociative Disorder closely related to Multiple Personality: "MPD . . . is common, especially in patients classically diagnosed as borderline. . . . . Borderlines do not have something wrong with their *personalities*. Neither do MPD patients. Both have dissociative disorders involving numerous psychic functions, including affect, behavior, memory, cognition, and perception" (Ross 1989: 152, 156).

This stance naturally results in a different sort of treatment than if BPD were dealt with by more traditional means. If the disorder gets redefined as one of the many possible consequences of PTSD or traumatic dissociation, then the trauma itself assumes great prominence whether its existence is immediately acknowledged by the patient or not; and, if redefined as Dissociative Identity Disorder, the presumption is strong that a hidden personality is responsible for the self-defeating borderline behavior. There is substantial disagreement about such things within psychiatry, and radical positions such as that quoted above (in fact many of the statements quoted above) should be seen in the context of sometimes virulent disputes within the profession. When it comes to the range of possible explanations of Borderline Personality Disorder, one bemused commentator observes that, at best, enhanced knowledge will emerge from such conflict, but "at worst separate 'Truths' are discovered and announced, and armed disciples (armed, that is, with words and reimbursement restrictions) will duke it out" (Kroll 1993: 212; see Kenny 1995).

And so, at the end, we are witness to professional disputes about the interpretation of misfortune. It is illuminating and sobering to see that— just as with the pluralistic medical systems of other societies—there are rival interpretations of misfortune in North America as well, even within the same realm of professional discourse. It might be thought that by calling attention to these things I am dismissing Western psychotherapy as "nothing but" witchdoctoring and divining. Not so, and in my view to maintain any such thing is ethnocentric, in that it implies some kind of inferiority in the therapeutic procedures of non-Western peoples or those out of the medical mainstream. What I have sought to describe are certain commonalties of process in the explanation and treatment of illness.

Yet, while there are commonalties of process, there are also differences in orientation that reflect the circumstances and cultural biases of the societies in question. Western "psychological" theories are characteristically more individualistic than those of Latin American and West African peasants; the former concentrate more on inner events than outward circumstances. The theory of traumatic memory to some extent reverses this tendency in so far as it domesticates individual pathology by placing it in a wider societal context.

Therapy is a *creative* process, but historical interpretation a difficult business. *Susto* is perhaps modeled on some generic human response to sudden fright, but in practice the relationship between trauma and suffering is ambiguous. The connection is closer in the case of some instances of PTSD, in that experience of disaster has very real and immediate effects. But when the supposed trauma happened long ago, and is known only via historical reconstruction, then the difference between the procedures applied to *susto* seems to me not very great. This is even more evident in determining the will of one's Destiny.

Western therapies based on the idea of traumatic memory attempt to establish meaningful relations between past and present in a culturally and socially appropriate way. They may even be based on valid science. Yet, in judging such things, we should not ignore the creative potential of psychological theory. In the above examples of *susto*, PTSD, Borderline Personality Disorder, and Bad Destiny, we have seen a number of possible and sometimes overlapping explanatory paradigms being brought to bear on particular problems: shaping *both* problem and outcome in the doing. Because of the two-way feedback between healer and client, the application of theory tends to give back results that confirm it. The unconscious gives back what we believe to be there.

When Borderline Personality Disorder is considered, the hermeneutic options expand along with the vagueness of the condition to which they are applied. Here therapy becomes much more obviously a creative process which imposes meaning on otherwise incoherent suffering. This may occur through the reconstruction of personal biography, utilizing a theory of mind that exploits the archaeological tradition of classical psychoanalysis. New identities are created in the process, and—as with African destiny concepts—responsibility for pathology and failure is diverted away from oneself while still explaining the existential paradoxes of life. In so far as this is successful, a deviant is converted into a victim, one stage of a healing journey though not the last.

The imagery of rite of passage is appropriate here, and is often found in the therapeutic literature itself. There are a certain number of "steps" in the healing process, there are certain "rituals" to go through—hypnosis for example—before reintegration of dissociated memories or the coming together of fragmented selves is complete. Therapeutic transformation can equal political conversion. To recognize the reality of abuse, not only in one's own life but as a general feature of contemporary society, is to become morally committed to fighting it and to see that there is a common cause in doing so. Unlike the case in Ghana in which a diagnosis of Bad Destiny exonerates society, here an equivalent diagnosis is used to condemn it. The theory of traumatic memory represents moral commitments based on perception of social evil. Another anthropologist, Monica Wilson, once wrote that witchcraft beliefs reflect the collective nightmares of society. So it is now.

References

American Psychiatric Association. 1994. *Diagnostic and Statistical Manual of Mental Disorders.* 4th Edition. Washington D.C.: American Psychiatric Association

Augustine, St. 1991. *Confessions.* Trans. by Henry Chadwick. Oxford: Oxford University Press.

Bascom, William.1969. *Ifa Divination: Communication Between Men and Gods in West Africa.* Bloomington: Indiana University Press.

Bass, Ellen & Laura Davis. 1988. *The Courage to Heal: A Guide for Women Survivors of Child Sexual Abuse.* New York: Harper & Row.

Crandon, Libbet. 1983. "Why Susto?" *Ethnology* 22: 153–167.

Davidson, Johnathan R. T. and Edna B. Foa. 1991. "Diagnostic Issues in Posttraumatic Stress Disorder: Considerations for the DSM-IV." *Journal of Abnormal Psychology* 100: 346–355.

Evans-Pritchard, E. E. 1937. *Witchcraft, Oracles and Magic among the Azande.* Oxford: Clarendon Press.

Fortes, Meyer. 1983. *Oedipus and Job in West African Religion.* Cambridge: Cambridge University Press.

Fraser, Sylvia. 1987. *My Father's House: A Memoir of Incest and Healing.* Toronto: Doubleday Canada.

Gardner, Richard A. 1991. *Sex Abuse Hysteria: Salem Witch Trials Revisited.* Cresskill, N.J.: Creative Therapeutics.

Gillies, Eva. 1976. "Causal Criteria in African Classification of Disease." In *Social Anthropology and Medicine.* Ed. by J. B. Loudon. New York: Academic Press.

Gillin, John. 1948. "Magical Fright." *Psychiatry* 11: 387–400.

Goldman, Laurence. 1993. *The Culture of Coincidence: Accident and Absolute Liability in Huli.* Oxford: Clarendon Press.

Good, Byron J. and Mary-Jo Delvecchio Good. 1982. "Toward a Meaning-Centered Analysis of Popular Illness Categories: 'Fright Illness' and

'Heart Distress' in Iran." In *Cultural Conceptions of Mental Health and Therapy*. Ed. by A. J. Marsella and G. M. White. Dordrecht: Reidel.

Gunderson, John G. and Alex N. Sabo. 1993. "The Phenomenological and Conceptual Interface between Borderline Personality Disorder and PTSD." *American Journal of Psychiatry* 150: 19–27.

Hacking, Ian. 1995. *Rewriting the Soul: Multiple Personality and the Sciences of Memory*. Princeton: Princeton University Press.

Herman, Judith. 1992. *Trauma and Recovery*. New York: Basic Books.

Herman, Judith, et. al. 1989. "Childhood Trauma in Borderline Personality Disorder." *American Journal of Psychiatry* 146: 490–495.

Herman, Judith and Mary R. Harvey. 1993. "The False Memory Debate: Social Science or Social Backlash." *Harvard Mental Health Letter* 9: 4–6.

Horton, Robin. 1961. "Destiny and the Unconscious in West Africa." *Africa* 31: 110–116.

Janet, Pierre. 1925. *Principles of Psychotherapy*. Tans. by H. M. & E. R. Guthrie. London: George Allen & Unwin.

Kenny, Michael G. 1986. *The Passion of Ansel Bourne: Multiple Personality in American Culture*. Washington D.C.: Smithsonian Institution Press.

———. 1995 (in press). "The Recovered Memory Controversy: An Anthropologist's View." *The Journal of Psychiatry and Law*.

Kroll, Jerome. 1993. "Etiologic Theories of Borderline Personality Disorder: A Commentary." In *Borderline Personality Disorder: Etiology and Treatment*. Ed. by J. Paris. Washington D.C.: American Psychiatric Press.

Lindy, Jacob, et al. 1984. "Building a Conceptual Bridge between Civilian Trauma and War Trauma: Preliminary Findings from a Clinical Sample of Vietnam Veterans." In *Post-Traumatic Stress Disorder: Psychological and Biological Sequelae*. Ed. by B. A. van der Kolk. Washington D.C.: American Psychiatric Press.

Logan, Michael H. 1993. "New Lines of Inquiry on the Illness of Susto." *Medical Anthropology* 15: 189–200.

Lopez Austin, A. 1988. *The Human Body and Ideology: Concepts of the Ancient Nahuas*. Trans. by Bernard & Thelma Ortiz de Montellano. Salt Lake City: University of Utah Press.

Mack, John E. 1975. "Borderline States: An Historical Perspective." In *Borderline States in Psychiatry*. Ed. by J. E. Mack. New York: Grune & Stratton.

Morrison, James. 1995. *DSM-IV Made Easy: The Clinician's Guide to Diagnosis*. New York & London: Guilford Press.

Ortiz de Montellano, Bernard. 1990. *Aztec Medicine, Health and Nutrition*. New Brunswick: Rutgers University Press.

O'Nell, Carl W. and Henry A. Selby. 1968. "Sex Differences in the Incidence of Susto in Two Zapotec Pueblos: An Analysis of the Relationships between Sex Role Expectations and a Folk Illness." *Ethnology* 7: 95–105.

Ogata, Susan N., et al. 1990. "Childhood Sexual and Physical Abuse in Adult Patients with Borderline Personality Disorder." *American Journal of Psychiatry* 147: 1008–1012.

Ross, Colin A. 1989. *Multiple Personality Disorder: Diagnosis, Clinical Features, and Treatment.* New York: John Wiley & Sons.

Rubel, Arthur A., et al. 1984. *Susto, A Folk Illness.* Berkeley & Los Angeles: University of California Press.

Saunders, Eleanor A. and Frances Saunders. 1993. "A Critique of Conceptual and Treatment Approaches to Borderline Psychopathology in Light of Findings about Childhood Abuse." *Psychiatry* 56: 188–203.

Scheper-Hughes, Nancy. 1992. *Death without Weeping: The Violence of Everyday Life in Brazil.* Berkeley & Los Angeles: University of California Press.

Scott, Wilbur J. 1990. "PTSD in DSM-III: A Case in the Politics of Diagnosis and Disease." *Social Problems* 37: 294–310.

Showalter, Elaine. 1985. *The Female Malady: Women, Madness, and English Culture, 1830–1980.* New York: Penguin.

Signorini, Italo. 1982. "Patterns of Fright: Multiple Concepts of Susto in a Nahua-Ladino Community of the Sierra de Puebla (Mexico)." *Ethnology* 21: 313–323.

Simmons, Debra. 1992. "Gender Issues and Borderline Personality Disorder: Why Do Females Dominate the Diagnosis?" *Archives of Psychiatric Nursing* 6: 219–223.

Spiegel, David and Etzel Cardena. 1991. "Disintegrated Experience: The Dissociative Disorders Revisited." *Journal of Abnormal Psychology* 100: 366–378.

Summerfield, Derek. 1993. "War and Posttraumatic Stress Disorder: The Question of Social Context." *Journal of Nervous and Mental Disease* 181: 522.

Terr, Lenore C. 1991. "Childhood Traumas: An Outline and Overview." *American Journal of Psychiatry* 148: 10–19.

———. 1994. *Unchained Memories: True Stories of Traumatic Memories Lost and Found.* New York: Basic Books.

Uzzell, Douglas. 1974. "Susto Revisited: Illness as Strategic Role." *American Ethnologist* 1: 369–378.

van der Kolk, Bessel. 1994. "The Body Keeps the Score: Memory and the Evolving Psychobiology of Posttraumatic Stress." *Harvard Review of Psychiatry* 1: 253–265.

van der Kolk, Bessel & Otto van der Hart. 1989. "Pierre Janet and the Breakdown of Adaptation in Psychological Trauma." *American Journal of Psychiatry* 146: 1530–1539.

Young, Alan. 1993. "A Description of How Ideology Shapes Knowledge of a Mental Disorder (Posttraumatic Stress Disorder)." In *Knowledge, Power, and Practice: The Anthropology of Medicine and Everyday Life.* Ed. by Shirley Lindenbaum and Margaret Lock. Berkeley & Los Angeles: University of California Press.

———. 1995. *The Harmony of Illusions: Inventing Post-Traumatic Stress Disorder.* Princeton: Princeton University Press.

———. ND. "Making Facts and Making Time in Psychiatric Research: An Essay in the Anthropology of Scientific Knowledge." Unpublished ms.

8

Landscapes of Memory
Trauma, Narrative, and Dissociation

Laurence J. Kirmayer

Introduction

In Georges Perec's shattering book *W or The Memory of Childhood*, we encounter two interleaved stories. One presents Perec's groping efforts to recall his childhood in wartime France—efforts that result only in a few fragmentary memories immediately taken apart by his own critical footnotes that correct the many imprecisions and confabulations. What gradually emerges is the story of a childhood lived at the margins of the Holocaust, of a father who dies in the Resistance, of a mother deported to die in a Nazi camp, of a Jewish boy raised by relatives as Catholic. Throughout, Perec struggles with absence: he fantasizes about a family life that never was, then lapses into a deep silence in which his mother is never mentioned again. The flat, matter-of-fact tone in which the story is told intensifies rather than veils his grief.

The second narrative, which alternates chapters with the first throughout the book, is also drawn from childhood reveries but, after a false start involving the search for a lost child, it becomes the fantasy of "W," an island nation devoted to the Olympic ideal of athletic competition.[1] Projected forward in the writer's imagination, the account of life in "W" grows increasingly bizarre and sinister until it converges on a portrait of a Nazi concentration camp.

The two narratives, personal history and fantasy, seem unrelated at first, going past each other like two ships in the fog. In the space between them, however, an ominous terror and grief are created that surpass what would be felt from either sentimental recollection or gothic tale of horror. In its carefully constructed gaps, Perec's narrative alludes to another untold story. This artful construction did not occur to Perec at first; he simply aimed to write a novel developing his adolescent fantasy of "W." As each chapter was completed, he published it as a serial in a literary magazine. When Perec found himself descending into a personal pain that was too unmanageable or unknown—particularly in the chapter that describes the methods of reproduction in "W"—he broke off the story and reentered psychoanalysis.[2] Later he solved the esthetic and psychological problem of finding distance from the text by constructing a fiction that affords the reader the experience of complicity in seeking out, and hiding from, memory.

Reading *W* as autobiography reminds us of the fundamental connection between memory and imagination, retelling and re-creating the self. Of course, the narrative based on "pure" fantasy is more seamless and integrated than the autobiographical narrative for which memory offers only snapshots, shadows, and feelings half-acknowledged and half-suppressed. Indeed, the very incompleteness and tentativeness of the autobiographical account attests to its veracity. Yet more of Perec's predicament—more of his self—is revealed in the fantasy story recovered and re-imagined from adolescence, as the transmuted fears of childhood drive the Olympic ideal toward a Nazi world of tortures and humiliations in the name of the athletic superman, impervious to any emotion other than lust for victory.

In Perec's story the greatest terror and loss are presented not in the explicit narrative of W but in the gaps between the two narratives, in the frailty and impersistence of memory and the felt absence of mother, family, and a safe world set against the unexpectedly dark journey of fantasy. Perec's fiction, then, serves to introduce the problem of the relation of narrative to remembering and forgetting and to that special type of forgetting—unexpected and precipitous—that is called dissociation.

In this chapter I discuss the representation of memory in narratives of trauma. Recent accounts of victims of childhood trauma will be contrasted with the testimony of survivors of the Holocaust. These accounts differ strikingly in the contours of the struggle to remember and forget. For the childhood trauma victim, the violence of traumatic events renders events difficult to remember, while for the Holocaust victim violence renders events ineradicable. Whatever the true (and still largely unknown) epidemiology of responses to trauma, what accounts for this stereotypical difference in current cultural representations of the two types of trauma narrative?

Survivors of the Holocaust are usually depicted as overwhelmed by memories and unwilling to recount their tale for fear of the pain it will re-evoke. Their problem is not the limits of memory but of language—the inadequacy of ordinary words to express all they have witnessed. The Holocaust presents an incomprehensible catastrophe that undermines the very possibility of coherent narrative (Funkenstein 1993).

In contrast, adults with a history of childhood abuse are often depicted as initially unaware of their traumatic experiences as memories. They suffer from dissociative disorders. They evince their traumatic past through symptoms, including physical and emotional pain, numbing, self-injury, substance abuse, lapses of memory, and changes of identity (Herman 1992; Terr 1994).

In both cases, symptoms are explained by trauma. However, for the Holocaust survivor, the reaction is one of being overwhelmed and then responding by numbing, detachment, or suppression so that one's story sits forever at the edges of consciousness to be worked around or told in fragments. For the survivor of childhood abuse, the response to overwhelming trauma is a form of mental escape by resolute partition of memory, self, and experience. There is no narrative of trauma then, no memory—only speaking in signs.

This difference may be understood as a consequence of mechanisms of memory stemming from different psychological defenses or from specific psychiatric disorders (post-traumatic stress disorder versus dissociative amnesia). This view treats trauma narratives as direct outcomes of psychobiological mechanisms of memory which, at present, remain largely hypothetical. In what follows, however, I shall argue that the distinctive qualities of trauma narratives can also be understood as differences in the culturally constructed *landscape of memory*, the metaphoric terrain that shapes the distance and effort required to remember affectively charged and socially defined events that initially may be vague, impressionistic, or simply absent from memory. Landscapes of memory are given shape by the personal and social significance of specific memories but also draw from *meta-memory*—implicit models of memory which influence what can be recalled and cited as veridical. Narratives of trauma may be understood then as cultural constructions of personal and historical memory.

Meta-Memory: Cultural Models of Remembering and Forgetting

The notion of memory is an hypostatization, turning a family of diverse processes into a thing by conflating the stories we tell about our past with the many ways in which we are changed by experience. Popular conceptions of memory make a number of assumptions not born out by experimental studies. In one common version, memories are "snapshots," laid down at the time of experience through a process of registration. They persist unchanged throughout our lives to be recalled when we look for them, like opening a photo album. If certain memories remain hidden or difficult to retrieve it is only because we are looking in the wrong place or, as we grow older, because of the accumulated clutter that must be cleared away. Of course, like photographs, memories may fade and this can limit the vividness and detail of recall.

Research contradicts this naive view of memory (Neisser 1992; 1994). Memory is anything but a photographic record of experience; it is a roadway full of potholes, badly in need of repair, worked on day and night by revisionist crews. What is registered is highly selective and thoroughly transformed by interpretation and semantic encoding at the moment of experience. What can be veridically recalled is limited and routinely reconstructed to fit models of what might have—*must* have—happened. When encouraged to flesh it out, we readily engage in imaginative elaboration and confabulation and, once we have done this, the bare bones memory is lost forever within the animated story we have constructed (Bartlett 1932; Loftus 1993).

Naive theories of memory also assume that memories are "time-stamped," and therefore offer themselves up in sequence. This sequence then provides a temporal structure for narrative. Each memory carries with it instructions for how to insert it into a larger narrative (like a piece of a puzzle with instructions on its back). Research suggests, however, that memory for the timing of events is not usually tied to images of the events themselves (Friedman 1993). Instead, the process typically works in the other direction: narrative structure supplies the temporal sequence of memory.

Similar processes of reconstruction, governed by different narrative templates, give rise to other aspects of memory. Memories are not stamped with their source, so that it is easy to forget where or how we learned something ("source amnesia") and to misremember inventions as actual events, constructing images to fit our knowledge and belief (Belli and Loftus 1994; Laurence and Perry 1983). To take a trivial example, many people who recall themselves swimming report seeing an image of their whole body as if from the air. Clearly, an imaginative construction has been substituted for veridical memory.

There are, of course, many forms of memory. The dominant cultural prototype of memory is declarative: we are able to describe what we know (semantic memory) and what we have experienced (episodic memory). The emphasis on declarative memory as the exemplar follows from our models of consciousness as representation. But we do not always have pictures for memories: often we have knowledge, skills, or dispositions to act which are represented by an image only after the fact. We are unable to remember the details of most of what we have lived through, although these events have surely formed us. There is much that we commemorate through our accent, posture, habits of gesture and thought—things we may be unaware of and forever unable to describe except in vague, abstract, or secondhand terms. These forms of nondeclarative or implicit memory have been called "procedural"—they can be shown but not directly described.

All forms of memory show great plasticity. The effects of imagination on reconstruction and recall are pervasive.[3] The tendency to underestimate this—and so to treat ordinary memory as veridical recall—probably reflects a more general tendency in contemporary Western culture to underestimate (and to pathologize) the role of imagination in normal psychological development (Watkins 1986). If memory is much less determinate than a snapshot of the past (as folk theory assumes), then the question of what engenders it is, perhaps, less crucial to its power and authenticity than what authorizes and stabilizes memory so that it becomes *my* memory and *the* memory of an event.

Folk models of memory govern what we try to remember, what we expect others to be able to remember, what we deem a memory and how we compose memories through narrative. Some types of events are meant to be easily remembered and others are not. Societies have a range of institutions, calendars, rituals, and practices to serve collective remembering (Connerton 1989). These may also anchor personal memory even as they serve to distort and change it.

Psychotherapy constitutes one important arena for the work of remembering in contemporary North American society. The experience of insight sought in psychodynamic psychotherapy is closely allied to the recovery of personal historical memory. In psychotherapy, the impress of past events is revealed in two ways: first, through the historical recall of declarative memory, in which events and feelings are described explicitly. The historical accounts produced in therapy are now widely recognized as narrative reconstructions (Spence 1982). Opinion differs, however, on the extent to which this reconstruction is based on episodic memory (that is, recollecting factual details of scenes and events) or semantic memory that recovers only abstract knowledge and meanings. In either case, reconstruction exerts a mutative effect on the past—supplying missing details in images of episodic memory and imputing meanings to events that were not present when they originally occurred (Lewis 1995).

A second dimension to personal history is revealed in the way we react rather than recollect. Psychodynamic theory allows much of our behavior to be interpreted as symptoms and signs that are residues of repressed memories, kept out of awareness by unconscious mechanisms of defense. Psychodynamically oriented clinicians claim that after long intervals of amnesia, repressed memories may be activated by idiosyncratic associations and more or less vividly recalled (Terr 1994). Unfortunately, there is little or no experimental evidence for repression and so the concept currently meets with great skepticism (Crews 1995; Holmes 1990; Loftus 1993; Merskey 1995; Pope and Hudson 1995).

Whatever the merits of repression theory, however, it is obvious our behavior tells a tale that, in some measure, is divorced from our conscious experience. Some of this behavior may be governed by hidden, unconscious, or repressed memories and images, but much of it is better understood as *procedural* and *distributed*—emerging out of interaction with others in a larger social context. In the therapeutic relationship, procedural memory is manifested not through recollection but through imaginative enactment. But the meanings of enactment reside as much in the social context and interpretive strategies of the listener/observer/interlocutor as they do in the past experience and current intentions of the speaker.

The context of retelling is crucial to the nature of memory. There are many possible situations of retelling, ranging from parenthetical remarks inserted into a conversation with one's doctor to explain bodily scars (Young 1989), the soliloquies of psychotherapy (Davies and Frawley 1994), courtroom depositions (Terr 1994), or videotaped testimonies to be stored in official archives to honor the dead or as a bulwark against future tyranny (Langer 1991). Indeed, even where retelling does not—and may never—occur, there is a "virtual space," a potential social context of retelling that influences the most private reconstructions of memory.

Narratives of Childhood Abuse: Forgetting to Remember

The struggle to recall distant, fragmentary, and unavailable memories is at the center of current professional texts and popular accounts of the pathology and treatment of the adult sequelae of childhood abuse (Briere 1993; Davies and Frawley 1994; Herman 1992; Terr 1994). This literature, and recent court cases, have spawned a controversy on the nature of "true" and "false" memories of childhood trauma. At issue is whether some individuals may forget about very significant events, such as childhood abuse, for decades, only to have them resurface in response to associative triggers or the recreation of elements of the original context. A skeptical interpretation of these delayed recollections argues that they are imaginative reconstructions or outright fabrications driven by leading questions and the demand characteristics of psychotherapy, courtrooms, and self-help groups (Crews 1995; Frankel 1993; Loftus 1993).

In the childhood trauma literature, traumatic memories are held to be fundamentally different from ordinary memories (e.g. Terr 1994). The intensity of emotion and pain that occurs with trauma engraves memories more deeply and indelibly than usual. The narrowing of attention in trauma and the subsequent warding off of the meaning of trauma may lead the bodily aspects of memory to persist even when the image or content of the memory is unavailable (van der Kolk and van der Hart 1995). This implies a kind of spectral splitting of the sensory, emotional, and cognitive aspects of experiences into different types of memories, which may persist as conditioned emotional responses, "emotional postures" (Griffith and Griffith 1994), or systematic misinterpretations of events. This same emotional intensity may lead memories to persist and to intrude on everyday awareness in the characteristic symptoms of posttraumatic stress disorder.

The theory of repression claims that when memories are laden with (or evocative of) intensely painful feelings, they may be warded off over long periods of time. The usual distinction between suppression and repression is that the former involves a conscious effort not to think of something while the latter is "unconscious," which in psychodynamic theory means both automatic (i.e. non-conscious) and motivated (that is, related to conflicts of desire). It is the fear of looking at traumatic memories that keeps them repressed. Repression differs, in turn, from dissociation, which implies a narrowing or splitting of consciousness so that some memories may be put aside.

Dissociation refers to a gap in the normal integration of memory, identity and experience (Spiegel and Cardeña 1991). As behavior, dissociation is defined by family resemblance among a wide range of phenomena, including psychogenic amnesias, conversion symptoms (e.g. hysterical blindness or paralysis), fugue states, and multiple personality (Kirmayer 1994). As a process, dissociation is offered as an explanation for forgetting, or interrupted access to memory, which is nonetheless registered and potentially available, indeed, demonstrably affecting past and present behavior and experience by its palpable absence.

In much recent literature, dissociation is closely linked with trauma (Herman 1992; Spiegel 1990). Dissociation is viewed as an adaptive response to overwhelming and inescapable threat or trauma. In effect, the victim escapes by walling off distressing experiences and memories or retreating to a corner of his or her mind.

In contrast to the elusiveness of repression, dissociative phenomena are readily reproduced in the laboratory with hypnosis.[4] Patients with dissociative disorders may be especially prone to use dissociation due to temperamental traits including openness to absorbing experiences, hypnotizability, or a "fantasy-prone" personality (Lynn and Rhue 1988). The direct linkage of trauma and dissociation appears simplistic in the face of research demonstrating the effects of temperament, family history, psychopathology, and current context on dissociation (Tilman, Nash and Lerner 1994).

Dissociation is often depicted in the literature as a rigid walling off of memories in an all or none fashion, but this does not accord well with either clinical or experimental evidence. In clinical reality, as in the laboratory, dissociation is found in all degrees of intensity in the same individual and is characterized more by its fluidity than by its rigid constancy. Dissociative experiences—as shifts in mental state or changes in voice—are not simply absences but can be accessed with appropriate rituals. When sufficient trust and safety have been established, patients with dissociative disorders are easily moved from one state to another, one memory to another, by implicit suggestions or shifts in metaphors for the self. This sensitivity of memory to the metaphoric implications of language is a crucial difference between accounts of repression and dissociation, as the former is portrayed as a rigid barrier overcome at a critical moment of de-repression while the latter involves fluid movements back and forth across an "amnestic barrier" that responds to shifts in metaphor with more or less permeability. Dissociation thus emerges as a more plausible mechanism than repression for psychogenic amnesias but one with quite different psychological and interpersonal dynamics than those posited for repression.

Research suggests that a variety of mechanisms may be at work in trauma-related amnesia or dissociated memories (Koss, Tromp and Tharan 1995). There may be effects on encoding and registration at the time of trauma, including a narrowing of attention, interference of emotion with information processing, and an alteration in self-consciousness (Christianson 1992). Subsequently, individuals may avoid thinking about painful events by selective deployment of attention (avoiding cues or situations liable to provide cues to remembering) and self-distraction. Traumatic memories may be isolated from other networks of association by interpreting them as dissonant or inconsistent with self-representation and personal history. Finally, memories may be actively suppressed by efforts to concentrate on alternatives, refusal to speak about them, and flat denials (to self or others) that they occurred. No matter how thin, such denials may undermine the processes of rehearsal and semantic bridge-building necessary for ready recall.

There are also factors that may influence traumatic memory at the time of recall. These include affect or mood state–dependent learning, whereby knowledge acquired in one affective state can only be accessed in a similar affective state (Bower 1981). Such mood state–dependent dissociation of learning or memory is usually partial or incomplete. In the case of traumatic memories, it is claimed that the greater intensity of emotion associated with trauma and its effects results in stronger dissociation, a steeper contour to the hills and vales of memory (Spiegel 1990). But mood is only one aspect of the context of retelling. Telling a story of trauma or reliving it occurs in a larger matrix of narrative and social praxis (Bartlett 1932; Bruner 1990). The form of narrative may also influence what can and cannot be recalled.

Although we do not know the effects of trauma on registration and recall, most of the arguments about narrowing of attention and affect state–dependence and defensive dealing with emotional context would make traumatic memories *more*, not less, malleable and influenced by imagination and context-sensitive reconstruction. Given this malleability and the vagaries of the reconstructive process, we should not be surprised that recollection of traumatic events waxes and wanes according to need and circumstance.[5]

The fragmented nature of dissociative narrative comes from the focusing of attention in the traumatic moment and from the subsequent absence of consensual social factors to help weave together the dispersed parts (Kirmayer 1992; 1994). Dissociation is a rupture in narrative, but it is also maintained by narrative because the shape of narrative around the dissociation protects (reveals and conceals) the gap. Dimensions of narrative relevant to processes of dissociation include coherence, voice, and time: that is, the extent to which the narrative of self is integrated or fragmented, univocal or polyvocal, and whether the flow of narrative time is progressive, regressive, or static. Narrative conventions may give rise to dissociation in several ways: by tolerating gaps in accounts of memory, identity, and experience when they occur; by expecting such gaps and creating a place for them in the story; by hiding gaps from others with diversions; or by hiding gaps from oneself by inventing alternate selves. The progression here from tolerance through expectation to concealment suggests a typology of dissociative processes based on social interaction.

What makes the dissociated moods, images, bodily feelings, and role enactments of dissociative identity disorder into a (weak) semblance of "personalities" is precisely their privileged access to autobiographical memories. To achieve this privileged access, memory must be partitioned and divided up among the putative selves. This may occur in the flow of experience or in the act of rehearsal and recollection.

Traumatic experience is not a story but a cascade of experiences, eruptions, crevasses, a sliding of tectonic plates that undergird the self. These disruptions then give rise to an effort to interpret and so to smooth, stabilize, and recalibrate. The effect of these processes is to create a specific narrative landscape. This landscape must fit with (and so is governed by) folk models of memory. Reconstructions of traumatic memory involve the building up of a landscape of local coherence to better manage or contain it, to present it convincingly to others and, finally, to have done with it. But, as the metaphor of landscape suggests, the narrative reconstructions of memory are not so much managed as lived in—offering vistas that reveal and conceal. Others may dwell within the same landscape, though, inevitably, they see it from different vantage points.

Holocaust Narratives: Writing the Unrightable

Trauma and its legacy through time raise profound questions about the relationship of narrative and self. Torture, violence, and abuse present challenges to constructivist theories in anthropology, since they represent the breakdown of the fabric of consensual reality. Victims report a degree of alienation and estrangement from self and others that throws into high relief the tacit dimensions of social life. Even witnesses at many removes from the scene of violence may experience vicarious pain and confusion that threaten the coherence of everyday life.

This challenge is nowhere more evident than in the testimonies of Holocaust survivors. Most accounts of the Holocaust in literature and mass media have used esthetic devices to mute and contain the chaos that persists closer to the experience. Recently, studies have appeared examining the qualities of Holocaust testimonies collected by interview and recorded on videotape for posterity (Greenspan 1992; Langer 1991; 1995). In these testimonies, the speaker does not have the same opportunities for careful composition and editing after-the-fact that characterize literary accounts (Young 1988). Consequently, these accounts emphasize the emotional difficulties of retelling and the profound effect of living with memories that subvert the everyday construction of the self.

Langer (1991) provides a searching analysis of some of the fourteen hundred testimonies in the Fortunoff Video Archives for Holocaust testimonies at Yale University. He organizes his discussion around the root metaphors of different types of memory revealed in the testimonies: deep memory, anguished memory, humiliated memory, tainted memory, unheroic memory. Each form is distinctive in that it involves some disruption or violation of the social conditions for "ordinary" memory. Each shows the link of memory to some affective process or pathology. If memories are narrative reconstructions, in this view each form of reconstruction (or failure of reconstruction) is governed by an underlying affective predicament or paradox that has intrapsychic, bodily, and social/political elements. The predicament that governs retelling is revealed by the emotions, poetic force, and gaps in the story. Take, for example, what Langer calls "humiliated memory":

> If anguished memory may be seen as discontent in search of a form, humiliated memory recalls an utter distress that shatters all molds designed to contain a unified and irreproachable image of the self. Its voice represents pure misery, even decades after the events that it narrates. Neither time nor amnesia soothes its gnawing. After hearing its testimony, we are less prone to dismiss as exaggeration the insistence by many surviving victims that the humiliations they endured in the camps were often worse than death. The details uncovered by humiliated memory dispute the claim still advanced by many commentators that the invincible spirit provided an armor invulnerable to Nazi assaults against the self (77).

> Like what I have called deep and anguished memory, humiliated memory is an especially intense form of uncompensating recall. Instead of restoring a sense of power or control over a disabling past (one of the presumed goals of therapy—and perhaps of history too), it achieves the reverse, reanimating the governing impotence of the worst moments in a distinctly non-therapeutic way (84).

In his metaphors, Langer puts affect before memory. When affect is put after memory, deferred, hidden, or obscured, we have the various methods of avoiding painful recollection.

> Numerous strategies are available to individuals who wish to escape the burden of a vexatious past: forget, repress, ignore, deny, or simply falsify the facts. For reasons difficult to ascertain, what I have called humiliated memory seems immune to these forms of evasion (96).

Langer invokes a range of methods by which memory may be evaded or occluded; yet "dissociate" is absent from this list, as it is from most literary and clinical accounts of Holocaust experience and pathology. Whereas Holocaust survivors might be expected to suffer from severe dissociation, they are described instead as suffering from painful recollections, anxiety, or numbing and emotional disconnection. In all research studies of Holocaust survivors published to date, mention of dissociative

183

pathology is muted or altogether absent (Eitinger 1980; Krystal 1988; Kuch & Cox 1992; Niederland 1968; Tilman, Nash & Lerner 1994).

Despite this absence, oral testimonies give striking examples of dereal-ization, depersonalization, duality of consciousness, and disturbed mem-ory in symptomatic narratives that closely resemble—yet remain distinct from—dissociation.

Asked if she lives with Auschwitz inside her, writer Charlotte Delbo (1995) replies:

> No—I live beside it. Auschwitz is there, fixed and unchangeable, but wrapped in the impervious skin of memory that segregates it-self from the present "me." Unlike the snake's skin, the skin of memory doesn't renew itself . . . I have the feeling . . . that the "self" who was in the camp isn't me, isn't the person who is here op-posite you. No, it's too unbelievable. And everything that hap-pened to this other "self," the one from Auschwitz, doesn't touch me now, doesn't concern me, so distinct are deep memory [m moire profound] and common memory [mémoire ordinarie] (quoted in: Langer 1991: 5).[6]

Delbo here describes depersonalization, derealization and a doubling of identity that, in another context, would surely be characterized as dis-sociative, yet her own awareness of this predicament prevents the label from being attached. The metaphors of doubling and self-estrangement break up the narrative representation of self; but the effect is conscious and self-reflective and so does not result in amnesia.

This same doubling or duality runs through many narratives. Langer suggests that the distinction between deep memory and common (ordi-nary) memory helps to explain the two strands found in Holocaust nar-ratives in which intense bodily experiences of reliving and narrative descriptions of the self from a more detached vantage point interfere with one another.

Even the sense of multiple voices within the person, characteristic of the most extreme form of dissociation, dissociative identity disorder (for-merly, multiple personality disorder), is approximated in the accounts of Holocaust survivors:

> As we listen to the shifting idioms of the multiple voices emerging from the same person, we are present at the birth of a self made per-manently provisional as a result of fragmentary excavations that never coalesce into a single, recognizable monument to the past (Langer 1991: 161).

The self is only whole (or undiminished) when it is allowed a coherent and spacious field of moral action. The disjunction between self at the time of trauma (e.g. life in a concentration camp) and at present shows the difficulty in linking the narratives and hence, the partial existence of two selves. These two selves live in two distinct worlds and are joined through the continuity of private pain and collective memory that spans the two worlds. The presence of an unbroken thread of pain gives rise to the nagging need to integrate the ruptured self. If either were suppressed there might be further fragmentation of memory and identity without the pressing need for integration. Indeed, this is the damaging consequence of the systematic attack on the heroic ego.

> The psychological consequences of the Nazi strategy to fragment identity by allying it with disunity instead of community is confirmed by Joseph K., who recalls placards posted in his town listing the names of ten residents who would be summarily executed if there were any attack on a German. Heroic endeavor, whether as resistance or sabotage, thus could become not only potential suicide but, as Joseph K. insists, a version of murder. . . . In excavating such impossible realities, unheroic memory suffocates the fertile concept of identity that we cherish as we listen (182).

When survivors speak of guilt, rage, or despair, their emotions are understood to be a pale shadow of the past; the magnitude of suffering, past and present, is understood to exceed what can be told in mere words.

> All such accounts are based on the attempt to give comprehensible, communicable form to memories that for survivors live on as the negation of comprehensible and communicable form. Set against those memories, all such accounts are attempts to "make a story" of what is "not a story" (Greenspan 1992: 145).[7]

To express strong emotion is still to experience human connection and struggle to give shape to one's suffering but, as the extremity of the situation builds in survivors" accounts,

> narrative unfolding stops, and instead of a plot's trajectory through foreground and background, we hear a staccato of snapshot images, each present and surrounding. While this way of recounting is, like the story mode, also a mediating form, it is as though memories start to retell themselves at these times. Crowding in at a faster pace than the recounter can speak them . . . (Greenspan 1992: 149)/

The image here is of the inrush of memory breaking down narrative, because narrative is an insufficient container or organizer for traumatic experience. But narrative is not only the conveyor of structure, smoothing, and holding, it can also create crevasses, ruptures, emptiness, and deep wells of nonbeing (Greenspan: 148). Elie Wiesel and other survivors speak of having died during the Holocaust yet continuing to live. Charlotte Delbo describes this experience of dying while alive as a recurrent event:

> The skin covering the memory of Auschwitz . . . is tough: Sometimes, however, it bursts, and gives back its contents. In a dream, the will is powerless. And in these dreams, there I see myself again, me, yes me, just as I know I was: scarcely able to stand . . . pierced with cold, filthy, gaunt, and the pain is so unbearable, so exactly the pain I suffered there, that I feel it again physically, I feel it again through my whole body, which becomes a block of pain, and I feel death seizing me, I feel myself die. Fortunately, in my anguish, I cry out. The cry awakens me, and I emerge from the nightmare, exhausted. It takes days for everything to return to normal, for memory to be "refilled" and for the skin of memory to mend itself. I become myself again, the one you know, who can speak to you of Auschwitz without showing any sign of distress or emotion (quoted in: Langer 1991: 6–7).

This account reveals the degree to which the "intrusions" of traumatic memory can make the self alien until the quotidian self can be reasserted only by isolating the unbearable feeling.

> As contrary as it is to our usual logic and experience, this simultaneity of being and not-being should be understood literally. The copresence of ongoing death and ongoing life—without resolution or higher synthesis—is, for survivors, embodied reality (Greenspan 1992: 148)

In the face of this breakdown of narrative coherence, Greenspan emphasizes the therapeutic value of having Holocaust survivors tell their stories. This recounting aims to break the silence that has overtaken survivors and that, in a way, has rendered them symptomatic. At the same time, the therapist's act of bearing witness provides a social context that allows the story to cohere both because of the emotional meaning of receiving another's empathic attention and because it invokes the tacit dimension of shared (or public) history. Even fragments can be read as a story if a larger narrative context is supplied by an audience primed by history.

Landscapes of Memory

In the face of such stark examples of altered identity, depersonalization, derealization, and intense motivation to forget, we must ask why Holocaust narratives emphasize recollection while the current literature of child abuse places so much emphasis on amnesia. The two types of narrative reflect different forms of pathology: post-traumatic stress disorder characterized by intrusions, and dissociative disorders characterized by gaps. Could there be a difference in the prevalence of each pathology in different traumatic situations? In the absence of any satisfactory epidemiology to answer this question, it is nevertheless instructive to consider some alternative explanations for the difference represented in the literature.

From a psychological point of view, what differentiates these narratives are differences in modes of attention and self-awareness.[8] These could reflect differences in personality traits; however, such individual differences would result in a difference between groups only if they influenced survival in the camps. Since dissociation is usually viewed as a useful strategy for surviving inescapable traumatic situations, Holocaust survivors might be expected to show *more*, not less of the requisite traits than other populations.

The two situations differ in the degree, type, and duration of trauma. Up to a certain level of severity or duration of trauma, individuals might respond one way and then switch to another pattern of response. For example, Terr (1994) claims that single traumatic events usually result in clear recollections and associated fears, while prolonged and repeated traumas may lead the person to develop more elaborate strategies of repression and dissociation. Again, Holocaust survivors should display more, not less dissociative pathology than childhood abuse survivors.

It might be argued that Holocaust and childhood trauma accounts differ because the trauma occurred at different ages. The traumas of the Holocaust were visited on all age groups but most of the testimonies we have are of survivors who were adolescents or adults at the time of the violence. When childhood Holocaust survivors are interviewed, some do indeed display difficulty in recollection (Kestenberg and Fogelman 1994; Stein 1993). But if coherent memories are never recovered, is this dissociative amnesia or simply the failure to register memories in a socially accessible, adult form, common to all childhood experience (Lewis 1995; White and Pillemer 1979)? The tendency in some recent work to use the same leading questions and techniques of imaginative elaboration now common in reconstructing childhood abuse memories, further clouds the issue (cf. Kestenberg and Fogelman 1994: xiii, 6–12).

While it is tempting to attribute differences between the literatures of childhood sexual abuse and Holocaust survivors to differences in the actual prevalence of experiences, available evidence is insufficient to support this conclusion. In the case of the Holocaust, as with clinical samples of patients with childhood abuse, we do not know how many experienced dissociation during or after their traumatic experiences but recovered and never sought help. An epidemiological survey might find similar levels of intrusive recollections and dissociative amnesias in both populations. Certainly, there are many—probably, the majority of—individuals who tell of their childhood abuse without dissociation. And there must be Holocaust survivors who have dissociated their experience and whose stories, therefore, have not been told. In fact, intrusions and amnestic gaps often co-exist in the same individual. The distinction between prototypical narratives then, may not reflect actual differences in psychopathology but rather differing expectations for recollection and different contexts for retelling.

This points toward a social explanation for the difference in prototypical narratives. The situation of the Holocaust survivor differs strikingly from the usual account of the adult victim of childhood abuse, now prone to dissociative disorders. While Holocaust stories involve bearing witness to what is widely, if not universally, recognized as a human catastrophe, personal stories of abuse are revelatory, shameful, and damaging to the individual and family. In the case of childhood abuse, it is precisely the distinctive qualities of the socially constructed relationship to the past that foster dissociation.

It is easy to forget when there is a tacit agreement not to remember. Terr (1994: 235ff) describes a situation where, with no ongoing family conflict or abuse, positive memories of a brother who died in childhood were forgotten by a child because his parents decided to avoid talking and thinking about the event. The memories were recovered later when the son, now an adult, insisted on a family ritual of remembering. Although the account is anecdotal, the experience is commonplace. That such family decisions can interfere with the recollection of ordinary—even positive—events without any stern injunctions reveals how easy it is to forget when there are no collective occasions for remembering. Like a magician performing sleight of hand, every gesture of social life then points us away from details which would provoke memory and recollection.

Stein (1993: 226ff) tells the story of forgetting (repressing?) a memory of being raped when he was eight, yet recollecting all the surrounding memories of his time in hiding as a child during the Holocaust. It was more difficult to recollect the shameful personal memory of this violence than the terrors and suffering shared with his older sister. Only when his sister, on her death bed, told him of this never-spoken-of traumatic event, did memories return.

This story of amnesia for childhood sexual trauma embedded in recollection of Holocaust experience points to the significance of telling one's story not only after a traumatic event but during its unfolding. Whole communities experienced the trauma of the Holocaust and so were able to talk about it openly or share tacit acknowledgment of its horrors. Whether the story was spoken aloud to others or told to oneself in internal monologue or dialogue, this narrative process served to maintain memory.

In situations where telling and even thinking are forbidden, where individuals are utterly alone (in prison, or the isolation of an abusive family), they still may construct a virtual space where their story can be narrated. When this virtual space is imagined as a social landscape, memory remains accessible. When the costs of recollection seem catastrophic for self or others, memory may be sequestered in a virtual (mental) space that is asocial, a space that closes in on itself through the conviction that no telling will ever be possible. Dissociation is the sequestration of memory in a virtual space shaped by the social demand—and personal decision—to remain silent, or to speak the unspeakable only with a voice one can disown.[9]

The historical circumstances of Holocaust survivors gave them little opportunity to dissociate. Instead, they felt compelled to tell their stories.[10] After liberation, survivors were witnesses to a public catastrophe. However, survivors soon learned to be selective in their retelling—lest they meet with incomprehension or others recoiling and avoiding them. They found themselves in what Langer calls a position of "moral quarantine," their stories too corrosive to the moral order. In this position the management of memory becomes more difficult. Survivors found they could not tell their stories again until a public literature of the Holocaust became more available, beginning in the 1960s with the publication of Hilberg's *The Destruction of the European Jews*. In recent years, there have been increasing numbers of Holocaust accounts, movies, monuments and public commemorations (Young 1988; 1993). Each collective act of remembering makes it more possible for individuals to recollect and tell their personal stories.

There is a crucial distinction between the social space in which the trauma occurred and the contemporary space in which it is (or is not) recalled. In the case of the dissociative disorder patient and the Holocaust victim, the difference is between a public space of solidarity and a private space of shame. Trauma shared by a whole community creates a potential public space for retelling. If a community agrees traumatic events occurred and weaves this fact into its identity, then collective memory survives and individual memory can find a place (albeit transformed) within that landscape. If a family or a community agrees that a trauma did not happen, then it vanishes from collective memory and the possibility for individual memory is severely strained.

A public space of trauma provides a consensual reality and collective memory through which the fragments of personal memory can be assembled, reconstructed, and displayed with a tacit assumption of validity. A private space of trauma places the victim in a predicament, since the validation of suffering depends on recovering enough memory to make it real for others, but this memory can be retrieved only by reliving or representing the place of victimization. Of course, this experience of reliving is vigorously resisted by rememberer and audience alike.

While "moral quarantine" makes Holocaust witnesses cautious in their accounts, they can afford to be reticent, since the underlying horror of their tale goes without saying. We are willing to listen to survivors tell their broken stories, and relive their stories as symptoms, because we grant the transhuman scale of what they have suffered. We do not see their failure to surpass their traumas and move on as a consequence of personal weakness but as the inhuman force of the evil they have endured. This is the blasted landscape in which the Holocaust narrative is inserted.

The landscape of "ordinary" family life in which memories of abuse must be situated does not allow the same tacit validation. The mode of remembering and telling one's story changes greatly when one faces the task of convincing a reluctant or skeptical listener of the reality of what one has experienced. The same terrible dread of annihilation felt by survivors of the Holocaust when they hear of those who seek to negate its reality is felt by victims of a severe childhood abuse when others minimize, trivialize, or place it on a continuum with ordinary evil. There is a need to have the rupture with ordinary experience acknowledged by others— even as this acknowledgment serves to make a bridge back to the quotidian.

Conclusion

I have contrasted two types of narrative: that of the Holocaust survivor whose suffering is (consciously) related to ineradicable memories, who suffers, in effect, from excess of memory and is driven by the need to commemorate collective history; and the narrative of the victim of childhood abuse who suffers from amnesia and must regain contested memory to reclaim and rebuild an uncertain self. Although these two very different situations are sometimes conflated for rhetorical purposes—for example, in Judith Herman's (1992) theory which treats both as causes of "complex posttraumatic stress disorder"—I have offered theoretical and empirical grounds for distinguishing the two at the level of the social and cultural shaping of memory.

Trauma victims may show either dissociation or intrusive memory. The difference between types of memory may be explained psychologically. On one currently popular account, trauma indelibly engraves episodic memories, but the intense affect associated with trauma may lead to affective state–dependent memory and dissociation or to repression. This simple conjunction of trauma and dissociation is complicated by individual differences in the propensity to use dissociation; those who are prone to dissociation may experience amnesias with little or no traumatic provocation. Those who are less prone to dissociation will tend to retain the memory of traumatic events and may be more likely to experience intrusive recollections or ruminations.

To this psychological account, I have tried to add a social dimension. Registration, rehearsal, and recall are governed by social contexts and cultural models for memories, narratives, and life stories. Such cultural models influence what is viewed as salient, how it is interpreted and encoded at the time of registration and, most important for long-term memories that serve autobiographical functions, what is socially possible to speak of and what must remain hidden and unacknowledged.

The distinction between forget, repress, ignore, and dissociate is not simply an arbitrary choice of metaphor. Each is a phenomenologically distinct form of not-remembering. Even where the mechanisms underlying the metaphor are unknown, the way we understand memory influences remembering itself, giving life to each metaphor. And each of these methods of evading memory is related to larger social and political circumstances surrounding memorable events and the circumstances of their recounting. As remembering is a social act, so too is forgetting. The contemporary landscape of memory is created through the modern *ars memoria*, which involve not so much feats of hypermnesia as of strategic forgetting.

The differences between types of memory in prototypical narratives of childhood abuse and Holocaust testimonials may then be understood less in terms of mental mechanisms *per se*, than in terms of the social conditions governing recollection and retelling. Recollection is based on the past context in which the story is historically rooted and the current context in which the story is retold.

Trauma narratives are rhetorical forms that emerge from the effort to anneal or bridge sundered parts of the self. Traumatic memories are imaginatively reconstructed along narrative lines guided by bodily experience and cultural models of memory and self. Dissociative amnesia then arises from embodied aspects of experience: the neurological capacity to forge coherence, the psychological capacity to meliorate pain with self-soothing, and the social capacity to speak the unspeakable, to tell a story no one wants to hear. The embodied basis of dissociative pathology includes both the rigidity or stuckness of the individual and the failure of the world to bear witness.

The social world fails to bear witness for many reasons. Even reparative accounts of the terrible things that happen to people (violations, traumas, losses) are warded off because of their capacity to create vicarious fear and pain and because they constitute a threat to current social and political arrangements. Psychotherapy aims to help individuals get unstuck by bearing witness to their suffering. To be most effective it must also support their efforts to be heard beyond the consulting room, in a local world.

Contemporary social movements empowering "victims" are part of this process—they enable recollection by providing therapist and client with a shared belief system, shared expectations, and a context in which the work of remembering can occur. The social movement creates and validates narrative forms through self-help groups, media presentations, and shifts in public attitudes and juridical practices. At the same time, of course, the reconstruction of memory in terms of victimhood may promote the alienation of families, over-simplify problems with complex origins and, ultimately, disempower those it aims to help by institutionalizing the position of victim.

If current accounts of childhood abuse exaggerate the prevalence of repression and dissociation, accounts of the Holocaust minimize the distortions of memory. The fundamental difference lies in the social context of retelling. In the case of Holocaust testimony, the enormity of the event always precedes the individual story, so that every detail becomes portentous. In the case of the victim of childhood abuse, the retelling involves an idiosyncratic personal history whose moral implications attack our complacent image of family life.

The injunction "never forget" made with regard to the Holocaust points to the ease with which even so extreme a rupture of experience can be forgotten, suppressed or mythologized until unrecognizable (Judt 1992; Vidal-Naquet 1992). The moral order requires memory, and memory, in turn, demands certain narrative forms. Martin Amis's book, *Time's Arrow* (1991) is a brilliant demonstration of the links between narrative, memory, and the moral order. The entire novel is written from the point of view of a consciousness inhabiting the body of a doctor moving backward in time from the moment of his death toward his birth. The protagonist cannot know who he is, because his past lies before him. As the story unfolds we come to see that this strange reversal mirrors the self-willed amnesia by which he has lived his life: emigrating, changing his name, forging a new identity, all to hide from the terrible fact of his past as a Nazi doctor. Eventually he confronts his past, returns to the crematorium where he consigned the disabled to death. Flakes of ash and curls of smoke coalesce and spiral downward into the smokestack of the crematorium to settle and thicken, reconstituting bodies which are pulled from the ovens like loaves of bread. Entropy itself is reversed, chaos stuffed back into its box. But this moment of renewal is fleeting, for time continues to move relentlessly backward carrying the Nazi doctor toward the annihilation of his own birth and conception.

Amis creates a world that is inhuman and absurd. The novel is a form of sadistic revenge exacted on the Nazi doctor, forced to live his life backwards in a grotesque and meaningless march toward nullity.[11] Time reversal turns choice into inevitability, creating a world where moral action is impossible. Amis's book drives home the impossibility of moral life under circumstances where history is denied. The moral function of memory is to compel us to confront what we—and all around us—wish to leave behind. It might seem that for memories to be true they must be unfettered. Yet the evidence is that memories are most fully and vividly accessed and developed when they fit cultural templates and have a receptive audience. Societies then must provide cultural forms and occasions for remembering. It is a paradox of freedom that the moral function of memory depends on the constraints of social and cultural worlds to provide a limited range of narrative forms with which to construct the coherent stories of our selves.

Notes

1. The pronunciation in French is "double V."
2. See Lejeune (1993) for an account of Perec's struggle in writing "W."
3. This is the major lesson of work on the "enhancement" of memory by hypnosis. Hypnosis encourages imaginative elaboration and confabulation, increasing the number of details recalled but not their accuracy (Orne, et al. 1988). These effects of hypnosis make its forensic use to enhance memory extremely dangerous and such applications have been widely prohibited.
4. Several authorities have challenged the equivalence of hypnotic and dissociative phenomena (e.g. Frankel 1990) but there remain close

parallels between the experiences and behaviors, their response to context and suggestion, and their correlation with specific personality traits. The major differences concern the spontaneity and intensity of clinical dissociative phenomena which may result from their association with strong emotion and motivation engendered by conflictual personal history.

5. Skeptics' incredulity about the very possibility of dissociative amnesia or repressed memories of horrific events, however, deserves just as much cultural critique as does the credulous belief in any recovered memory as veridical. Dissociative amnesia is easy to demonstrate in the laboratory with hypnosis. Lack of ability to demonstrate repression experimentally in the laboratory is cause for skepticism but many psychological phenomena are difficult to reproduce outside their real-life social contexts. Repression contravenes the commonsense notion that the persistence and salience of memory is directly proportional to the intensity of the stimulus event: big events yield big memories. Perhaps a more important reason for this skepticism is the challenge that repression presents to the cherished notion that we are in charge of our own memories and our own best biographers. The skeptical view therefore appears commonsensical and parsimonious in the absence of scientific proof of repression.

6. Delbo again: "When I speak to you of Auschwitz, my words don't come from deep memory; they come, so to speak, from external memory [*mémoire externe*], intellectual memory, reflective memory." And Langer continues, "Refining the opposition between deep and common memory, she develops a parallel distinction between what we might call 'thinking memory' and what she labels 'sense memory' ('*mémoire des sens*')." This distinction recalls that of declarative (descriptive, semantic) versus procedural (episodic, bodily) memory. Pain (*sens*) has made memory itself an object to be dissected. But *mémoire des sens* is also "memory of meanings," putting the body at the center of meaning as articulate witness to the past even in its mute survival.

7. "Leon, the survivor who contributed the idea of 'making a story' of what is 'not a story,' . . . [recalled] returning to a ghetto that had been liquidated only hours before . . . : 'the scene coming back from the arms factory into the ghetto. And the grayness of the morning. And those dozens of bodies wherever you turned . . . .

You're *supposed* to react! You're supposed to run up! And race! Yell! Scream! Utter! Emote! Show *anything* about it! Anything whether it is— . . . .

Entering the ghetto in a dead silence. Those columns marching in . . . . Maybe a poet can evoke something approaching it, but even sound would be out of place. There's no sound actually. There is no sound. It would have to be a silent poem" (Greenspan 1992 145–146). Just so—the poet Paul Celan used shards of metaphor and silence to transcend the limits of narrative.

8. It is striking that the emptiness of dissociative gaps and the richness of fantasy are closely related. Both involve the same processes of absorption: in the one case the gaps are explored like the ragged cavity of a tooth that the tongue returns to again and again, magnifying its contours with attention; in the other, the emptiness is entered like a cave to discover images on its walls.

9. Familial abuse presents the child with the added problem of integrating contradictory images of the aggressing parent as also loving and kind and of the non-aggressing parent as failing to protect and colluding with abuse. Dissociation provides a strategy for managing the intense dissonance created by this contradiction.

10. "Whatever the specific purposes, many survivors recall a period immediately after liberation when they were simply compelled to speak about what they had witnessed and survived" (Greenspan 1992, p. 147).

11. Amis's reversal of time is not an arbitrary punishment for the Nazi criminal but exactly the sort of destruction of meaning visited upon the victims. Speaking of the sense of time in the camps, Chaim E. says: "You were not thinking for tomorrow because tomorrow's thoughts were bad. Today was already better than tomorrow" (Langer 1992, p. 180). Langer speaks of the "counter-time" of Auschwitz.

References

Amis, Martin. 1991. *Time's Arrow or The Nature of the Offence.* London: Penguin Books.

Bartlett, F. C. 1932. *Remembering.* Cambridge: Cambridge University Press.

Belli, R. F., and Elizabeth F. Loftus. 1994. "Recovered Memories of Childhood Abuse: A Source Monitoring Perspective." In *Dissociation: Clinical and Theoretical Perspectives.* Ed. by S. J. Lynn and J. W. Rhue. New York: Guilford.

Bower, Gordon H. 1981. "Mood and Memory." *American Psychologist* 36 (2): 129–148.

Briere, John. 1993. *Child Abuse Trauma: Theory and Treatment of the Lasting Effects.* Newbury Park: Sage Publications.

Bruner, Jerome. 1990. *Acts of Meaning.* Cambridge: Harvard University Press.

Christianson, S. A. 1992. "Emotional Stress and Eyewitness Memory: A Critical Review." *Psychological Bulletin.* 112 (2): 284–309.

Connerton, P. 1989. *How Societies Remember.* Cambridge: Cambridge University Press.

Crews, F. 1995. *The Memory Wars: Freud's Legacy in Dispute.* New York: The New York Review of Books.

Davies, J. M., and M. G. Frawley. 1994. *Treating the Adult Survivor of Childhood Sexual Abuse: A Psychoanalytic Perspective.* New York: Basic Books.

Delbo, C. 1995. *Auschwitz and After.* New Haven: Yale University Press.

Eitinger, L. 1980. "The Concentration Camp Syndrome and Its Late Sequelae." In *Survivors, Victims and Perpetrators.* Ed. by J. Dimsdale. Washington, D.C.: Hemisphere.

Frankel, Fred H. 1993. "Adult Reconstructions of Childhood Events in the Multiple Personality Literature." *American Journal of Psychiatry* 150: 954–958.

Friedman, William J. 1993. "Memory for the Time of Past Events." *Psychological Bulletin* 113 (1): 44–66.

Funkenstein, A. 1993. "The Incomprehensible Catastrophe." In *The Narrative Study of Lives.* Ed. by R. Josselson and A. Lieblich. Newbury Park, CA: Sage.

Greenspan, H. 1992. "Lives as Texts: Symptoms as Modes of Recounting in the Life Histories of Holocaust Survivors." In *Storied Lives: The Cultural Politics of Self-Understanding.* Ed. by G. C. Rosenwald and R. L. Ochberg. New Haven: Yale University Press.

Griffith, James L., and Melissa E. Griffith. 1994. *The Body Speaks: Therapeutic Dialogues for Mind-Body Problems.* New York: Basic Books.

Herman, Judith L. 1992. *Trauma and Recovery.* Boston: Harvard University Press

Holmes, D. S. 1990. "The Evidence for Repression: An Examination of 60 Years of Research." In *Repression and Dissociation: Implications for Personality Theory, Psychopathology, and Health.* Ed. by J. L. Singer. Chicago: University of Chicago Press.

Judt, Tony. 1992. "The Past Is Another Country: Myth and Memory in Postwar Europe." *D¾dalus* 121 (4): 83–118.

Kestenberg, J., and E. Fogelman, eds. 1994. *Children During the Nazi Reign.* Westport, CT: Praeger.

Kirmayer, L. J. 1992. "Social Constructions of Hypnosis." *International Journal of Clinical and Experimental Hypnosis* 40 (4): 276–300.

———. 1994. "Pacing the Void: Social and Cultural Dimensions of Dissociation." In *Dissociation: Culture, Mind and Body.* Ed. by D. Spiegel. Washington: American Psychiatric Press.

Koss, M. P., Tromp, S. and Tharan, M. 1995. "Traumatic Memories: Empirical Foundations, Forensic and Clinical Implications." *Clinical Psychology Science and Practice* 2: 111–132.

Krystal, Henry. 1988. *Integration and Self-Healing: Affect, Trauma, Alexithymia.* Hillsdale, N.J.: Analytic Press.

Kuch, K. and B. J. Cox. 1992. "Symptoms of PTSD in 124 Survivors of the Holocaust." *American Journal of Psychiatry* 149: 337–340.

Langer, Lawrence L. 1991. *Holocaust Testimonials: The Ruins of Memory.* New Haven: Yale University Press.

Langer, L. 1995. *Admitting the Holocaust: Collected Essays.* New York: Oxford University Press.

Laurence, J.-P., and Campbell Perry. 1983. "Hypnotically Created Memory among Highly Hypnotizable Subjects." *Science* 222: 523–524.

Lejeune, P. 1993. "W or The Memory of Childhood." *Review of Contemporary Fiction* 13 (1): 88–97.

Lewis, M. 1995. "Memory and Psychoanalysis: A New Look at Infantile Amnesia and Transference." *Journal of the American Academy of Child Psychiatry* 34 (4): 405–417.

Loftus, Elizabeth F. 1993. "The Reality of Repressed Memories." *American Psychologist* 48: 518–537.

Lynn, S. J., and J. W. Rhue. 1988. "Fantasy Proneness: Hypnosis, Developmental Antecedents, and Psychopathology." *American Psychologist* 43 (1): 35–44.

Merskey, H. 1995. "Multiple Personality Disorder and False Memory Syndrome." *British Journal of Psychiatry* 166: 281–283.

Neisser, Ulric. 1982. *Memory Observed: Remembering in Natural Contexts.* San Francisco: W. H. Freeman.

———. 1994. "Self-Narratives: True and False." In *The Remembering Self: Construction and Accuracy in the Self-Narrative.* Ed. by U. Neisser and R. Fivush. New York: Cambridge University Press.

Niederland, W. G. 1968. "The Psychiatric Evaluation of Emotional Disorders in Survivors of Nazi Persecution." In *Massive Psychic Trauma.* Ed. by H. Krystal. New York: International Universities Press.

Orne, Martin T., W. G. Whitehouse, David F. Dinges, and Emily C. Orne. 1988. "Reconstructing Memory through Hypnosis: Forensic and Clinical Implications." In *Hypnosis and Memory.* Ed. by H. M. Pettinati. New York: Guilford Press.

Perec, Georges. 1988. *W or The Memory of Childhood.* Boston: David R. Godine.

Pope, H. G., Jr., and J. I. Hudson. 1995. "Can Memories of Childhood Sexual Abuse Be Repressed?" *Psychological Medicine* 25: 121–126.

Spence, Donald P. 1982. *Narrative Truth and Historical Truth: Meaning and Interpretation in Psychoanalysis*. New York: W. W. Norton.

Spiegel, David. 1990. "Hypnosis, Dissociation, and Trauma: Hidden and Overt Observers." In *Repression and Dissociation: Implications for Personality Theory, Psychopathology, and Health*. Ed. by J. L. Singer. Chicago: University of Chicago Press.

————, and Etzel Carde–a. 1991. "Disintegrated Experience: The Dissociative Disorders Revisited." *Journal of Abnormal Psychology* 100 (3): 366–378.

Stein, A. 1993. *Hidden Children: Forgotten Survivors of the Holocaust*. Toronto: Penguin Books Canada.

Terr, Lenore. 1994. *Unchained Memories: True Stories of Traumatic Memories, Lost and Found*. New York: Basic Books.

Tilman, Jane G., Michael R. Nash, and Paul M. Lerner. 1994. "Does Trauma Cause Dissociative Pathology?" In *Dissociation: Clinical and Theoretical Perspectives*. Ed. by S. J. Lynn and J. W. Rhue. New York: Guilford.

Van der Kolk, B. and Van der Hart, . 1995. "The Intrusive Past: The Flexibilitiy of Memory and the Engraving of Trauma." In *Trauma: Explorations in Memory*. Ed. by C. Caruth. Baltimore: Johns Hopkins Press.

Vidal-Naquet, P. 1992. *Assassins of Memory: Essays on the Denial of the Holocaust*. New York: Columbia University Press.

Watkins, Mary. 1986. *Invisible Guests: The Development of Imaginal Dialogues*. Hillsdale, N.J.: Analytic Press.

White, S. H., and D. B. Pillemer. 1979. "Childhood Amnesia and the Development of a Socially Accessible Memory System." In *Functional Disorders of Memory*. Ed. by J. F. Kihlstrom and F. J. Evans. Hillsdale, New Jersey: Lawrence Erlbaum.

Young, James E. 1988. *Writing and Rewriting the Holocaust: Narrative and the Consequences of Interpretation*. Bloomington: Indiana University Press.

————. 1993. *The Texture of Memory: Holocaust Memorials and Meaning*. New Haven: Yale University Press.

Young, K. 1989. "Narrative Embodiments: Enclaves of the Self in the Realm of Medicine." In *Texts of Identity*. Ed. by J. Shotter and K. J. Gergen. London: Sage Publications.

9

Missions to the Past
Poland in Contemporary Jewish Thought and Deed

Jack Kugelmass

History in the Age of the Post-Histoire

The French social historian Pierre Nora writes that *lieux de mémoire* or sites of memory—museums, archives, festivals, and the like, "are fundamentally remains, the ultimate embodiments of a memorial consciousness that has barely survived in a historical age that calls out for memory because it has abandoned it" (1989: 12). In like manner, the psycho-historian Saul Fried-lander notes the emergence of two contradictory tendencies in Western so-cieties since the 1960s: an abundance of deliberate evocations of the past via media productions, museums, and memorials; and a growing irrele-vance of historical consciousness as if we have entered an age which is es-sentially post-historical. "The common denominator of these contradictory aspects is the overriding presence of the past within the commercially dom-inated sector of the culture industry. . . . In this framework the past ap-pears as both pervasive and apparently irrelevant" (1993: 58–59).

Similar assessments concerning the jettisoning of the past can be heard from social critics across the political spectrum. In his masterful critique of American historical theme parks, the Marxist historian Michael Wallace warns against giving over the task of writing history to commercial corpora-tions (1986: 178–79). If the left is critical of what passes for history, conserv-ative historians are repulsed. Indeed, Daniel Boorstin sees a general decline in meaning altogether in contemporary culture. Citizens pursue pseudo events rather than real experience. Tourism, for example, has replaced travel; the experience itself consists of little more than preformulated tid bits not much different from a visit to an upscale shopping mall (1964: 79–80).

Tourism is not unrelated to the issue of history, because tourist sites are often either packaged as, or are indeed relics of this past. In regard to Jewish tourism this is particularly so because when Jews travel they frequently exhibit some interest in visiting synagogues (Loeb 1977: 187) or meeting local Jews, whom they typically view as historical relics. Over the past few years, I have become interested in the "going home" phenomenon, exemplified both in Jewish return visits to the Old World and in the changing representations of the old country through stage, film, and book on the part of North American Jews from the very beginning of mass migration until today (Kugelmass and Shandler 1989). Disconnected from the Old World irrevocably now because of the Holocaust, and unable to maintain an architecture of memory domestically because of an almost uncanny degree of economic success and mobility, North American Jews have an apparent need to reestablish sites of memory and that need has taken on considerable urgency in recent years.

In this essay I intend to take issue with those who believe that history has been entirely relegated to postmodernity's junk pile. Ethnic groups have a unique and collective commitment to memory—indeed, one might take that as their most salient characteristic—but that memory should be understood less as a thing that can be passed intact from one generation to the next (Fischer 1987), or even as a constant force within the trajectory of a group (I would like to distinguish a sense of the importance of the past or tradition from the substance of tradition) than as a continual process of engagement and disengagement, of remembering and forgetting propelled in either direction by overarching social, political, and economic forces. In recent years, Jews have started visiting Eastern Europe en masse and doing so less as tourists than as pilgrims. They come to see the past, to pay homage to ancestors and to heal what they have increasingly come to realize is a radical rupture in the memory fabric of their culture. But as I intend to argue, such pilgrimages themselves can be subdivided between those reclaiming a connection to East European roots, and those seeking to reappropriate those roots and replant them, sometimes quite literally, in less hostile soil.

In an editorial written shortly after visiting Auschwitz, Hershel Shanks, the publisher of a popular American Jewish magazine, writes,

> People ask me, how was it? What was it like? All the words are wrong.
> So when I have to react in a word or two to casual, friendly inquiries, this is what I say: 'Strangely enriching. You must go.' (1990: 4).

Tens of thousands of North American and Israeli Jews now visit Eastern Europe each summer. Many go as individuals or on family tours determined to recover on film whatever traces remain of ancestral homes. A surprising number are survivors. Some are prompted by children curious to know about their parents' war-time lives; others, realizing that they are reaching the end of their active life are determined to introduce their own children to those who hid them during the war, or to visit with their families the places of childhood and adolescence that permanently marked their lives. But by far the largest number had no such experience themselves. They are North American and Israeli Jews of all ages, typically part of tour groups organized by synagogues, schools, and youth movements. Indeed, over the past few years considerable effort has been made by tour operators to offer subsidized, one-week packages for rabbis and other Jewish professionals who are then expected to organize similar tours for their congregants. Frequently, participants write about their experiences, and I have been collecting such accounts and whenever possible interviewing for additional information.

If there is any way to sum up what I have read, it is this: for Jews, visiting the death camps of Poland has become obligatory, as if there were no other way to really know the recent past. Ultimately, it is the very seriousness of such visits that distinguishes Jewish travel to Poland from tourism. Many of those who go, especially those who travel as part of institutionally organized tour groups—the majority of Jewish travelers to Poland—do so to participate in a secular ritual, one that confirms who they are as Jews, and perhaps even more so as North American or Israeli Jews. I use the term "secular ritual" (Falk Moore and Myerhoff 1977: 7) here for several reasons: first, I want to distinguish the visits clearly from the traditional ritual of pilgrimage which has a long-standing place within East European and North African Jewish culture, including appropriate prayers and prescribed modes of behavior. For even though these secular rituals do not comply with traditional forms, they do appropriate them and in part invent whole new meanings. Participants in a United Synagogue Youth tour at Treblinka, for example, are handed small index cards and are told to scatter throughout the site and to write a note to someone who died in the camp—an act clearly copied from the hasidic custom of writing *kvitlekh*, but for the sake, here, of expressing solidarity between the living and the dead rather than to ask for divine intervention. Secondly, we might consider the missions' relative shallowness when compared to more traditional pilgrimages. Ritual's sense of efficacy derives from an elaborate cosmology. Secular ritual is much narrower in scope, reflecting a movement away from a traditional religious world view among contemporary Jews. Finally, we also need to recognize that such tours are not unique events, and that the concept of secular ritual lets us distinguish the collective from the strictly personal. Indeed, most visitors follow a well-trod route, and if they do not recite exactly the same prayers or read the same poems and narrative accounts, the texts are largely interchangeable.

Participants on memorial tours are frequently required to engage in practices that they might prefer to avoid in their every day lives: e.g., attending services three times daily, eating strictly kosher food prepackaged in Western Europe, attending lectures and evening discussions, and enduring sometimes arduous travel schedules. But for those who give themselves over to the experience, such practices contribute to their "time out of time" quality. Their very liminality suggests to participants that what they are experiencing is marked in a special way.

Indeed, the journeys themselves are generally called "missions" by both organizers and participants. At the same time, the shared nature of the experience has tremendous potential for generating catharsis. Participants are encouraged to talk about their feelings, to discuss what they have seen either during the travel time between the site and the hotel, or in evening group discussions.

Almost immediately, these activities demand engagement even to the point of forcing participants to experience themselves as Holocaust victims. At Auschwitz-Birkenau, a member of a Montreal synagogue group watched her fellow participants march towards the destroyed crematoria. As they walked she could see the men at some distance. Crossing her vision was a barbed wire fence and she commented to others near her that for a moment she imagined the men actually imprisoned in the camp. One traveler on a different journey, reflecting on the previous day's tour of Cracow and Kazimierz, writes:

> Last night I was transported from 1987 to earlier times: before the war and even back to the eighteenth and nineteenth centuries. In that way I have become part of Polish hasidic life, and I also enter the world of my grandparents Dora and Josef.
>
> Today we go to Auschwitz. By the time we enter, I have changed from being a "surviving grandson" to being equal, arriving at the gates from the past in the past. Only now can I finally die with Josef, Dora, and my father Hans. Later as I walk back through the camp entrance at Birkenau, I am reborn, in my present life. As witness, not as survivor. (Dekro 1988: 11)

A participant on the international Jewish youth "March of the Living" writes of seeing the piles of shoes in Majdanek:

I glance at my own shoe, expecting it to be far different than those in this ocean of death, and my breath catches in my throat as I see my shoe, though lighter in color, is almost the same style as one, no, two, three of the shoes I see: it seems as though every shoe here is my shoe.

I wish I could throw my shoes into this pile, to grasp and feel each shoe, to jump into this sea, to become a part of it, to take it with me. (Horn 1992: 16)

The receptiveness North American Jews now have towards such experiences did not occur without considerable prompting long before they ever set foot on Polish soil. And clearly the media are important here: the broadcasting of *Roots, Holocaust, Shoah*, and even the Eichmann trial a decade or so earlier are all cases in point (Friedlander 1993: 46). But one wonders if the neglect of the Holocaust by North American Jews in the immediate decades after the war were not simply lack of knowledge or even lack of an accessible literature of destruction (Nathan Glazer cited in Gans 1979: 207)—even if the facts were known it still required a narrative framework to integrate those facts into the popular imagination—but the result of a very close Jewish identification with the dominant paradigm of North American culture. Military and economic might are persuasive even when the potential threat they pose is directed elsewhere. And that identification stems from two generations of rapid and self-desired Americanization. After all, the New World stood for progress, and Jews who came to North America *en masse* beginning more than a century ago came here fully prepared to be caught within that web of belief. And if nostalgia for the Old World periodically entered their minds, it quickly dissipated since, as numerous memoirs make clear, Jews were cognizant long before the Holocaust of the kind of life they would have led had their East European parents not ventured across the ocean. The result, of course, was a readiness to shed the past and much that reminded them of it while reshaping their religion, its ancillary customs, and codes of behavior to a society that billed itself as pluralist. And relative to Europe if not to much of the rest of the world it was.

It has been argued that "a myth of progress makes the loss of memory less troubling" (Terdiman 1993: 24). But the shattering of that myth which occurred during the political and economic upheavals during the 1960s (particularly in the United States in response to the Vietnam debacle) has made Jews cognizant that they had indeed lost something. In earlier writing I argued that there are various underlying social factors that produced this transformation in world view (Kugelmass 1992, 1994). Let me briefly review several of these here and then suggest some additional

factors that relate more to the realm of ideas than to the political and economic underpinnings of society.

Fear of Assimilation

Holocaust consciousness emerges at the very moment when North American Jews find themselves ensconced within society's mainstream. Herbert
Gans (1979: 207–8) argues that the Holocaust meets "a need for the
threat of group destruction," a need stemming from increasing intermar-
riage; a decline in religious observance; and the fear that a lack of overt
anti-Semitism has made the boundaries between Jew and non-Jew too permeable. In the words of Jacob Neusner, "The central issue facing Judaism
in our day is whether a long-beleaguered faith can endure the conclusion
of its perilous age." Or witness any number of episodes on popular American television shows which address the issue of Jewish non-celebration of
Christmas. These invariably resolve the conflict generated by intermar-
riage through a degree of mutual tolerance: the Jew agrees to abandon a
taboo against complying with the worship of foreign gods; the non-Jew
celebrates Hanukkah. Seen within this context, the importance of the
Holocaust in general and of Poland in particular as a place of pilgrimage
is that it represents a journey to a simpler past.

Symbolic Ethnicity

Although North American Jewish pilgrimages to Poland began as induce-
ments for securing donations from a wealthy and often non-observant
elite within the Jewish community, it is striking how common they have
become. They are now so central to the Jewish experience that increasingly children are sent on them as part of their religious or ethnic education. The March of the Living was organized in the late 1980s to include
thousands of Jewish school children from across North America. So suc-
cesful was the event that rabbis who participated have begun to take their
congregations on similar pilgrimages and the event has been repeated
with ever larger numbers of Jewish children participating from around
the world. These examples point to two interrelated aspects of what Herbert Gans refers to as the emergence of "symbolic ethnicity": one is the
heightened value placed on rites of passage in Jewish ritual since they are
generally less demanding than calendrical rites; the other is the tendency
for ethnics in general to express their identity by trips to the "old country"
(Gans 1979: 204–5). In this latter sense one might believe that contem-

porary North American Jews are simply doing what all other ethnic groups do. But there are significant differences: first, for the majority of North American Jews, the population that constitutes the old country no longer exists; and second, for many of those who go on such missions, Israel has come to be considered the new old country. Visits "home" are less about going home to Poland than about going home to Israel. I shall have more to say about this shortly.

Conflict

Of course cultural symbols are often intricately tied to political and economic conflict (Cohen 1974). The expansion of rites connected to the Holocaust, in particular the rite of pilgrimage to Poland and to the death camp, emerged simultaneously with, and at least to some degree in response to, two conflicts with profoundly disquieting implications for North American Jews. One is the Arab-Israeli conflict, and the other is rising ethnic tension in the United States. In addition I would suggest that American society increasingly attributes a positive valence to victimhood and this, at the very least, sets the stage for public displays that in an earlier era would have been scorned or shunned. One cannot help but think that the increasing popularity of events such as the "March of the Living" is growing in direct proportion to the ambiguousness of the Middle East situation. As long as Israel was perceived as a David against Goliath, there was no need for a ritual to convince participants and spectators of its vulnerability. But with the increasing perception of Israel as Goliath—the use of stones by Palestinians is also a rhetorical strategy—there is increasing need for Jews to formulate a counter-rhetoric of remembered victimization. Moreover, this strategy did not arise spontaneously among North American Jewry, but has had the active support of Israeli and American Zionist organizations, hence the typical conclusion of the "mission" by touring Israel. Visits to Poland's death camps by high school students were already part of Israeli public culture by the mid 1960s—two decades before similar events were staged by North American Jews.

By evoking the Holocaust dramaturgically, that is, by going to the site of the event and reconstituting the reality of the time and place, North American Jews are not only invoking the spirits of the tribe, that is, wresting claim to their martyrdom, they are also making past time present. And in doing that they are symbolically reversing reality, transposing themselves from what they are currently perceived as—in the North American case highly privileged and in the Israeli case oppressive—and presenting themselves as the diametric opposite of privilege, of what they in fact were. And it is this image of the self which has been, and continues to be, central to the Jewish world view. In stressing the political component of the rite of pilgrimage, I do not mean to suggest that there is anything cynical at work here. On the contrary, those who perform these rites do so out of conviction, because they offer a way out of a difficult moral dilemma and allow Jews to steer a course somewhere between hegemonic and oppositional culture. Moreover, these rites are performed primarily for fellow Jews: they are intra- rather than inter-tribal. And they have the same agenda as all ritual, namely to bridge fundamental discontinuities in life: those between American and East European Jewry, between post-war and pre-war Jewry, the living and the dead, between power and power-lessness. They are an attempt to counteract fragmentation and the loss of belief that modernity itself has brought on and the possibility that such disbelief will cause the complete demise of the tribe.

Overcoming the "Myth of the War Experience"

Certainly one reason for the earlier neglect of the Holocaust in North American Jewish thought had to do with the more general response to a war in which tens of millions were killed. Few North American families— both Jewish and non-Jewish alike, remained untouched by the war's destructiveness, even those a continent removed from the battlefields. That global "death immersion" (Lifton 1977) prompted both a strong post-war commitment to "normalcy" as domesticity and a concomitant degree of "psychic numbing" (Lifton 1969) without which, the horror of senseless death would have completely subverted the "Myth of the War Experience" (Mosse 1990: 7–8), a myth which, at least in America, lingered until the Vietnam War. But if myths of heroic death may have helped people cope with the loss of human life (and in formerly occupied Europe for the relative passivity of citizens) such myths could only marginalize the survivors. War, according to Jean Bethke Elshtain, is the cultural property of a people (cited in Jeffords 1989: 182), and in the aftermath of World War II the property of survivors was of no particular value. Noting that survivors had very limited ability to affect their own fate and the fate of those they loved, Lawrence Langer speaks of the diminished self of unheroic memory (1991: 176–77). Survivors were seen as passive victims (in contemporary terms feminized victims rather than heroic soldiers) and therefore themselves responsible for the trauma they experienced.

Despite psychic numbing and a masculinist mythology that turned collective memory of the war into a fairy tale–like triumph of good over evil, some people managed to give voice to the war's darker side. Even before the war was over, many survivors were concerned that their story be told and began to wage a persistent struggle against the "holes of oblivion" (Arendt 1979: 232) to which their loved ones, indeed their entire way of life, had been relegated. Outside of Israel, where state ritual could also be brought to bear on behalf of memory, narrative constituted the only available weapon in that struggle. Initially much of survivor testimony was framed by the limiting factors of the particular language and cultural community from which it sprang—during the late 1940s and '50s survivor accounts were largely written in Yiddish and to a lesser degree Hebrew. Typically, they appeared in collective volumes known as *yisker-bikher* (memorial books) commemorating hundreds of individual East European communities (Kugelmass and Boyarin 1983). But testimony gradually radiated outward to address ever-wider audiences as survivors resettled and their access to the west—socially, economically, and culturally—became more secure. The current prominence of survivor accounts suggests both the social ensconcement of the community that generated it and a fundamental change in North American attitudes toward war and death in the intervening years between the end of World War II and the present, a change made possible in large measure through the decline of empire and a concomitant redefining of masculinity and heroic memory.

Bearing Witness

A good deal has been written on the need to bear witness as a motivating force behind survivor testimony. In "The Survivor," the final chapter of *Death in Life*, Robert J. Lifton considered this need an outgrowth of the survivors' sense of an organic balance between the living and the dead. That their survival could only have occurred through the demise of others resulted in underlying and persistent guilt. Although a sense of guilt is common in any survival experience, how much more so when surviving literally depended on the selection for death of others—often friends and relatives—seemingly less fit to live (1969: 488–92). In a chapter titled "Life in Death" in his book *The Survivor* (a title clearly intended to challenge Lifton's earlier work), Terrence des Pres disputed the legitimacy of employing the concept of guilt in a situation where defilement—according to Paul Ricoeur a basic symbol of evil—is real rather than symbolic (1977: 76). During the Holocaust myth was transmogrified into history, the camps and related experiences of capture, imprisonment, and escape were literal rather than symbolic descents into Hell, followed, at least in survivors' accounts, by Redemption. Moreover, according to des Pres, surviving was possible only through the cooperative work of many; the need to bear witness stems not from feelings of guilt but rather from the need to fulfill a moral obligation to the dead. In bearing witness the survivor not only speaks for those who no longer can, but also for humanity more generally, warning of the consequences to human survival when men, acting like gods, believe that all things are possible.

Despite their use of different explanatory models, Lifton's and des Pres's formulations have striking similarities in regard to the Holocaust's implications for the future of humankind. Eschewing psychoanalytic explanations, des Pres argued that the mechanism generating testimony draws from animal behavior and is socio-biological rather than cultural in origin; the will to bear witness is comparable to an animal's scream or call to its group. That warning on the human level transmits information that is vital for human survival (1977: 235–37). For Lifton, concern for the future underlies his own activism on behalf of nuclear disarmament. Indeed, using the nuclear metaphor, he suggests that identification guilt radiates outward from the dead to survivors and, through ever-widening circles, ultimately encompasses the rest of the world. The existence of such patterns of identification "suggests that the guilt associated with identification provides an important basis for the ultimate symbolic connection of all human behavior" (1969: 499).

A New Mythology

Despite the elegance of des Pres's analysis, because it is ultimately bounded by the literary nature of his project, it falls short of Lifton's formulation for understanding social behavior, and along with it the subject of this essay. Indeed, there are two facets of Lifton's formulation that have particular significance for understanding the emergence of social memory about the Holocaust. By isolating survivors, the psychic numbing that radiated outward to envelope us all stymied the symbolic connection between us and them. But that connection has become an increasingly urgent one in recent years. I have already outlined some of the reasons that underlie that urgency for North American Jews. But Lifton sees a direct connection between the absence of an emotional sense of what nuclear weapons can do—the threat of annihilation that hangs continuously over all of our heads—and the "technical-professional focus and perceived ideological imperative" of the Third Reich's killing machine that continues today in our scientific effort towards weapons of mass destruction. As a result, according to Lifton, "It is no exaggeration to say that psychic numbing is one of the great problems of our age" (508–9). Interestingly, and this has direct bearing on my argument, the very pervasiveness of psychic numbing makes us value experiences that enable us to break out of it. For some survivors such breaking out occurs through frequent ruminations on their own death immersion, while "those [including those not directly affected by the Holocaust] who open themselves up, even momentarily and from afar, to the actualities of death encounters, can undergo an intense personal experience which includes elements of catharsis and purification" (509).

A final point in Lifton's formulation that has striking resonance with the importance of Jewish visits to the death camps is the fixation on death imagery as fulfillment of the survivor's obligation to "remember everything":

> Hence the sacredness of the literal details of his death encounter ... and the worshipful stasis surrounding its image. Indeed we begin to understand why religious and political movements take shape as forms of survival: the significance of the witnessing of the death of Jesus for the emergence of Christianity, and that of the surviving of the Long March for Chinese Communism. The survivor may become a "disciple" not only of a dead leader, or of the collective "dead," but of the death immersion itself. (1977: 528)

When Jews today believe that awareness of the Holocaust is an important way to revitalize their culture, one can only wonder how much Holocaust consciousness is a revitalization and how much it is a radical reformulation based upon foundations very different from biblical and/or rabbinic Judaism.

History as the cornerstone of Jewish identity is hardly a new phenomenon (although this particular aspect of it—the death spell—is indeed peculiar). As Yoseph Hayim Yerushalmi argues in *Zakhor*, for Jewish historians of the nineteenth century, because of "an ever-growing decay of Jewish group memory," particularly that connected to Jewish tradition, history became "the faith of fallen Jews" (1982: 86). But there is a difference between collective memory and critical history, and certainly there is a difference between those who see themselves as fallen and those who do not. The former is a prerogative of select intellectuals. Critical history, therefore, can hardly serve as the faith of the many. But Yerushalmi does not limit his analysis strictly to an elite. Indeed, reflecting on the lack of resonance historical scholarship has for contemporary Jews, he compares post-Holocaust Jewry with the Spanish exiles of the sixteenth century, noting an unwillingness to confront history directly and seeming "to await a new metahistorical myth, for which the novel provides at least a temporary modern surrogate" (1982: 98).

Although I would agree that in the contemporary world popular arts are surrogates for myth, why limit such myths to the domain of the novel?

Are not film and now television the stages upon which the image of the past is given dramatic shape? And is it possible to understand the behavior and perceptions of North American Jews without considering the impact of media spectaculars such as *Roots, Holocaust,* and *Schindler's List?*

Performance

If critical history stands so much at odds with collective memory or myth, then perhaps stage rather than museum is the correct metaphor for looking at the relationship of Eastern Europe to its North American Jewish public. Poland, for example, is filled with ready-made props—ruined synagogues, doorposts with impressions from mezuzahs, crumbling cemeteries, and death camps. These objects are deafening in their silence; they are often scriptless since almost no one within Poland is capable of writing texts and labels to the country's Jewish monuments. And, Poland's viability as stage is enhanced by the fact that the country is nearly devoid of actors who might contest the presence of these foreign visitors, or attempt to wrest control of the performance. Here what most North American Jews are performing is, if not an actual engagement with history as many of us might advocate, then at least an attempt to piece together the icons of the past, to retrieve or reclaim them and to reassemble them, albeit within a framework which inscribes their meaning through the present.

Paul Connerton (1989) makes a persuasive argument for the performative nature of social memory; without bodily practices, he suggests, tribal memory cannot be maintained. Perhaps, then, the corporeal nature of marches to the camps constitutes the surest way for North American Jews to remember the fate of European Jewry. If so, we ought to consider the emergence of these pilgrimages in the face of a growing discontinuity between experiential memory—that of both the survivors themselves and North American Jews who lived through the war and its aftermath—and social memory, that is, the meaning of these events for all Jews, particularly those whose knowledge of the events is gleaned from others, in succeeding generations. As the distance between the present and the war grows, there is bound to occur an increasing awareness of a crisis of continuity. How are those who, for the most part, did not themselves witness the war, yet are convinced of its significance, to pass the memory of those events and their consequences to succeeding generations?

Moreover, given the "excess" that the Holocaust carries with it (Friedlander 1992: 19–20) and the concomitant challenge such excess poses to scholarly let alone lay understanding, these rites have very special significance because they do what endless study and discussion cannot do nearly as convincingly. They create meaning. And they do so in two ways. First they give form, substance, and focus to otherwise abstract and diffuse cultural orientations (Ortner 1978: 5), particularly to the awareness North American Jews have toward the past and future and their sense of the need for individuals to exert considerable effort and self-sacrifice in order to guarantee a collective future. Second, the rites are constructed dialogically (Schieffelin 1985; Young 1988: 192), requiring the creative input of participants, who interact with existing monuments through prayer, the reading of poems and memoirs, and photography, and who consecrate sites of martyrdom simply by visiting places overlooked by other visitors. In both these ways, performance itself is meaningful.

Although the same claim for a discursive thrust towards synthesis could be made for even the most nostalgic reflections (Stewart 1988), these rituals stand out both because they are collectively formulated and because they are rituals, and have as their underlying concern the matter of healing ruptures in the cultural system of knowing, and through it, the promotion of group continuity. Consequently, the pilgrimages are much less oriented towards the present via the past than they are towards the future via the past. Their work, to borrow a phrase from Richard Schechner, "is to 're-present' a past for the future (performance-to-be)" (Schechner 1985: 51). In part a meditation on the past and in part a scripted play about the present, the rites I have described are also very much rehearsals of what North American Jews are intent on becoming, or perhaps more accurately stated, intent on not becoming.

Given the fact that a great many of these "missions"—particularly those organized by Jewish institutions—begin by visiting Poland (thus entering the abyss of despair) and then conclude by touring Israel (thus experiencing redemption), their underlying message is a warning both against the danger posed by the diaspora itself, and of the need to reinforce Jewish solidarity through the agency of a separate state.

So mythic history is alive and well even within the age of post-histoire. But historical memory relegated to mythic paradigms is stripped of its ability to disturb, to force us into recognizing at least some of the "might have beens" that lie beneath the surface of our own present day reality.

Genealogical Memory

In earlier writing on Jewish visits to Poland, I was quick to pronounce judgment on the misuse of, or, better stated, disregard for, much of Polish Jewish history and culture that these visits promote. Perhaps a fairer appraisal requires recognition that not all itineraries are the same, and many of those

211

who go to Eastern Europe do so not as participants in institutional missions but as family historians determined to find a connection to a past they hardly know, to locate ancestral towns, to recover, even through purchase, heirlooms that were never passed down or were simply lost in transmission. Thus Billy Crystal in his 1989 autobiographical film "Midnight Train to Moscow" found surviving Russian family members through the work of a genealogist cousin. Countless Jewish families now have similar cousins. Indeed, in the opinion of librarians and archivists at major Jewish collections, such cousins have become like a plague. Genealogy has become a passion among Jews, with annual four-day conventions at luxurious hotels in various cities in North America and Israel and workshops on anything from how to copy photographs to how best to travel in remote regions of the pale. What impresses me about this phenomenon is its banality. If Holocaust pilgrims seek to enter mythic space and time, genealogists are motivated by something as ordinary as the desire to know who their grandparents were and how they lived. In that quest, they not only draw upon the greatest body of folk ethnography ever collected—the *yisker-bikher*—but they are (to the extent possible given their cultural, linguistic, and historical distance from the Old World), attempting to contribute to the very same project undertaken by the authors of the *yisker-bikher*. Indeed, this is not just by accident. It is genealogists who have rediscovered these books and created a market for them where none had previously existed. It is they who are now commissioning the translation and republication of these volumes. And it is they, too, who are writing new *yisker-bikher* for towns that previously had none.

This simultaneous emergence of Jewish genealogy and Holocaust consciousness suggests the existence of a larger memory project, which would, perhaps, explain historian Saul Friedlander's conundrum about Holocaust consciousness in Israel increasing even as the mythic vessel to contain it—catastrophe and redemption—is dissipating (1993: 45). Or perhaps Friedlander is wrong. The critical framework of intellectuals probably finds little resonance with laypersons, and Holocaust consciousness, popular arts, and secular rituals are, indeed, effective means of reinforcing seemingly outworn paradigms. Whatever the case, one can only marvel at the presence of mythic structures in contemporary Jewish thought, and marvel too at the near heroic efforts of those individuals determined to reclaim a past that long before and even well after the Holocaust, most Jews were quite determined to forget.

Notes

Research for this essay was made possible by grants from the Lucius N. Littauer Foundation, Inc., the Memorial Foundation for Jewish Culture, the

National Endowment for the Humanities, and the Wisconsin Alumni Research Foundation of the University of Wisconsin, Madison. I would like to thank the Center for Jewish Research at the Jagiellonian University in Cracow and the following people who read and commented on drafts of two larger versions of this essay titled "The Rites of the Tribe: American Jewish Tourism to Poland." Among them are Michael Fischer, Kostek Gebert, Harvey Goldberg, Mark Kaminsky, Rudy Koshar, Herbert Lewis, George Mosse, Peter Novick, Frank Salomon, and James Young.

References

Arendt, Hannah. 1979. *Eichmann in Jerusalem.* New York: Penguin Books.

Benjamin, Walter. 1985. *Illuminations.* New York: Schocken Books.

Cohen, Abner. 1974. *Urban Ethnicity.* London: Tavistock.

Connerton, Paul. 1989. *How Societies Remember.* New York: Cambridge University Press.

Dekro, Jeffrey. 1988. "First Time Home: Poland Leaves Its Mark on a Visitor." *Reconstructionist* LIV (Oct–Nov): 9–11, 14.

Des Pres, Terrence. 1977. *The Survivor: An Anatomy of Life in the Death Camps.* New York: Pocket Books.

Falk Moore, Sally, and Barbara Myerhoff. 1977. *Secular Ritual.* Amsterdam: Van Gorcum.

Fein, Leonard. 1988. *Where Are We?: The Inner Life of America's Jews.* New York: Harper and Row.

Friedlander, Saul. 1993. *Memory, History, and the Extermination of the Jews of Europe.* Bloomington: Indiana University Press.

———, ed. 1992. *Probing the Limits of Representation: Nazism and the "Final Solution."* Cambridge: Harvard University Press.

Gans, Herbert J. 1979. "Symbolic Ethnicity: The Future of Ethnic Groups and Cultures in America." In Gans, et al., *On the Making of Americans: Essays in Honor of David Riesman.* Philadelphia: University of Pennsylvania Press.

Horn, Dara. 1992. "On Filling Shoes." *Hadassah Magazine,* November, 16–22.

Hynes, Samuel. 1995. "So Many Men, So Many Wars: 50 Years of Remembering World War II." *New York Times,* 30 April: 12–17.

Jeffords, Susan. 1989. *The Remasculinization of America: Gender and the Vietnam War.* Bloomington: Indiana University Press.

Kugelmass, Jack. 1992. "The Rites of the Tribe." In *Museums and Communities: The Politics of Public Culture.* Ed. Ivan Karp, Christine Mullen Kreamer, and Steven D. Lavine. Washington, D.C.: Smithsonian Institution Press.

————, ed. 1994. *Going Home: How Jews Invent Their Old Countries.* Evanston: Northwestern University Press.

Kugelmass, Jack, and Jonathan Boyarin. 1983. *From a Ruined Garden: The Memorial Books of Polish Jewry.* New York: Schocken Books.

Kugelmass, Jack, and Jeffrey Shandler. 1989. *Going Home: How American Jews Invent the Old World.* (Exhibition catalog) New York: YIVO Institute.

Langer, Lawrence. 1991. *Holocaust Testimonies: The Ruins of Memory.* New Haven: Yale University Press.

Lifton, Robert J. 1969. *Death in Life: Survivors of Hiroshima.* New York: Vintage Books.

Loeb, Laurence. 1977. "Creating Antiques for Fun and Profit: Encounters Between Iranian Jewish Merchants and Touring Coreligionists." Ed. Valence L. Smith. *Hosts and Guests: The Anthropology of Tourism.* Philadelphia: University of Pennsylvania Press.

Marrus, Michael. 1991. "The Use and Misuse of the Holocaust." In *Lessons and Legacies: The Meaning of the Holocaust in a Changing World.* Ed. Peter Hayes. Evanston: Northwestern University Press.

Mosse, George. 1990. *Fallen Soldiers: Reshaping the Memory of the World Wars.* New York: Oxford University Press.

Nora, Pierre. 1989. "Les lieux de mémoire." *Representations* (Spring): 7–25.

Ortner, Sherry. 1978. *Sherpas through Their Rituals.* New York: Cambridge University Press.

Segev, Tom. 1993. *The Seventh Million: The Israelis and the Holocaust.* New York: Hill and Wang.

Schechner, Richard. 1985. *Between Theater and Anthropology.* Philadelphia: University of Pennsylvania Press.

Schieffelin, Edward. 1985. "Performance and the Cultural Construction of Reality." *American Ethnologist* 12 (November): 707–24.

Shanks, Hershel. 1990. *Moment* (February): 4–5.

Silberman, Charles. 1985. *A Certain People: American Jews and Their Lives Today.* New York: Summit Books.

Stewart, Kathleen. 1988. "Nostalgia—A Polemic." *Cultural Anthropology* 3 (3): 227–41.

Terdiman, Richard. 1993. *Present/Past: Modernity and the Memory Crisis.* Ithaca, N.Y.: Cornell University Press.

Wallace, Michael. 1986. "Mickey Mouse History: Portraying the Past in Disney World." In *History Museums in the United States: A Critical Assessment.* Ed. Warren Leon and Roy Rosenzweig. Urbana: University of Illinois Press.

Yerushalmi, Yosef Hayim. 1982. *Zakhor: Jewish History and Jewish Memory.* Seattle: University of Washington Press.

Young, James. 1988. *Writing and Rewriting the Holocaust.* Bloomington: Indiana University Press.

10

Internal and External Memory
Different Ways of Being in History

Maurice Bloch

> Il y a . . . aussi de l'histoire dans les sociétés unilinéaires.
> Cependant, chez elles, la descendance, autrement dit les liens
> généalogiques, ne sont pas des moyens au service de la créa-
> tion historique. Celle-ci se produit du dehors—par l'effet des
> guerres, épidémies, migrations, disettes, etc.—plutôt que du
> dedans. En ce sens le cognatisme quand il apparaît, offre à la
> société le moyen d'intérioriser l'histoire . . . .
> ——Claude Lévi-Strauss

It is common to see the study of long-term semantic memory as a
privileged area for the examination of the link between the individual and
the social. This point was made by Bartlett (1932), Vigotsky (Wertsch
1985), and Luria (1976), three psychologists who were unusual for their
time in their desire to link the individual and the social. Subsequently
Sperber, in an article considering the links between psychology and anthropology (Sperber 1985), has seen memory as the key area for the study
of the articulation between public and private representations. Finally,
and more specifically in psychology, there has been a general new tendency to move the study of memory out of the laboratory into the real
world. This tendency originates in its modern formulation in the work of
Neisser (1978) and is well manifested in such textbooks as Baddeley's *The
Psychology of Memory* (1976) and Cohen's *Memory in the Real World* (1990).
However, once psychologists have crossed the boundary between the lab-

215

oratory and the outside they find themselves in an environment where there is no longer a defined frontier limiting what they should be concerned with, and they plunge headlong into a consideration of how people in the world retain the past, not only as individuals but also as members of groups, who then employ supra-individual mnemonic systems and devices such as little poems and material objects. In other words psychologists stumble, almost by accident, but in a way which in principle should be very laudable, into territory normally occupied by anthropologists and historians.

Yet in spite of the general feeling that in the study of memory we have an area where psychology, with its concern with individual representations, and subjects such as anthropology or history, which traditionally deal with shared representations, might join up, the actual theoretical link between the disciplines is in reality plainly absent.

Psychologists give a nod in the direction of the fact that some aspects of memory become public representation, but, in reality, except perhaps for Bartlett, this does not fundamentally affect their approach to memory, while anthropologists and historians acknowledge that remembering and recalling are first of all individual activities, a fact they note by, for example, a mention of Bartlett and Luria in their early chapters (usually ignoring subsequent psychological work), only to forget the psychological aspect completely when they get down to business.

In order to clear the ground whereby a more genuine and fruitful theoretical and empirical connection might be made, I shall criticize the way the psychologists have approached the more social aspects of memory. A criticism of the anthropologists and historians from the point of view of the psychologists is equally necessary, though this will have to be considered elsewhere (Bloch 1993 and n.d.).

The problem with psychologists' approach to memory in the real world comes, I believe, from their failure to grasp the full complexity of the engagement of the mind in culture and history, and, in particular, their failure to understand that culture and history are not just something created by people but that they are, to a certain extent, that which creates persons.

Both psychologists and some anthropologists take a largely technological approach to memory. Thus Baddeley and Cohen first consider the neural processes which might make memory possible, then they consider how this "faculty" is used to coordinate action, next they consider the character of long-term memory and its limitations, and finally they turn to mnemonic objects and social practices, which they visualize as being merely "the extension of the brain." For them the socially instituted practices of memory are merely a primitive form of artificial intelligence in that they simply concern two processes, first, the process of making individual representations into public representations and, secondly, the process of storing these public representations. For such writers mnemonics are external extensions of the brain in much the same way that tools and weapons are extensions of the arm.

This approach is again evident in many recent studies of literacy, most particularly in the work of Goody (1977) and Olson (1977). There, literacy is merely seen as a particularly effective mnemonic device, i.e., an artificial memory with an infinite storage potential which does not deteriorate.

Such writers, then, first try to understand the workings of the mind/brain in a historical and cultural vacuum and then, following an acknowledged or unacknowledged evolutionary program, try to see how social and cultural institutions, as they have evolved, have extended the biological potential of the individual.

This is much too simple. First of all, technological potential never explains the uses to which technology is put. Secondly, the phenomenological maintenance of past states is, in real circumstances, largely determined by history or a people's view of themselves in history and hence, via notions of persons and places, various views of ethics and intentions (Bloch 1989a). If we want to move from concerns with potentials to concerns with the nature of the actual engagement of people in history, as the movement from the private to the public requires, then we must look to the varied context-specific ways in which people see themselves in the real world and how their abilities are engaged in the context of their own theories, purposes, and conditions.

It is for this reason that I want to compare folk theories of memory or, what amounts to much the same, folk theories of sources of knowledge and wisdom. First of all, I wish to do this to show how these folk theories are of a different kind to the theories of psychologists because they never consider potentialities without also taking into account moral purposes. Secondly, I want to show that, while psychologists tend to consider the actor, the external world, and the relation between the two as unproblematic, the people I shall discuss think of themselves, their body, their mind, their knowledge, and their material culture as part of a history which began before they were born and will continue after their death.

At the very least, the point in discussing these folk theories of the place of the "person in history" would be to show precisely the difference in ways of approaching the matter between psychologists and the people about whom I am talking, but I would argue there might be other advantages. First of all, these people may well have something to teach the psychologists. Secondly, even if ordinary people are wrong to see things in such subtle ways, and psychologists are right in seeing matters so simply, people's own evaluation and theories of knowledge and memory affect how they treat and value these matters and must, therefore, be of relevance to those who study them.

§

I begin the examination of folk theories of memory and the place of the person in history by going back to two familiar writers for whom the divorce of morals from the question of remembering would not even be considered.

In a recently published, wideranging book, *Ancient and Medieval Memories: Studies in the Reconstruction of the Past* (1992), Janet Coleman, a historian of ideas, contrasts with remarkable clarity Plato's and Aristotle's theories of memory.

Plato was above all concerned with the absolute transcendental truth of what has been called the "forms." For him nothing new of importance was ever learned during life. Humans, because they are humans, know everything of significance from the first. Unfortunately they forget and their original knowledge becomes vitiated by events and time so they need to learn anew, but in fact, what they are really doing when they think they are learning is remembering in the sense of recalling what they already knew. Thus when we learn something significant we are merely recalling original and unchanging truth, which, because it is absolutely true, must originate beyond human experience, time-bound as this must be.

Aristotle on the other hand believed that people were largely created by what they learned, and their minds were matured by new knowledge that shaped them as they remembered it and used what they remembered. The mind for him was like wax, which became permanently imprinted with new information but was represented there according to the mind's own capacity to represent sensual experience. According to him, when a person is trying to remember, what he or she does is merely search for the imprint of past information or events, which may be unfortunately overlaid by more recent memories and information, thus making it difficult to find.

These two theories are linked to many other aspects of the philosophy of the two thinkers, but clearly, as Coleman shows, the difference has implications for their respective views of history. The Platonist sees particular events as swirling unimportantly around the person while the duty of that person is, above all, that he/she should retain this human identity and protect the true knowledge it implies from the injuries of events. The Aristotelian on the other hand cannot consider him or herself ultimately aloof from history. They should be actively seeking to deliberate and make choices about good events and knowledge so as to be continually

218

created and recreated, made and remade through practical reasoning in the process of history. The Aristotelian is in a permanent transformational dialectic with the world and others. Practical wisdom is not absolute and finite for him but is being continually renegotiated through enlightening experience. For the Aristotelian living should not be a matter of holding oneself back since the very physical being is inevitably, continually shaped by the response to events in a way that will remain in the mind as permanent imprints.

These two types of theories of memory are therefore inseparably linked to differing concepts of the person, of the cosmos, of morality. In this placing of memory in a wider context the philosophers are very like the ordinary people whom anthropologists study and to whom I shall shortly turn, since ordinary people and philosophers together approach the matter one way, while modern psychologists take a very different path when they forget the more encompassing totality that gives the very concept of memory its significance. However, in stressing this resemblance between the works of philosophers and the thought of ordinary people as studied by anthropologists, one should not also forget that there are great differences. In particular ordinary people's knowledge is a complex mixture of implicit and explicit knowledge that is very different from the totally explicit theories of such philosophers as Plato and Aristotle.

I now turn to the ethnographic examples, starting with two deliberately contrasting examples for which I rely on the analyses and documentation found in two recently completed theses in the anthropology department of the London School of Economics.

The first is a study by Gabrielle vom Bruck of the historical and contemporary place of the descendants of the Prophet Mohammed, the Sadah, in northern Yemen. We should note, however, that many of the aspects stressed by vom Bruck would also be valid for similar groups in the Arab world as a whole.

According to the generally accepted history of Yemen, the Sadah, one of the groups of the descendants of the Prophet Mohammed, established themselves among the local tribes in the ninth century A.D., first as peacemakers and then, under the leadership of their head, the Imam, as rulers of what became the Yemeni Imamate.

As descendants of the Prophet, the Sadah are privileged vessels of divine and legal knowledge by the very fact of their ancestry. But, as vom Bruck shows, the idea of a descent group distinguished by their sacred wisdom carries within itself contradiction. Put simply the problem in such a conception is that wisdom is something which is learned and holiness is something which is practiced and therefore these qualities do not necessarily imply a particular descent affiliation. For example, one might be

219

wise and holy and not be a member of the Sadah, or one might be a descendant of the Prophet but lazy and so ignorant.

The potential contradiction in the two aspects of this elite is apparent to all, but for members of the Sadah and for believers in their preeminence in religious matters it is implicitly avoided in the following way. Descendants of the Prophet, because of his original contact with God, have by that fact something in their inherited potential which makes them, in normal circumstances, develop holiness and wisdom more than other, lesser people. The belief in such a potential and the theory of mind it implies is somewhat similar to the belief in innate abilities of the Platonists or more recently of those psychologists who, largely following Chomsky, stress the innate potentialities of persons to develop particular types of knowledge. Such knowledge will not develop without being given a chance but, if a member of the Sadah is properly taught in a good environment, then, they will most probably become that divine paragon that their holy ancestry innately disposes them to becoming.

There are many facets to such a belief. Inevitably, who one's parents are is critical for the Sadah. Only if one's father is a descendant of the Prophet will one be a member of the Sadah and therefore have the special potential for holy wisdom. Indeed even paternity may not be quite enough, and so, to make doubly sure it is even better if one's mother is also a member of the Sadah. Thus, implied in the psychological theory of holy predisposition is a theory about the nature and character of kinship and conception. This theory is quite specific and is based on the presumption of the determining potential of birth and more particularly of the preeminent, though not exclusive, relevance of paternity. These notions are, of course, common to all the Arab world and indeed to many societies with descent groups, but they are used as the grounding of the more specific formulation of identity used by the Sadah.

There are however yet further implications to all this. Linked with this theory of the mind and descent is a theory about learning and the nature of such mnemonic devices as writing.

Eickelman (1978) stresses three characteristic features of learning in the Muslim world: the emphasis on learning by rote, its rigorous discipline, and its lack of explanation. The reasons for these characteristics is that for Muslims the truth is found in the words of God, which the text fixes, and that, therefore, the purpose of learning is, above all, the preservation of the presence of the divine message among Muslims through time. The purpose is to achieve what in Islamic theory is called "mnemonic domination" (Eickelman 1978: 489). The mind of the pupils is infinitely inferior to the mind that created the Quran because of the immeasurable distance that exists between God and humans. It is therefore important to place the holy message in these inferior minds, not so that the pupils will "make it their own," as our educationalist would say, but so that the text will make the mind of the pupils its own, and thereby make the pupils people of Islam. The learning has to conquer the recalcitrant self, not the other way round. This also explains the importance of memorizing the text and not merely reading it. In such a system writing is not to be seen as a substitute to internalization, as Goody would have it; rather it is merely one device which facilitates the internalization, or rather the molding, of the recipient. A similar point was made recently with great clarity by Mary Carruthers (1990) dealing with the somewhat similar notions of European Medieval literacy.

Now, of course, in the case of the descendants of the Prophet, learning in a Quranic school has a further twist to that which it had in the medieval Christian world or, for that matter, for Muslims who are not descendants of the Prophet. For the Sadah learning Islamic wisdom is less of a struggle since it is being implanted in ground which already awaits it. Learning Muslim wisdom by the Sadah represents the meeting of the externally unchanged scripture, maintained through the device of writing, with the internally unchanged potential for knowing it, transmitted to them through the biology of reproduction and descent. What is learned by the Sadah is learned particularly deeply and significantly since they are taking into themselves what is already in themselves as a potential. Madelung, writing about them, quotes Muslim writers saying that "knowledge grows in the breast of the prophet's descendants as rain causes the fruit to grow" (Madelung 1965: 48). For the Sadah there is, therefore, nothing in the process of learning or of bodily growth and reproduction which creates anew what was not already potentially there. The creation of Islamic learning has occurred once and for all, and many Muslims believe that all possible future and past knowledge is found in the Quran. Learning and producing children are processes of maintenance of the divine so that what has been, is, and will not decay. The idea that the knowledge and truth are being continually created as the result of a creative and ongoing dialectic would be a terrible sacrilege.

It is because of this idea that the conceptualization of the presence of the Sadah in history becomes fascinating. History in Yemen, just as much as anywhere else, has been a continual turmoil of events. In particular the Sadah have been buffeted by the twentieth century. Until the middle of this century Yemen, under the rule of the Sadah and the Imam, was quite isolated from the rest of the world. However, even then, the outside world impinged. New ideas, especially new pan-Arab and socialist ideas from progressive centers such as Egypt, were having an effect, at least on a small intelligentsia. Second, the fact of having to deal with external powers

221

made the Imam behave even more like a political leader and less like a religious one, and he therefore lost legitimacy in the process. Both these factors and others combined in the events of the 1962 revolution that overthrew the Imamate and led to strong and, to a certain extent, continuing persecution of the Sadah.

The Sadah's reaction to this difficult situation is sensitively documented by vom Bruck, and she identifies a dual response. On the one hand, the Sadah had to adapt to oppressive force and had to compromise. But they also tried to maintain themselves unchanged as best they could, largely through various practices such as endogamy or, in some cases, partial or total immigration. This was their duty.

They, the unchanging continuation of the chosen vessel of God, the upholders of ultimate truth, know that governments, states, polities, and intellectual fashions come and go but they do and should remain. Their presence, strengthened by the learning which has naturally found a home in them, is ultimately beyond historical accident. They will always be required, if not temporarily by humans, at least by God. Truth for them, as Plato would have agreed, is always beyond events and the concept of a historical truth; or, as a part of it, the Sadah exist beyond history, like God. They have been here since the Prophet and in their essentials they remain. Events swirl around them, but they are a fixed content which must be continually rediscovered so that the wisdom of God can recreate society as the learned Quran should construct the minds of the pupils. They are both in history and out of it, or rather they are in other people's history while they remain unchanged. To them, therefore, the particular events of history are external.

Now let me turn to a very different ethnographic example, that of a group of poor peasants and urban dwellers in a part of the central Philippines, Bicol, recently analyzed by Fenella Cannell. As was the case for my discussion of the Sadah of Yemen in relation to the rest of the Arab world, many of the characteristics Cannell stresses for the Bicolanos are common to other Christian lowland (i.e. non-tribal) Filipinos.

Cannell stresses how the Bicolano poor represent themselves as people "who have nothing." They describe themselves, not entirely inaccurately, as people who have been, and are, at the mercy of more powerful others: rich landowners, powerful government officials, but also outside colonial powers: Spain and America. This image is also consistent with their view of the supernatural world since they similarly see saints and spirits as powerful others whom they have to accommodate and modify. The reaction of the ordinary Bicolanos to events brought about by these powerful others, whether in the past or now, is not to hold themselves aloof, but to allow these events continually to mold them, though in the process of adapting, they will also, from their position of initial weakness, gradually and continually change these more powerful forces through a humble and somewhat ironic negotiation, in order to create a somewhat more equitable *modus vivendi*. By contrast to the Sadah, they do not value or are not interested in an eternal irreducible essence in themselves, an essence which will ultimately reassert itself unchanged after the vagaries of the moment have passed. The ordinary Bicolano do not construct an imaginary pre-colonial, pre-compromise state to which they want to return like nineteenth-century European romantics or Muslim fundamentalists; rather they represent their role in history as having been willing to let powerful outsiders transform them to the core and in the process having also somewhat modified those who thought they were merely conquerors. In this way they are Catholic because they accepted Spanish Catholicism though in their acceptance they created, in a way that they do not choose to stress, something new. Similarly, they watch foreign television programs in order to adapt and mold themselves to these models as best they might. They particularly value beauty contests of all kinds because, as Cannell shows with delightful empathy, these give them a chance to appear, even if only for a sharply delineated moment, like these foreign and powerful models which they can control by their somewhat ironic participation.

In many ways this willing adaptation to foreign or urban models seems, to the Bicolanos at least, a response caused by their weakness in the historical process which they feel, perhaps rightly, is increasing. Cannell argues that this idiom of increasing powerlessness is also reflected in their relation to the supernatural, and she stresses how they talk, for example in their discussion of the changes in the nature of spirit mediumship, of their growing lack of control—but all this however is only a first step.

Cannell goes on to stress the significance of the idea of "negotiation" as being central to their view of how to deal with these more powerful others. The actor starts in a position of inferiority and oppression but with time and patience he/she engages the superior in a negotiation which becomes a relationship of exchange, if always unequal exchange. One transforms oneself to accommodate the superior in oneself but as this occurs one engages their pity and so one gradually builds oneself up through the accumulation of accepted experiences. As a result the negotiation from weakness becomes the basis for becoming a subject in one's own right through creative, adaptive transformation.

In many ways the Bicolano emphasis on the value of becoming and on metamorphosis has a similar place to the emphasis on an absolute eternal truth in the Muslim societies discussed above (though of course it could not be more different in terms of content). In the Philippines it is as though nothing is fixed forever, events will bring new imprints on the wax that is a person and so form him/her into something which did not exist before. But then the imprints of the past will be gradually covered and partially obscured by other imprints, as the person is continually and gradually transformed in history from one state to another—as he/she constructs meaning through selective recollection. One could say of the Filipinos, then, that they are Aristotelians to the Yemenis Platonists.

For them the distant past is a weak and fading memory gradually replaced by newer constituting events. Unlike the Sadah "they" were not there in the past and "they" will not be there in the future. Rather, for them, there were people in the past who became them, and as a result of events, the descendants they will produce will become gradually different through the effect of events and time.

With this type of idea we would not expect the kind of mnemonic objects that must be preserved unchanged, such as the religious texts of Islam that ensure the continuing molding of the present exactly to the pattern of the past. Indeed there is a striking absence of a conservationist spirit about the lowland Philippines that makes their villages and towns poor tourist attractions. In the area where Cannell worked, however, there was an object which at first sight seemed to be of this kind. This was a statue of a saint (actually of Christ) which was the focus of pilgrimage. But, as Cannell points out, even here the idea of transformation and becoming had penetrated, since the saint was thought of as having grown up (literally the wood got bigger and more recognizable) in the recent past but by now was entering a period of decline and shrinking through old age.

The Bicolanos' own explanation of their cultural malleability is in terms of their weakness, poverty, and negotiating ability and, indeed, the particular group that Cannell studied is both far from the centers of power and yet open, without protection, to all the whims and winds of external influence. However, there probably is more to the matter than can be explained in purely political terms.

I pointed out above how the Sadah's view of the way they are in history seems to accord well with their view of kinship, which we can call loosely the descent type. In such a system birth transmits essential and immutable qualities and gives potentialities that, if only given the right environment, will develop of themselves. This implies, as Fortes stressed in his discussion of unilineal descent groups (Fortes 1953), that each individual is a replacement of his forebears, or the vessel in which the eternal element is given a temporary incarnation. Of course such a type of kinship system and theory of the person and the body is very widespread, far beyond the Mediterranean world into Africa and Asia. However, the particular form of this general cultural complex, which is illustrated in the case of the Sadah, is especially interesting in that it gives the classical idea of descent an extreme, and therefore particularly clear, formulation. There is therefore an elective affinity between the Sadah's view of their place in history and their theory of kinship, and the same is probably true of the Bicolanos' concept of their malleable response to history and their kinship ideas. This means that although one can understand their views of the past in terms of their situation in the face of colonial powers, a fuller explanation of their understanding of their place in history needs to take into account aspects of their culture which probably have a much longer history than that of the colonial Philippines.

It is my guess that a relationship exists between the particular formulation of the Filipino's relation to events and much more general Southeast Asian ideas about the body and kinship.

In a recent general statement about kinship in Southeast Asia, J. Fox says, "I think it is true for the Austronesian world [which includes the Philippines] that one's social identity is not given at birth. One gets the 'impression' if you read some of the old classical African monographs that a person's identity has been defined by the fact of being born into a lineage. Now my view would be that especially in the Austronesian world social identity is not fixed. You are launched . . . you are on a path" (Fox 1987: 174). Such a view would indeed fit the Merina of Madagascar to which I turn below, where I argue that kinship is created little by little throughout life and is only fixed after death in the final placing of the dead in the tomb. It will, I would guess also, largely fit for the people studied by Cannell, and this is suggested in Cannell's forthcoming discussion of Bicolano marriage. Such a view of kinship, created not through birth but through a continual becoming, brought about through contact with the coexisting world, accords well with a view of one's place in history that results from a continual negotiation, which ultimately creates permanent cumulative transformation through the taking on of new appearances, which you become but which in the process you also make your own. The Filipino's view of the past and its continuing changing imprint on them seems coherent not only with their understanding of their place in history but with their understanding of the nature of reproduction, of birth, of the character of mind and of their body. For them history is internal since events are continually changing them down to the very roots of their being since they are not defined by birth but are through life in a continual process of growing definition.

The cases of the Sadah of Yemen and of the Bicolanos of the Philippines are therefore in many ways opposites, and I must admit that for the sake of a short presentation I have pushed the contrasts to extremes, ignoring some elements where the two are not quite so distinct. However there are systems which, even at the schematic level of this essay, seem genuinely intermediate.

As an example of these I take a group of people living in Madagascar, the Merina (Bloch 1971, 1986). As was the case for the Yemenis in relation to the Arab world as a whole, and for the Bicolanos for the Philippines, much of what I have to say would apply to other peoples in Madagascar and possibly beyond. In fact I am much helped here by some of the ideas formulated in another recent thesis by R. Astuti concerning a quite different Malagasy groups to the Merina; the Vezo, fishing peoples of the west coast of Madagascar (Astuti 1991).

The Merina are a group of people who were the subjects of a kingdom which developed in the eighteenth century by incorporating various other groups and political entities.

In many ways their kinship system corresponds well to the Austronesian patterns as characterized by Fox in that birth does not determine the person. The Merina stress how the newborn child is all soft, her kinship alignments relatively open. For example (as is the case with the Vezo), whether she will be linked to her father's side of the family is a matter which remains open for negotiation. Adoption is always possible and common and very often leads to the original parentage being forgotten.

Accompanying this view of the nature of kinship is an attitude to history which has many similarities to that of the Bicolanos. The Merina have been very willing recipients of foreign ways of doing things. They became Christians enthusiastically long before colonization. They adopted foreign dress, types of houses, and hairstyles remarkably easily. They were very willing to emigrate to parts of Madagascar outside Imerina and very soon to France, where they have long formed an active and relatively prosperous community. The Merina, a little like the Filipinos, are normally above all interested in transformation and appearance, in the transformation brought about by growth, the transformation of the growing unity of families brought about by marriage, the transformations brought about in their own identity by events. For them transformation, movement, unencumbered enjoyment of the possibilities of present situations, and being alive are two sides of the same coin. In this respect they are Aristotelians.

But unlike the Filipinos discussed by Cannell there is another aspect to their representation of their experience of history. Talking of the Vezo, Astuti says that for them one belongs to a descent group only after death and this would, with modifications, be true of most Malagasy. Among the Merina the monumental tombs represent the immortalization of the descent group, its unchanging permanence through time, but also its immobile localization in a piece of territory with which it has been and will

226

always be placed forever. Merina tombs are megalithic structures intended to last forever. These tombs are not just containers; in fact they conceptually merge the stone container with the members of the group that are continually being placed there, after the living have ended the mobility implied by the fact that they are alive, and after the dry parts of their body have been separated from the wet parts through the rituals which follow death.

As dried parts of tombs the Merina thus have a permanent place in history. Their tomb and, in a sense, the fact that they were there in the past in that particular locality, as events flowed around them, ensure that they will remain there in the future so long as the new generations have their remains placed in the tomb and so long as the living maintain the material structure.

This permanence in history is, however, very different to the permanence in history of the Yemeni Sadah. It is not "as a special kind of human being" that they were there in the past, and will and should be there in the future; it is as dead, dried objects which contrast dramatically with living people.

There is however for the Merina a relationship between the living, mutable, and mobile being, endlessly modified by the moment and the imprint these moments leave on it, and the steady object in the tomb. Throughout life (including the period immediately after life) the one type of being becomes the other. As the living person goes through life and moves towards final burial in the tomb, a journey which will only be completed after death, the steady dead being is gradually taking over the fluid living being. The process of gradual invasion is caused by a person receiving blessing since for the Merina blessing involves the living coming into contact with the tomb, which in a sense, little by little, places itself in the body of the maturing individual. In this way a cycle is established so that the living become the dead and the dead become the living.

What this means is that living people are dual. The young are more "live, mutable, mobile beings," while the old gradually contain more of the unchanging tomb in themselves, though the final transformation of the living into the tomb object is a fairly brutal process, carried out in the ritual of secondary burial (Bloch 1971). The gradually changing mixture which are living people is therefore first of all conceptualized in terms of the body, but it also has many other aspects. For example, it is also manifested in terms of a dualism in ways of speaking between ordinary speech and the ancestral oratory of the old.

Above all it is a dualism of knowledge and mind. On the one hand there is knowledge concerning day-to-day practical matters, which should be dealt with through the maximum ingenuity and flexibility of thought,

227

and on the other hand, there is knowledge consisting of immobile ancestral traditions which should be merely repeated but not changed. This contrast is actually made explicit by the Merina themselves as well as by other Malagasy people (Beaujard 1991) who contrast in every possible way tales, which are intended to entertain, amuse, and provoke thought, which they say are not about truth but about "lying," and what is called *Tantara*, which is ancestral knowledge and which is categorically true.

This emphasis on truth immediately reminds us of the Sadah and, for that matter, of Plato, and we can see that a notion of truth integral with certain types of or aspects of being inevitably determines whether history is inside oneself or outside. As truth bearers, or as future dried ancestral bones in and merged with the localized tomb, the Merina, like the stones of the tomb itself, should be unaffected by the swirl of events. In this way, for them history is external. However, they are not really like the Sadah. The Sadah in their lives are, and should be, vessels of immutable holy wisdom. In their person they are permanently true because of their birth which has given them the potential truly to learn and know the holy scriptures. As "living people" therefore the Sadah are only in history in the way a rock is in the middle of a stream. This is not true of the Merina. As "living people" they are like the Bicolanos, made by events; it is only fully as dead people that they will become that transcendental permanence that is the stones of the tomb. But then it will not be *them* but something that has grown in them as they have become more mature, older, and which, after death, will finally dominate as the final remains of their live selves, the wet elements, are completely removed. The Merina tomb is therefore not a memorial of the dead, it is a memorial of the way the living have been abolished by transcendental stone.

This may all sound very abstract but it takes many very concrete forms. For example, the Merina who live in France seem apparently and easily totally French in their culture, their values, and their aspiration. But there is one great difference: they all, at amazingly great expense, will arrange for their corpses to be flown back to Madagascar so that, in the end, they will be back as part of permanent stone structures in the soil of their ancestral land. The Merina living in France are, therefore, in a particularly dramatic way, which nonetheless is common to all Merina, participating in two different ways in two kinds of histories at once. One is a history in France, where like Aristotelians they learn and are internally transformed by the flow of events, and the other is a history in Madagascar that remains external, since irrespective of what happens they are still in the same place they always have been and in a substance, stone, which, like Platonic truth, is absolute and unchanging. But in fact they do not participate in this static existence in Madagascar as live, wet beings but as dead, dry, lithic beings, since for them being alive is about movement and change and sensual pleasure (Bloch 1989b).

§

What do these three examples show? First of all that there is no one way of relating to the past and the future and therefore of being in history. There is, therefore, no one way by which one wants to inscribe memory in the public world. For example if we consider things which could be called mnemonic objects: the Quran of the Sadah, the saint of the Bicolanos, and the tombs of the Merina, we can see that their purposes and their characteristics are completely different. There is no point in trying to understand what such objects can do as markers of the past if we consider them as simply memory devices, without also considering the more general contexts given above. There is not a generalized need of human beings to remember the past. And, in any case, as Bartlett stressed long ago, the devices which select from the past what is to be remembered also inevitably involve selecting what of the past is to be obliterated, for example the soft parts of the body of the Merina. When we consider the social actor's attitude to the distant past it becomes clear that one's effort involves not simply finding ways of remembering better, as is the aim of the psychologists' imaginary actor, but also, and equally, finding ways to forget it.

One fundamental problem in linking together the concepts of memory offered by, on the one hand, most psychologists, and, on the other, most anthropologists and historians, therefore seems to lie with the psychologists' much too simple notion of the person. Psychologists, and others like them, tend to imagine as unproblematic that entity which acts on the external or simply and passively responds to the external. When a psychologist is looking at short-term memory, or at working memory, she can get away with this. The totally unconscious use of memory involved in carrying out practical tasks may probably be satisfactorily studied without taking into account the cultural and historical specificities which construct the actor. However as soon as we move to long-term memories such as autobiographic memory and the long-term semantic memory of a historical past, a memorizing which extends memory well beyond the life of the individual, the problem of the nature of the subject must come to the fore.

Such recalling defines the person in relation to time by invoking, or not invoking, notions of a past interaction with an external world which contains truth and falsehoods, permanent and impermanent elements, which is, or is not, in a state of continual creative dialectic flux. These ways of remembering the past not only create the imagined external world but

229

they create the imagined nature of the actor in the past, which, insofar as this actor is seen as a predecessor, refers also to those living in the present. As the member of the Sadah chooses to fix wisdom that has come from the past in his receptive body, he is defining the kind of person he really was in the past. He is constructing the kind of person he will be in the future. And sandwiched in between these two, as a filling of infinitely small depth, he is defining himself as a permannent, unchanging person in history. When the Bicolano imagine themselves sandwiched between their malleable forebears in the colonial past and consequently their malleable successors in the future they are constructing themselves in the present as a completely different filling to the sandwich than do the Sadah, and again the same is true of the Merina except that they, perhaps, see themselves as a single filling shared by two different sandwiches. These different definitions of the self mean that we cannot assume a priori that we know what the person is, irrespective of cultural or historical context. I am not arguing, however, as would a cultural relativist, that there is nothing else to actors than these historically constructed self-definitions; indeed the relation of these definitions to aspects of the person which are not so fundamentally determined by specific histories is precisely an area of potential cooperation between psychologists, anthropologists, and historians, but this kind of joint project cannot begin if we do not take on board the relevance of these self-definitions for constructing the actor. The three examples I have given here of culturally defined actors are not anything like the hypothesized, generalized, and unspecific actor of psychology manuals, who is envisaged merely as an accumulator and maximizer of unproblematic memories, irrespective of content. Indeed we may suspect that this image even may itself not be as scientific and culture-free as psychologists implicitly assume since it too may have something to do with the culture in which it was produced, in this case the image of the individual as fundamentally an economic maximizer.

No human scientist can therefore ignore how people represent themselves to themselves in history because it is, to a certain extent, in terms of these representations that they will react to revolutions, migration, or colonial conquests, as we have seen it to be the case for the examples I have discussed here.

Clearly the problem of linking up the notion of memory offered by psychologists on the one hand, and, on the other, anthropologists and historians is therefore difficult but also thought-provoking. There are two problems. The first, I have discussed here. The second I have not.

If psychologists concerned themselves merely with working and short-term memory they might get away with their rather simple notion of actors, but they do not so limit themselves and they want to, and do, move from private representations to public representations. If they do this, as I have tried to show, then they must take into account the kind of matters discussed here.

However, before anthropologists and historians become too pleased with themselves in having taught the psychologists a lesson, they should remember the second problem which I have not discussed here and which might temper their self-satisfaction. If historians and anthropologists confined themselves merely to public "representations" of the past they perhaps could ignore what psychologists have been showing concerning the place of memory in practical action. But they don't; they want to understand the mental character of what people remember and the significance this has for the form and perhaps the content of what is remembered; they want to see how the mental presence of the past affects what people do, and in this aspect of their work they will have to learn many lessons from the psychologists. I have not discussed this side of things, and in many ways the debate has been admirably opened by Sperber (1975).

In other words the study of memory may well be a privileged area for seeing how public, historically created, cultural representations join private representations, but before we can go forward in this joint enterprise with any success, much preliminary but essential theoretical groundwork needs to be done. I have attempted to do a little of this here.

Notes

This is a slightly revised version of the Edward Westermarck Memorial Lecture, presented in Helsinki, January 31, 1992. I would like to acknowledge the help of Dr. F. Cannell, Dr. J. Coleman, and Dr. G. vom Bruck for reading and commenting in a very useful manner on earlier drafts. My account of their work is however my own and the reader who really wants to know what they say should turn to their texts.

References

Astuti, R. 1991. "Learning to Be Vezo: The Construction of the Person among Fishing People of Western Madagascar." Unpublished thesis, London University.

Baddeley, A. J. 1976. *The Psychology of Memory*. London: Harper and Row.

Bartlett, F. C. 1932. *Remembering: A Study of Experimental and Social Psychology*. Cambridge: Cambridge University Press.

Beaujard, P. 1991. *Mythe et Société à Madagascar (Tanala de l'Ikongo)*. Paris: L'Harmattan.

Bloch, M. 1986. *From Blessing to Violence: History and Ideology in the Circumcision Ritual of the Merina of Madagascar*. Cambridge: Cambridge University Press.

———. 1989a. "Literacy and Enlightenment." In *Literacy and Society*. Ed. M. Trolle-Larsen and K. Sousboe. Publications of the Centre for Research in the Humanities, Copenhagen.

———. 1989b. "The Symbolism of Money in Imerina." In *Money and the Morality of Exchange*. Ed. M. Bloch and J. Parry. Cambridge: Cambridge University Press.

———. 1993. "Time Narratives and the Multiplicity of Representations of the Past." *Bulletin of the Institute of Ethnology*. Academica Sinica N. 75.

———. n.d. "Autobiographical Memory and the Historical Memory of the More Distant Past." MS.

Bruck, G. vom. 1991. "Descent and Religious Knowledge: 'Houses of Learning' in Modern Sana'a." Unpublished thesis, London University.

Cannell, F. 1992. "Catholicism, Spirit Mediumship and the Ideal of Beauty in a Bicolano Community: Philippines." Unpublished thesis, London University.

Carruthers, M. 1990. *The Book of Memory: A Study of Memory in Medieval Culture*. Cambridge: Cambridge University Press.

Cohen, G. 1990. *Memory in the Real World*. Hove and London: Lawrence Erlbaum Associates.

Coleman, J. 1992. *Ancient and Medieval Memories: Studies in the Reconstruction of the Past*. Cambridge: Cambridge University Press.

Eickelman, D. F. 1978. "The Art of Memory: Islamic Education and Social Reproduction." *Comparative Studies in Society and History* 20: 485–516.

Fortes, M. 1953. "The Structure of Unilineal Descent Groups." *American Anthropologist* 55: 17–41.

Fox, J. 1987. "The House as a Type of Social Organization on the Island of Roti, Indonesia." In *De la Hutte au Palais*. Ed. C. MacDonald. Paris: C.N.R.S.

Goody, J. 1977. *The Domestication of the Savage Mind*. Cambridge: Cambridge University Press.

Lévi-Strauss, C. 1984. *Paroles Données*. Paris: Plon.

Luria, A. R. 1976. *Cognitive Development: Its Structural and Social Foundations*. Cambridge, Mass.: Harvard University Press.

Madelung, W. 1965. *Der Imam al Oasim. Ibn Ibrahim und die Glaubenslehre der Zaiditen*. Berlin: de Gruyter.

Neisser, U. 1978. "Memory, What Are the Important Questions?" In *Practical Aspects of Memory.* Ed. M. M. Gruneberg, P. E. Morris, and R. N. Sykes. London: Academic Press.

Olson, D. R. 1977. "From Utterance to Text: The Bias of Language, in Speech and Writing." *Harvard Educational Review* 47: 257–81.

Sperber, D. 1975. "Anthropology and Psychology: Towards an Epidemiology of Representations." *Man* 20: 73–89.

Wertsch, J. V. 1985. *Vigotsky and the Social Formation of Mind.* Cambridge, Mass.: Harvard University Press.

11

The Past Imperfect
Remembering As Moral Practice

Michael Lambek

> The self we know in self-knowledge can't be construed as an
> object. Being a self is a matter of how things matter to us.
> ——Ernst Tugendhat, *Selbsbewusstein und Selbstbestimmung,* as
> paraphrased by Charles Taylor, *Sources of the Self*

> It is time to rescue the phenomenon of memory from being
> regarded merely as a psychological faculty and to see it as an
> essential element of the finite historical being of man.
> ——Hans-Georg Gadamer, *Truth and Method*

> To remember at all . . . is to become enmeshed in the thicket
> of the past.
> ——Edward Casey, *Remembering*

Hacking's critique of the prevalent assumption that memory is an appropriate object of scientific knowledge leaves us seeking a more appropriate
way to approach the subject. I propose that one interesting way to understand memory is as a form of moral practice. The argument has two strands:
that we think about memory as a human, cultural practice rather than a natural object or process; and that the kind of practice it is be understood as
moral rather than simply technical, intellectual, or instrumental.
    I build my case by alternating pieces of abstract argument with frag-
ments of ethnography from fieldwork among Malagasy speakers on the is-

land of Mayotte and in northwest Madagascar.[1] The ethnography, which is suggestive rather than decisive in this form, draws particularly on my reflections on spirit possession, which is common in the area. In brief, possession refers to the relations that particular disembodied creatures ("spirits") engage with particular human hosts, such that the host is periodically "absent" from her own body, replaced by the voice and persona of the spirit.[2] On the surface spirits resemble the distinct alters of multiple personality disorder described by Antze (this volume) and there is a similar gender distribution and similar expressions of liveliness and sometimes of child personas (Hacking 1995: 76). But the possessed do not generally suffer the extreme anguish of at least some people with MPD; cases of possession are treated by means of a standardized ceremonial scenario and generally lead to a socially and psychologically positive outcome; the spirits are drawn from a public repertoire and legitimated as distinct from their hosts; and the spirits do not memorialize private suffering so much as they speak to the wider family and community. Their message is, in part, one of the prevalence of suffering (rather than its individuality) and also of the transcendence of suffering (rather than its fixation). Possession leads to greater rather than lesser connection to others. Spirit possession is in many ways a moral discourse, exploring the ambiguities of power (Lambek 1981). Here I speak only about the connection to issues of memory.

§

A few days following my return to Mayotte (Comoro Archipelago, Western Indian Ocean) in 1980, after a four-year absence, my mentor Tumbu took me aside, fixed me with a penetrating look, and asked whether I hadn't forgotten to greet anyone. I was delighted when he reminded me of my social ties to the spirits that possessed his wife Mohedja. (I had not forgotten them, but was waiting to see what would progress.) I had to call them soon, he said, because they could not appear once Ramadan began.[3] When Mohedja's spirits rose in succession we greeted each other as old friends; such affirmation was a fulfillment of moral obligations entered into some years earlier. During our conversation I was introduced to a new spirit of Mohedja's, Zaliata, who had not yet held her ceremony. Zaliata asked whether I would sponsor it. Although sponsorship is expensive, I took this as a positive overture. Sponsorship is usually taken by the spouse or close kin of a host and is an affirmation of ties and indeed a way of consolidating them. Moreover, Mohedja knew this would provide me with further opportunity to see a possession ceremony from the inside, as it were. I agreed, but cautiously. My visit in 1980 was only of several weeks' duration and much of that during Ramadan. I had no way of knowing whether I would ever return to Mayotte and indeed at the time I thought of the visit as possibly my last one, intended to close off unfinished business and say good-bye. I explained to Zaliata that I might not be in a position to hold the ceremony and that she must not exhibit impatience nor make Mohedja ill in the meantime as spirits who have not held their ceremonies often do. The spirit agreed to this condition and we parted.

The spirit's request meant that business in Mayotte was not finished (how could relations among friends ever be?) and I thought about it often in subsequent years. When I returned to Mayotte again in 1985, urged on in part by the memory of Zaliata's outstanding request, I called up Zaliata and said I intended to keep my commitment. But at this, there arose unexpected difficulties. Mohedja's adult daughters objected. What disconcerted them most, I think, and what surprised me most, was that the situation was so unexpected. They had not even known of Zaliata's existence, they said, or at least they had not remembered that she possessed their mother. The simple fact of the matter was that Zaliata had never once risen in Mohedja during my five year absence nor had any illness or communication been laid to her door. Mohedja's other spirits had risen during this time. However, Zaliata arrived promptly at my request and remembered our agreement perfectly. Indeed, Zaliata's absence in the intervening years had been precisely an index of the retention of the memory of our contract. Her appearance in my absence would have been pointless since only I could carry through with the next stage of the possession script.

Mohedja's daughters attempted to dissuade their mother and her spirit from undergoing the new ceremony. I was embarrassed by the turn of events, apologized to the daughters, and told Mohedja I would be happy with either outcome. Mohedja agreed with her daughters' decision, but immediately thereafter fell sick, her symptoms testifying to the violation of the agreement. Zaliata remained stubborn and refused to accept the daughters' arguments. Mohedja's daughters became reconciled to the situation and helped me sponsor the ceremony. Mohedja herself danced blissfully in trance.[4]

§

Let us distinguish two broad conceptualizations of memory. One of these, dominant in America now, emphasizes the role of memory in the expression and validation of the discrete, private individual. Memory here is simultaneously objective and subjective; this conjunction may be what gives memory such discursive power. Memory is subjective in that it is uniquely ours, something which distinguishes each of us from others and which defines who we are and how we see things. It is something that each of us "possesses" and that validates our unique presence as an independent witness, whether as bystander, agent, or victim. Yet this possession is objectified in a number of ways. Memory is pluralized, thus rendered discrete, transactable, and even commodifiable. Memories are objects, not acts. Advertising brochures tell us we can collect them on foreign beaches, produce them during candlelit dinners, and capture them on film, but when they are contested they appear more like unshreddable bureaucratic files. To the degree that memory is conceptualized as an act it is a passive one, analogous to a video camera left running in a corner of the room, recording or re-viewing, but not shaping experience. But this means that memory is judged entirely according to objective criteria, how well it conforms with "the facts." Our memories may be depicted as complete or incomplete, but never as subtle, tactful, or reasonable, well or poorly crafted, elegantly or clumsily performed. They are accurate or inaccurate, but never justified or unjustified. Finally, memory is evaluated objectively because, as Hacking has been at pains to show (above and 1995), it has become an object of professional knowledge about which experts can discover the timeless truth. Moreover, memory is understood as no mere human product but as constitutive in a causal sense of who we are as individuals and as societies or ethnic groups. In the extreme, the conflation of excessive subjectivity and objectivity leads people to identify with their hypostatized memories.

The analogies to the files and video camera are not, of course, arbitrary. Our reified, naturalized concept of memory is undoubtedly linked to our technological capacities, especially to reproduction by means of the camera.[5] The memory constructs of other societies are linked to *their* cultural means of inscription, storage, and access (such as spirit possession). My point is not that diverse cultural technologies provide more or less accurate and complete memory, but that they provide diverse ways of imagining memory and hence distinctive qualitative emphases. The objectifying devices of contemporary Western memory production have at least three significant qualities that distinguish them from the idea of memory as ongoing practice: they freeze words and images; they put frames around them; and they render remembering mechanical and impersonal (Casey 1987: 270, 298). This enables us to resituate memory ostensibly outside engaged experience and the give and take of social relations. An inherently and preeminently temporally constituted process like remembering is thus detemporalized. This is nonsense, but it is difficult to see it as such when authoritative discourses in psychiatry, law, and history so often attempt to validate it.[6]

Let us try to imagine memory in another way, one which resists the extremes of both excessive subjectivity and excessive objectivity; one which situates memory in time and sees it as a function of social relationships, in part a mutual affirmation of past interaction, in part the traces of our introjection of one another. There is a sense that in the ordinary course of events the memories of parties to a social relationship ought to be compatible with each other. People ought to maintain their relationships over time and be able to take up where they left off, to acknowledge the commitments they have made to one another. The intermittent quality of the appearance of spirits and hosts (not to mention anthropologists) and their respective consciousness serves to heighten these qualities of memory, but they are implicit in friendship, kinship relations, marriage alliances, and, indeed, any system of reciprocity.

Memory in this model is less a completely private yet potentially objective phenomenon stored *within* the mind and capable of remaining there than it is activated implicitly or explicitly *between* people, a confirmation of the sense of continuity (caring) and discontinuity (mourning) that each person experiences in their relations with others, and likely acknowledged by additional parties.[7] Memory here is more intersubjective and dialogical than exclusively individual, more act (remembering) than object, and more ongoing engagement than passive absorption and playback. Applying this to contemporary psychotherapy one could say that what occurs is not necessarily the replacement of amnesia by memory, false memories by true ones (or vice versa), so much as the alternation of social contracts, for example, in gross terms, the displacing of family relationships by those with the therapist; a reformulating of social ties and commitments. The value of articulating a particular version of the past would be explicitly connected to its moral ends and consequences for relations in the present.

Such an argument recognizes that how we view memory, and how we remember, have implications for how we view the person, and vice versa. It leads us away from understanding memory as a purely "natural" or "automatic" activity (analogous, say, to digestion) and the product of unmediated gaze, and hence away from accuracy as the only criterion by which to evaluate memory, toward seeing memory as always and inevitably culturally and socially mediated and hence subject to evaluation along a number of dimensions whose relative importance are open for debate. It is not to deny the importance of accuracy, but to recognize *why* we consider accuracy important. The questions to ask of any given acts of memory are what is affirmed and what is denied.

Such an approach treats memory not as a neutral representation, more or less accurate, of the past, but as a claim or set of claims, more or less firm, more or less justified, more or less appropriate, about it. Both remembering and forgetting may be claims, motivated acts of some sort;

this indeed is Freud's argument regarding forgetting. In this sense neither memories nor their gaps should be taken at face value, not even after therapy or inquisition and validation by other kinds of experts. Like speech, memory contains both semantic and pragmatic dimensions, and constitutes both locutionary and illocutionary acts. As Antze argues (this volume), to remember is never solely to report on the past so much as to establish one's relationship toward it. Memory is never out of time and never morally or pragmatically neutral.[8]

The same argument applies when we move from instances of remembering to formal discourses of memory. Any invocation of "memory," whether in psychology, psychotherapy, psychiatry, neurology, history, or anthropology, is "motivated" by claims regarding time, person, consciousness, reality, truth, and the like. Hence, to break through the theoretical circle of self-validating disciplinary analogies may require, short of sheer brilliance, borrowing ideas from the equally self-validating but substantively distinct analogies of other times and places.

The illustration from Mayotte draws upon the usual, doubtless exaggerated, comparison between the individualist West and the socially embedded Rest. Yet I use it less to provide a sense of difference than as a source for insight about Western experience. There are also plenty of Western models at hand, ranging from Halbwachs (1980) on collective memory or Mead (1934) on intersubjectivity, to Janet on memory as an act (see Leys above) and contemporary debates in psychoanalytic theory between proponents of the classical drive model and what Stephen Mitchell (1988) refers to as the relational model. My argument may be faulted for resting on ideal types. But the public discussion we have now is largely restricted to understanding memory through the ideological, albeit implicit, lens of a possessive individualism. What happens if we reconstitute the discourse of memory in the key of object relations?

§

We have seen that spirits retain specific memories and thereby index the social relations to which they pertain. They provide, in effect, a sort of "parking" function between rounds of communication. This is, however, far from the whole story; spirits are memorable in and of themselves. Above all, they are memorable irruptions in the personal lives of their hosts. Mohedja and Tumbu can tell stories about the arrival of each of their spirits. Each is linked to a specific phase of their lives, particular problems, projects, and relationships at the time (such as Mohedja's relationship with me), often to serious illness and conflict. The spirit condenses these memories in its person. Each subsequent intervention on the part of the spirit draws out (rediscovers and extends) the narrative of which it is the central character

240

and the relationship to the world of which it is the embodiment, and also provides the occasion for reinterpretation. Moreover, with the hindsight of having a spirit one can reinterpret past events, knowing now, as one did not then, that they may have been caused or influenced by the spirit before it had chosen to make itself fully known to the host. Spirits thus aid in constructing and authorizing revisionary accounts of the personal past. At the same time, however, they are not, in Paul Antze's useful phrase (personal communication 1994), memorials *to* the past. What counts is not only how they entered the hosts (pain, victimization), but their progress through the ceremonial scenario and the commitments engaged upon thereafter. Spirits provide their hosts both new channels of communication and internalized self-objects, enabling continuous adaptation to the present and engendering a working-through process.[9] Central to spirits are their narrative and performative functions. Spirits are vehicles *for* memory rather than the frozen remnants of memory.[10]

§

Higher order consciousness, consciousness of being conscious, requires the representation of a self. The self-representation of this self, its consciousness of temporal and spatial existence, is memory. Memory in this sense, argues Oliver Sacks (1993) in his review of the work of Gerald Edelman, is something neither deposited in the brain nor having a specific location within it. It is, rather, a symbolic practice.

What are the relations among memory, consciousness, and the symbolic vehicles, of which perhaps the most important is narrative?[11] Benedict Anderson (1991) argues that narrative enters precisely to replace memory, that is, that the presence of a narrative is an index of having forgotten the original experience. Thus he takes memory as somehow continuous and literal as opposed to "imagined." I suggest that neither of these pictures of memory, whether as direct, literal, and subjective, or as narrated, imagined, and objectified, is sufficient. The literalist picture ignores the fact that our experience of memory is generally indirect, by means of recall, recollection, or reminiscence (cf. Casey 1987).[12] At the same time, it would be a mistake to go to the opposite extreme and mistake the fluidity of memory for the detached objectifications of collective memorials (including here the overly coherent narratives produced in some forms of North American psychotherapy). It seems more interesting to take these ideal typical pictures of memory as poles and to focus on the movement between them, on how one goes from the one to the other and back, how private experience and public narrative mutually inform each other. In other words, whereas Anderson distinguishes memory from (fixed) narrative, we also need to distinguish it from the immediacy of direct experience. Memory, as suggested above, concerns the consciousness of being conscious. Hence, we need to retain for memory the idea of perspective or clearing of space, the view of there from over here, of situated distance (cf. Kirmayer's landscape).

It follows that we must understand memory as *essentially incomplete*; memory is perspectival and the perspective is a continuously shifting one. The voicing of memory is transitional, no longer fully subjective and not yet fully objective before it is legitimated in collective constructions like history textbooks, ritual commemorations, or legal testimony (or vice versa). Active memory (like acts of spirit possession and talk about spirits) lies between primary experience and the routinized "forgetting" that Anderson describes.

Anderson's memory that we cannot recapture and hence must replace by narrative is analogous to Freud's understanding of dreams. The experience of dreaming is not based upon a concrete, bounded narrative or image that we can then repeat verbatim; instead, the telling replaces the dream. In other words, it is impossible to know where the images perceived or originating in sleep break off and those in waking life, elicited in what is ostensibly a reproduction but becomes its own creative process, begin. Once formulated in words, it is this version we remember, the representation, not the original experience. What we call the dream is actually the highly mediated retelling. Similarly, memory can be understood as acts of narrative, re-tellings, a point Freud grasped in his formulation of screen memories, that is, memories of memories.[13] Accessible memory has no unmediated essence, either as subjective experience or as objective fact, but is always in the act of being made.

These points help us reflect on the differences between history and memory as constituted in contemporary discourse. For many people, history is secondary to memory in not being based on direct continuous experience, on I-witnessing. This valuation implies a dangerously literalist view of memory, the kind one might find in a court of law. It neglects the fact that, as Terdiman puts it, representation can never be identical reproduction (1993: 59). If the first person account has a certain kind of legitimacy of the "I-was-there" sort, conversely documentation provides a counterweight of its own. Thus the opposite tack on the comparison of history and memory, as oral historians have learned to their chagrin, is to trust only what has been recorded in writing, since, as it is said, memory is notoriously "unreliable," whereas, presumably, the texts stick to their stories. Here we have, in a nutshell, one of the salient distinctions between texts and practice.[14]

In contrast to Anderson (but in his spirit) I refer to narratives as vehicles of memory but recognize that they can become more or less objectified, more or less detached from the process of remembering. This view of remembering as symbolic practice understands neither personal memory nor scholarly history as literal; to the degree that both are narrativized constructions the categorical distinction between them begins to dissolve. The critical distinction is one of fluidity, the degree to which any particular narrative is open to continuous reformulation, any event or document to reinterpretation and how such changes are legitimated.

§

Spirits are memorable not only for what they evoke about the host's experience but because they are themselves historical or mythic figures. If in Western discourse it makes sense to distinguish memory from history (although I have begun to deconstruct the opposition), this is less obvious in places where history is less text-mediated than voiced and embodied. When the spirits are persons from the past, once living figures who re-emerge after death, the narratives they evoke include dimensions of broad collective interest. This is crucial in Madagascar where the *trumba* spirits who possess people are the ancestors of living royalty; the spirits draw their collective import both from contemporary political circumstances and from past events in which they were live agents. Each spirit is vehicle for a history that is preserved, in part, through relations between contemporary hosts and the figures from the past who possess them. Taken together, the roster of spirits and the ways they interact with each other provide a collective historical memory. Spirits wear the clothing of the time when they were alive, speak the languages of the past, embody past habits, customs, and comportment; they continue to enact the concerns, relationships, and perspectives of the past. They are thus "living history" in a strong sense; they bring forward and force people to acknowledge the commitments of and to the past. The past is never completely over; it continues to shape the present, even as it is distinct from it, and at the same time it is available to be addressed by the present. Conversely, remembering entails engagement with the past.

§

Memory of any kind implies a self or subject who perceives the memory or does the remembering. Today our understanding of the nature of this self is increasingly dependent upon reference to memory—I am the product of who I was and what I experienced—just as the nature of memory is implied and constituted by the theory of the self or subject—you should remember what your therapist or civics instructor thinks you can because that is the way people or nations are. I take memory to be an intrinsic part of selfhood (such that memory and identity serve to mutually validate

243

each other), but I also take these to be culturally somewhat variable (cf. Bloch this volume). Thus the contemporary North American invocation of memory tells us about the boundedness and singularity of a particular subject and relationship of self and others. The cultural variability in identity supports the argument for the sort of dialectical relationship between narrative and experience I have suggested.

The practice of memory operates in partly similar ways for individual and collective subjects. In each case we narrate and represent our identity, and then reproduce these representations, by means of the public idioms and tools at our disposal. We create imagined communities (in Anderson's brilliant coinage) and imagined selves and then attempt to live accordingly. In neither case is it useful for the theoretician to start from a pre-given primordial or essential identity existing apart from the ongoing construction of itself. As Anderson argues, it is out of oblivion that narratives spring. It is precisely because I *cannot* remember in direct, unmediated fashion the experience of my childhood, that is, can no longer experience as a child, and because I cannot remember directly the events that lead from the infant to the man, that I rely upon a narrative construction to realize this continuity. Individual memory, like the narration of the collective we call history, is never literal reproduction, but an artifice to render the continuity in change realistic.

In addition to being a necessary response to oblivion, such artifice also works in part by means of selective oblivion, or censorship. Objectified narrative may be understood less as an inadequate replacement for direct experience than as a purification of it, a transformation of pain into art. Narrated memory is a creative distillation and transformation of past experience, a poiesis (cf. Terdiman 1993). As Gadamer puts it, "Only by forgetting does the mind have . . . the capacity to see everything with fresh eyes, so that what is long familiar combines with the new into a many levelled unity" (1985: 16). In the best of circumstances, this may be sublimation, but even neurotic or hysteric symptoms have a symbolic consistency, as Freud demonstrated.[15]

This argument needs to be supplemented by another explanation for oblivion that suggests that foundational experiences become constitutive *of* the self in such a manner that they are no longer accessible *to* it. To the degree that the subject is constituted through such assimilative *forgetting*, conscious memory might be conceived as the unresolved, the residual. In this sense, conscious memory is significant less as the trace of the past than as the kernel of the future (cf. Kugelmass, this volume). Such a model acknowledges the relevance of two senses of "memory," as suggested by Anderson's original argument; however it requires at least two senses of "forgetting" as well.

Not only does the constitution of the collective subject work analogously to the constitution of the individual one in general, but particular self experiences and discourses of the self provide idioms for narrating collective experience and identity. This is immediately evident in the application of a term like "collective memory" and is well-developed in arguments that the concept of the modern nation is modeled on the ideology of collective individualism (Handler 1988). It is found also in the iconic representation of history by "great men," including the *trumba* spirits. Likewise, the discourses of collective identity offer a language for expressing selfhood via kinship, ethnicity, gender, race, and class, or newer conceptualizations like sexual orientation and postcolonial subject, or my own transposition of "imagined community" to "imagined self." In other words, images of individual identities constitute a totemic system, so to speak, of collectivities, and vice versa. In both the individual and the collective case we have today in the West the conceptualization of highly bounded entities distinguished from one another by their property (Handler 1988), property that includes inviolable, sacred memories belonging to their rightful owners.[16] However, while such explicit memories may be extremely salient, they are poetic rather than literal and not necessarily as foundational as their subjects claim.

§

The narratives most salient to the Antankarana of northwestern Madagascar today refer to events that took place in the first half of the nineteenth century, specifically to the incursions of the Merina on their territory. At one point some members of the royal descent group were pressed against an inlet of the sea. Rather than submit to the enemy, they plunged into the water, where many of them drowned or were eaten by fish. Sometime thereafter the martyrs began to reappear, possessing living Antankarana as *trumba* spirits. Every year the Antankarana monarch holds a bathing ritual at which hundreds of people gather at the beach and the possessed plunge into the water. Royal bathing rituals have significance throughout Madagascar; the Antankarana version reenacts the death of the martyrs while also celebrating the emergence, empowerment, and renewal of the spirits. The ceremony is a positive, revitalizing one, constituting an ongoing exchange among the king, the people, the ancestors, and the spirits, but it also memorializes the historical trauma. Merina are not allowed at the site.

The martyrs appear on many occasions. Their pathos is reinforced by the fact that, like all *trumba*, they portray themselves at the point of death, mimetically reproducing the manner of their dying in the way they contort the bodies of their hosts on entry (Andrew Walsh, personal communication 1995) and smearing these bodies with white clay to indicate the extent of their wounds. Moreover while most spirits exemplify generational succession and continuity, this group of spirits stands out by being composed of a core set of siblings, all of whom died at once. Gathered together in public spaces, the spirits provide a kind of snapshot of a traumatic moment in northern Malagasy history which is still significant today. However, these Sea Dwellers (*Antandrano*), as they are called, come not to grieve but to engage in the passions of life. They make music, sing, dance and drink, engage playfully with the living, and often assist them with their personal troubles.

Here, in contrast to the view propounded by Michelet at about the same time the martyrs were drowning (Anderson 1991: 198), history does not speak for the dead who cannot speak for themselves. Northwestern Malagasy not only speak to the dead, they speak as the dead; in other words, the dead do speak for themselves. The royal dead are not framed and frozen in objectified, textualized memory, but rendered active in the present. Reciprocally, contemporary Malagasy live not only in the present but in the past. *They do not possess memories, rather they are possessed by them.* Put another way, time is not fully consecutive; the past is not finished and done with, receding ever further into the distance, but (in grammatical terms) imperfect. In the daily interactions of spirits with living people and the many phases of the ritual cycle I cannot describe here, past and present interpenetrate.[17] Historical memory is not determined by a fixed representation that is to be judged entirely by its accuracy but is a mutual tuning constituted in well-crafted and elegantly performed symbolic and moral practice.

§

To speak of memory as symbolically mediated rather than literal is not to endorse the idea that anything goes, that we have no grounds on which to discriminate when memories conflict. Nor is it to suggest that the most coherent narrative is the most adequate. Indeed, if anything the reverse— the smoother the story, the more evident that it is the product of secondary reworking. What symbolic mediation suggests is that any account of the past is organized by means of certain cultural conventions (cf. Kirmayer, this volume). Central among these will be what Bakhtin (1981) has called the chronotope, that is the particular space-time continuum in which the action of any narrative (whether inscribed in writing, embodied in ceremonies, or voiced and under continuous reconstruction) is construed. The chronotope provides a useful analytical device for comparing the worlds in which the subjects of memory, the heroes of the narratives, subsist and, moving up a level of abstraction, which link the events of the memories to the events of their recounting.[18] Malagasy historical chronotopes differ strikingly from European ones.

§

As the concept of the chronotope suggests, space and time are not abstracted from one another in northwest Madagascar. Remembering is carried forward via weekly and lunar cycles, the opening and shutting of gates, the crossing of thresholds, the raising and collapse of vertical posts. Travel between shrines and the annual transport of certain royal artifacts across the countryside reinscribe political relations of the Sakalava monarchy, indexing simultaneously both past constitutions and present lines of power.[19] And while spirit possession is open to virtually anyone (subject to the will of the spirits; hosts do not consciously seek possession), the bearing of memory is spatially and socially distributed.

During the eighteenth century the Sakalava in the region of present day Mahajanga formed the most powerful kingdom on the island. They were weakened by competition from the British-supported Merina, the collapse of the slave trade, and the advent of French colonialism. The polity fragmented into a number of smaller kingdoms and royal factions who share a common historical tradition and idiom for articulating it. The Sakalava polity was supported by a subtle organic division of labor among its component descent groups that is still evident in the distribution of memory-bearing tasks. Doing fieldwork among Sakalava, it is extremely difficult to get a reasonably full account of the past from any single informant. This is not only for the common reason that different people present versions that support their own interests, but because the responsibility for remembering is itself divided up in complex ways, both by task and by subject. People often do not know the nature of their neighbors' contributions (or at least do not feel they have the right to represent them), but taken together, over many hundreds of square kilometers, there is a remarkable tuning. In particular, the role of each distinctive royal personage from the past is maintained somewhere.

Local mediums, shrine managers, and guardians each play their part without knowledge of the whole. Yet in the ensemble a tremendous amount of history is articulated. Not surprisingly, much of this history concerns trauma and its overcoming. The trauma is not only that of war, as in the case of the Water Dwelling spirits (who are also recalled by Sakalava), but emerges from the "family romance" of generations of royalty. I give a brief illustration, drawing upon a single excerpt from but one story. Returning from battle and being informed by one of his sons of infidelity in his absence, a king brutally murdered his wife. Although this event is purported to have taken place some ten generations ago (mid-eighteenth century), it continues to be reexperienced by generations of spirit mediums. The medium of the murdered wife is said to reside at the woman's tomb and may never enter the city of Mahajanga, which houses the shrine containing her husband's relics. Should she do so, she suffers terribly. So does the medium of the husband if he is reminded of his past actions. The memory is kept alive less in the words of the story, which by no means everyone knows or has the right to tell, than in the embodied comportment and pain of a few localized mediums and tomb guardians. In similar fashion, the memory of each former monarch is kept alive and orchestrated with the others. Succession to mediumship is not determined by objective, ascriptive criteria. For the individual host, possession by a particular spirit—bearing a particular identity and trauma—connects his or her personal life to the wider historical narrative in a complex manner, conjoining private suffering with public performance, and individual quests with collective projects.

§

If memory is approached as claims, then it is understood to have addressees, interlocutors who can in turn support or confirm, cast doubt upon or challenge them. Memory is constituted in such dialogical relations (Bakhtin 1981), even if as a form of internal resistance to the claims of others. In using a language of claims I am on dangerous ground, possibly approaching the forensic approach I decried earlier. One difference is that the people who engage in litigating memory often view their claims as mere descriptions of fact. More significant, however, is that the view of practice I have been developing far exceeds the instrumental. If memory is motivated, it is by no means only for private, selfish, or confrontational ends; nor, as the Malagasy case suggests, need the subject be as discretely bounded as we imagine.

We tend to view knowledge as objective fact, true or false, whose accuracy can be judged in a court of law or a psychological experiment. But much of experience is not like that. Memories are eyewitness accounts (assuming sight is the privileged sense; often it is not) only if the emphasis is put on the witnessing, a moral act, rather than on the eye. Rather than treat memory as a discrete thing, stored and retrieved, or as the biologically innate processes of storage and retrieval waiting to be discovered by the experiments of the psychologist, I have been arguing that we understand it as a culturally mediated expression of the temporal dimension of experience, in particular of social commitments and identifications. Remembering comprises contextually situated assertions of continuity on the part of subjects and claims about the significance of past experience. Such tacit assertions and claims, based as much on cumulative wisdom and moral vision as on individual interest, form a kind of moral practice.

If, as Charles Taylor (1989) argues, our life narration and our sense of self are inextricably linked to our sense of the good, the chronotope of memory must be a moral space. Taylor posits three axes of moral thinking, namely respect for others, understandings of what makes a full life, and dignity, i.e., "the characteristics by which we think of ourselves as commanding (or failing to command) the respect of those around us." These axes exist in every culture but differ in how they are conceived, how they relate to each other, and in their relative importance (1989: 15–16).

Taylor argues for "the essential link between identity and a kind of orientation. To know who you are is to be oriented in moral space, a space in which questions arise about what is good or bad, what is worth doing and what not, what has meaning and importance for you and what is trivial and secondary" (ibid.: 28). If the spatial analogy is explicit, there is surely also a temporal dimension and an orientation toward the past as well as toward the future. "To know who I am is a species of knowing where I stand. My identity is defined by the *commitments* and *identifications* which provide the frame or horizon within which I can try to determine from case to case what is good, or valuable, or what ought to be done, or what I endorse or oppose. In other words, it is the horizon within which I am capable of taking a stand" (ibid.: 27, my emphasis).

My argument throughout has been in line with Taylor's staunchly nonreductionist view: "We are selves only in that certain issues matter for us. What I am as a self, my identity, is essentially defined by the way things have significance for me . . . these things have significance for me, and the issue of my identity is worked out, only through a language of interpretation which I have come to accept as a valid articulation of these issues. To ask what a person is, in abstraction from his or her self-interpretations, is to ask a fundamentally misguided question, one to which there couldn't in principle be an answer" (ibid.: 34).

If remembering is a moral and identity-building act, so to be sure, is forgetting. Freud saw it as an act of "moral cowardice" (SEII: 123) that hysterics could not remember those feelings or ideas that ran counter to the ego. At the same time, it was a sign of moral character that the incompatible idea was disposed of by conversion rather than acted upon (SEII: 157). Central to Freud's later understanding of the genesis of the person is the idea that we must have a history that we get wrong. Similarly, two commentators on nationalism, Anderson (1991) and Hobsbawm (1992), draw on Renan's remarks of 1882: "*Or, l'essence d'une nation est que tous les individus aient beaucoup de choses en commun et aussi que tous aient oublié bien des choses,*" recognizing that the ethical quandaries of the historian and psychoanalyst are similar. In telling the stories of their subjects, must both remember the very things those subjects are determined to forget?

Is their responsibility to support current identity politics or to break through the defenses in order to reposition the subject for new self-interpretations or radical change?[20]

§

The picture I have been trying to draw of memory as moral practice is elegantly captured by the Aristotelian ideal of *phronesis*. Although for Aristotle "practical wisdom is a kind of awareness of order, the correct order of ends in my life, which integrates all my goals and desires into a unified whole in which each has proper weight," he rejects Plato's linkage of this to our awareness of the unchanging and eternal order of the cosmos. "Our grasp of the right order and priority of ends in life cannot be of this kind. It is an understanding of the ever-changing, in which particular cases and predicaments are never exhaustively characterized in general rules. The practically wise man (*phronimos*) [or woman] has a knowledge of how to behave in each particular circumstance which can never be equated with or reduced to a knowledge of general truths. Practical wisdom (*phronesis*) is a not fully articulable sense rather than a kind of science" (Taylor 1989: 125).[21] Our relationship to the past is ever-changing. How we acknowledge this relationship—via—memory is a form of *phronesis*.

Taylor's last sentence returns us to Hacking. How we view the subject of memory, what we seek from it as intellectuals, equally depends on our moral orientation and not simply on rational reflection and scientific inquiry. It depends, for example, on whether we are romantics, "yearning after a richer past, one fuller of meaning, from the standpoint of an empty or shallow present" (Taylor 1988: 464), or whether we seek to decenter present subjects. To recognize this is to recognize that memory can be invoked by theorists for various ends, and that these choices are ultimately moral choices. As *phronesis* rather than *episteme* they are not to be judged solely according to their conformity to an externally existing reality, but also as constituents of that social reality.

Notes

An earlier version of this paper was presented at the Canadian Anthropology Society annual meeting, May 1993. I am indebted to Paul Antze for many useful discussions on memory that make this paper a kind of co-construction, although he is absolved of responsibility. I thank also Ian Hacking, Gavin Smith, Jackie Solway, Emmanuel Tehindrazanarivelo, and Andrew Walsh for their criticism and encouragement.

1. Fieldwork has been generously supported by the NSF and the Canada Council (1975–76), the University of Toronto (1980), the National Geographic Society (1985), and the Social Sciences and Humanities Research Council of Canada (1985, 1990–96).
2. For more comprehensive accounts of possession in Mayotte see Lambek (1981 and 1993). Among the vast number of contributions to spirit possession elsewhere Boddy (1989) and Crapanzano and Garrison (1977) provide particularly rich accounts.
3. Thus, incidentally, possession "remembers" Islam (cf. Lambek 1993).
4. Memory is a function of the person and the relationships and contexts to which she commits. Each of Mohedja's spirits retains its own memories and thus memory is one of the means by which the distinctions between the spirits, and between the spirit and host, are legitimated. However spirits are no mere fragments of the individual self. A given spirit can have a relationship with more than one host. When spirits shift between hosts, ideally the memory goes along with them. Thus a spirit possessing Mohedja ought to remember clients who had approached it when it was active in Mohedja's mother. The demand for such continuity is an ideal, a function of the claim to identity.
5. And, of course, computer storage. Hacking points out that the memory "flashback" is derived from the movies (1995: 252).
6. Terdiman (1993, chapt. 2) addresses the temporality of memory production by means of an insightful application of Marx.
7. Caring and mourning are drawn from Casey's remarkable discussion of what he calls "the thick autonomy of memory" (1987: 276), a phenomenologically derived depiction which has much in common with the one developed here.
8. For parallel arguments see Schafer (1976) on agency in psychoanalysis; Fingarette (1969) on avowal and disavowal; Felman and Laub (1992) on witnessing and testimony. Hacking (1995: chapt. 17) turns to the way agency is attributed in memory to past actors and how the availability of new forms for describing actions can transform memory.
9. I cannot develop this here. Often a spirit has appeared in a close senior relative before moving to the current host. Social and psychological implications of communication and succession are variously addressed in Lambek (1981, 1988, 1993), and a book in progress.
10. The contrast with the case of the Moroccan man, Tuhami, who was bothered by spirits but never engaged in full-blown possession (Crapanzano 1980) is instructive.
11. In the ensuing discussion "narrative" stands metonymically for any form or vehicle through which memory is expressed. Narrative is not

the only vehicle of memory, but I take it to be prototypical and for the purposes of my argument I ignore most of the differences between inscriptive and embodied remembrance (De Boeck 1995) or between recalling and remembering (Bloch n.d.). Non-semantic vehicles such as smells may be highly evocative but their source is external; to the degree that they remain meaningful, they quickly get woven into narratives or scenes. The smell of a certain disinfectant powerfully evokes images of the high, white interior walls of my grandmother's house, and then of events that transpired within them, but an image of the walls never produces the smell for me.

12. For Anderson (and for those who subscribe to the romantic view of unspoiled premodern communities) memory would be simply continuity or repetition. But once the repetition becomes conscious of itself as repetition it is no longer an exact copy. Cf. Leys, this volume.

13. Or fantasies remembered as real. As Terdiman puts it, "memory cannot distinguish between the register of facts and that of interpretations" (1993: 346).

14. Historians' attempts to legitimate their craft by insisting on the value of history over memory resemble the attempts of anthropologists and sociologists to distinguish their insights from "common sense" or "common knowledge." Such questionable delegitimation of lay knowledge is opposed by arguments which carry the opposite risk, namely romanticization. Memory is a popular topic in social history and anthropology today precisely because it is seen as a privileged site of resistance to hegemonic narratives. For more nuanced approaches, see the essays in Sider and Smith, eds. (in press).

15. Unfortunately, when subject to excessive external influence, both collective and individual narrated memories may resemble less art than kitsch.

16. In extreme cases this connection is essentialized, envisioned as somehow biological. For critiques see, inter alia, James (1995) and Suleri (1992).

17. The cycle is addressed in the forthcoming doctoral thesis of Andrew Walsh (University of Toronto) as well as Lambek and Walsh n.d. See also Feeley-Harnik (1991).

18. See also the extensive work of Hayden White (1973, 1987) on the narrative construction of historical texts.

19. Groupings in Madagascar, whether the macro ones we misconceptualize as ethnic or tribal, or the more restricted ones we call clans, are generally not firmly bounded discrete entities. Affiliation is non-exclusive and is acquired primarily through bilateral descent but also through living in a particular place and subscribing to local customs,

taboos, and the authority of local royalty. In trying to distinguish Antankarana or Sakalava it seems least misleading to characterize them as those people who subscribe to a respective narrative or repertoire of narratives about themselves (Lambek n.d.; Lambek and Walsh n.d.).

20. Smith (in press) provides a reflection on the historical issue with reference to class rather than nation.

21. See also the extended discussion in Gadamer (1985: 278ff) whose application of Aristotelian ethics to the hermeneutic problem "that the same tradition must always be understood in a different way" must be highly relevant to understanding memory.

References

Anderson, Benedict. 1991. *Imagined Communities*. 2nd edition. London: Verso.

Bakhtin, Mikhail. 1981. *The Dialogic Imagination*. Ed. Michael Holquist, trans. Caryl Emerson and M. Holquist. Austin: Univ. of Texas Press.

Bloch, Maurice. n.d. "Autobiographical Memory and the Historical Memory of the More Distant Past." Manuscript.

Boddy, Janice. 1989. *Wombs and Alien Spirits*. Madison: Univ. of Wisconsin Press.

Casey, Edward. 1987. *Remembering: A Phenomenological Study*. Bloomington: Indiana Univ. Press.

Crapanzano, Vincent. 1980. *Tuhami*. Chicago: Univ. of Chicago Press.

———, and Vivian Garrison, eds. *Case Studies in Spirit Possession*. New York: Wiley.

De Boeck, Filip. 1995. "Bodies of Remembrance: Knowledge, Experience and the Growing of Memory in Luunda Ritual Performance." In *Rites et Ritualisation*. Edited Georges Thinès and Luc de Heusch. Paris: J. Vrin.

Feeley-Harnik, Gillian. 1991. *A Green Estate*. Washington, D.C.: Smithsonian.

Felman, Shoshana, and Dori Laub. 1992. *Testimony: Crises of Witnessing in Literature, Psychoanalysis, and History*. New York: Routledge.

Fingarette, Herbert. 1969. *Self-Deception*. London: Routledge & Kegan Paul.

Freud, Sigmund. *The Standard Edition of the Collected Works*, Vol. 2.

Gadamer, Hans-Georg. 1985. *Truth and Method*. New York: Crossroad.

Hacking, Ian. 1995. *Rewriting the Soul*. Princeton: Princeton Univ. Press.

Halbwachs, Maurice. 1980 [1950]. *The Collective Memory*. Translated F. J. and V. Y. Ditter. New York: Harper.

Handler, Richard. 1988. *Nationalism and the Politics of Culture*. Madison: Univ. of Wisconsin Press.

Hobsbawm, Eric. 1992. "The Opiate Ethnicity." *Alphabet City* 2: 8–11.

James, Wendy. 1995. "Whatever Happened to the Enlightenment?" Introduction to *The Pursuit of Certainty*. London: Routledge.

Lambek, Michael. 1981. *Human Spirits: A Cultural Account of Trance in Mayotte*. New York: Cambridge University Press.

———. 1988. "Spirit Possession, Spirit Succession." *American Ethnologist* 15 (4): 710–31.

———. 1993. *Knowledge and Practice in Mayotte: Local Discourses of Islam, Sorcery, and Spirit Possession*. Toronto: Univ. of Toronto Press.

———. n.d. "The Poiesis of Sakalava History." Manuscript presented to the 1995 Satterthwaite Colloquium.

———, and Andrew Walsh. n.d. "The Imagined Community of the Antankarana: Ritual, Identity, and History in Northern Madagascar." Forthcoming, *Journal of Religion in Africa*.

Mead, George Herbert. 1934. *Mind, Self, and Society*. Ed. Charles Morris. Chicago: Univ. of Chicago Press.

Mitchell, Stephen. 1988. *Relational Concepts in Psychoanalysis*. Cambridge, Mass.: Harvard Univ. Press.

Sacks, Oliver. 1993. "Making Up the Mind." *NYRB* (April 8) XL (7): 42–49.

Schafer, Roy. 1976. *A New Language for Psychoanalysis*. New Haven: Yale Univ. Press.

Sider, Gerald, and Gavin Smith, eds. In press. *Between History and Histories: The Production of Silences and Commemorations*. Toronto: Univ. of Toronto Press.

Smith, Gavin. In press."Pandora's History: Central Peruvian Peasants and the Re-covering of the Past." In Sider and Smith, *Between History and Histories: The Production of Silences and Commemorations*. Toronto: Univ. of Toronto Press.

Suleri, Sara. 1992. "Woman Skin Deep: Feminism and the Postcolonial Condition." *Critical Inquiry* 18 (Summer): 756–69.

Taylor, Charles. 1989. *Sources of the Self*. Cambridge: Harvard Univ. Press.

Terdiman, Richard. 1993. *Present Past: Modernity and the Memory Crisis*. Ithaca, N.Y.: Cornell Univ. Press.

White, Hayden. 1973. *Metahistory*. Baltimore: Johns Hopkins Univ. Press.

———. 1987. *The Content of the Form: Narrative Discourse and Historical Representation*. Baltimore: Johns Hopkins Univ. Press.

Contributors

PAUL ANTZE teaches in the Division of Social Science and in the Graduate Programs in Anthropology and Social and Political Thought at York University, Toronto. He was until recently President of the Canadian Association for Medical Anthropology. He has written about cultural aspects of popular therapeutic movements in North America and is currently at work on a book about the culture of support groups and networks for people with Multiple Personality Disorder.

MAURICE BLOCH is Professor of Anthropology in the University of London at the London School of Economics. His most recent book is *Prey into Hunter: The Politics of Religious Experience* (Cambridge University Press, 1992). Earlier works include *Placing the Dead* (Seminar Press, 1971) and *Ritual, History and Power* (Athlone, 1989).

GLYNIS GEORGE recently defended her doctoral dissertation on "Gender and the Politics of Culture in Western Newfoundland" in the Department of Anthropology at the University of Toronto. She is currently teaching in the Women's Studies Program at McMaster University in Hamilton, Ontario.

IAN HACKING is University Professor of Philosophy at University of Toronto. His most recent book is *Rewriting the Soul: Multiple Personality and the Sciences of Memory* (Princeton, 1995). Earlier works include *Le plus pur nominalisme* (L'eclat: Paris, 1993), *The Taming of Chance* (Cambridge, 1990), and *Representing and Intervening* (Cambridge, 1983).

MICHAEL G. KENNY has a D.Phil in Social Anthropology from Oxford Unversity and is Professor in the Department of Sociology and Anthropology at Simon Fraser University, Burnaby, British Columbia. He is author of *The Passion of Ansel Bourne: Multiple Personality in American Culture* (Smithsonian, 1986), a study of the cultural roots of a distinctive psychiatric disorder closely related to the problem of traumatic memory.

LAURENCE J. KIRMAYER is Professor and Director of the Division of Social and Transcultural Psychiatry, Department of Psychiatry, McGill University, and the Editor-in Chief of *Transcultural Psychiatric Research Review*. He directs the Culture and Mental Health Research Unit of the Department of Psychiatry, Sir Mortimer B. Davis–Jewish General Hospital in Montreal. He has written extensively in the areas of cultural psychiatry, psychosomatic medicine, and psychotherapy. He is a co-editor of the volume *Current Concepts of Somatization* and the author of a forthcoming book, *Healing and the Invention of Metaphor*.

JACK KUGELMASS is Professor of Anthropology, Folklore, and Jewish Studies at the University of Wisconsin–Madison. His contribution to this volume is from a longer work in progress, *The Rites of the Tribe*, to be published by the University of Wisconsin Press.

MICHAEL LAMBEK is Professor of Anthropology, University of Toronto. He is the author of *Human Spirits: A Cultural Account of Trance in Mayotte* (*Comoro Islands*) (Cambridge University Press, 1981) and of *Knowledge and Practice in Mayotte: Local Discourses of Islam, Sorcery, and Spirit Possession*, a volume in the *Anthropological Horizons* series that he edits for the University of Toronto Press (1993).

RUTH LEYS is Associate Professor in the Humanities Center at the Johns Hopkins University. She is the editor, with Rand B. Evans, of *Defining American Psychology: The Correspondence between Adolf Meyer and Edward Bradford Tichener* (1990) and author of *From Sympathy to Reflex: Marshall Hall and His Critics* (1991). She is currently preparing a book (tentatively titled *Incurable Wounds; Traumatic Cures*) which examines the history of conceptualizations of psychic trauma, dissociation, repetition, and memory.

ALLAN YOUNG is a Professor of Anthropology in the Departments of Anthropology, Psychiatry, and Social Studies of Medicine at McGill University. He is the author of *The Harmony of Illusions: Inventing Post-Traumatic Stress Disorder* (Princeton University Press, 1995). His current research is in the ethnography and history of psychiatry; his earlier research focused on indigenous medical beliefs and practices in Ethiopia.

DONNA J. YOUNG is a graduate student in Anthropology at the University of Toronto and is completing a doctoral dissertation on the cultural implications of social change for impoverished New Brunswick women. She currently teaches in the Department of Anthropology at the University of New Brunswick.

Author Index

Subject Index